Our Lord Jesus Christ *"...bore our sin in His own body on the tree, that we, having died in our sins, might live for righteousness..."*
(II Peter 2:24)

Lord Jesus, *"...You are my rock and my fortress; therefore, for Your name's sake, lead me and guide me. Pull me out of the net which they have secretly laid for me, for You are my strength. Into Your hand I commit my spirit; You have redeemed me, O LORD God of truth."*
(Psalm 31:3)

Acknowledgements

Thank you from the depth of our hearts, our precious children and spouses and grandchildren for loving us unconditionally! Thank you for all your prayers, for faithfully supporting us as we've served the Lord in ministry. As we've told you so many times, you are priceless treasures to us—Michele, Mac, and Sean; Joe Jr., Carolin, Shane, and Ryan; Michael, Angie, Kristen, and Brandon—for which we thank the Lord. And, what joy we have in knowing that He will surely reward you all abundantly—on earth and in heaven—for so patiently walking in love with us all these years! Indeed, He will surely bless you for so willingly standing behind us and encouraging us in the ministry to which God called us so many years ago. We can never thank you enough! God bless you abundantly!

And, our hearts are filled with great gratitude to all of you brothers and sisters in Christ who have so faithfully and lovingly supported our ministry and us with your prayers and love-offerings over so many years. Thank you so very much for helping us share God's wondrous truths with hurting souls so that they have freedom from the enemy, plus God's joy and peace that passes all understanding. It causes us great joy to know that because the Lord knows of your loving kindness and willing sacrifices, He will surely reward you—on earth and in heaven. Thank you again from the bottom of our hearts! God bless you abundantly!

It is with much gratitude that we also thank you who have shared copies of your counseling notes with us, which you took during some of our counseling workshops, for they were of great help in getting us started in writing this book. And, with great gratitude, we thank you who have so lovingly spent your precious time and energy in critiquing the book before its printing. We are delighted to know that the Lord will surely reward you, on earth and in heaven, for sharing these wonderful love-labor-gifts with our ministry and us. Thank you again from the bottom of our hearts! God bless you abundantly!

And, last but most surely not least, we humbly thank our precious Lord Jesus for saving our souls, rescuing us from Satan, and for allowing us the privilege of being used as His "tools" to share His tools of truth—how He sets Satan's captives free. What joy it gives us to know that He will use "More Tools for Liberating the Bruised" to bless and help set many souls free. We thank our precious Savior and Lord again for everything—from the bottom of our hearts!

With our enormous gratitude and love,
Joe and Rita

More Tools for Liberating the Bruised

Authors: Rev. Dr. Joe and Rita F. Allbright

More Tools *for Liberating the* Bruised

PRINTED IN THE UNITED STATES OF AMERICA
BY SMOOTH SAILING PRESS

Smooth Sailing Press
9306 Max Conrad Drive / Suite C / Spring, Texas 77379
(281) 251-0830
www.smoothsailingpress.com

ISBN: 978-1-933660-91-2

SMOOTH SAILING
PRESS
www.smoothsailingpress.com

Foreword
Testimonies from Souls Set Free Through Jesus Christ

In prayerfully seeking God's wisdom as to who should write the forward, instead of a single person coming to our minds—a crowd of souls came who were once held tightly in Satan's stronghold. Indeed, who better to testify to the validity of God's truths shared in "Liberating the Bruised" and workshops that led them to freedom, peace and joy? And the Lord told us to share some testimonies that represent "an anonymous crowd of both counselees and ministers/counselors"—from a variety of Christ-based denominations! We thank this precious crowd for sharing their testimonies of what Jesus has done for them!

"I thank God that He led me to a counselor who knew about you, Brother Joe! I was so full of hopelessness that I was suicidal. I am so thankful that after I went though the steps, I found freedom! If I had continued the way Satan was leading me, I would have died and missed the joy of sharing my testimony with others about how Jesus gives hope and can truly set Satan's captives free! I am so excited! Thank you for obeying the Lord and writing 'Liberating the Bruised' and teaching others about God's wonderful truths!"

"Dr. Joe, I just want to thank you for writing 'Liberating the Bruised!' I was so desperate for help, and when I did as you suggested, "snuggled up to Jesus" and read your book and very seriously applied His truths to my life—it truly saved my life! Thank you! I know first hand that He can do the same for others if they snuggle up to Him and apply His truths to their lives! And, I am very happy to hear that you plan to share additional counseling information and prayers in another book! I look forward to reading it and sharing it with others! God bless you!"

"I am so thankful, my dear brother Joe, that the Lord placed a very caring minister on my pathway who had studied your teachings—which are quite eye-openers to say the least! I had no idea how Satan could manipulate and control a Christian—until it happened to me! I thought people who claimed they were Christians but displayed behavior extremely contrary to God's ways were actually lost! But when the minister asked me to read your book so I would understand your counseling procedures, I understood the truth! He then took me through the counseling procedures and I was led out of captivity! I was no longer withdrawn from the world, depressed, hiding "in the bottle," and feeling like I was worthless to God and everyone else! My eyes and heart were even opened to the amazing truth that God could even use me to help others find freedom as I did! So, I just want to thank you for sharing God's truths with me and others like me! God bless you, brother!"

"How very, very grateful I am to you for counseling me and leading me to freedom from Satan's stronghold! Thank you for not being ashamed of the Gospel—nor of the truth about our mighty battle with Satan! Thank you for boldly sharing God's unpopular, uncompromising truths that most certainly can set Satan's captives free—if they take the Lord at His entire Word and obey Him! I had been to so many other ministers and counselors, who sincerely wanted to help me, but they didn't know about the deeper, root things you teach in your book—the wounded personalities, the flip-side and iniquities of the fathers connected to ancestral demons! I truly cannot thank you enough for taking time to write 'Liberating the Bruised' and for holding the workshops! Thank you for not only helping me and my family, but also for helping so many of God's children find peace and freedom to walk joyfully in God's will for their dear lives! God bless you!"

"My dear Dr. Joe, I really shudder, thinking of what would have happened had you not counseled me! I'm so grateful that the Lord led me to you, to your ministry! For I know I would have lost my family and my ministry, and in despair, would have more than likely killed myself! I thank God often each day for His mercy on me and for leading you into this very needed spiritual warfare ministry! Thank you for sacrificing so much time in penning and publishing 'Liberating the Bruised' in order to share what the Lord taught you about our enemy and how we can absolutely, totally defeat him! I am now able to be the spiritually healthy husband, father, and pastor God intended! With joyful gratitude, my family, my flock, and I thank you! May God bless you and Rita for your love and commitment to Him!"

"Thank you, Dr. Joe, for not being selfish with God's truths! Thank you for blessing my husband and me, our children, and our grandchildren—our future generations! We are all eternally grateful to you! God bless you and Rita as you carry on His work!"

Also from the crowd comes forth a beautiful testimony from a dear brother, Pastor Bill Stallings, a Southern Baptist Minister, who is Associate Pastor of Chester Second Baptist Church in Chester, South Carolina. He and his dear fellow pastors have graciously given us permission to include their church's name and contact information, with hopes of encouraging other ministers and counselors to read his testimony, and prayerfully study God's truths shared in both of Joe's books which led to

Pastor Bill's own freedom.   Brother Bill and the other pastors' desire for other pastors and counselors to experience the same joys they have been blessed to experience by leading bruised people on their mission field to freedom from the enemy, Satan. Pastor Bill and his fellow pastors are well-balanced in God's Word, not off to extremes in either direction. They do not water down the Word, nor do they add to it—they have determined to obey the Lord's words: *"Be diligent to present yourself approved to God, a worker who does not need to be ashamed, rightly dividing the word of truth."* (II Timothy 2:15) And now, Brother Bill Stalling's powerful testimony:

"Greetings in the name of our Lord.

"I was born and raised in North Carolina and like so many Southern Baptists, our family sporadically attended church. I eventually became saved at the age of 13 at a youth retreat. There has never been any doubt of the legitimacy of my salvation experience within me but, like so many new believers today, there was no follow up or discipleship available. Very soon the Enemy began to creep into the areas of my life where I was weak, vulnerable or still sinful. Even though my eternal destiny was secure by my profession of faith, my daily walk continued to be a struggle and I never felt *"whole."* I was somewhat bewildered because *"all things did not become new"* as I tried to reconcile that with my experience. In some areas yes, there was immediate and drastic change, but in others, there was still great difficulty regardless of how much I disciplined myself, studied or prayed.

"I was born the youngest of four children to a mentally ill mother who was in and out of hospitals for much of my life, and even today at seventy-one years old still has episodes of which lead to her going to care facilities. She has mental issues running back several generations on her father's side and a sister, who is a few years older than she, is in an institution today. On my father's side there is a long history of both emotional and physical abuse which included substance abuse. Epilepsy also ran on my father's side. He himself was an epileptic and it affected two of my brothers, but by the grace of God it skipped me and my precious children – my daughter Kristin, now age twenty-four, and my son Landon, age twenty.

"Our home life was one borne out of secrecy and control as my father attempted to keep the Christian facade up as he took us to church on occasion, only to have the family issues continue to surface from time to time by the children either running away from home or being brought home by police for things such as substance abuse, breaking and entering and just general behavioral issues leading to embarrassment which eventually led us away from church altogether. In 1980, my parents lost one of their children, my eldest brother, due to a drowning accident. This would be the first of many children they would lose through accidents. In 1985, my second bother died in another tragic drowning accident.   Then, ten years later in 1995, my sister died in a one-vehicle drunk-driving accident.   From the time my first brother died, our home life completely unraveled as my father overcompensated for his own pain while dealing with his mentally ill wife and trying to figure out what to do.

"My father dominated me in every respect as he saw his world come apart and his frustration turned into physical and emotional abuse. By this time I was the only one left at home at 14 years old. None of us along the way received any type of secular counseling as it was unpopular to the church and often came with a stigma attached so we simply learned to cope in our own ways which led to deeply embedded sinful ways of dealing with our emotions and the anguish that was going on inside. No counseling was offered by our church other than the proverbial message of *"in time God will heal."* However, I found that time does not heal all wounds, but only added to the pain, the dysfunction and confusion of my life. My father's continued emotional and verbal abuse escalated more and more as well as did the physical. By the time I was seventeen, I was gripped by fear, anger, anxiety, insecurity, nightmares and a sense of dooming failure which was coupled with hopelessness and a spirit of futility as I lived in constant fear that I too would be dead by the time I was 30 years old. I simply could not live beyond that which I had come to believe about myself and our family's history.

"As I continued to mature I became performance-oriented in all aspects of my life. There was no room for mediocrity, and failure was not an option in any area whether it be work or recreation. During the early years of my marriage I attempted suicide and sought to destroy myself as well as my precious wife, Teri Lyn — to whom I've been married for twenty-six years this August 2011. Like my father, I learned to conceal everything from everyone out of fear of judgment and shame. I suffered in silence and kept all the childhood experiences inside so much that I never even told my wife about the abuse and the mental torment that I experienced on a continuous basis, which began from the time I awoke in the morning to the time I fell asleep with exhaustion at night. It took some 15 years into our marriage following my own healing before I was able to share. I learned how to cope the best I could while living in a state of denial, yet all along I knew deep within me that there was *"something which was not right,"* but I did not know what to do or where to go for help. Fear of exposure kept me in an emotional prison, isolated from experiencing true intimacy with God. I had so many structures built into my heart and mind from habitual patterns of thinking that I could not enter into meaningful relationships with people on a deeper level. All relationships were about "an inch deep and a mile wide" due to the lack of my ability to trust and I could not put myself into any position of which I thought would carry any form of personal risk. I avoided all social gatherings except for those of which I could manage to find a way out, and I often found myself depressed. I tried to reconcile the Word against my present experience, as I was told as a Christian that I should have joy, but that certainly was not always my experience as I strained to endure and I didn't understand why.

"I studied the scriptures looking for some self-help and cried out to God because I didn't dare ask anyone out of fear of rejection which would only add to the guilt and shame that I was already carrying. I knew that I could ask for forgiveness from those things that I had committed, but found no way to reconcile the sins and hurts committed against me or find any rational reason as to why they affected me for so long and how tight a grip they seemed to have on me as they continued to linger and control me in so many ways.

"Later the Lord called me into full-time ministry where I continued to seek answers and grow in my faith. Much to my regret at that present time, I had somehow managed to open a very small window into my life and a select few were able to see that there was *"something in my life that needed healing."* I do not know how I let that happen because I had worked so hard to make sure it didn't. However, the Lord wanted my healing nonetheless and because of that He sent a lady to our church who was doing ministry. I serve on a three-pastor staff with each of us having different and varying gifts and responsibilities, but somehow I was left out of the planning and scheduling of this Christian lady who was to come to our congregation and offer some help for people whom we had worked with for <u>years</u> but had failed to lead them to freedom from Satan's strongholds. These people were held in strongholds connected to sexual molestation, child abuse, marital problems, adultery, pornography, drug abuse, SRA, and issues with bipolar. Many were heavily medicated and some had actually become "professional counselees" who knew the scriptures as well as any pastor, yet could not get free and walk with any dominion of power and authority in their life or with personal integrity. We were putting *"band aids on gaping wounds"* at best and ended up seeing the same people revolving through our office doors. Many of them finally left the church because they had come to the last place that they thought would and could offer some hope and help, yet only to leave disappointed and disillusioned. All of this was taking place around us while I myself was *"standing up on the outside, but falling down on the inside"*.

"I knew in my heart that the Lord wanted me free from my own silent cry and as usual, I learned to run when these issues began to surface or felt as if *"my inner self"* was about to be an open book and then only to be flooded with deep feelings of the coming shame. After discovering the actual reason for the lady's ministry visit, I made it a point to be out of the office during the time the Christian lady-counselor would be there in hopes I could prevent myself from running into her until she left and avoid the *"looking into my soul that I so feared."* However, by the end of the week and after much pressing from the Lord I agreed I would see her. I went to see her very reluctantly with my mind made up I was just simply going to *"go through the motions"* so I could return to my prison. Yes, it was a prison, but at least it was a familiar prison and I knew my way around. As strange as it may seem, I desperately wanted freedom, but feared what freedom might look and feel like as I had no idea what total freedom might cost me.

"As I began receiving ministry I knew it was of the Lord and that He was drawing me to Himself. It was my time for healing, however for the very first time I heard the enemy speak to me with a voice of authority as I began giving myself to the Lord in ministry. It was a very clear and distinct voice which said "Don't you dare tell...you will never get free!" At this point, I, for the very first moment in my life, realized that I had been caught up in a spiritual battle since I was a child and that I had no chance of winning or becoming free outside of deliverance by the power of God. The lady counselor had studied God's truths taught in Dr. Allbright's book, which led to my freedom from performance orientation, arrested development, anxiety and depression, suspicion which bordered on paranoia, anger, and fear of authority. Today I am 46 years old, healed and whole and serve with greater joy and anticipation of the things God has for me as I too minister to the needs of our people in this way.

"After my healing I was asked to share what God did for me with the others who gave themselves to this ministry as well. There was so much the Lord had healed and so much that had been *"upside down"* for so long that He *"righted,"* that it was not only overwhelming to talk about, but to be able to share with others as to the depth of my healing was difficult to put into words. One of the pastors in our meeting time said to me, *'We knew all along that you needed help, but because you were so wounded we knew you couldn't and wouldn't let any of us in to help, therefore we purposefully didn't include you in the planning and scheduling because we knew you would run.'* Their response, which was out of love, was also followed by, *'Bill, we knew there were people here who needed this ministry in their life, but you needed it the most. We also knew that it was you that God was going to use in this ministry to help and heal others.'* I was absolutely blown away, first by the love of God because of the great care and enduring love He had for my healing, but also for the love I could feel from them for the very first time. And, for the very first time my life, my past made sense and was reconciled. I was able to see what and why it was that I never could seem to step up into my ministry as God had designed for me.

"My spiritual ministry gift is that of the teacher so as you could imagine I struggled with my theology as I served in a Southern Baptist Church; however I could not deny what had taken place in my life. I wrestled with God because I wanted to make certain that I was following the scriptures and anguished over it all. I did however finally have to put down my pride and seek God and the scriptures without my preconceived ideas or traditional teachings. I searched the scriptures diligently for His truth and I ended up coming to a great peace that God is not obligated to heal only in the realm of which I am able to believe at the present moment. I am a student of the Word and if a person is willing to search they will find that Dr. Joe Allbright's teachings are biblical and sound in the faith as well. The problem we have as the Body of Christ is that we have believed the lie from the Enemy that deliverance is a thing of the past or it's regulated to third world countries. The Lord is able to reach across time and space and heal the damage done by our past mistakes or sins committed by our ancestors of which we suffer the lingering consequences. *Is it so hard to believe that we receive blessings from our fathers and forefathers, yet deny the curses that come from them as well?*

"As pastors to our congregation we continued to fail in our counseling methods with the most difficult problems that some were facing. After no measurable lasting progress we either blamed our sheep for their lack of love for the Lord, their undisciplined life and we ended up only having them leave the church burdened down with guilt and shame with no answers for their problems and with a greater sense of hopelessness. Many times we were faced with the reality of what to do next as we then began to see the same families with children who carried the same issues. It's heartbreaking that we as pastors have even gone so far that when we are unable to help, that we would send them to a psychiatrist or a psychologist because we feel powerless to offer any hope. Unfortunately many end up on medication with a dull and slumbering spirit that is all but dead to the voice of God.

"We are in a small bedroom community in rural South Carolina governed by church tradition where it seems that men's traditions are held in honor, while the works and power of God have been regulated to the lower shelf. Our church today is an outreach and a hospital for the hurting, walking wounded and the imprisoned. We, as expected, are and have been ridiculed for our non-compliance to the status quo by the churched or religious community. We have an excellent reputation however with the unchurched in our community because they are being saved, loved and healed here and then equipped for the Kingdom and released to live out their faith as the Father desires. We as a church are willing to pay that price if it means God's people are set free and are able to embrace their walk with God which in turn changes the world.

"Dr. Allbright's ministry has enabled a disproportional amount of our men who are being set free and are now reclaiming their role as high priest of their families and who now know the love of their Heavenly Father and can, in turn, be a father to their children. We have men who are compassionate and tender with their wives who were themselves abused and abusive and can now look at and treat their wives with honor and love the same way Jesus does. Our children are learning to have respect for their parents, respect for themselves, respect for the holiness of marriage and for authority and yet are secure in who they are because Dad has been healed and made whole through this ministry.

"There is so much more that God is actively doing because we have decided that God's plan and truths of yesterday still meet the needs of people today. We have had to pay a high price in other areas as well, but in each of them the Kingdom gain has far outreached our level of risk. God has met us at every opportunity and opposition and He has gone before us countless times as we have simply sought to pursue what He wanted to do in us and through this ministry here. My prayer is that, we as pastors will have a heart like God when we see the sheep stricken, oppressed and wearing sackcloth of ashes instead of a garland of praise and offer help, healing and cleansing to them."

In His Service,
Pastor Bill Stallings

Chester Second Baptist Church - 803-377-7149
P. O. Box 115, Chester, S.C. 29706
www.chestersecondbaptist.com

Preface

Before you read this book, Rita and I believe that you should know a little more about my background than what I shared in my first book, plus some of hers as well. For, it was out of my past pain and suffering—and also painful experiences that Rita went through—that the Lord taught us both His ways—shared some of His tools—and brought forth our empathy and compassion for hurting, troubled souls. In later years, He led us into ministry where we were in the pastorate a number of years, then into my preaching revivals and counseling one-on-one. He then led me to write "Liberating the Bruised," and then, led Rita and me to share additional counseling tools in this second book, "More Tools for Liberating the Bruised." Upon surrendering to write this book, we felt it was a mandate from the Lord and while writing it, we had an urgency to hasten to complete the work. We are well up in years—in our seventies—and are still fairly active, but our bodies are clearly in the God-ordained aging process—evidence that it is appointed unto us once to die! We neither know what our appointed times are to move into heaven, nor how long our bodies will cooperate with our willing hearts and minds to continue effectively in service for Him. The point is, that we are only two people in a world packed so very full of hurting people, that we know by sharing the tools the Lord has placed in our hands, God's ministry through us is being multiplied! We find much joy in knowing that by sharing these tools now, they can continue to be passed on to others so many more souls can be rescued from Satan's captivity! We hope that as you read from whence we came, understand our hearts, that you will be encouraged to submit to the Lord, resist the enemy, and find joy as you walk in God's will for your precious life on this needy mission field!

I was born in an old, small, frame house on the Old Love Lady Road, five miles outside a small east Texas town named Crockett. I was born to a share-cropper and his wife who already had a two-year-old son. My dad died of tuberculosis, nine days before my first birthday. Being a share-cropper, his death brought not only the loss of a dad and provider, but also the loss of a house to live in. For about a year, my mother, brother, and I lived with various relatives, but they were having tough times too, so we couldn't stay. Then, we came to Houston where Mother (with only an eighth-grade education) had been given a job with a family as their live-in maid, but we boys weren't allowed to live there with her. So, she chose to give us away. A preacher and his wife had brought us all to the house where I was given to an older couple, who lived in Houston's Heights area. We had never met the couple, even though the woman was my mother's stepsister. My brother and I were in the front yard, and watched our mother ride off with the couple who was taking her to her live-in job. I was crying hard, begging, ***"Mama, don't go! Mama, don't go!"*** She didn't even look back at me through the car window or wave good-bye. To me as a toddler, it appeared that she wasn't sad about leaving me. My brother, sitting above me in a tree, said, "Shut up you crybaby! Mama's never coming back!" Surely, my crying wasn't helping to console him! He was hurting badly too, crying on the inside! He was just "keeping a stiff upper lip," refusing to expose his feelings at that time! But, in his adulthood—even far into his old age—angry, bitter words about our mother giving us away surfaced, proving that he still clung tightly to his childhood hurts - his pain of rejection. I was left at the couple's house. My brother, age four, was taken to live in a far away town with a farming family and he labored very hard for many years in their fields.

When I was eight years old—one week after Christmas—my foster dad, "Daddy Martin," died, leaving "Mama Bea" to soon have to start looking for work. By the time I was nine, "Mama Bea" had gone to work as a practical nurse, going from home to home and caring for rich ladies and their new babies for two-week stays. The first week, she would spend twenty-four hours a day with them. The second week, she would spend about fourteen hours a day. The third week, she would start all over again with a new job. I went to bed almost every night with a little dog named Tiny in one hand and a thirty-two revolver in the other. With the covers pulled over my head—I hoped a stranger wouldn't pull them down in the night and do harm to me. I lived my life in total worry and fear. In my teens, I was sometimes told that my middle name must be "Worry".

My mother came back into my life when I was ten, bringing with her my brother, whom I had seen only about six times during the eight years I had lived with Mama Bea. She had learned that the farming couple who took my brother in was abusive and overworked him. She and my brother crowded into the little two-bedroom home with Mama Bea and me, and none of us got along very well—tempers readily flew! My mother had a job at a nearby bakery, so we were with her evenings and weekends. A caring family started picking me up to take me to church through Baptist Temple's bus ministry in Houston's Heights. I was led to the Lord at age ten, by Dr. T. C. Jester, in Baptist Temple's parsonage on a Saturday afternoon, October 12, 1946, and was baptized October 13, 1946. My mother was saved that day also.

When I was eleven, my mother met and married our new milkman, who delivered milk to the house twice a week. He had been married and divorced three times. He had no children and didn't want any, yet he married a lady with two—and there was a great deal of disunity going on in the house! The four of us lived with Mama Bea until I was thirteen years old, and then we moved into our own home. But, after about a year and a half, my step-dad was called back into the Air Force, and he and my mother were eventually stationed in London, England. I was sent back to live with Mama Bea, while my mother sent my brother to live with a man we called "Uncle Steve"—who, grievously enough, was a homosexual. Shortly thereafter, Mama Bea became ill and had to have major surgery, a situation which forced me to drop out of school at fifteen years of age—at the end of my ninth grade year—to get a job to support us. My brother, age seventeen, helped me find work at Texas Pipe Bending Company, where he worked. From that day forward, I was never out of the workaday world.

I was enjoying attending church and youth fellowships at Baptist Temple, where I had gotten saved. During a revival being held there, the Lord clearly spoke to my heart, calling me at age eighteen to preach the Gospel. However, during the invitation, as I walked with a willing heart down the aisle to surrender to God's call, the enemy pointed out friends my age sitting in the congregation who had already surrendered to preaching and music ministries and were in the midst of getting their college and seminary education. The enemy reminded me that I wasn't as educated as they—and he even told me that I wasn't handsome enough to stand behind a pulpit to proclaim God's Word! My willing enthusiasm to serve the Lord was squelched and buried in condemnation before I reached the preacher waiting at the front of the sanctuary that Sunday morning. When he asked me why I had come forward, I lied, telling him that I had come to rededicate my life. I would carefully guard this experience with secrecy for fifteen years.

At Baptist Temple, when I was twenty years old, I met my one-and-only wife, Rita, who was eighteen. We married, October 11, 1957, when I was twenty-one, and she was nineteen. Rita and her brother and two sisters were brought up in a very loving Christian home—certainly not perfect but it was evident that they were full of unconditional love for one another. On both her father and mother's sides of the family, their extended family—a dear grandmother, many uncles, aunts and cousins—also loved one another unconditionally—"warts and all!" What Rita didn't know about me when we married was that my family was quite unlike hers. Mine was dysfunctional, and I was not the confident, in-control person I appeared to be. Instead, I was very insecure on the inside! Neither did Rita know "my secret"—that God had called me to preach during the revival. We thought it very "special" to later determine that Rita had accepted the Lord as her Savior at age sixteen, during the very same revival. When she accepted the Lord as her Savior, she was so overwhelmed by God's love and forgiveness, she was crying uncontrollably as her heart was brimming over with love for and gratitude to Him. She had an enthusiastic willingness to be God's missionary—wherever He wanted to send her.

While both of us understood Satan, the Tempter, was God's enemy and ours—we did not realize how he could so cunningly and viciously manipulate us away from God's pathways! The truth later became evident with both of us, that Satan wanted neither of us to be used by the Lord! Satan was quite convincing with his words of condemnation—assuring each of us in his cunning ways, that neither of us were adequate tools the Lord would ever want to use! Just as he had convinced me as I walked the aisle to surrender, a couple of weeks after Rita's salvation, he had convinced her that she was too little (four foot eleven and a half inches tall at the time—now aged, four foot ten) and she was surely not smart enough to be a missionary. So, with sorrow and disappointment in her heart, she resolved to be grateful for the privilege of "at least" teaching intermediate age girls in Sunday school—in the same department where I was teaching boys.

When Rita and I married, she didn't know about my past hurts, nor my secret—that I had begun a fifteen-year run from God's will—and she surely would not have imagined that during our marriage, her "good ole Baptist boy" would eventually become a drunk for five years! I was an accountant when we married, then later entered the life insurance business and became very successful and made a lot of money. Secretly, I was still harboring in my heart the deep hurt from my mother giving me away. When I was an adult, while talking with her about "the old days" and her giving my brother and me away, she spoke very matter-of-fact without showing any sorrow, "It was just what I <u>had</u> to do." Even though I was happily married, down deep inside, I was tormented with feelings of loneliness—questioning, "Should I have even been born?" I felt like I just didn't fit comfortably into this world.

Due to the overwhelming feelings of inferiority, insecurity, and inadequacy, those fifteen years running from God's will were characterized by my needing to be in control of my life—and to show people that I could excel, and be financially successful and secure! In addition, I stayed in a defense mode to make sure no one else ever hurt me again like my mother did! Ultimately, the pressures of trying to excel and be socially accepted became overwhelming. The demands I put on myself to sell life insurance put me in a pressure cooker, and with the company pressing me to socially drink and wine and dine my clients, I was an easy target for alcohol to become my coping mechanism! I learned that it helped numb the pain buried deeply inside my heart, yet I was still capable of putting forth boldness as I muddled through each day.

In the midst of those fifteen years, the Lord blessed Rita and me with three very precious, wonderful children, Michele Renee, Joe Edward, Jr., and Michael Glenn. In spite of Rita's really enjoying being a wife and mother, from childhood up into adulthood, she had suffered verbal rejection upon repeatedly hearing since childhood, "You're too little to do this! You're not smart enough to do that!" When various pressures came, Rita weakened and began to entertain Satan's suggestions that she was a lesser wife and mother than other women. He began to bombard her with so many words of condemnation; she began entertaining his suggestions about suicide! Upon starting to make preparations for it, the Lord spoke to her heart, overwhelming her with His loving words of truth, that she would be sinning against God and that her sin would bring great hurt and harm to her precious children. With many tears, she repented and began to lean more on the Lord and develop a closer walk with Him. However, while she had dealt with the "suicide" issue, the hurts of so many rejections remained buried deeply in her heart, with the unforgiveness growing into anger and bitterness toward a person who served to continually put her down.

One day, her heart reached a dangerous point—like a volcano on the brink of erupting with a vengeance toward Joe's step-aunt who almost daily reminded her of her small stature and of her not measuring up to what she expected of her as a wife to Joe and mother to the children! As was the "custom," Joe, Rita and the children were at the step-aunt's house for Sunday lunch after church. As usual, the step-aunt was washing dishes while Rita dried them and put them away. However, this was actually a pleasant time for all that day! The step-aunt had not said anything unkind to Rita to stir up any ill thoughts toward her. Rita was calmly drying a handful of cooking utensils. As she began passing behind the step-aunt, to put the utensils—one of which was a large butcher knife—in a drawer on the other side of the kitchen sink, Rita was shocked when she was bombarded with temptation to take vengeance that was so cold-heartedly evil. For, clearly she heard the enemy suggest: "Stick it in her!" Rita froze in place behind the step-aunt as the Lord spoke to her of the ugly truth about the hurts she had so tightly clung to in her heart since childhood. From the first hurt, like a snowball growing larger and larger as it rolls downhill, it had grown from hurt, to unforgiveness, anger, bitterness and eventually, vengeance. Instantly, in the privacy of Rita's heart, she wept bitterly before the Lord, confessing her wicked sin of holding onto the hurt and harboring unforgiveness toward another person in her heart.

The step-aunt was completely unaware of this explosive, critical meeting Rita was having with the Lord. She knew nothing of the silent battle that had been going on in Rita's heart—and she never did. Rita had never displayed any retaliation at the step-aunt, therefore, the Lord instructed Rita's not to share what had happened—that the step-aunt would not have understood and would have only been hit hard with "hurt" in the process. Rita earnestly repented and forgave the step-aunt, plus all others who had hurt her in the past. She shuddered to think of how wicked those sins were before the Lord and asked Him to remove them all—"tear it all out of me—replace them with Your love for all Your people—even my enemies!" Quickly, sweet release and peace swept over her as she not only experienced God's forgiveness but His amazing love pouring out of her heart for the step-aunt! She felt joy that she could see her with God's eyes, hear her with His ears, and understand and love her with His heart, which continued through many years that followed! Rita cherished the Lord and His mercy, always remembering: "Amazing grace, how sweet the sound that saves a wretch like me!"

It was not long after this that I started drinking, which was surely a great heartbreak to Rita. But, she was snuggled up very closely to the Lord, desiring to live in His will, and she remained a faithful, good wife and mother. My children didn't even know that I drank alcohol, much less that I was an alcoholic, until the end of my fifteen-year run and I gave my testimony for the first time at church. When I came in drunk from wining and dining my clients late at night, Rita had already put the children to bed. I was sober when I left for work in the morning. And when I was sick in the morning, suffering hangover-headaches, Rita simply explained to the children that Daddy was sick (spiritually) and asked them to "play the whisper game." I did care so deeply about my family that I didn't drink at the house.

During those five years of my coming home sloppy drunk in wee-hour mornings, Rita always welcomed me at the door with open arms, saying, "Honey, I'm so glad you're home safely." I'd stagger through the door and she would help me to bed while hiding tears. Out of her love for the Lord and me, I'm so grateful that she chose not to expose my sins to our children, and instead, was determined to teach the children to love, respect and honor their earthly father. Rather than become angry and bitter, she chose to obey God and consistently resisted the temptation to try to change me by "preaching sermonettes" at me! She took her sorrows, her heartaches to the only One she knew could comfort her and change me—the Lord Jesus—and left the convicting and changing up to Him. She knew through her own experience that He had convicted and changed her—so He could get through to Joe, too! In fact, while Rita was tearfully conversing with the Lord about her burden for me, He told her, "You just love 'my little boy' and let me tend to him—while we work on your issues!" At that time, we had not yet learned about "the core personalities that God created from the foundation of the world!" Truly, it was the core, Joe Allbright that Rita had fallen in love with! Just as God does—Rita loved me, just hated my sin!

And, the Lord Himself, out of His love, persistently talked to me, scolded me and even spanked me, as loving fathers do! On my way home one night from wining and dining clients, in a drunken state, weaving on the highway as I headed home, I lost control of the car, hit a guard rail, and spun around facing headlights of oncoming traffic. No seat belts then, no air bags; I found myself in the back seat with blood running down my face. As I struggled to get back to the front seat—not even sure where I was—God spoke to me as clearly as if He were broadcasting "breaking news" through the car radio, declaring, "Joe Allbright, you become who I saved you to be, or I'll just kill you and take you on home with me!" Now some folks would mistakenly think God sounded like He was being mean to me. But, on the contrary, I immediately knew that God was most surely not being mean to me! For I immediately understood that my heavenly Father allowed that accident to happen as a "spanking" to get His little boy's undivided attention! Even though His message held a warning that if I didn't repent and get onto His mission fields He would "kill me," the threat of being killed was not what overwhelmed me and caused me to repent. I was not afraid of dying! I had been driving drunk for so long, knowing I could kill myself in an accident—and from there go to heaven! No, what ministered to my heart was my Father's love in the midst of the spanking that ministered to my heart! For when He declared that He would take me on home with Him in spite of my disobedience—my long run from His will—His merciful love melted my heart! He said that He would take me home to live with Him, my heavenly Papa. I surrendered my all to Him.

Up until then, Rita had been both a mom and a dad to the children. But, during those days, our children still knew that I loved them very dearly. So, the only way I actually hurt my children in their early years was by my long hours of work robbing them of quality time with me. I gave them lots of nice things, but not the more precious things—quality times with their dad. By the time Michele was twelve, I had quit drinking. I am so grateful to my Lord that while my children were still young, I was able to ask and receive their forgiveness for neglecting them in some areas! I was so blessed to be able to express my love for them in many words and deeds long before they "left the nest!" And, now Rita and I are blessed with wonderful, healthy relationships with our children, their spouses, and our five grandchildren! Each one of them is a priceless treasure to us, straight from the Lord!

How very happy we are that we allowed the Lord at last to have His way with us—with His little clay vessels! Never have I regretted surrendering on April 9, 1969, at Oak Ridge Baptist Church, just outside Conroe, Texas, to preach His Gospel! I served in the pastorate for more than seven years (in three churches). Many souls were led to Jesus as God preached messages through me. But, I made a lot of mistakes—sins for which God has forgiven me—and He knows if I could go back in time, I would strive to walk in His Spirit consistently! Oh, how thankful I am for God's patience and mercy! Rita and I—and our children—were so blessed to be with those precious brothers and sisters in those churches! What joy it will be for all of us to live together in heaven!

Then, God placed me in this preaching and counseling ministry where I've been since 1976. Since then, I have earned four degrees, the last from Trinity Theological Seminary—Doctor of Ministry in Counseling. During this time, Rita and I have had the privilege and pleasure of seeing so many sin-sick, broken-hearted, hurting souls find freedom through the ministry appointed unto us! What joy it has been to offer souls hope by sharing God's tools through biblical counseling at no charge! And, what joy it is for us to be able to share these tools with you in print! If Satan has hindered you in any way from walking in God's will and possessing His peace and joy, we hope that the first book and this second book together will enable you to reclaim what is rightfully yours! We hope that the tools within them will lead you to your freedom, peace and joy through Jesus Christ! And if you are a minister, missionary, counselor or lay-counselor who has a heart for encouraging and helping to rescue perishing souls, care for the spiritually dying, we hope that these tools—many of which helped Rita and me long ago—will likewise go on to help many, many souls for many years to come! God bless you as you stay snuggled up to Him, walking with and obeying Him on this mission field as you sojourn toward your heavenly home!

As you study "More Tools for Liberating the Bruised" we hope that you will perceive the deep love we have in our hearts for the Lord and His people! We hope that you will fully understand that it is our love for the Lord and His people that motivated us to obey the Lord's will for us to share His instructions on how to help precious souls overcome the enemy. Earnestly we have prayed for God's wisdom to be taught in this book from cover to cover—biblically based, not "personal opinions." While we were writing down God's truths pertaining to counseling procedures that lead Satan's captivated souls to freedom, peace and joy, the Lord cautioned us not to end the book with the counseling procedures. He convicted our hearts to go beyond and address negative learned behavior patterns and external temptation that all Christians experience until they move into heaven. We obeyed. After writing that portion of the book, then He prompted our hearts to go even further into areas where Satan has relentlessly battled and trod upon God's family who are meeting in church buildings, which has long been a burden to our hearts. No doubt about it, at that point, we were convinced that the enemy would prefer that we share no more about how all Christians can walk victoriously in Christ over the Devil and his cohorts.

The Lord reminded us that an uninvited guest, Satan, is a faithful attendee of church where Christian soldiers gather to meet with their Commander and Chief—for training and service. Within those walls, Satan's intentions are to hinder the lost from accepting Christ and to deter all Christians from walking in obedience to Christ on their individual mission fields on earth. Once again, our deep love for our Commander and Chief motivated and urged us to lovingly share additional topics with God's soldiers—the Church body—even though we knew the topic would even be unpopular and controversial with some of our fellow believers. Many people have heard Joe's statement: **"The worst enemy you can have is a friend who won't tell you the truth—in love!"** If we truly love others, we will tell them the truth, in love—in spite of the risks of offending them and being rejected. Jesus loves everyone. He is The Way, The Truth, and The Life. There is no fault in Him, yet *"He is despised and rejected by men, a Man of sorrows and acquainted with grief...He was wounded for our transgressions, He was bruised for our iniquities."* (Isaiah 53:3 and 5b) *"...the soldiers of the governor took Jesus into the Praetorium and gathered the whole garrison around Him. And they stripped Him and put a scarlet robe on Him. When they had twisted a crown of thorns, they put it on His head, and a reed in His right hand. And they bowed the knee before Him and mocked Him, saying 'Hail, King of the Jews!' Then they spat on Him, and took the reed and struck Him on the head. And when they had mocked Him, they took the robe off Him, put His own clothes on Him, and led Him away to be crucified."* (Matthew 27:27-31)

All of that did not stop our perfect, loving Lord from willingly sacrificing Himself for the sake of every soul. Not one of us is capable of comprehending the immeasurable amount of suffering He endured in our behalf! Therefore, how dare we not be willing to run any risks of being rejected and out of our gratitude, share His truths in love without reservation? Motivated again by our love for our Savior and His people, we determined not to fall short of obediently sharing additional biblical truths with great hope of bringing freedom, peace, joy, and unity amongst our beloved Church family.

Our prayer is that all readers will welcome, study, and apply all of God's love-lessons of truths written to us all for our good. These treasures of truth serve the purposes of admonishing, edifying, encouraging, and building up our beloved Church family—welcoming freedom, peace, joy and unity into God's family! We are all uniquely called according to God's purposes. And lessons in I Corinthians 12:12-31 teach vital lessons about "Unity and Diversity in One Body." Each one of us is a vital member of God's family and together, jointly, we are representatives of the body of Christ. We are supposed to be functioning in unity so that the world can see the love of Jesus in us. No differently that a physical body has ears, eyes, nose, and limbs, we each have important functions within God's family!

For a variety of reasons, the reputation broadcasted from all too many church walls the church walls is that of a crippled body. Our desire is that all God's people will humble themselves, love the Lord with all their hearts, and walk together in obedience and unity with our Lord. Oh that the outside world would begin hearing of transformation, restoration taking place within those walls, God's people united in love. In doing so, we know each "member" would know the peace and joy of fulfilling God's will for their lives! Oh that we will all obediently love one another as

Christ loves us and display the love of Christ so that the world may know Him! **May God's tools of truth in this book encourage you as you walk in His will for your precious life!**

"Therefore if there is any consolation in Christ, if any comfort of love, if any fellowship of the Spirit, if any affection and mercy, fulfill my joy by being like-minded, having the same love, being of one accord, of one mind. Let nothing be done through selfish ambition or conceit, but in lowliness of mind let each esteem others better than himself. Let each of you look out not only for his own interests, but also for the interest of others." (Philippians 2:1-4)

"For we are His workmanship, created in Christ Jesus for good works, which God prepared beforehand that we should walk in them." (Ephesians 2:10)

NOTES

Scripture quotes, unless otherwise stated, were taken from:

Table of Contents

Introduction
More Tools for Liberating the Bruised

Jesus, our Master Carpenter!

"...He came to His own country and His disciples followed Him. And when the Sabbath had come, He began to teach in the synagogue. And many hearing Him were astonished, saying, 'Where did this Man get these things? And what wisdom is this which is given Him, that such mighty works are performed by His hands! Is this not the carpenter, the son of Mary, and brother of James, Joses, Judas, and Simon? And are not His sisters here with us?' So they were offended with Him.

"But Jesus said to them, 'A prophet is not without honor except in his own country, among his own relatives and in his own house.' Now He could do no mighty work there, except that He laid His hands on a few sick people and healed them. And He marveled because of their unbelief. Then He went about the villages in a circuit, teaching And He called the twelve to Himself, and began to send them out two by two..." (Mark 6:1-7)

Jesus, our Master Carpenter, generously leaves His unique tool box of truth and wisdom open that all may freely use—or reject. Our Master Carpenter willingly died on man's cruel tool of the Cross so those who choose to believe can be saved and Satan's captives may be set free! We are amazingly blessed to have access to our Master Carpenter Jesus and His tool box! May we not neglect our treasure and wisely use His tools—His Word—according to His instructions!

Romans 10:17 declares *"...faith comes by hearing, and hearing by the word of God!"* So it is very clear that the proclaimed and written Word of God is how God draws people to Himself! God's spoken and written Word is His means through which He teaches His people His ways—His commandments, statutes, and judgments. He says that when His people willingly apply—perform—His teachings to their precious lives, what He says He will do for them, He will do. We read proof here:

"Seek the LORD while He may be found, call upon Him while He is near. Let the wicked forsake his way, and the unrighteous man his thoughts; let him return to the LORD, and He will have mercy on him; and to our God, for He will abundantly pardon. 'For My thoughts are not your thoughts, nor are your ways My ways,' says the LORD, 'For as the heavens are higher than the earth, so are My ways higher than your ways, and My thoughts than your thoughts. For as the rain comes down and the snow from heaven, and do not return there, but water the earth, and make it

bring forth bud, that it may give seed to the sower and bread to the eater, **so shall My word be that goes forth from My mouth; it shall not return to Me void, but it shall accomplish what I please, and it shall prosper in the thing for which I sent it. For you shall go out with joy, and be led out with peace....'"** (Isaiah 55:6-12a)

Therefore, notice that we have been convicted in our hearts that as we are sharing God's counseling tools with you, we are to quote many scriptures from the Word of God as evidence of what is being taught. After making a statement with a scripture references following it, many people are very prone not to stop, look it up and read it! They may sincerely plan to go back and read it later—but many never slow down to get back to it.

In fact, only recently a counselor said, *"Bro. Joe, I love 'Liberating the Bruised!" It has helped me personally so much, and also for a number of years, the many people I have counseled! And, now, at last, I'm planning to take time to go back and read all the scripture references posted in it, for I didn't do it while reading the book."* You can understand why we feel that it is important actually to quote many of the powerful scriptures—lessons of truth—thus, making them handy for you to read as you study the counseling procedures and other teachings in this book. Concerning our vocabulary, the Lord impressed us to make these tools "an easy read" so that no one has to take time to look up a word in the dictionary!

Now let's begin in God's Word! Our Lord Jesus stood up in the Temple and opened the book of the prophet Isaiah, and this is what He read: **"The Spirit of the Lord is upon Me, because He hath anointed Me to preach the gospel to the poor; He hath sent me to heal the brokenhearted, to preach deliverance to the captives, and recovering of sight to the blind, to set at liberty them that are bruised, to preach the acceptable year of the Lord."** (Luke 4:18-19; Scofield Study Bible, King James with word changes.)

When the Lord instructed me to write the first book on spiritual warfare for counseling hurting people, I was reading that scripture and when I read **"...to set at liberty them that are Bruised,"** He spoke to my heart, giving me the title of the book, **"Liberating the Bruised,"** which was published in 1997. In some translations the word "oppressed" is used rather than bruised, but nonetheless, oppressed or bruised reflects "hurting." After writing the book, over the years the Lord taught me additional valuable counseling tools, which I began using during counseling. Then the first morning of one of the workshops, I shared some of these new tools which were recorded on a set of five "Counseling the Bruised" CDs, which became a little partner to "Liberating the Bruised." During counseling sessions, when some vital steps had been taken, I would sometimes pause, turn to the ministers and counselors, saying, "Now be sure to put that information in your counseling tool box!"

During workshops, quite a few people began approaching me, urging and encouraging me to write another book so I could share in print the counseling procedures along with the example prayers that I pray while working with counselees. I was definitely not eager to write another book. I was more focused on what God called me to be, a preacher, a speaking prophet! It is there that I am most comfortable! In all honesty, I felt if ministers and counselors would just read "Liberating the Bruised," they would be driven to take seriously the necessity to be still and know Him—to listen to Him—because the Lord Himself would most surely teach them what He has taught me! In James 1:5, to all Christians He says: ***"If any of you lack wisdom, let him ask of God, who gives to all liberally and without reproach, and it will be given to him."***

Much to my discouragement, the number of persons urging, encouraging and begging me to share what God has taught me, increased rather than decreased! Then, a number of persons who had attended my workshops began offering to share the notes that they had taken during workshops, so I wouldn't have to start totally from scratch. I would at least have a portion of track to start running on! These offers were followed with more urging, encouraging and begging! Then, straight from the Lord Himself came urging and encouraging words to my heart! I came under conviction that it would be selfish for me not to share "my tools" that the Lord had given me, tools which have been proven to help so very many souls find freedom from their torment, their bondage which led them to freedom with peace and joy. In my counseling I had seen how God's teachings had led so many of them to live fulfilled lives as they began walking in God's will! Ministers and counselors had observed the same as they had read and applied God's teachings shared in my first book. How dare I remain selfish with these additional tools as if they are "mine, all mine"? **They are really God's tools—tools that set Satan's captives free—that He has entrusted to my hands!**

I willingly chose to surrender and make myself available to the Lord in the area of writing even though it is not my comfort zone! I chose to obey my Lord Jesus because I love Him with all my heart, soul, mind, and strength! How dare I say "No!" to Him? When I willingly surrendered myself to obey Him, to my heart came peace and encouragement to share His tools that He placed in my care! He further encouraged me by reminding me that in sharing, not only would many ministers and counselors be blessed to have His tools in their ministry, but also the precious souls to whom they minister would surely be blessed!

After I willingly surrendered to share the tools, the Lord began speaking to my heart about Rita helping me to compile the book. She has been my precious partner and wife since 1957. Outside of the Lord Jesus Christ, Rita is the love of my life. She has faithfully served alongside me in ministry for over forty years, and she has a God-given writing ability. Years ago, Rita wrote a book—*Such As I Have, Give I Thee*—which is out of print at this time. (By the way, Lord willing, having it reprinted and available will be our next project.) Without hesitation Rita agreed to partner with me in compiling all these tools for us to share with others. What better partner could I have to write this book? We had peace and an excitement about being used of the Lord—being in the bulls-eye center of God's will! Together we began working where our Father is working—sharing His tools! Then God gave us the title: "More Tools for Liberating the Bruised."

The Lord also vanquished my great concerns that in writing this book, people would make the very serious error of thinking "More Tools for Liberating the Bruised" was a replacement for "Liberating the Bruised." I was very confident that the first book was a vital forerunner, containing many deep truths about spiritual warfare, all quite beneficial in giving a broader understanding of the additional biblical truths shared in its new partner, "More Tools for Liberating the Bruised." The first book covers studies on **"The Origin of Demonology," "Old Testament Scriptural Accounts of Demons,"** as well as the **"New Testament Scriptural Accounts of Demons."** It also contains an in-depth study on the **"The Fall and Restoration of Man"** and **"Restoring True Worship."** It also contains **biblical teachings about counseling procedures,** which are also illustrated through **actual case studies of some of my counselees.**

Therefore, I cannot stress enough the fact that many souls over the years have testified that they were set free having learned and applied the truths shared in "Liberating the Bruised." While my first book is no less helpful and continues to point many people to complete freedom through our Lord Jesus, the new tools book does offer some possible detours that moves the counseling forward at a little bit quicker pace. This evidence was encouraging because feeling that time is of the essence these days, it could help more people! **However, I strongly caution all of you dear ministers and counselors not to be impatient and in doing so, yield to temptation and fall into Satan's snare to take shortcuts and unwise detours that lead to dead ends which cause you to waste time finding your way back! Remember, Satan delights in seeing you go off on "wild goose chases!"** I'm confident that as you take time to diligently study the two books, the biblical content will be a blessing that leads you to very fruitful counseling sessions where you will experience over and over again the joy of seeing God's precious children set free from Satan's strongholds!

I want us to pause a moment and prayerfully consider **what God has to say about the importance of Godly, biblical counseling.** Without a doubt, God has given His Church a mandate to make counseling available to our fellow believers as well as non-believers, witnessing and offering help to them. Please meditate on God's words of instruction to us:

> *"You will guide me with Your **counsel**, and afterward receive me to glory."*
> (Psalm 73:24)

> *"Your testimonies also are my delight, and my **counselors**."* (Psalm 119:24)

> *"A wise man will hear, and will increase learning; and a man of understanding will attain **wise counsel**."* (Proverbs 1:5)

> *"**They would have none of my counsel**, and despised my every rebuke. Therefore, they shall eat the fruit of their own way, and be filled to the full with their own fancies. For the turning away of the simple will slay them, and the complacency of fools will destroy them; but **whoever listens to me will dwell safely, and will be secure without fear of evil**."* (Proverbs 1:30-33)

> *"Where there is **no counsel, the people fall**; but in the **multitude of counselors there is safety**."* (Proverbs 11:14)

> *"**Without counsel**, plans go awry, but in the **multitude of counselors** they are established."* (Proverbs 15:22)

> *"Now why do you cry aloud? Is there no king in your midst? **Has your counselor perished?** For pangs have seized you like a woman in labor."* (Micah 4:9)

> *"Finally, my brethren, be strong in the Lord, and in the power of His might. **Put on the whole armor of God, that ye may be able to stand against the wiles of the devil.** For we do not wrestle against flesh and blood, but against principalities, against powers, against the rulers of the darkness of this age, against spiritual hosts of wickedness in the heavenly places. Therefore take up the whole armor of God, that you may be able to withstand in the evil day, and having done all, to stand. Stand, therefore, having girded your waist with truth, having put on the breastplate of righteousness, and shod your feet with the preparation of the gospel of peace; above all, taking the shield of faith with which you will be able to quench all the fiery darts of the wicked one. And take the helmet of salvation, and the sword of the Spirit, which is the word of God; **praying always with all prayer and supplication in the Spirit, being watchful to this end with all perseverance and supplication for all saints**."* (Ephesians 6:10-18)

Let each of us carefully consider the sometimes neglected, latter portion of the last sentence concerning spiritual warfare. There is a very **critical** truth involved with the instructions for us to be **"watching with all perseverance."** For it teaches each of us **personally ("me, myself, and I"), the importance of being clean before the Lord in order to care for others. The following scripture comes to mind that stresses this necessity for cleanliness of our hearts and cautions us not to look at others with critical spirits, thoughts and words of condemnation, but rather for us to be driven by the compassion of Jesus to offer them help—display efforts to rescue them from the enemy:**

> *"**Judge not, that you be not judged. For with what judgment you judge, you will be judged; and with the measure you use, it will be measured back to you. And why do you look at the speck in your brother's eye, but do not consider the plank in your own eye? Or how can you say to your brother, 'Let me removed the speck from your eye'; and look, a plank is in your own eye? Hypocrite! First remove the plank from your own eye, and then you will see clearly to remove the speck from your brother's eye.**"* (Matthew 7:1-5)

Oh that all of us would persevere to have clean, pure hearts, void of "planks" and critical spirits, and persevere to see others with God's eyes, hear them with God's ears, and understand and love them with God's heart. Oh that all of us would constantly stay on guard against the deceits of the enemy **so that our hearts can remain pure for our own sake as well as other souls**, as the following scripture teaches:

31

"Brethren, if a man is overtaken in any trespass, you who are spiritual restore such a one in the spirit of gentleness, considering yourself lest you also be tempted. Bear one another's burdens, and so fulfill the law of Christ. For if anyone thinks himself to be something, when he is nothing, he deceives himself. But *let each one examine his own work,* and then he will have rejoicing in himself alone, and not in another. For each one shall bear his own load. Let him who is taught the word share in all good things with him who teaches. Do not be deceived, God is not mocked; for whatever a man sows, that he will also reap. For he who sows to his flesh will of the flesh reap corruption, but he who sows to the Spirit will of the Spirit reap everlasting life. And, let us not grow weary while doing good, for in due season we shall reap if we do not lose heart. Therefore, as we have opportunity, let us do good to all, especially to those who are of the household of faith."* (Galatians 6:1-10)

We are all called according to God's purpose in this life. (II Timothy 1:9) **No matter what mission field we serve Him on, our enemy Satan will tempt us from time to time to grow weary in well-doing!** The mission field of counseling is no exception, as many of you can more than likely testify! In counseling sessions, it is often grievous to one's heart to learn of the backgrounds of people who have gone through abusive times. It is certainly equally grievous to counsel those who have been the abusers who cannot go back in time and simply erase their ill deeds. Indeed, out of our love and devotion to our Lord and Savior, we should choose to "not grow weary in well-doing." I can testify that in depending on the Lord to renew my strength and restore the joy of my salvation, in choosing to "keep on keeping on," my heart is always rewarded by seeing souls find freedom, peace and joy. That makes it worth it all!

Indeed, not one of us should grow weary in well-doing, for the laborers in the fields are still all too few. As sheep in God's flock, when passing through wearisome times, may we never fail to take times of refreshing with "The Shepherd," for He alone can restore our strength! *"The Lord is my Shepherd; I shall not want. He makes me to lie down in green pastures; He leads me beside the still waters."* (Psalm 23:1)

While some choose to rely on the Lord's strength to keep on keeping on, other ministers and counselors have grown weary and spend as little time as necessary getting into and dealing with the critical, unpleasant problems of people—thus neglecting them. In their weariness, suffering with "burnout," they attempt to console their people with, "I'm praying for you! God bless!" To the opposite extreme, Satan has also succeeded in putting ministers and counselors on "guilt trips"—making them think they are sinning if they don't jump to attention when troubled people holler and cry!

This is why it is critical for ministers and counselors to rely on the Lord for wisdom to govern their schedules and keep their priorities in proper order! I cannot stress enough the importance of **(1) with pure hearts, putting God first!** (Please note that I did not say "ministry first"!) Then **(2) immediate family—for God ordained the family before He established the larger "Church**

family," and next **(3) the mission field beyond your house**, on the job site, and various pathways on which the Lord places you while sojourning toward your heavenly home.

Keeping this in mind, I strongly caution ministers and counselors to depend on the Holy Spirit in their hearts to govern their schedules rather than letting their counselees, and even other ministries and personal activities, govern their time. As many ministers and counselors have probably experienced, "enough is never enough" in this pressure-cooker world! With so many people being in the "I want it now!" mind set, some hurting people are very prone to put the pressure on their pastors and counselors! These counselees who have the attitude, "It's all about ME! I'm hurting worse than anyone else! You HAVE to help me NOW!" Some throw in the threat of suicide with hopes of putting more pressure on the counselor! Please prayerfully read this scripture as you parallel "time" with "precious oil":

> *"And being in Bethany in the house of Simon the leper, as He sat at the table, a woman came having an alabaster flask of very costly oil of spikenard. Then she broke the flask and poured it on His head. But there were some who were indignant among themselves, and said, 'Why was this fragrant oil wasted? For it might have been sold for more than three hundred denarii and given to the poor.' And they criticized her sharply. But Jesus said, 'Let her alone. Why do you trouble her? She has done a good work for Me. For you have the poor with you always, and whenever you wish you may do them good; but Me you do not have always. She has done what she could. She has come beforehand to anoint My body for burial. Assuredly, I say to you, wherever this gospel is preached in the whole world, what this woman has done will also be told as a memorial to her.'"* (Mark 14:3-9)

There are times when it may appear to others that pastors and counselors are neglecting people, thus they suffer criticism. When we read in this passage of scripture about the lady being criticized for neglecting the poor, we know that Jesus was about to be crucified. She knew his life was in danger and she seized the moment to express her deep love for Jesus. The timing of her ministering to Jesus was perfect and counted as a beautiful sacrifice unto the Lord, even though some were full of indignation and criticism! So pastors and counselors should remember that no matter what they do, they will have critics—so do God's will and have peace and joy no matter what others say!

This brings me to another crucial point about God's wonderful servants who are committed to serving Him and helping His people. In order for them to be able to hear the voice of the Lord clearly guiding them in their hearts, they must have clean hearts! For their sake as well as for the sake of everyone on their pathways, they, too, should most definitely be free from any bondage within themselves! Otherwise, they make themselves extremely vulnerable to temptation, critical problems, and destruction of not only their testimony for Christ, but also of the joy of walking with the Lord.

Satan is thrilled to see the reputations and ministries of God's pastors and counselors destroyed and displayed before others to be mocked. My heart is grieved, knowing that this has happened in all too many churches and ministries. We must all heed God's warning in I Peter 5:8, **"Be sober, be vigilant, because your adversary, the devil, like a roaring lion walketh about, seeking whom he may devour,"** or we can be assured that he will most surely attempt to catch us in his snare!

Ministers and counselors—for their own sakes as well as the people to whom they minister—must have all their "known" sins sincerely confessed! They dare not expect to accomplish God's will if they are stubbornly remaining in sin! Our Lord stresses the importance of confessing sin—even "unforgiveness" hidden in their hearts—as we read:

> *"And whenever you stand praying, if you have anything against anyone, forgive him, that your Father in heaven may also forgive you your trespasses. But if you do not forgive, neither will your Father in heaven forgive your trespasses."* (Mark 11:25-26)

We find in God's Word the qualifications of all ministers, bishops, deacons...all overseers of the flock in I Timothy 3:1-13, which declares that their lives should be right before the Lord, not double-tongued, not given to wine, not violent, not greedy for money, not covetous; gentle, humble, not quarrelsome, and one who rules his own house well.

> *"(...if a man does not know how to rule his own house, how will he take care of the church of God?); not a novice...lest being puffed up with pride he fall into the same condemnation as the devil. Moreover he must have a good testimony among those who are outside, lest he fall into reproach and the snare of the devil."* (I Timothy 3:5-7)

And, he is to be bold in the faith and love others!

> *"Love has been perfected among us in this: that we may have boldness in the day of judgment; because as He is, so are we in this world. There is no fear in love; but perfect love casts out fear, because fear involves torment. But he who fears has not been made perfect in love. We love Him because He first loved us. If someone says, 'I love God,' and hates his brother, he is a liar; for he who does not love his brother whom he has seen, how can he love God whom he has not seen? And this commandment we have from Him: that he who loves God must love his brother also."* (I John 4:17-21)

Oh how I long for God's biblical counseling to be taught and practiced in the Church—in churches where it ought to be! It should be a priority, but instead, in all too many churches, all other activities are far above it. To my surprise and sorrow one day I heard a pastor say that he does not counsel because he would have to "clean up his life." Sadly, he is only one of many pastors who are in bondage today. Many under shepherds are so burdened down with hustle-bustle schedules that they have no time to listen to cries from their sheep's broken hearts. Many really don't care, therefore, they don't offer to listen to the cries, wipe their tears and offer solutions. While some counseling is offered in some churches, some limit the time—and charge by the hour. For the most part, those needing counseling are referred out to individual Christian counseling ministries and to secular counseling as well. Oh, that we would have Godly counselors in "God's house" in these critical times when our world is so full of hurting souls who are held captive by the merciless enemy.

Please know that I am extremely grateful to all of you who have willingly surrendered to God's calling to proclaim the Gospel and do not compromise and depart from preaching sound doctrine. To those of you who have willingly surrendered to Christian counseling ministry, and offer it in the boundaries of sound doctrine, I am extremely grateful to you as well! God bless you! I encourage you all to be steadfast in your calling. Stay snuggled up to the Lord, consistently live a clean, pure life that exemplifies Christ and glorifies His name. In doing so, I know you will experience the peace and joy of daily walking God's will, including the joy of helping people find their freedom in Christ!

Dear pastors, ministers, missionaries, and counselors, it is a deep desire of my heart, and Rita's, that "More Tools for Liberating the Bruised," partnered with "Liberating the Bruised" will truly be a blessing to you and to your ministry. It brings us both joy to know that the Lord knows of your labors and sacrifices and will bless you as you willingly serve Him in the battle against the enemy!

Chapter One
Legal Rights Tools of God, Satan and Christians

Truly blessed are those whose God is the Lord! Blessed are those people who know His laws, recognize them as love-laws, and out of their love for Him abide by them! Blessed are those people—those Christians—who trust Him to be their Defense Attorney and Supreme Judge against the prosecuting attorney—the enemy and accuser of the brethren!

"Rejoice in the LORD, O you righteous! For praise from the upright is beautiful. Praise the LORD with the harp; make melody to Him with an instrument of ten strings. Sing to Him a new song; play skillfully with a shout of joy. For the word of the LORD is right. And all His work is done in truth. He loves righteousness and justice; the earth is full of the goodness of the LORD. By the word of the LORD the heavens were made, and all the host of them by the breath of His mouth. He gathers the waters of the sea together as a heap; He lays up the deep in storehouses. Let all the earth fear the LORD; let all the inhabitants of the world stand in awe of Him. For He spoke, and it was done; He commanded, and it stood fast. The LORD brings the counsel of the nations to nothing; He makes the plans of the people of no effect. The counsel of the LORD stands forever, the plans of His heart to all generations. Blessed is the nation whose God is the LORD, the people He has chosen as His own inheritance. The LORD looks from heaven; He sees all the sons of men. From the place of His dwelling He looks on all the inhabitants of the earth; He fashions their hearts individually; He considers all their works. No king is saved by the multitude of an army; a mighty man is not delivered by great strength. A horse is a vain hope for safety; neither shall it deliver any by its great strength. Behold, the eye of the LORD is on those who fear Him, on those who hope in His mercy, to deliver their soul from death, and to keep them alive in famine. Our soul waits for the LORD; He is our help and our shield. For our heart shall rejoice in Him. Because we have trusted in His holy name. Let Your mercy, O LORD, be upon us, just as we hope in You." (Psalm 33:1-22)

"As it is written: There is none righteous, no, not one; there is none who understands; there is none who seeks after God. They have all turned aside; they have together become unprofitable; there is none who does good, no not one. Their throat is an open tomb; with their tongues they have practiced deceit; the poison of asps is under their lips; whose mouth is full of cursing and bitterness. Their feet are swift to shed blood; destruction and misery are in their ways; and the way of peace they have not known. There is no fear of God before their eyes...all have sinned and fall short of the glory of God." (Romans 3:10-18; 23)

Yet, *"God so loved the world, that He gave His only begotten Son, that whoever believes in Him should not perish but have everlasting life. For God did not send His Son into the world to condemn the world, but that the world through Him might be saved. He who believes in Him is not condemned; but he who does not believe is condemned already because he has not believed in the name of the only begotten Son of God. And this is the condemnation, that the light has come into the world, and men loved darkness rather than light, because their deeds were evil."* (John 3:16-19)

From the beginning, mankind has always had the God-given legal right—the freedom—to choose for or against God. Had He made us robots, we would not know the peace and joy of coming to know Him personally as our heavenly Father—as our Savior and Lord! Grievously enough, as we've just read, the Bible clearly reports of mankind repeatedly choosing to rebel and reject God—and rejecting God's priceless "Tool"—the sinless Lamb of God—who could extract their very souls from Satan's grasp and Hell itself! Out of our Creator's amazing love and grace He chose to sacrifice His Son to pay for our sins, while mankind has created useful tools, as well as tools to be used for evil. In times when Jesus walked the earth, the Jews fashioned with their hands whips, typically having three thongs, for scourging. While Jewish law set a limit on how many times a person could be struck with the whip—no more than 40 times—the Romans set none. It was simply determined by the man in charge over the event. On the end of the thongs the Romans attached jagged pieces of bone or metal to add more painful cruelty to their tool. With wood and metals, they used anvils and tongs to form tools—swords, hammers, nails and crosses for executions. Mankind blindfolded the Lamb of God and they even struck Him with the palms of their bare hands! They scourged Him on His bare back with great cruelty, and created a crown from a very thorny vine and pressed it upon His brow—and mocked Him, saying "Hail! King of the Jews"—and they pierced His side with a sword. Yes, mankind's tools were unmercifully used to torture and crucify our Savior—the sinless Lamb of God.

It's a sad truth that we Christians fail to keep to the forefront of our minds not only how Jesus suffered, bled and died physically for us on Calvary, but that He who was without sin took upon Himself the grotesque horror of all mankind's sins. What He felt is truly impossible to adequately describe, but we are brought to at least understand somewhat as we read what Jesus declared on the cross: *"Now from the sixth hour until the ninth hour there was darkness over all the land. And about the ninth hour Jesus cried out with a loud voice, saying, 'Eli, Eli, lama sabachthani?' that is 'My God, My God, why have You forsaken Me?"* (Matthew 27:45-46) He was expressing the grief of being in a sin-state—covered with our sins—that brings a void, a separation from Holy God! Before Jesus suffered this, while on earth, He suffered rejection, verbal abuse, mockery, unfair judgments and words of condemnation that He endured—on our behalf!

"He is despised and rejected by men, a Man of sorrows, and acquainted with grief. And we hid, as it were, our faces from Him; He was despised, and we did not esteem Him. Surely He has borne our griefs and carried our sorrows; yet we esteemed Him stricken, smitten by God, and afflicted. But He was wounded for our transgressions,

He was bruised for our iniquities; the chastisement for our peace was upon Him, and by His stripes we are healed. All we like sheep have gone astray; we have turned, every one, to his own way; and the LORD has laid on Him the iniquity of us all." (Isaiah 53:3-6)

Most surely, we Christians fail to remember often enough His awesome mercy and grace upon us! When things aren't going according to our desires, may we as Christians pause often to remember that it was our sins, our iniquities, that nailed our Savior to the cross! As Isaiah said: **"...we are all like an unclean thing, and all our righteousnesses are like filthy rags!"** (Isaiah 64:6a) We should take time to remember *"...it was Caiaphas who advised the Jews that it was expedient that one man should die for the people."* (John 18:14)

And, after Jesus was tried, Pilate said, *"I find no fault in Him at all."* (John 18:38) But then, Pilate let mankind vote, saying, *"'But you have a custom that I should release someone to you at the Passover. Do you therefore want me to release to you the King of the Jews?' Then they **all** cried again, saying, 'Not this Man, but Barabbas!' Now Barabbas was a robber. So then Pilate took Jesus and scourged Him. And the soldiers twisted a crown of thorns and put it on His head, and they put on Him a purple robe. Then they said, 'Hail, King of the Jews!' And they struck Him with their hands. Pilate then went out again, and said to them, 'Behold, I am bringing Him out to you, that you may know that I find no fault in Him."* (John18:39-40; 19:1-4)

We heard this saying that expressed this truth quite well some time ago: "Jesus came to pay a debt He didn't owe because we owed a debt we couldn't pay!" What an amazing, awesome love of God—how can we neglect to be full of gratitude and love Him with all our being, all the days of our lives? Indeed, the sacrificial Lamb of God is God's gift to the world—a priceless tool that can extract every believer from Satan's stronghold and secure their place in heaven forever! May we as Christians not fail to think often on these truths, and to teach others, our counselees, truth about what Jesus did for sinners such as we! May we apply them personally and teach others as Jesus said to the scribe: *"...The first of all the commandments is: 'Hear, O Israel, the LORD our God, the LORD is one. And you shall love the LORD your God with all your heart, with all your soul, with all your mind, and with all your strength.' This is the first commandment. And the second, like it, is this: 'you shall love your neighbor as yourself.' There is no other commandment greater than these."* (Mark 12:29-31)

As a minister and Christian counselor, my heart has been heavy over the years to observe so much immaturity on the part of Christians who have long had the opportunity to draw nigh unto the Lord, study His Word, and grow to spiritual maturity. I think it is partly because they fail to remember the above subject, thus they are not motivated by deep gratitude and love for the Lord. I have also seen some Christians who "know the Word well" but they still "don't walk it to the fullest"—they only walk on the "easiest, most pleasant paths." I'm very sad to say that some of these immature Christians are even in places of service, such as ministers, teachers, missionaries, and counselors! Becoming complacent in immaturity, they have left themselves in vulnerable, even dangerous positions where the enemy more easily tempts and deters them from God's will! Some have even been drawn into lifestyles that have destroyed their reputations and testimonies for Christ. Scripture below, in Hebrews 5:12-14, tells of such immaturity in persons in those days who should have been mature—and grievously so, it applies to today!

> *"For though by this time you ought to be teachers, you need someone to teach you again the first principles of the oracles of God; and you have come to need milk and not solid food. For everyone who partakes only of milk is unskilled in the word of righteousness, for he is a babe. But solid food belongs to those who are of full age, that is, those who by reason of use have their senses exercised to discern both good and evil."* (Hebrews 5:12-14)

Poor spiritual health, like poor physical health, comes from picking at one's "food," leaving the healthy diet and just drinking "the milk." This makes one vulnerable to suffer malnutrition! Good spiritual health comes by eating well-balanced "meals" and chewing the "meat" well—even if it seems tough—and swallowing the wholesome "meal" in its entirety! Sadly enough, too many Christians are like "picky" children—they aren't "cleaning their plates!"

A. LEGAL RIGHTS TOOLS OF SOVEREIGN GOD, JEHOVAH

LEGAL RIGHTS TOOL OF GOD: JESUS OUR TEACHER, OUR SAVIOR

We read in the book of John, when Jesus was on the earth that Nicodemus, a ruler of the Jews, had wisely observed Jesus. Then he came seeking Jesus by night, and stated to Him: *"Rabbi, **we know that You are a teacher come from God**; for no one can do these signs that You do unless God is with Him."* (John 3:2b) We know the wonderful story of Nicodemus who then came to believe and trust in the Lord Jesus as His Messiah, His Savior and Lord!

It is my great concern that some Christians, including ministers, teachers, missionaries, and counselors, have not snuggled up to the Lord and taken seriously **the necessity for them to learn from our Master Teacher who can ground them in sound doctrine**. Therefore, they are left wide open for Satan to gain ground in their own lives. Some precious Christians have even been sorely deceived into thinking themselves as powerful tools appointed by God rather than tools powered by God's guidance and wisdom. Some are deceived into thinking themselves as smart or smarter than God, and arrogantly voice, "I command by-my-faith, in Jesus' name, that You do thus-and-so!"—so often giving orders to their Potter that are not in His will.

This has happened so much in the public eye that Satan takes joy in using it to bring confusion and skepticism to Christianity as a whole. These precious well-meaning Christians have been cunningly detoured away from being Christ-like examples for the younger Christians, weaker brethren, and for Christians who are being held tight in Satan's strongholds. They have become stumbling blocks! Coming straight from the mouth of our perfect Lord Jesus—in whom there was no sin—comes the following message that emphasizes the fact that all Christians are to listen for wisdom to be given from God, not from any human reasoning that may "sound good!" If Jesus found it necessary to seek the will of the Father during His earthly walk, how dare we venture to think that we should not do the same? For, when Jesus was on earth, he declared this:

> *"I can of Myself do nothing. As I hear, I judge; and My judgment is righteous, because I do not seek My own will but the will of the Father who sent Me."* (John 5:30)

Therefore, it is so critical that we as Christians depend moment by moment on our Lord Jesus Christ who lives in the form of the Holy Spirit in our hearts to give us wisdom! Otherwise, we are in danger of being carried away with unsound doctrine, as we find proclaimers of God's truths, evangelists, pastors, and teachers who were being warned about in Ephesians 4:11-16:

> *"And He Himself gave some to be apostles, some prophets, some evangelists, and some pastors and teachers,* **for the equipping of the saints, for the work of the ministry, for the edifying of the body of Christ, till we all come to the unity of the faith and of the knowledge of the Son of God**, *to a perfect man, to the measure of the stature of the fullness of Christ: that* **we should no longer be children, tossed to and fro and carried about with every wind of doctrine, by the trickery of men, in the cunning craftiness of deceitful plotting, but speaking the truth in love, may grow up in all things into Him who is the head—Christ**—*from whom the whole body joined and knit together by what every joint supplies, according to the effective working by which every part does its share, causes growth of the body for the edifying of itself in love."*

Powerful message for all Christians, indeed! We are to "grow up in the Lord," be "in unity together with Christ" and be "keepers of our brothers and sisters!" We are responsible to share our testimony and train babes in Christ up in the way that they should go. It is our responsibility to teach them how awesome our Almighty God is, how fully trustworthy He is, and likewise, teach them that through their authority in Him, they can stand strong in the war against unsound doctrine—against the enemy spewing deceit! Far too many Christians have already been blown about! Far too many have been hindered from learning about God's legal tools—weapons of war— that they can use to stand against the enemy. And, neither have they learned that the enemy has acquired some legal tools that he claims for his own and quite effectively uses to defeat Christians. All Christians should know God well, mature in Him, and be trained by Him to discern both good and evil—and then share those powerful weapons of truth with others!

LEGAL RIGHTS TOOLS OF GOD: SOVEREIGNTY AND AUTHORITY OVER ALL

Therefore, let us begin our study to get to know our awesome God Almighty better and in doing so, learn more about His legal tools, weapons of war, the power of His might. In order to do that, let us obey Him as He directs us in His own words: **"Be still, and know that I am God; I will be** *exalted among the nations, I will be exalted in the earth! The Lord of hosts is with us; The God of Jacob is our refuge. Selah."* (Psalm 46:10-11) Let us remember that the word "Selah" means to "pause and think on these things."

I believe that when Christians take time to pause at length to better know our sovereign Lord they will be **(1)** drawn to have an **attitude of far greater respect and awesome reverence** before their Creator, their sovereign God. When they understand and believe these awesome truths **(2)** they will **be far more grateful to God for His great, sacrificial love for them, and for His mercy and grace upon them**. Then **(3) their trust in the Lord will increase, thus, their confidence will increase in knowing who they really are in Jesus Christ, children of God**. And **(4)** upon better understanding the **privilege of their salvation—their legal tool "their position in Jesus Christ," they have no cause to fear the Devil**! They can, indeed, learn to discern good from evil! They will understand that Christians' *"...weapons are not carnal but mighty through God to the pulling down of strongholds!"* (II Corinthians 10:4) Having this greater understanding, when confronted with the enemy, Satan, they can know without doubt that through Jesus Christ, they can resist, rebuke, and defeat him consistently if they choose to do so. They will know how to legally claim back the tools that were legally acquired from them by Satan. The key lies in their choices to believe, trust in, listen to and obey their Creator, the Almighty, sovereign God who holds the most powerful tools, or yield to, listen to and obey the enemy who is all too eager to legally claim control of God's precious children!

What I desire for you as ministers and counselors to glean from this—and to teach others—is that our God Jehovah is sovereign, the Almighty, the Powerful One, the Mighty One, and that Satan, the Devil can do nothing in our God's universe without His permission! We read in John 1:1: *"In the beginning was the Word, and the Word was with God, and the Word was God."* (John 1:1) We read in Matthew 28:19: *"'Go therefore and make disciples of all the nations, baptizing them in the name of **the Father and the Son and of the Holy Spirit**, teaching them to observe all things that I have commanded you; and lo, I am with you always, even to the end of the age.' Amen."* These two scriptures confirm that our God is **"the Word and the Trinity"—God the Father, the Son, and the Holy Spirit**. No matter what anyone else thinks the truth is, **OUR GOD—IN THREE PERSONS—HAS THE FINAL SAY IN EVERYTHING!** After a thorough study of God's Word—His sovereignty—one would be foolish not to come to the logical conclusion that the Lord God Almighty is God, Creator and Ruler of all the universe. Let us begin by taking a close look at what God has to say through His Word about His legal tools!

Our God, the Word, our Creator, our God in three persons, spoke and it all began. In the midst of His awesome creation came rebellion, enemies and wars. As I've shared before, over many years my heart has been grieved to see so many of God's servants in various positions of leadership fall into Satan's deceptive snares that he actually acquired "legally" for a wide variety of reasons! For all too many years, the subject of spiritual warfare has not been taught to babes in Christ, thus, all too many have been sorely deceived, tricked by the enemy, and held tightly in his strongholds! Sadly enough, he continues to set snares and succeed in capturing precious Christians! If Christians are to stand strong as they journey on this earth through storms of life—through trials and tribulations—**I deem it essential** for them not only **(1)** to know the Lord, God Almighty extremely well, but also **(2)** to understand who God's enemy is—who is also their enemy, and **(3)** to understand their legal rights to stand against this enemy! No doubt, far too many Christians do not realize that God has already established legal rights tools for all believers that they can use to defend themselves and conquer the enemy! I believe one of the main hindrances to their living lives victoriously over the enemy is that they do not really know their God and Savior Jesus nearly as well as they should! While the Lord dwells in their hearts, it's as if He dwells in a corner of their hearts, available only for special occasions! It's as if they do not love Him with ALL of their hearts as He desires them to do so! Our sovereign God, Jehovah, our Lord Jesus is available to communicate with them 24 hours in every day, yet they treat Him as if He has to schedule an appointment with them! Yet, our Lord is always available to teach, guide, warn against temptation, and convict His children when they have yielded and stepped out into dangerous territory, giving the enemy opportunity to bring them down! What an awesome opportunity each one robs from themself when choosing not to seek to know their sovereign God better!

Even though the word **"sovereign"** does not occur in any form in our English Bible, it conveys biblical thought of **the supreme authority of God**. In the Greek, He is called, **"pantokrator, Almighty"** [3841] in II Corinthians 6:18, *"I will be a Father to you, and you shall be My sons and daughters, says **the Lord God Almighty**.* [3841] In the book of Revelation it is used eight times. (Rev. 1:8; 4:8; 11:17; 15:3; 16:7, 14; 19:15; 21:22)

We see in I Timothy 6:15, *"...which He will manifest in His own time, He who is the blessed and only **potentate** [1413] **Dunástes**, "Possessor of power or authority, referring to the Lord as absolute ruler; the King of kings, and Lord of lords." Also, in Ephesians 1:11, we read:

> *"In Him also we have obtained an inheritance, being predestinated according to the purpose of Him who works all things according to the counsel of His own will."*
> (The Zondervan Pictorial Bible Dictionary, page 807)

In the Hebrew **"Šadday"** [7706]: a masculine noun and name for God means "Shaddai, Almighty." The word occurred only forty-eight times in the Hebrew Bible, but thirty-one times in the book of Job. We find people of faith in the Old Testament referring to Him as El Shaddai, God Almighty! When the Lord appeared to Abraham when he was ninety-nine years old, God identified Himself as El Shaddi, God Almighty. (Genesis 17:1) And, we read in Genesis 28:1-3; 35:11 that all three patriarchs knew Him by this name, as did Joseph in Genesis 48:3; cf. Exodus 6:3. Hebrew **"Yehowah"** [3068] is a noun meaning "God." It is the name for God in the Jewish language. It's the name that God used when He revealed Himself to Moses. Before the renaissance, it was written without vowels, YHWH. (The Complete Word Study Dictionary Old Testament Baker; Carpenter. Page 1105, A.M.G. Publishers, Chattanooga, TN 37422, U.S.A.)

LEGAL RIGHTS TOOLS OF GOD: HE IS LORD, GOD, JEHOVAH

It is fairly well accepted by most Bible scholars that its meaning is that God has always been in existence; and we read, *"And God said to Moses, 'I AM WHO I AM.' And He said, 'Thus you shall say to the children of Israel, 'I AM has sent me to you.'"* (Exodus 3:14) He is the one who was, who is, and who will always be. Different translations of the Bible render the divine names: Lord, God, and Jehovah.

Deuteronomy 4:39: *"Therefore, know this day, and consider it in your heart, that the LORD Himself is God in heaven above and on the earth beneath; there is no other."*

I Chronicles 29:11-12: *"Yours, O LORD is the greatness, the power and the glory, the victory and the majesty; for all that is in heaven and in earth is Yours; Yours is the kingdom O LORD, and You are exalted as head over all. Both riches and honor come from You and You reign over all. In Your hand is power and might; in Your hand it is to make great and to give strength to all."*

Job 9:12: *"If He takes away, who can hinder Him? Who can say to Him, what are You doing?"*

Psalm 29:10: *"The LORD sat enthroned at the flood, and the Lord sits as King forever."*

Psalm 47:2-4: *"For the LORD Most High is awesome; He is a great King over all the earth. He will subdue the peoples under us, and the nations under our feet. He will choose our inheritance for us, the excellence of Jacob who He loves. Selah."*

Psalms 47:8-9: *"God reigns over the nations; God sits on His holy throne. The princes of the people have gathered together, the people of the God of Abraham. For the shields of the earth belong to God; He is greatly exalted."*

Psalms 83:18: *"That they may know that You, whose name alone is the LORD, are the Most High over all the earth."*

Psalms 93:1-2: *"The LORD reigns, He is clothed with majesty; the LORD is clothed, He has girded Himself with strength. Surely the world is established, so that it cannot be moved. Your throne is established from of old; You are from everlasting."*

Psalm 135:6: *"Whatever the LORD pleases He does, in heaven and in earth, in the seas and in all deep places."*

Psalm 147:4-5: *"He counts the number of the stars; He calls them all by name. Great is our LORD and mighty in power; His understanding is infinite."*

Daniel 2:20b-22: *"...Blessed be the name of God forever and ever, for wisdom and might are His. And He changes the times and the seasons; He removes kings and raises up kings; He gives wisdom to the wise and knowledge to those who have understanding. He reveals deep and secret things; He knows what is in the darkness, and light dwells with Him."*

At this point, I think it important for us to pause and take time to focus on the realization that this awesome, sovereign God that Daniel spoke about is part of the Trinity—the Father, the Son, and the Holy Spirit! Indeed, how awesome to know that we human beings have the privilege of knowing and having a relationship with the Father, the Son and the Holy Spirit! For, *"in the beginning was the Word, and the Word was with God, and the Word was God. He was in the beginning with God. All things were made through Him, and without Him nothing was made that was made.* **In Him was life, and the life was the light of men.** *And, the light shines in the darkness, and the darkness did not comprehend it."* (John 1:1-5) Jesus said to us, *"As long as I am in the world, I am the light of the world."* (John 9:5)

What powerful truth! And, it is amazingly wonderful to think of the Trinity, the Father, the Son, and the Holy Spirit, while being ONE, yet serving unique purposes in three forms! Indeed, as determined when learning of **the sovereignty of God—there is none like Him**! Some people rob themselves of grasping these amazing truths about the Trinity—mistakenly thinking that Jesus did not come into existence until He was born, crucified, buried and was resurrected! The three-in-one have always been in existence and have never been sitting around twiddling their thumbs! Take time to meditate on the time when King Nebuchadnezzar had kidnapped the three young Jewish men, Shadrach, Meshach and Abed-Nego, and was using them as his slaves. He counted them as very good servants, but when the day came that they refused to bow down and worship the king's gods, in fury, he had them bound and cast into the fiery furnace. However, read the transformation of his view of those young men and the Almighty God in whom they trusted as their authority:

"Then King Nebuchadnezzar was astonished; and he rose in haste and spoke, saying to his counselors, 'Did we not cast three men bound into the midst of the fire?' They answered and said to the king, 'True, O king.' 'Look!' he answered, 'I see four men loose, walking in the midst of the fire; and they are not hurt, and the form of the fourth is like the **Son of God.** *' Then Nebuchadnezzar went near the mouth of the burning fiery furnace and spoke, saying 'Shadrach, Meshach, and Abed-Nego, servants of the* **Most High God**, *come out, and come here.' Then Shadrach, Meshach, and Abed-Nego came from the midst of the fire. And the satraps, administrators, governors, and the kings' counselors gathered together, and they saw these men on whose bodies the fire had no power; the hair of their head was not singed nor were their garments affected, and the smell of fire was not on them. Nebuchadnezzar spoke, saying,* **'Blessed be the God of Shadrach,**

Meshach, and Abed-Nego, who sent His Angel and delivered His servants who trusted in Him, and they have frustrated the king's word, and yielded their bodies, that they should not serve nor worship any god except their own God!" (Daniel 3:24-28)

God Almighty most surely demonstrated His power and authority so well, that Nebuchadnezzar established a decree that no one in his kingdom even speak anything negative against Shadrach, Meshach, and Abed-Nego's God! He promoted the young men to higher positions in the province of Babylon, too!

Later, we read Daniel 4:34-35: *"And at the end of the time, I, Nebuchadnezzar, lifted my eyes to heaven, and my understanding returned to me; and I blessed the Most High and praised and honored Him who lives forever: for His dominion is an everlasting dominion, and His kingdom is from generation to generation. All the inhabitants of the earth are reputed as nothing; He does according to His will in the array of heaven and among the inhabitants of the earth. No one can restrain His hand or say to Him, What have You done?"*

What **a wonderful example of believers being redeemed, claimed and kept by Jesus** even before He descended from heaven to walk among men and die! What power and authority the Trinity— our God the Father, the Son, and the Holy Spirit—holds, indeed! Most surely, our God Almighty is like none other!

Matthew 6:9-13: *"In this manner, therefore, pray: Our Father in heaven, Hallowed be Your name. Your kingdom come, Your will be done on earth as it is in heaven. Give us this day our daily bread. And forgive our debts as we forgive our debtors. And do not lead us into temptation, but deliver us from the evil one, for Yours is the kingdom and the power and the glory forever, Amen."*

Acts 17:24: *"God, who made the world and everything in it, since He is LORD of heaven on earth, does not dwell in temples made with hands."*

There is no doubt that our God's mercy is under His sovereign will! We read in Romans 9:14-24:

"What shall we say then? Is there unrighteousness with God? Certainly not! For He says to Moses, 'I will have mercy on whomever I will have mercy, and I will have compassion on whomever I will have compassion.' So then it is not of him who wills, nor of him who runs, but of God who shows mercy. For the Scripture says to Pharaoh, 'For this very purpose, I have raised you up, that I may show My power in you, and that My name may be declared in all the earth. Therefore He has mercy on whom He wills, and whom He wills He hardens. You will say to me then, 'Why does He still find fault? For who has resisted His will?' But indeed, O man, who are you to reply against God? Will the thing formed say to Him who formed it,

'Why have you made me like this?' Does not the potter have power over the clay, from the same lump to make one vessel for honor and another for dishonor? What if God wanting to show His wrath and to make His power known, endured with much longsuffering the vessels of wrath prepared for destruction, and that He might make known the riches of His glory on the vessels of mercy, which He had prepared beforehand for glory, even us whom He called, not of the Jews only, but also of the Gentiles?"

B. SATAN'S LEGAL RIGHTS—TOOLS OF WAR

This is what sovereign God says about the kings, princes, leaders of the world who choose to come up against Him and His people—war against them—but as we see, in the end, sovereign God rules over them and they are defeated!

ENEMIES OF SOVEREIGN GOD

II Kings 19:28: *"Because your rage against Me and your tumult have come up to My ears, therefore, I will put My hook in your nose and My bridle in your lips and I will turn you back by the way which you came."* (Also, Isaiah 37:29)

Proverbs 21:1: *"The king's heart is in the hand of the LORD, like the rivers of water; He turns it wherever He wishes."*

Isaiah 44:24-25: *"Thus says the LORD, Your Redeemer, and He who formed you from the womb: I am the LORD who makes all things, who stretches out the heavens all alone, who spreads abroad the earth by Myself, who frustrates the signs of the babblers, and drives diviners mad; who turns wise men backward and makes their knowledge foolishness."*

I Samuel 2:6-10: *"the LORD kills and makes alive; He brings down to the grave and brings up. The LORD makes poor and makes rich; He brings low and lifts up. He raises the poor from the dust and lifts the beggar from the ash heap, to set them among princes and make them inherit the throne of glory. For the pillars of the earth are the LORD's, and He has set the world upon them. He will guard the feet of His saints, but the wicked shall be silent in darkness. For by strength, no man shall prevail. The adversaries of the Lord shall be broken in pieces; from heaven He will thunder against them. The LORD will judge the ends of the earth. He will give strength to His king and exalt the horn of His anointed."*

It is extremely tragic for persons to choose not to believe that the Lord Jesus, our Creator, Almighty God, Jehovah is above all, for in yielding to and believing the Devil who has been broadcasting lies since before Adam and Eve, they rob themselves of the blessings of truth! Let us take time to look closely at that liar, the arch enemy of God and mankind, so that as Christian soldiers, we will come to a full understanding of who we are really up against—how our enemy can come to attain legal rights tools, authority and power over God's people if we let him!

SATAN'S TOOLS OF WAR, CLAIMED, KEPT OR FORFEITED

No different from any physical war that one is engaged in, the more we know about our enemy, Satan the Devil, the more we know about his strengths as well as his weaknesses, the vulnerable places in his armor. As Christian soldiers properly attired in our own uniforms, holding fast to our armor, we can take necessary strategic steps that will enable us to defeat him—and reclaim any ground that he has conquered and taken from us! As strong Christian soldiers, we are studying this subject not only for our sakes, but for the sake of our weaker, bruised brothers and sisters—so we can, indeed, march them boldly to their liberation! After we have made a thorough investigation of our enemy and his band of soldiers following his command, then we will thoroughly investigate the options Christian soldiers have! We will learn how to properly use our weapons—our tools of war! We will also study the strategic plan of advancement in order to defeat the enemy, which our Commander, our Lord, God Almighty has so clearly laid out for us in His Word!

Let us engage now in learning what we are up against in this spiritual battle by studying a couple of the enemy commander's names, "Satan" and "Devil":

Šāṯān [7854] is the Hebrew name that means opponent, adversary, and accuser. (The Complete Word Study Old Testament Zodhiates With Greek Parallel; AMB Publishers, Chattanooga, TN 87422, U.S.A.) See Job 1:6-7, Matthew 4:10; I Peter 5:8, which refer to him as an adversary.

Devil, Gr., **Diabolos** [1228] means one who falsely accuses, he seeks to divide people and does not need an excuse. He is an accuser, a slanderer. I Tim. 3:11; II Tim. 3:3; Titus 2:3 (The Complete Word Study New Testament Zodhiates With Greek Parallel; AMB Publishers, Chattanooga, TN 87422, U.S.A.) Also see Temptation, Matthew 4:1 and Luke 4:2, 13.

MISTAKEN IDENTITY

Before I continue sharing other names of Satan, I feel it is necessary for me to clarify that Satan is often misidentified as a king and an angel that is mentioned in the Bible. The name in Hebrew is **abaddon** and it means **destruction**, and in Greek, **appollyon** which means **destroyer**. This king, or angel, is over the Abyss—the bottomless pit—but take note that he is not Satan the Devil.

My desire is not to do a complete word study on the various names of God's arch-enemy and our enemy. However, in order to expose how he and his demon spirits are able to approach, attack and interact with the lives of mankind—both unbelievers and believers—I want to proceed with a biblical investigation of him and his various names in addition to his more commonly known names, Satan and Devil. In doing this—we will far better understand the enemy and his cohorts' warfare tactics, their strategies and weapons that they use.   Let us now review the various names and descriptions by which our enemy is known and spoken of in God's Word, which will enable us to know our enemy all the better.

1.   A liar and the father of all lies (John 8:44)
2.   Accuser of our brethren (Revelation 12:10)
3.   Adversary (I Peter 5:8)
4.   Angel of light (II Corinthians 11:14
5.   Beelzebub (or Beelzeboul), the ruler of demons (Matthew 12:24)
6.   Belial, Gr. (955) "worthlessness" (II Corinthians 6:15)
7.   Deceiver of the world (II John 7; Revelation 12:9)
8.   Great dragon; serpent of old; Devil; Satan (Revelation 12:9)
9.   Lucifer "Day Star" (English Standard Version; Scofield Study Bible 2002 addition of
       New King James)
10. Lucifer, son of the morning (which means "Day Star"; Isaiah 14:12)
11. Murderer (John 8:44)
12. Old serpent (Genesis 3:4; Revelation 12:9)
13. Prince and power of the air, the spirit who now works in the sons of disobedience
       (Ephesians 2:2)
14. Rulers of the darkness of this age; spiritual hosts of wickedness in heavenly places
       (Ephesians 6:12)
15. Ruler of this world (John 12:31; 14:30; 16:11)
16. Serpent (Genesis 3:4; II Corinthians 11:3, 14)
17. Tempter (Matthew 4:3)
18. The god of this age (II Corinthians 4:3-4)
19. Wicked one (Matthew 13:19)

Evil spirits, demon spirits, ancestral demons and generational demons all fall into the same category.   They all work for their "father-god," Satan, helping him to torment, manipulate and motivate mankind to sin, to fail, and to destroy themselves.

In my first book, "Liberating the Bruised," with much hope of settling debates on the subject, I shared a great deal of information about whether or not Christians can be demonized. I also shared a great deal of information about ancestral demons. Since the book is currently in print, I think it very unwise to take up additional space repeating the information in this book. "Liberating the Bruised" and "More Tools for Liberating the Bruised" are partners, each blending their valuable purposes together as one!

I do want to take a moment to share an illustration to help clarify how a Christian can be "demonized" or "demon possessed." "Possession" does not necessarily mean "ownership," but it does carry the meaning of "control of something." Let's say that you want to use my car to take a trip to Kalamazoo. I "own" the car, but I hand you my car keys, you get in behind the wheel, I sit in the passenger seat, and off we go to Kalamazoo and to any other place you choose to drive while sitting in the driver's seat. You do not own "my car!" I do! Likewise, when a Christian relinquishes his car keys to Satan, he's allowing Satan to control the wheel while the Christian sits in the passenger seat! As long as Satan is allowed to sit in the driver's seat, Satan drives the person onto highways of his choice. That Christian has given Satan "temporary possession" to manipulate and control his vehicle—but take care to understand that it is not ownership! The Christian has already been bought with a price—Jesus' shed blood on Calvary—and cannot be stolen away permanently! When the Christian decides he is sick and tired of relinquishing his vehicle's keys and being driven around by the enemy, he can call upon the Lord Jesus, deal with his issues, get his keys back and regain control!

Let's continue on to learn more about that enemy who delights in being given keys and driving God's children around!

SATAN FORFEITED HIS HEAVENLY HOME

In the book of John, when Jesus was speaking to the Jews who were nonbelievers and desiring to kill Him, He told them that they were of "their father the devil" who "does not stand in the truth, because there is no truth in him." He was referring to the fallen angel named "Day Star" and "son of the morning"—who is also called " Lucifer" in some translations. He fell under God's condemnation due to ambitious pride as he sought to be elevated as a god—one to be adored and worshiped by others. He lusted for a position where he would be adored and worshiped like our sovereign God, Jehovah. His arrogant desire was for God to be dethroned and worship him. As we read evidence of that when Satan was tempting Jesus in chapter four of Matthew, keep in mind that Jesus was God in the flesh:

> *"For it pleased the Father that in Him all the fullness should dwell, and by Him to reconcile all things to Himself, by Him, whether things on earth or things in heaven, having made peace through the blood of His cross...For in Him dwells all the fullness of the Godhead bodily."* (Colossians 1:19; 2:9)

> *"Again, the devil took Him up on an exceedingly high mountain, and showed Him all the kingdoms of the world and their glory. **And he said to Him, 'All these things will I give You <u>if You will fall down and worship me</u>.'** Then Jesus said to him, 'Away with you, Satan! For it is written, You shall worship the Lord your God, and Him only you shall serve.' Then the devil left Him and behold, angels came and ministered to Him."* (Matthew 4:8-11; also see Mark 1:12-13; Luke 4:1-13)

Satan's desires and his doom are reflected in Isaiah 14:12-14:

> *"How you are fallen from heaven, O Lucifer, son of the morning! How you are cut down to the ground. You who weakened the nations! For you have said in your heart: 'I will **ascend** into heaven, I will **exalt my throne above the stars of God**; I will also **sit on the mount of the congregation on the farthest sides of the north**; I*

will **ascend above the heights of the clouds, I will be like the Most High**.' *Yet you shall be brought down to Sheol, to the lowest depths of the Pit."*

God Almighty literally stripped Lucifer of his honorable names, "Son of the Morning" and "Day Star." As we continue reading in Isaiah 14:16-17, we see that by his evil choices he was stripped of a reputation carrying any sign of edification or glory:

*"Those who see you will gaze at you, and consider you, saying, 'Is this the **man** who made the earth tremble, who shook kingdoms, who made the world as a wilderness and destroyed its cities, who did not open the house of his prisoners?'"*

While I firmly believe that Isaiah 14:12-14 and Ezekiel 28:12-15 are speaking about Lucifer and his being cast out of heaven, there are liberal scholars who contend that the King of Babylon and King of Tyre were simply kings and had nothing to do with the fall of Lucifer—who after his fall was known as Satan and the Devil. Others who are seriously conservative Bible scholars believe—as I do—that these scriptures contain clear revelation of Satan's origin—and his self-imposed destruction in the end for himself and his large band of rebels! Before we move further, let us take a look at what he was like before he chose to sin against his Creator, God. **It becomes clear as we read God's description of Lucifer that we cannot begin to imagine how awesomely beautiful he was and what beautiful music he was capable of producing. How very tragic that out of his pride, he gave that all up and brought self-condemnation upon himself by his choice to consistently sin and rebel against God! Iniquity grew to self-destruction in his heart!**

*"Thus says the Lord God: 'You were **the seal of perfection, full of wisdom and perfect in beauty. You were in Eden, the garden of God**; every precious stone was your covering; the sardius, topaz, and diamond, beryl, onyx, and jasper, sapphire, turquoise, and emerald with gold. **The workmanship of your timbrels and pipes was prepared for you on the day you were created.** You were the anointed cherub who covers; I established you; you were on the holy mountain of God; you walked back and forth in the midst of fiery stones. **You were perfect in your ways from the day you were created, till iniquity was found in you**...Your heart was lifted up because of your beauty; you corrupted your wisdom for the sake of your splendor...you have become a horror, and shall be no more forever.'"* (Ezekiel 28:12b-15, 17a, 19b)

Just as we have a Holy War going on down here on earth now, a war between good and evil, a Holy War went on in heaven before Satan and his co-workers were cast out.

For we read in Revelation 12:7-9: *"And **war broke out in heaven**: Michael and his angels fought with the dragon; and **the dragon and his angels fought, but they did not prevail**, nor was a place found for them in heaven any longer. So the great dragon was cast out, that serpent of old, called the Devil and Satan, who deceives the whole world; **he was cast to the earth, and his angels were cast out with him**."*

For now, our all-wise, Almighty God still permits him to play a unique part in this age, amidst mankind, but only for a temporary period of time on this earth. Think on this: Before the time of Adam and Eve, in heaven's amazingly glorious setting, God gave all the angels a choice to love Him and live in heaven forever, or reject Him. Michael and his band of angels, along with Gabriel and his band of angels, chose to love and to obey God. However, Lucifer and his band of angels adored themselves and chose not to love Him. In fact, they rebelled against Him and set out to take over and rule heaven. Now, the setting is in reverse. Earth-dwelling souls this side of heaven, from Adam and Eve to present times, all have a choice to accept and love the Lord, which assures each of them of a move into heaven where they'll live forever. Those choosing to rebel against the Lord will join Satan and his fallen angels when they move into their new—and permanent—home, the lake of fire!

We know that when God kicked Lucifer and his co-workers out of heaven to go to and fro on the earth for God's designated period of time, it was for a good reason. It has to do with freedom of choice! From Adam and Eve on up to the last human being born on earth, humans have freedom of choice to believe and trust in God or to choose to yield to temptation, the whispered suggestions of Satan and follow his leading. This time for humans on earth has to do with **giving people a choice to believe in God—and find salvation by believing this:**

> *"...God so loved the world that He gave His only begotten Son, that whoever believes in Him should not perish but have everlasting life, for God did not send His Son into the world to condemn the world but that the world through Him might be saved.* **He who believes in Him is not condemned;** *but* **he who does not believe is condemned already,** *because he has not believed in the name of the only begotten Son of God. And this is the condemnation, that the light has come into the world, and men loved darkness rather than light, because their deeds were evil. For everyone practicing evil hates the light and does not come to the light, lest his deeds should be exposed, but he who does the truth comes to the light, that his deeds may be clearly seen, that they have been done in God."* (John 3:16-21)

We know that when our Lord Jesus died for us on the cross, Satan was judged and defeated (John 12:30-33). However, until we all get to move to heaven, he is still permitted to stir up trouble and war against God and His people, just as he did at one time in heaven! What joy to know, though, that we do not have to give in to his cunning words of temptation, and that God gives us instructions in His Word about how we can resist and defeat him. Let's proceed to see what else God has to teach us about him.

SATAN'S LEGAL RIGHTS TOOLS OF WAR: TEMPTATION, LIES, AND DECEPTION

God Word reveals that Satan is the ruler of a powerful kingdom—which stands against the kingdom of God. (Matthew 12:26; Luke 11:18a). Satan exercises his authority in several different realms. He is over a huge organization of spiritual beings, his angels. (Matthew 25:41) As the prince and power of the air (Ephesians 2:2), he powerfully directs his organized host of wicked spirits in the heavenlies to do his bidding, warring against and tempting souls. (Ephesians 6:12) Peter makes it clear in his sermon to the Gentiles in the house of Cornelius, in Acts 10:38, that Jesus through power of the Holy Spirit ministered to a number of people oppressed by the Devil because of the work that he and his wicked spirits had done. This allows us to see that **Satan, the old Devil, is not omnipresent, omniscient, nor omnipotent! He must rely on all of his co-workers, demon spirits to assist him in his work. Satan cannot read our minds—only God can read our minds!** However, Satan and his troops are quite experienced at **darting here and there while spying on us**!

Soldiers at war on earth find it very beneficial to study as much as they can about their enemies in order to know their strengths and weaknesses. Therefore, keen observations and spying becomes quite helpful! Likewise, you can be assured that our enemy, the Devil and his soldiers are spying on us, observing our strengths as well as our weaknesses and vulnerable places in the armor of Christian soldiers! No doubt, they "watch our walk and listen to our talk!" So, for us as Christians to be able fight effectively, it is of utmost necessity for us to also study our enemies' strengths and weaknesses—"spy" on them!

You can be assured that Satan and his army are each well equipped with powerful weapons, a variety of temptation-tools. Most surely, they are not reluctant to fire their weapons of temptation at their prey! Along with his army, Satan takes full advantage of the time he has left on earth to influence, tempt, and dominate as much of lost humanity as he can! He is arrogantly marching forth as "ruler of this world!" (John 12:31; 14:30; 16:11) He has organized a world system based on his own principles, which, through Jesus Christ we have victory over! (II Corinthians 4:3-4; Colossians 1:13; I John 2:15-17) Even though we are secure in the fact that we'll go to heaven when we die, we're still in the midst of spiritual warfare as we read these verses of scripture:

> *"We know that whoever is born of God does not sin; but he who has been born of God keeps himself, and the wicked one does not touch him. We know that we are of God, and **the whole world lies under the sway of the wicked one**. And we know that the Son of God has come and has given us an understanding, that we may know Him who is true; and we are in Him who is true, in His Son Jesus Christ. This is the true God and eternal life. Little children, keep yourselves from idols."* (I John 5:18-21)

With Satan choosing to be the enemy of God and all human beings whom God created, he is most diligently focusing on tempting souls to come over to his side. Grievously enough, he is quite good at the act of tempting, which, by the way means **"enticing, desired, influenced by exciting hope or desire."** Let us remember that Satan doesn't necessarily tempt souls "to be bad, to be evil," for temptation is typically dressed in various fashions of "rewards!" He has an exhaustive large selection of "worldly pleasures" for them to choose from—and upon their pursuing these "pleasures," evil behaviors are born!

We read in II Thessalonians 2:9-12: *"The coming of the lawless one is according to the working of Satan, with **all power, signs, and lying wonders**, and with **all unrighteous deception** among those who perish, **because they did not receive the love of the truth, that they might be saved**. And for this reason God will send them strong delusion, that they should believe the lie, that they all may be condemned **who did not believe the truth** but **had pleasure in unrighteousness**."*

In Revelation 12:9: he is called the **"deceiver of the whole world,"** presenting temptation in some cunning, clever fashion. Not only does he capture some souls and uses them for extremely evil deeds, he uses some of his captives as false prophets, wolves in sheep's clothing! In II Corinthians 11:13-15, we read: **"...such are false apostles, deceitful workers, transforming themselves into apostles of Christ. And no wonder! For Satan himself transforms himself into an angel of light. Therefore it is no great thing if his ministers also transform themselves into ministers of righteousness, whose end will be according to their works."** Indeed, Satan is as God said, an angel of light! The enemy does not just casually stroll up to a person to offer them delightful treats with no strings attached! There are evil motives to his madness! His war tactics are to sneak up on his opponent as we read in John 10:10, *"The **thief** does not come except **to steal**, and **to kill**, and **to destroy**..."* while our Lord says *"...I have come that they may have life and that they may have it more abundantly."* The Lord goes on to say in John 10:11-13: *"I am the good shepherd. The good shepherd gives His life for the sheep. But a hireling, he who is not the shepherd, one who does not own the sheep, sees the wolf coming and leaves the sheep and flees; and the wolf catches the sheep and scatters them. The hireling flees because he is a hireling and does not care about the sheep."* Our Lord surely warned us that there would be false prophets, wolves in sheep's clothing—of which there have, indeed, been all too many! How tragic that these souls had the opportunity to know, love and follow the Lord, yet chose to know, love and follow the deceitful enemy—who in the end, defeated and destroyed them with great pleasure!

We read of Jesus encouraging **believers**: *"Then Jesus said to those Jews who believed Him, '**If you abide in My word, you are My disciples indeed. And you shall know the truth, and the truth shall make you free**.' They answered Him, 'We are Abraham's descendants, and have never been in bondage to anyone. How can you say, 'You will be made free'?' Jesus answered them, 'Most assuredly, I say to you, **whoever commits sin is a slave of sin**. And a slave does not abide in the house forever, but a son abides forever. Therefore **if the Son makes you free, you shall be free indeed**.'"* (John 8:31-36)

Then, we read of Jesus speaking to **nonbelievers**: *"**You are of your father the devil, and the desires of your father you want to do**. He was a murderer from the beginning, and does not stand in the truth, because there is no truth in him. When he speaks a lie, he speaks from his own resources, for he is a liar and the father of it. But because I tell the truth, you do not believe Me. Which of you convicts Me of sin? And if I tell the truth, why do you not believe Me? He who is of God hears God's words; therefore **you do not hear, because you are not of God**."* (John 8:44-47)

SATAN'S TOOLS OF AUTHORITY, LEGALLY CLAIMED

When a person consistently chooses to turn from God and he yields to Satan's temptation, sinning repeatedly, deliberately rejecting and disobeying the Lord, **iniquity forms in his heart**. He has literally opened the door of his life to Satan, allowing him to legally claim him as his slave! This can apply to a lost person rejecting Christ, but it can also apply to a Christian, repeatedly disobeying the Lord! Remember that God does not create robots, He creates people—each one having the right to choose a lifestyle for himself! Of course the enemy lies in wait—seeking whom he may devour! (I Peter 5:8) The enemy always has high hopes of capturing his prey to use for his evil purposes!

From the beginning, when Adam and Eve were in the Garden of Eden, he was there to tempt, to entice with rewards and benefits. God had placed two trees in the midst of the garden, The Tree of Life and The Tree of Knowledge of Good and Evil. They could eat of every tree in the garden but the Tree of Good and Evil. God warned them not to eat of that tree, for they would most surely die! This couple was in a setting of delightful perfection, they had the awesome privilege of walking and talking with God! They had all that they needed and more, and were told to **leave only ONE thing alone**. Satan, the tempter pointed it out to them in such a way that it appeared God was a liar and was depriving them of something! But as we recall, when the cunning serpent tempted Eve, he was lying and knew if she took heed to his lie, she and Adam would be deprived of being glorified—made more splendid, like God! From the Devil's experience in heaven—from whence he was kicked out—he knew full well that God would keep His Word! So he cleverly lied to Eve, told her what she wanted to hear—that **she and Adam could have it all!** They would receive delightful rewards by not believing God and choosing to disobey Him. They would find pleasure by eating from the tree—and surely would not die! For we read:

> *"Then the serpent said to the woman, 'You will not surely die. For God knows that in the day you eat of it your eyes will be opened, and you will be like God, knowing good and evil.' So when the woman saw the tree was good for food, that it was pleasant to the eyes, and a tree desirable to make one wise, she took of its fruit and ate. She also gave to her husband with her, and he ate."* (Genesis 3:4-6)

Sadly, they chose to believe the enemy rather than the God who loved them. Do you see that they were just like prideful Satan when he resided in heaven; he was not satisfied to live with God in the glory of heaven, but rather wanted to be elevated to not only be like God, but to be positioned over Him. He wanted to be the boss! Satan has not changed. He still wants to be in charge and his sales pitch has not changed! He tempts precious souls to desire to be elevated above others and to gain rewards for themselves. Upon their considering his suggestions, they succumb to pride, greed, and selfishness and then Satan has them right where he wants them—in his powerful snare!

SATAN'S TOOLS OF AUTHORITY, LEGALLY CLAIMED BUT FORFEITED

For a time, due to yielding to temptation, Saul of Tarsus was a slave of the Devil who thoroughly enjoyed using him to perform his elaborate, systematic plan of action! He, no doubt, delighted in issuing orders to Saul and watching him obey them by participating in the persecutions and executions of Christians. However, in this case, the Devil ended up forfeiting his claim to Saul! While the Devil was working on Saul, the Lord was convicting Saul of his lost, sinful state and calling him unto Himself! What joy to read a portion of the testimony of Saul (now Paul) concerning his wonderful transformation, his conversion:

> *"Indeed, I myself thought I must do many things contrary to the name of Jesus of Nazareth. This I also did in Jerusalem, and many of the saints I shut up in prison, having received authority from the chief priests; and when they were put to death, I cast my vote against them. And I punished them often in every synagogue and compelled them to blaspheme; and being exceedingly enraged against them, I persecuted them even to foreign cities. While thus occupied, as I journeyed to Damascus with authority and commission for the chief priests, at midday, O king, along the road I saw a light from heaven, brighter than the sun, shining around me and those who journeyed with me. And when we all had fallen to the ground, I heard a voice speaking to me and saying in the Hebrew language, 'Saul, Saul, why are you persecuting Me? It is hard for you to kick against the goads.' So I said, 'Who are You, LORD?' And He said, 'I am Jesus, whom you are persecuting. But rise and stand on your feet; for I have appeared to you for this purpose, to make you a minister and a witness both of the things which you have seen and of the things which I will yet reveal to you. I will deliver you from the Jewish people, as well as from the Gentiles, to whom I now send you, to open their eyes, in order to turn them from darkness to light, and from the power of Satan to God, that they may receive forgiveness of sins and an inheritance among those who are sanctified by faith in Me.'"* (Acts 26: 9-18)

This scripture definitely reveals that God knows the hidden parts of our soul! When He told Saul that He knew it was hard for him to "kick against the goads"—it let Saul know—and tells us— that the Lord knew that Saul had been listening to Him and that he was under heavy conviction of his sins! What joy that Saul chose to turn from his wicked ways, repent and receive the Lord Jesus as his Savior – his promised Messiah! Therefore, the Devil had to forfeit all the legal rights of authority that he had once claimed on Saul, his slave!

SATAN'S TOOLS OF AUTHORITY, LEGALLY CLAIMED AND KEPT

Because our sovereign God does not violate anyone's freedom of choice, including whether or not to accept or reject Him, Satan is then permitted to hang onto and claim the legal rights of authority to manipulate and govern a person until he repents and deals with his issues. It's critical that we remember that while this can hold true for a rebellious Christian, he cannot touch the Christian's salvation—his blessed assurance of going to heaven when he dies! While Satan most surely is not pleased at all over that truth, he glories in the fact that he grieves the heart of the Christian's Lord and Savior! Satan pridefully delights in controlling lost souls who are in his clutches by their very own choices! When they have stubbornly refused to believe in our God Almighty, we read of God permitting Satan, the god of this age, to keep blindness in the eyes of these unbelievers, in II Corinthians 4:3-4:

> *"But even our gospel is veiled, it is veiled to those who are perishing, **whose minds the god of this age has blinded**, who do not believe, lest the light of the gospel of the glory of Christ, who is the image of God, should shine on them."*

Thus, Satan has claimed and kept his legal rights of authority over these rebellious souls.

SATAN'S TOOLS OF TEMPTATION OFFERED TO JESUS, DECLINED!

As we read earlier about God permitting Satan to use his warfare tool of temptation on our precious Lord Jesus on earth, he took full advantage of the opportunity! When we read portions of this event, we see that he boasted of his having convinced Adam and Eve to listen to and obey him instead of their heavenly Father. Then we read that God allowed Satan to tempt Jesus for forty days. We read a portion of it that reveals Satan boasting to Jesus of his holding some power and authority while tempting Him in Luke 4:5-6: ***"Then the devil, taking Him up on a high mountain, showed Him all the kingdoms of the world in a moment of time. And the devil said to Him, 'All this authority I will give You, and their glory; for this has been delivered to me, and I give it to whomever I wish."*** However, in the next verse, Luke 4:7, we read that there was a **"catch"** to his offer: ***"Therefore, <u>if You will worship before me</u>, all will be Yours."*** What would the outcome be?

Can you see that with Satan having been cast out of heaven, stripped of his heavenly position and lovely name "Day Star" and he became the darkness of evil, he wanted the God of light to worship the god of darkness? In essence, he was desiring for Jesus—the Father, Son and Holy Spirit—to swap places with him! Gratitude should spill from our hearts continually that our sinless Jesus rightfully exercised His authority as He turned Satan's offer down, declaring: ***"...Get behind Me, Satan! For it is written, 'You shall worship the Lord your God, and Him only you shall serve."*** (Luke 4:8)

How tragic that Adam and Eve didn't turn Satan's offer down! They took, they bit, they ate of The Tree of Knowledge of Good and Evil. When Satan tempted them, upon their choosing to disobey God, He had no other alternative but to cast them out of the Garden of Eden so they would not live for eternity in a sinful state. Satan won, he legally claimed his tool of authority over Adam and Eve. Therefore, Adam and Eve forfeited their legal rights to their dominion—their authority over the earth and the things in it. At that time, everything went out of kilter. Through them, all mankind suffered the fallout, generation through generation. Creation suffered the fallout also, groaning within itself! (Romans 8:22) As you study human behavior and creatures in nature today, you can clearly see evidence of this! How grateful we are in knowing that our sinless Lord Jesus declined Satan's offer! For our sakes, He laid down His life that we might live—and **He was bruised for our transgressions!**

As we view the spiritual condition of the world today, we can so very clearly see evidence that so many souls have stubbornly chosen against God and are now veiled in blindness. We are, indeed, in the midst of a Holy War—Satan against God, nonbelievers against believers. How tragic that the precious people that our Creator formed are so divided—by the choices of so many to become the enemy of God! How tragic that in spite of the preaching of God's Word and His written Word being available that tells what happened to the rebellious angels who were cast out of heaven, they still reject Him! The angels were without excuse—people on this side of heaven are without excuse! Just as God lovingly warned Adam and Eve of the danger of yielding to temptation and disobeying His Holy rules—established for their own well-being—God has warned every soul here on earth. Evidence of these truths are seen in II Peter 3:9: ***The Lord is not slack concerning His promise as some count slackness, but is longsuffering toward us, not willing that any should perish but that all should come to repentance.*** It most surely grieves Him when His precious clay vessels choose against Him. In Jeremiah 29:11-14a, we read what God thinks about us:

> *"...**I know the thoughts I think toward you, says the LORD, thoughts of peace and not of evil, to give you a future and a hope**. Then you will call upon Me and go and pray to Me, and I will listen to you. And, **you will seek Me and find Me, when you search for Me with all your heart**. I will be found by you, says the Lord, and **I will bring you back from your captivity**...."*

SATAN, GOD'S TOOL OF AFFLICTION
FOR TESTINGS AND TESTIMONIES

Upon reading the entire book of Job, first of all, it is quite evident that **Job truly loved God with all his being!** During God's conversation with Satan, God Himself stated: ***"...My servant Job...there is none like him on the earth, a blameless and upright man, one who fears God and shuns evil...."*** (Job 1:8) To this, the enemy Satan mockingly responded, declaring his opinion that Job would not love God so much and be so faithful to Him had God not built a protective hedge around him! Satan saw that Job was in a perfect setting—like unto Adam and Eve's garden—so Satan declared that it was no wonder that his faith in God was strong!

As the rest of this true event unfolds, what a powerful, perfect testimonial the story of Job carries as a lesson for us: God—out of His all-knowing-wisdom—actually allows Satan to negatively affect and attack a believer's finances, means of making a living, family, friends, and health, **for goodly purposes**! Now, take care to understand that while **God permitted Satan some leeway to afflict His righteous man**, He certainly held tight to His sovereign, divine authority to put **restrictions on Satan**! For we read in Job 1:12: *"And the Lord said to Satan, 'Behold all that he has is in your power; only do not lay a hand on his person.' So Satan went out from the presence of the Lord."*

Then, in Job 2:6, we read: *"And the Lord said to Satan, 'Behold, he is in your hand, but spare his life.'"* **Our times are most surely in God's hands, and only He has the legal right to determine when each person is allowed to leave this earth!**

Now let us all take a moment to remember some very important truths if we're going to contain peace and joy in our hearts, no matter what's going on "round about us!" When God's ways do not match up to our human reasoning and we don't understand the whys, we should embrace the truth of the matter: God is right, we are wrong! Period—exclamation point! **When we venture into the territory of questioning our Creator—arguing with Him—with a lack of faith and trust in the Lord—we are pleasing Satan!**

Keeping that in the forefront of our minds, let us try to put ourselves in Job's sandals when **God let down the hedge** and allowed Satan to serve as a **tester-tool of Job's faith**. Little did Job know that his choices would not only serve as a powerful testimony to everyone in his part of the world, but into all the world, down through the ages to this very point in history—and beyond! Haughty Satan assumed he could cause Job so much pain and suffering that he would cry out with pain and self-pity, thus even harbor anger, bitterness and unforgiveness toward God. He felt confident that Job would lose his faith and trust in God's love and care for him. However, as we read Job's story in its entirety, we see that Job's faith, his trust in God, was not lessened though he was most surely severely tested through **(1)** loss of family, **(2)** loss of property and wealth, **(3)** rejection and persecution by wife and friends, and **(4)** his body racked with extreme physical pain. All of his oxen and donkeys were stolen, all but one of his servants were killed, and all of his sons and daughters were killed, yet as we read of his response, we learn of his great respect for and trust in God—His sovereignty!

> *"Then Job arose, tore his robe, and shaved his head: and **he fell to the ground and worshiped**. And he said, 'Naked I came from my mother's womb, and naked shall I return there. **The Lord gave, and the Lord has taken away; blessed be the name of the Lord**.'"* (Job 1:20-21)

What a great faith, what a great trust Job had in the Lord, his God Almighty! While in the midst of his suffering, he expressed his heart's desire for the Lord Himself to be blessed! Having suffered such great losses, we read that while he was suffering such horrible pain with boils all over his body and scraping them with a broken piece of pottery as he sat in ashes, *"...his wife said to him, 'Do you still hold fast to your integrity? Curse God and die!"* We read: *"But he said to her, 'You speak as one of the foolish women speaks. Shall we indeed accept good from God, and shall we not accept adversity? In all this Job did not sin with his lips."* (Job 2:9-10)

After Job suffered the pain of his wife angrily voicing her lack of trust and wise understanding for the God he loved and trusted, Job's friends then paid him a visit. At first they sympathized and mourned with him in the midst of his sufferings, but then told him that he must be suffering because of some sin in his life for which he was not willing to admit to and repent! Now keep in mind that these friends were believers in the same God whom Job worshiped. They were "counselors" who were expected to give people Godly counsel, sound doctrine for solutions to problems, and help and comfort in times of need and sorrow.

Instead, in poetic form at length they elaborated on some truths while blending in generous amounts of human reasoning. In their self-righteousness, they cast words of condemnation upon their friend Job. They reasoned that the measure of a person's sin would be equal to the measure of suffering he would be dealt, thus judged by Job's great suffering that his sins must be great! They wrongfully declared that the innocent person, one who is right with God is exempt from all sufferings!

However, our dear, wise brother Job knew that they were wrong, just as his wife was! All were guilty of yielding to temptation to blend truth with lies! During many conversations with his three friends, we find Job telling his counselor-friends: *"I have heard many such things; miserable comforters are you all! Shall words of wind have an end?"* (Job 16:2-3) Indeed, in error, they were unwisely "puffing wind!" In spite of all this rejection from wife and friends, Job remained firm in his conviction that both the righteous and the wicked suffer adversities. He trusted that God allowed all the "bad" things to happen to him for His good reasons—even if he didn't understand. We read of the genuineness of Job's convictions and dedication to God as we read his own words: *"Though He slay me, yet will I trust Him. Even so, I will defend my own ways before Him. He also shall be my salvation, for a hypocrite could not come before Him."* (Job 13:15-16) What a powerful statement that not only expressed his great faith and conviction about the truth of the matter about adversities, but clearly stated that his Almighty, sovereign God alone is his judge and his salvation!

Job's great understanding about the difference between himself and sovereign God is seen in Job 42:1-6 when he declares that God is sovereign and that he is in low esteem, reflecting his humility. We read of Job voicing his thoughts, how he felt, when he was in such physical torment and anguish, in Job 3:3: *"May the day perish on which I was born, and the night in which it was said, a male child is conceived."* Later, in Job 9:2b, he says: *"...how can a man be righteous before the Lord?"* In Job 9:14-15, we read: *"How then can I answer Him, and choose my words to reason with Him? For though I were righteous, I could not answer Him; I would beg mercy of my Judge."* And he continues in Job 9:32-33: *"For He is not a man, as I am, that I may answer Him, and that we should go to court together. Nor is there any mediator between us, who may lay his hand on us both."* He declares in Job 28:28: *"Behold, the fear of the Lord, that is wisdom, and to depart from evil is understanding."*

In Job 29:2 and 5a, we find Job voicing how he felt—like God had forsaken him—in the midst of the tremendous amount of suffering, physically as well as emotionally from all the words of condemnation blasted upon him by his self-righteous wife and friends: *"Oh, that I were as in months past, as in the days when God watched over me...when the Almighty was yet with me."* Can you imagine the heart-wrenching afflictions, and hurtful sins of his wife and friends that were cast upon him? He had yielded to entertaining the negative thought that perhaps God was now far away from him. After God preached a good long sermon to him (Job 38 and 39), Job replied:

"I know that You can do everything, and that no purpose of Yours can be withheld from You. You asked, 'Who is this who hides counsel without knowledge?' Therefore I have uttered what I did not understand, things too wonderful for me, which I did not know. Listen, please, and let me speak; You said, 'I will question you, and you will answer Me.' I have heard of You by the hearing of the ear, but now my eye sees You, therefore I abhor myself, and repent in dust and ashes." (Job 42:2-6)

Now we come to another critical point and vital lesson in this matter! Job did not have thoughts of condemnation toward his critical friends, but rather a ready attitude of forgiveness! He clearly desired to be clean before the Lord himself, and expressed his earnest desire for them to be clean before the Lord also, for their own sakes! For as we have gotten to know Job better, it's evident that while he shared his convictions about these matters and confronted his friends about their own attitudes and behavior, **Job was truly a Godly, nouthetic counselor—confronting with scripture out of love to bring about a needed change. He was sharing God's solutions of truth in love while leaving the judging of their sins up to sovereign God—the Judge of all judges!** Job knew quite well that God would speak directly to them about the sins that He needed to confront them about! Most surely, that is exactly what we see God doing when we read Job 42:7-17:

*"...the LORD said to Eliphaz the Temanite, 'My wrath is aroused against you and your two friends, for you have not spoken of Me what is right, as My servant Job has. Now therefore, take for yourselves seven bulls and seven rams, go to My servant Job, and offer up for yourselves a burnt offering; and My servant Job shall pray for you. For I will accept him, lest I deal with you according to your folly; because you have not spoken of Me what is right, as My servant Job has. So Eliphaz the Temanite and Bildad the Shuhite and Zophar the Naamathite went and did as the Lord commanded them; for the Lord had accepted Job. **And the Lord restored Job's losses when he prayed for his friends. Indeed the LORD gave Job twice as much as he had before.** Then all his brothers, all his sisters, and all those who had been his acquaintances before, came to him and ate food with him in his house; and they consoled him and comforted him for all the adversity that the LORD had brought upon him. Each one gave him a piece of silver and each a ring of gold. Now the LORD blessed the latter days of Job more than his beginning; for he had fourteen thousand sheep, six thousand camels, one thousand yoke of oxen, and one thousand female donkeys. He also had seven sons and three daughters. And he called the name of the first Jemimah, the name of the second Keziah, and the name of the third Keren-Happuch. In all the land were found no women so beautiful as the daughters of Job; and their father gave them an inheritance among their brothers. And after this Job lived one hundred and forty years, and saw his children and grandchildren for four generations. So Job died, old and full of days."*

A very interesting truth is found as we look more deeply at how God blessed Job by doubling his possessions, but not his ten children. Why did God only give him ten more children rather than twenty? **Because he had not permanently lost those ten children. Job knew that he would see them again in heaven!** The additional ten children would also go to heaven, thus, Job would have twenty children! We see that Job had the same confidence of this truth as we read what David said after the death of his baby son. You recall that David had an affair with Bathsheba, the wife of Uriah, whom he had killed. From the affair, Bathsheba gave birth to a very sickly son. In II Samuel 12:16 we read of David appealing to the Lord to let him live: *"David therefore pleaded with God for the child, and fasted and went in and lay all night on the ground."* After seven days, the child died, II Samuel 12:20-23 reveals David's heart: *"So David arose from the ground, washed and anointed himself, and changed his clothes; and went into the house of the Lord and worshiped. Then he went to his own house; and when he requested, they set food before him, and he ate. Then his servants said to him, 'What is this that you have done? You fasted and wept for the child while he was alive, but when the child died, you arose and ate food.' And he said, 'While the child was alive, I fasted and wept; for I said, 'Who can tell whether the Lord will be gracious to me, that the child may live? But now he is dead; why should I fast?* **Can I bring him back again? I shall go to him, but he shall not return to me***.'"* What blessed assurance in knowing this—and that the iniquities of the father and son did not keep them out of heaven!

Job had that same confidence that he would one day go to his children in heaven! What a wonderful testimony of faith our brother Job had, which not only brought God's approval and blessing to him, but to his friends and to his family, for generations to come. This is truly an example of a man who, out of his great love for God, chose to make the right choices. God said: *"Trust in the Lord with all your heart, and lean not on your own understanding; in all your ways acknowledge Him, and He shall direct your paths. Do not be wise in your own eyes; fear the Lord and depart from evil. It will be health to your flesh, and strength to your bones."* (Proverbs 3:5-8) Job did that! Job also fulfilled these commandments: *"...You shall* **love the Lord your God with all your heart, with all your soul, and with all your mind***. This is the first and great commandment. And the second is like it: You shall* **love your neighbor as yourself***. On these two commandments hang all the Law and the Prophets."* (Matthew 22:37-40) Job's life is a perfect example of living a Christ-like life before others, no matter what temptations, trials, and tribulations may come that ask for willing obedience to sacrifice self for the sake of others.

WHY DOES GOD LET BAD THINGS HAPPEN TO GOOD PEOPLE?

This is a perfect time to share some truths about why God sometimes allows "bad" things to happen to both "good" and "bad" people. We should keep in mind what we're told in Matthew 5:45b: *"...He makes His sun rise on the evil and on the good, and sends rain on the just and on the unjust."* Let us not forget that He's not a respecter of persons—He loves and blesses all the precious humans He created! While He does not share every reason why He lets "bad things" happen to all, He will give us enough wisdom about it to give us peace in the midst of "bad circumstances" if we listen to Him! While seeking understanding, we should always keep such "bad matters" under the umbrella of "everyone has a freedom of choice, which affects others—innocent bystanders included." For instance, God does not want a person to rob and kill another person, but that person has the freedom to do so! When it comes to physical sufferings—health issues— afflicting good and bad people, even today, God still—like in Job's time—uses them for a variety of good reasons! As an example, let's look at three main purposes that God has for allowing such things:

1. God may allow something "bad" to happen to a lost person but it is for a good reason! It serves as a tool for Him to gain his undivided attention, which will draw him under conviction of his lost state. He will have an opportunity to be still and consider repenting and accepting the Lord Jesus as his Savior. In the reverse—God showers blessings upon a lost person to show him His loving kindness—His love, mercy and grace upon him! God knows best how to get the attention of each of His children!

2. God may allow a "bad" thing to happen to a back-slidden Christian to draw him to attention concerning sin in his life that is hindering him from walking peacefully and joyfully in God's will for his life. Like a good Father—when His gentle pleas fall on deaf ears, out of His loving concern, He gets their attention by spanking His rebellious children!

3. There are times when God allows "bad" things to happen to Godly people like Job, Christians who love the Lord their God with all their heart, soul and mind for His goodly purposes—testing and testimonies! Let us not forget what Paul said when he had a physical problem that God did not choose to remove from him: *"And lest I should be exalted above measure by the abundance of the revelations, **a thorn in the flesh** was given to me, **a messenger of Satan to buffet me, lest I be exalted above measure.** Concerning this thing I pleaded with the Lord three times that it might depart from me. And He said to me, 'My grace is sufficient for you, for My strength is made perfect in weakness.' Therefore most gladly I will rather boast in my infirmities, that the power of Christ may rest upon me. Therefore, I take pleasure in infirmities, in reproaches, in needs, in persecutions, and in distresses, for Christ's sake. For when I am weak, then I am strong."* (II Corinthians 12:7-10) Like myself, many believe that we're given **a clue to what Paul's affliction was** as we consider that **others, such as Timothy, served as his penman.** For we read in Galatians 6:11: *"See what **large letters** I have written to you **with my own hand!**"* So he **may have had a serious vision problem when it came to reading and writing**—perhaps extreme "farsightedness." It was bothersome enough that Paul conversed with the Lord, made his appeals, got God's answer—"No"—three times and Paul then dropped the subject. **Then Paul not only willingly continued to walk with the "thorn in his flesh" in God's will, but he actually relaxed and took pleasure in accepting and living inside God's decision!** Whether God used this "thorn" solely for testimony to others of his willingness to serve in spite of "a thorn" and/or to keep Paul humble—that's God's business. Job and Paul demonstrated that they loved the Lord their God with all their hearts, souls, minds, and strength!

Like Job and Paul, down through the years and in present times, as other strong believers pass through the "bad" times, their response will speak loudly through their unwavering display of **a) gratitude to the Lord for the blessings** He has bestowed on them, and their **b) trust in Him as they refuse to doubt that He is trustworthy**, and their **c) deep love and adoration for the Lord—no matter what trials and tribulations are going on!** We have heard of Christians sharing their testimonies while going through sorrowful experiences and some on their death beds, which deeply touched hearts of lost persons and they received Jesus as their Savior. Stories have been told of Christian women who while being raped, told the rapists they forgive them and that Jesus loves them and desires that they be saved— that they go to heaven when they die. Some of these precious women have lived, some have died. And some of these rapist have repented of their sins and received the Lord as their Savior while some have not. The rapists who chose to repent have been transformed into a new creation in Jesus Christ, but while still on earth, they have to submit to the law, pay the consequences of their sin, and be held in prison. However, those prisoners can share their testimonies in those prison walls—their mission fields!

Let us take a moment to look at the disciples questioning Jesus about a "bad, negative" thing that happened to someone and see what He says: *"Now as Jesus passed by, He saw a man who was blind from birth. And His disciples asked Him saying, 'Rabbi, who sinned, this man or his parents, that he was born blind?' Jesus answered, 'Neither this man nor his parents sinned, but that the works of God should be revealed in him."* (John 9:1-3) There are a few points in the complete story of this blind man that are crucial to gaining a better understanding of why both good and bad things happen to both good and bad people. **First**, we see that **the "cause" of the man's blindness was not due to his parents' nor his sin! Secondly**, through Jesus' teachings and His unimaginably high number of miracles, He demonstrated His power—truth that He was God housed in a clay vessel—the promised Messiah! **Thirdly**, the arrogant, hypocritical Pharisees declared to the man who had shared how Jesus gave him sight: *"Give **God** the glory! We know that this **Man** is a sinner."* (John 9:24) The now-sighted man stuck to his true story, testifying before the Pharisees: *"'Since the world began it has been unheard of that anyone opened the eyes of one who was born blind. If this Man were not from God, He could do nothing.'"* (John 9:32-33) With that, the Pharisees promptly excommunicated him! They were physically sighted but spiritually blind—clean on the outside, filthy on the inside. (See Matthew 23.)

Take care to note that this man perceived that "Jesus was of God—a man of God," but he had not yet perceived Him as his promised Messiah! **Jesus healed a non-believer!** Upon Jesus' hearing of the man being excommunicated, He went to the man and asked him: *"'Do you believe in the **Son of God**?' He answered and said, 'Who is He, Lord, that I may believe in Him?' And Jesus said to him, 'You have both seen Him and it is He who is talking with you.' Then he said, 'Lord, I believe!' and he worshiped Him."* (John 9:35-38) A lost, blind person healed, then saved!

Then, we read, *"Then some of the Pharisees who were with Him heard these words, and said to Him, 'Are we blind also?' Jesus said to them, 'If you were blind, you would have no sin; but now you say, 'We see.' Therefore your sin remains."* (John 9:40-41) So we have seen that the blindness of the man was a tool that God saw fit to use to show Himself as the Son of God—to bring salvation to those who are willingly to accept Him—and further the Gospel to future generations!

In this present generation there are two very precious Christians who come to mind who are wonderful examples of how God can use "earthly negatives" to invite people to turn them into "His heavenly positives!" Each of them had two choices: **(1)** become bitterly angry at God and let the enemy use the negative circumstances to drive them to their beds, and wheelchairs, to waste away in self-pity. Or, **(2)** receive the Lord as their Savior, trust Him without questioning or arguing, and willingly accept the "negative condition" of their clay vessel and trust that He will enable them to fulfill His purpose in life!

One such person was born in 1949 a healthy little girl, and while a lost seventeen-year-old in 1967, she dove into a lake, broke her neck and would be housed in a quadriplegic body the rest of her earthly life—unable to use her arms or legs. In time, she accepted the Lord as her Savior and she chose not to give into temptation to engage in self-pity. Instead, this delightful lady, **Joni Eareckson Tada**, joyfully testifies of her love for the Lord Jesus and willingly committed her life to serving Him. Joni sings, speaks internationally, teaches Bible, and has written many children's books and books that minister to people with disabilities. During Joni's two-year rehabilitation, she learned how to hold an artist's brush between her teeth and paint beautiful artwork—which is sold through her ministry today. **Our dear sister Joni posted this scripture on her website:** *"To keep me from becoming conceited because of these surpassingly great revelations, there was given me a thorn in my flesh, a messenger of Satan, to torment me."* (II Corinthians 12:7) She determined that the enemy would not claim victory over God's precious clay vessel! What a glory she is unto the Lord, a beautiful instrument of the Lord, blessing so many souls all over the world! In 1982, the Lord blessed her with a wonderful husband, Ken Tada, who retired from teaching and serves alongside his beloved Joni. You can type Joni's full name in the web box and find much inspirational information about her and the tremendous ministry to which God called her!

Another powerful testimony is that of our precious brother, **Nick Vujicic**, age 26, who, without any medical reason, was born without arms or legs, to a precious Christian couple who loved the Lord and received Nick as God's gift to them, just as they had their "whole" children born before him. Nick had the same two choices that our sister Joni did, to waste away in self-pity, or to find peace, joy and freedom in Christ! He chose to receive the Lord as his Savior and joyfully he submitted himself for His Potter to use in His plan! And God has used him in 19 nations to draw many lost souls to Jesus—in churches, schools, orphanages, prisons, hospitals, stadiums and one-on-one! A scripture posted on his website (www.lifewithoutlimbs.com) from Jeremiah 29:11 reads: *"For I know the plans I have for you, declares the LORD, plans to prosper you and not to harm you, plans to give you hope and a future."* Most surely, Nick has found his hope and future in Jesus Christ—his mission in life! He says that one of his favorite scriptures in the Bible is Psalm 139:17-18: *"How precious to me are your thoughts, O God! How vast is the sum of them! Were I to count them, they would outnumber the grains of sand."* Nick says that his greatest joy in life is to introduce Jesus to those he meets and tell them about His great desire to know them personally by allowing Him to be their Lord and Savior. Truly, Nick is a beautiful instrument of the Lord, inviting so many souls to meet and know Christ. He once said that when he arrives in heaven, God is going to ask him, **"...who did you bring with you?"** Your heart will be blessed if you go to Nick's website and learn more about Nick, his testimony, and the marvelous ministry to which God has called him!

So when "bad" things happen to others, we should take great care not to jump to conclusions born of the flesh—human reasoning—like Job's friends did! Instead, we should remember that He is the Potter, we are the clay as Isaiah 64:8 says, **"But now, O LORD, You are our Father; we are the clay, and You our potter; and all we are the work of Your hand."** (Also see Exodus 4:11; Romans 9:20-21). We should all prayerfully and humbly seek God's wisdom in how we can minister to and encourage souls who find themselves in "bad, negative positions!" Each of us can choose to be a pliable piece of clay in His hands, or a rebellious one. It has been said that God won't use an unrepentant dirty clay vessel, but He can still use a "broken one" as they come to Him for restoration! How vital, indeed, it is for us to pray that He would make us sensitive to His voice of wisdom as we make ourselves available to encourage and help—to love one another as Christ loves us!

In I Peter 1:6-8 we read what God has to say through Peter about faithful Christians who are unwavering in their gratitude, trust, and love for the Lord—and are serving the Lord, yet they are enduring hardships, trials, tribulations, and persecutions in the midst of this Holy War! **"In this you greatly rejoice, though now for a little while, if need be, you have been grieved by various trials, that the genuineness of your faith, being much more precious than gold that perishes, though it is tested by fire, may be found to praise, honor, and glory at the revelation of Jesus Christ, whom having not seen you love. Though now you do not see Him, yet believing, you rejoice with joy inexpressible and full of glory."**

SATAN, SOWING TARES AMONG THE WHEAT, FOR A TIME

Until our Lord Jesus comes for us, corporately or individually, it is critical that we understand and help our counselees and other Christians as well—to understand that we are most definitely in a Holy War! The Lord wants all Christians to realize they are Christian soldiers, sorely needed to go forth with God's truths in the fields, for the enemy is casting lies in the fields, day and night! All Christians are missionaries, fully armed with the Gospel of truth and adequately equipped with personal testimonies of God's saving grace! Satan and his evil army buddies are dedicated to their cause—to shoot down God's Christian soldiers with their lies! Oh, that all Christian soldiers would embrace the fact that through Christ, they are more than conquerors, they can serve in God's army without fear and trembling!

SATAN'S TOOLS, BURNING WITH HIM FOREVER

What a relief to know that our King of kings and His Christian soldiers win the final war, and Satan, his army, and non-believing people who joined Satan's army in their rebellion against God, lose! What relief to know that they and their evil tools—weapons of war—are cast into the lake of fire, never to torment anyone again! Until that time, though we live in the midst of a blend of believers and non-believers—people who love the Lord Jesus and people who hate Him. Oh, that Christian soldiers would serve our King more diligently than Satan's soldiers serve him! How encouraging it is for Christians to read Jesus' words concerning this:

> *"He answered and said unto them: 'He who sows good seed is the Son of Man. The field is the world, the good seeds are the sons of the kingdom, but the tares are the sons of the wicked one. The enemy who sowed them is the devil, the harvest is the end of the age. The Son of Man will send out His angels, and they will gather out of His kingdom all things that offend, and those who practice lawlessness, and will cast them into the furnace of fire. There will be wailing and gnashing of teeth. Then the righteous will shine forth as the sun in the kingdom of their Father. He who has ears to hear, let him hear!* (Matt. 13:37-43)

Of course, at this time, we are still stationed on this earth and are engaged in battle against these evil forces. Having investigated our enemy and his co-workers so that we know them, their tactics, and strategies well, let us move forward with confidence as Christians soldiers for our King, our Lord Jesus on this battlefield! **Let us examine the fantastic tools of war that our King Jesus has provided for us to use in battle to defeat our enemies who still lie in wait!**

C.   CHRISTIANS' LEGAL RIGHTS AND TOOLS OF WAR

As Christians, we are given legal rights through Jesus Christ to stand strong against the enemy! If we choose to stand our legal ground out of our love and gratitude to Him, He readily equips us with His tools of war—mighty weapons that serve to defend us against the enemy! As each of us choose to listen to and obey Him, we can walk in victory over the enemy and declare: ***"I can do all things through Christ who strengthens me."*** (Philippians 4:13) How comforting to know He is not fickle-minded! **We can count on Him to be faithful, and faithfully warn us when the enemy sets out to capture us!** We read this in Hebrews 13:8-9a: *"Jesus Christ is the same yesterday, today, and forever. Do not be carried about with various and strange doctrines. For it is good that the heart be established by grace...."* How important it is for us to understand that **He understands what we are going through** on earth—**He understands the warfare that we are engaged in,** for we read this in Hebrews: ***"For we do not have a High Priest who cannot sympathize with our weaknesses, but was in all points tempted as we are, yet without sin."***

As we read in Matthew 4, Jesus clearly recognized when Satan was using his war-tools of temptation against Him! He knew full well that his evil strategies carried hope of luring Jesus away from His purpose in life. In his abominable pride, Satan was even hoping that he could claim Jesus as his servant who would bow down and worship him! Satan still had the same thoughts that he had when he was a resident in heaven—no repentance found in him. However, no doubt, once again, he was greatly disappointed when Jesus declared to him: *"...You shall not tempt the Lord your God."* (Matthew 4:7) Do you see that Jesus did not even take a moment to consider yielding to temptation? He immediately rebuked Satan! Yes, Jesus had fasted for forty days and forty nights and He was exhausted and hungry—but out of His love for all sinners, He had already chosen to stand in His sinless authority against the enemy! He gave no ground to the enemy, thus Satan had no legal rights to claim Him—as Jesus said in John 14:30: *"I will no longer talk much with you, for the ruler of this world is coming, and **he has nothing in Me**."*

LEGAL RIGHTS TOOLS, REDEEMED, CLAIMED AND KEPT BY JESUS

In our Lord's very own words, we find evidence that He chose to resist temptation from the enemy and willingly died on the cross that we might live! Therefore, we Christians have the legal right and authority through Jesus Christ, the Light of the World, our Redeemer, to go to heaven to live with Him when we die! **Our legal rights tool is Jesus in whom we believe! We are given that legal right through our belief in Jesus Christ who shed His blood, died in our place on Calvary, and paid our sin-debt in full!** For God says clearly: *"For God so loved the world that He gave His only begotten Son, that whoever believes in Him should not perish but have eternal life. For God sent not His Son into the world to condemn the world, but that the world through Him might be saved."* (John 3:16-17)

> Peter said: *"Let it be known to you all, and to all the people of Israel, that by the name of Jesus Christ of Nazareth, whom you crucified, whom God raised from the dead, by Him this man stands here before you whole. This is the stone which was rejected by you builders, which has become the chief cornerstone. Nor is there **salvation** in any other, for there is no other name under heaven given among men by which we must be saved."* (Acts 4:10-12)

> *"And this is the testimony: that God has given us **eternal life**, and this life is in His Son. He who has the Son has life; he who does not have the Son of God does not have life. These things I have written to you who believe in the name of the Son of God, that you may **know that you have eternal life**, and that you may continue to believe in the name of the Son of God."* (I John 5:11-13)

> *"...you were not **redeemed** with corruptible things, like silver or gold, from your aimless conduct received by tradition from your fathers, but **with the precious blood of Christ**, as a lamb without blemish and without spot."* (I Peter 1:18-20)

Our God-given legal rights mercifully come through our authority in Jesus Christ: *"And Jesus came and spoke to them, saying, "**All authority has been given to Me in heaven and on earth**. Go therefore and make disciples of all the nations, baptizing them in the name of the Father and of the Son and of the Holy Spirit, teaching them to observe all things that I have commanded you; and lo, I am with you always, even to the end of the age."* (Matthew 28:18-20)

When the Lord speaks of His authority over all, He does not only mean that He has the power and authority to save us and take us to heaven, but He also has the authority to give us power over the temptations of the enemy while we're sojourning on earth on our way to heaven! Through Jesus Christ, we can resist the enemy and walk in victory! Paul said: *"...**the Lord will deliver me from every evil work**, and preserve me for His heavenly kingdom. To Him be glory forever and ever. Amen!"* (II Timothy 4:18)

Freedom is provided for believers! Christians do not have to be held all their earthly lives in the strongholds of the enemy! Our Lord says: *"If you abide in My word, you are My disciples indeed. And you shall know the truth and the truth shall make you free. Therefore, **if the Son makes you free, you shall be free indeed**."* (John 8:31b-32, 36)

SAVED BY GRACE NOT BY WORKS,
TO WALK IN GOOD WORKS

How merciful for our Lord to allow us to be saved by His grace! Out of our gratitude, love and adoration, we should choose—like our Jesus did—to resist Satan's offers of temptation, which could only bring shame to our Lord and Savior, Jesus Christ! In addition, out of our gratitude, love and adoration we should let our testimony flow in a steady walk of "good works!" How wonderful to know that we do not have to attempt to earn our way to heaven! We read of our Lord's confirmation of that in His Word:

> *"....you He made alive, who were dead in trespasses and sins, in which you once walked according to the course of this world, according to the prince of the power of the air, the spirit who now works in the sons of disobedience, among whom also we all once conducted ourselves in the lusts of our flesh, fulfilling the desires of the flesh and of the mind, and were by nature children of wrath, just as the others. But God, who is rich in mercy because of His great love with which He loved us, even when we were dead in trespasses, made us alive together with Christ (by grace you have been saved), and raised us up together, and **made us sit together in the heavenly places in Christ Jesus**, that in the ages to come He might show the exceeding riches of His grace in His kindness toward us in Christ Jesus. For **by grace you have been saved through faith, and that not of yourselves; it is the gift of God, not of works, lest anyone should boast**. For we are His workmanship, created in Christ Jesus for good works, which God prepared beforehand that we should walk in them."* (Ephesians 2:1-10)

Did you notice that Jesus said God had prepared beforehand that we should walk in good works? His plans for us were already well established in heaven—long before we were born! We are most surely saved by grace and called according to His purposes to do good works! Out of our gratitude for salvation, we should desire to willingly work for our heavenly Father, our Lord Jesus Christ on whatever mission field He places us! All Christians are missionaries, scattered on a wide variety of mission fields in this sin-filled world, equipped to share salvation's plan and to help others as the Lord directs. When we arrive in heaven, the Lord will give rewards for the good works that we've done—crowns which we will have the privilege of casting at the feet of the King of kings and Lord of lords! (See II Corinthians 5:10; Revelation 4:9-11)

While surely there are obedient servants of the Lord who will receive many crowns, which they will have the joy of casting at the feet of Jesus, there are others who did very little or nothing at all concerning the cause of Christ. It's important for all of us to take care not to venture into God's judging territory! There are some souls who, for various reasons, have not even had the opportunity or privilege of serving the Lord. The thief on the Cross is a very good example of that. The thief who received the Lord as his Savior as he was dying on the cross beside Jesus, heard Jesus promise that he would be with Him in Paradise! (Luke 23:43) We read of the Lord's merciful judgment in I Corinthians 3:13-15:

> *"Each one's work will become clear; for the Day will declare it because it will be revealed by fire; and the fire will test each one's work, of what sort it is. If anyone's work which he has built on it endures, he will receive a reward. If anyone's work is burned, he will suffer loss; but **he himself will be saved, yet so as through fire.**"*

How awesome that we have the promise of our merciful sovereign Savior that we go to heaven when we die! What wonderful words of life these are:

> *"Now this I say, brethren, that flesh and blood cannot inherit the kingdom of God; nor does corruption inherit incorruption. Behold, I tell you a mystery; we shall not all sleep, but we shall all be changed in a moment, in the twinkling of an eye, at the last trumpet. For the trumpet will sound, and the dead will be raised incorruptible, and we shall be changed. For this corruptible must put on incorruption and this mortal must put on immortality. So when this corruptible has put on incorruption and this mortal has put on immortality, then shall be brought to pass the saying that is written: death is swallowed up in victory. O death, where is your sting. O Hades, where is your victory. The sting of death is sin and the strength of sin is the law. But, thanks be to God who gives us the victory through our Lord Jesus Christ. Therefore, **my beloved brethren, be steadfast, immovable, always abounding in the work of the Lord, knowing that your labor is not in vain in the Lord.**"* (I Corinthians 15:50-58)

SATAN AND INIQUITY CANNOT
KEEP CHRISTIANS OUT OF HEAVEN

The Lord permits Satan to oppose the righteous. In Zechariah 3:1-5, we read that truth about our Old Testament believers: *"Then he showed me Joshua the high priest standing before the Angel of the Lord, and Satan standing at his right hand to oppose him. And the Lord said to Satan, 'The Lord rebuke you, Satan! The Lord who has chosen Jerusalem rebuke you! Is this not a brand plucked from the fire?'* **Now Joshua was clothed with filthy garments, and was standing before the Angel.** *Then He answered and spoke to those who stood before Him, saying,* **'Take away the filthy garment from him.'** *And to him He said,* **'See, I have removed your iniquity from you, and I will clothe you with rich robes.'** *And I said, 'Let them put a clean turban on his head.' So they put a clean turban on his head, and they put the clothes on him. And the Angel of the Lord stood by."* **What joy to know that in this case, Satan had no authority, no legal rights over Joshua. Most surely, he didn't have a leg to stand on before our Lord!** And we also read:

> *"Blessed is he whose transgression is forgiven, whose sin is covered. Blessed is the man to whom the LORD does not impute iniquity, and in whose spirit there is no deceit. When I kept silent, my bones grew old through my groaning all the day long. For day and night Your hand was heavy upon me; my vitality was turned into the drought of summer." Selah "I acknowledged my sin to You, and my iniquity I have not hidden. I said, I will confess my transgressions to the LORD, and You forgave the iniquity of my sin. Selah."* (Psalm 32:1-5)

NEUTRALITY IS NOT AN OPTION

All humans, from Adam and Eve to the last person born on the earth will either go to live in heaven with our Lord Jesus, or they will go to the lake of fire to dwell with the Devil and his followers. For God says to Christians:

> *"When the Son of Man comes in His glory, and all the holy angels with Him, then He will sit on the throne of His glory. All the nations will be gathered before Him, and He will separate them one from another, as a shepherd divides his sheep from the goats. And the King will say to those on His right hand, 'Come, you blessed of My Father, inherit the kingdom prepared for you from the foundation of the world."* And then God says to those who have chosen to reject and rebel against Him: *"...Depart from Me, you cursed, into the everlasting fire prepared for the devil and his angels...and these will go away into everlasting punishment, but the righteous into eternal life."* (Matthew 25:31-34; 41, 46)

How comforting to know that we are the sheep of our Good Shepherd who says:

> *"My sheep hear My voice, and I know them, and they follow Me. And I give them eternal life, and they shall never perish; neither shall anyone snatch them out of My*

hand. My Father, who has given them to Me, is greater than all; and no one is able to snatch them out of My Father's hand. I and My Father are one." (John 10:27-30)

SECURE, IN OR OUT OF GOD'S WILL

As Christians we are tightly secure in God's flock, but our Good Shepherd has warned us that until we move into heaven, our enemy Satan the Devil is relentless in seeking to discourage and hinder all of God's sheep and His little lambs from walking in God's will! For we read:

> *"**Shepherd the flock of God** which is among you, **serving as overseers, not by compulsion, but willingly**, not for dishonest gain but eagerly; nor as being lords over those entrusted to you but **being examples** to the flock; and when the Chief Shepherd appears, you will receive the crown of glory that does not fade away. Likewise you younger people [lambs], submit yourselves to your elders. Yes, all of you be submissive to one another, and **be clothed with humility** for God resists the proud but gives grace to the humble. Therefore, humble yourselves under the mighty hand of God, that He may exalt you in due time, casting all your care upon Him, for He cares for you. **Be sober, be vigilant; because your adversary the devil walks about like a roaring lion, seeking whom he may devour. Resist him, steadfast in the faith....**"* (I Peter 5:2-9a)

EXERCISING AUTHORITY IN CHRIST WITH TRUTH BEFORE HIS THRONE

What wonderful truths to teach others, to teach counselees, that when they desire to have clean hearts before the Lord, as they humbly yet confidently and boldly come before the Lord Jesus, as they confess their sins, they will most surely find forgiveness! As they plead their case before Him, they will find grace and wisdom—and solutions to problems! For this truth is stated in Hebrews 4:16: *"Let us therefore come boldly to the throne of grace, that we may obtain mercy and find grace to help in time of need."*

What wondrous authority we have in Jesus! Satan, the accuser of the brethren does not have a chance to win his case against his prey when they are of repentant hearts and longing to be right with the Lord! In counseling sessions, as the counselees and I are dealing with their issues, presenting their cases before our Judge who sits on His throne, victory always comes! Our fair and just Judge transforms the counseling room into His courtroom, which is quite unique from the courtrooms of men! While Satan stands as "prosecuting attorney" against the Christian, our sovereign Jesus Christ is both "Defense Attorney" and "Judge!" In His courtroom the law stands that every person must tell the truth, including the prosecuting attorney, Satan! Our Defense Attorney and Judge always rules in favor of the Christian! What a joy it is when Satan the adversary loses his case each time when the Christian is desperate and repentant!

"Righteousness and justice are the foundation of Your throne; mercy and truth go before Your face. Blessed are the people who know the joyful sound! They walk, O LORD, in the light of Your countenance. In Your name they rejoice all day long, and in Your righteousness they are exalted. For You are the glory of their strength. And in Your favor our horn is exalted. For our shield belongs to the LORD, and our king to the Holy One of Israel." (Psalm 89:14-18)

How thankful we are to the Judge and our Defense Attorney that out of His love and mercy for sinners, He chose to be: *"...wounded for our transgressions, He was bruised for our iniquities: the chastisement for our peace was upon Him; and by His stripes we are healed."* (Isaiah 53:5) **Through His sacrifice for us** *"...in all these things we are more than conquerors through Him who loved us."* (Romans 8:37)

CHRISTIANS' LEGAL RIGHTS
THROUGH CHRIST OVER SATAN

Our Lord Jesus clearly states in His Word that not only are Christians positioned with Him in His legal rights, His power and authority, but we can walk in our God-given authority and do the works of our heavenly Father—of our Lord Jesus. Take care to absorb into your heart this scripture:

*"Do you not believe that I am in the Father, and the Father in Me? The words that I speak to you I do not speak on My own authority; but **the Father who dwells in Me does the works. Believe Me that I am in the Father and the Father in Me,** or else believe Me for the sake of the works themselves. **Most assuredly, I say to you, he who believes in Me, the works that I do he will do also; and greater works than these he will do because I go to My Father."*** (John 14:10-12)

How amazing that just as Jesus and the Father are One, we Christians have the Lord Jesus, His Holy Spirit living within us! How humbling it is to know that He wants to use us in carrying on His work—sharing salvation's plan and sharing the good news that Jesus can liberate the bruised—set Satan's captives free! We have the legal rights through Jesus Christ to claim back all ground from the enemy! Through our position in Jesus Christ we have that legal right!

It is awesome to comprehend our position in Christ! If we as Christians are "seated in heavenly places," it certainly stands as truth that we have full authority over the enemy, doesn't it? We read: *"You have put all things in subjection under His [Jesus'] feet. For in that He put all in subjection under Him, He left nothing that is not put under Him...."* (Hebrews 2:8) Knowing this, we can understand that we most surely have power over Satan and his demonic forces. This is confirmed as we read the following scripture, which accents the fact that **we should be exercising our legal rights over the enemy as well as watching out for our brothers and sisters—we are keepers of our brothers and sisters!**

73

In Ephesians 1:15-23 we read of Paul's prayer concerning spiritual wisdom: *"Therefore I also, after I heard of your faith in the Lord Jesus and your love for all the saints, do not cease to give thanks for you, making mention of you in my prayers: that the God of our Lord Jesus Christ, the Father of glory, may give to you the spirit of wisdom and revelation in the knowledge of Him, the eyes of your understanding being enlightened; that you may know what is the hope of His calling, what are the riches of the glory of His inheritance in the saints, and what is the exceeding greatness of His power toward us who believe, according to the working of His mighty power which He worked in Christ when He raised Him from the dead and seated Him at His right hand in the heavenly places, far above all principality and power and might and dominion, and every name that is named, not only in this age but also in that which is to come. And He put all things under His feet, and gave Him to be head over all things to the church, which is His body, the fullness of Him who fills all in all."*

We also read in Ephesians 6:10-18: *"...My brethren, be strong in the Lord and in the power of His might. Put on the whole armor of God, that you may be able to stand against the wiles of the devil. For we do not wrestle against flesh and blood, but against principalities, against powers, against the rulers of the darkness of this age, against spiritual hosts of wickedness in the heavenly places. Stand therefore, having girded your waist with truth, having put on the breastplate of righteousness, and having shod your feet with the preparation of the gospel of peace; above all, taking the shield of faith with which you will be able to quench all the fiery darts of the wicked one. And take the helmet of salvation, and the sword of the Spirit, which is the Word of God; praying always with all prayer and supplication in the Spirit, **being watchful to this end with all perseverance and supplication for all the saints**."*

How humbling to think of our Lord Jesus giving us the legal rights, power and authority to live in victory over the enemy, and to be able to help others find victory in Jesus! As we read the following passage about what our Lord Jesus did, it should be so encouraging to us to walk boldly in our legal rights, our power and authority in Jesus to help set Satan's captives free!

*"Then He went down to Capernaum, a city of Galilee, and was teaching them on the Sabbaths. And **they were astonished at His teachings, for His word was with authority**. Now in the synagogue there was a man who had a spirit of an unclean demon. And he cried out with a loud voice, saying, 'Let us alone! What have we to do with You, Jesus of Nazareth? Did You come to destroy us? I know who You are—the Holy One of God!' But Jesus rebuked him, saying, 'Be quiet, and come out of him!" And when the demon had thrown him in their midst, it came out of him and did not hurt him. Then they were all amazed and spoke among themselves, saying **'What a word this is! For with authority and power He commands the unclean spirits, and they come out.'"** (Luke 4:31-36)*

74

We Christians are without excuse to walk in our legal rights, our power, and our authority through Jesus Christ. Therefore, as ministers and counselors, we should with joy obey the Lord, stand strong in the power of His might and take full advantage of exercising our God-given legal rights because:

> *"The Spirit of the Lord is upon Me, because He has anointed Me to preach the gospel to the poor; He has sent Me to heal the brokenhearted, to proclaim liberty to the captives and recovery of sight to the blind, to set at liberty those who are oppressed [bruised]; to proclaim the acceptable year of the Lord."* (Luke 4:18-19)

God's precious Christians, through Jesus Christ, hold the wonderful privilege of having legal rights, power and authority over the enemy, Satan the Devil! Keeping that in mind, we will now move to the next chapter where we will examine how the "Four Pillars Supporting the Biblical Counseling Platform" provide very useful tools for counseling ministries!

Chapter Two
FOUR PILLARS SUPPORTING THE BIBLICAL COUNSELING PLATFORM

There are four major subjects in the Bible—which I call four pillars—that support the platform of biblical counseling. God's truths within these four supporting pillars offer us the power and authority to walk in victory over the enemy—if we choose to accept and apply them with willing hearts. I have been in the ministry since 1969 and ten years later, in 1979, I began focusing more diligently on the counseling ministry. During all these years, the Lord has taught me some counseling tools that are vital to helping people! But He has also taught me that in order for people to receive counseling successfully—through any ministry—Amos 3:3 must be met first! God asks, *"Can two walk together, unless they are agreed?"* Of course, the answer is **"No!"** And it is critical for us to remember that **the Lord says where there is unity, He commands a blessing**! (See Psalm 133:1-3)

For this reason, when the time comes for me to work with the counselee, it is essential that he has not only read my first book, but that he has **either** listened to the teachings on my set-of-five "Counseling the Bruised" CDs and reviewed the small accompanying syllabus, **or** has read "More Tools for Liberating the Bruised." The CDs and syllabus contain basic information about the "Four Pillars Supporting the Biblical Counseling Platform" that the Lord taught me after I wrote the first book. With the counselee doing this beforehand, it will **(1)** save one-on-one counseling time, **(2)** give him a much better understanding of spiritual warfare in relation to his spiritual condition and the hope for victory that is in Jesus Christ, and as he willingly submits to counseling, **(3)** we will have the confidence that there is a meeting of our minds—unity, which God will bless! Things will go so much more smoothly when we stand together in unity on theology as we work, for we have the God-given rights, authority and boldness to be able to deal with the biblical responsibilities that must be met! I usually make this statement to my counselee: "If you are not willing and eager to receive this type of biblical counseling, then it will be like pouring water on a rock—it will just splatter on us and waste your time and mine!"

I will now explain the four pillars that support the biblical counseling platform, on which we can stand boldly on our biblical authority and lead a counselee to freedom.

A. THE INIQUITY OF THE FATHERS PILLAR

As we consider these four pillars, the first one that we will look at is, **the Iniquity of the Fathers Pillar**. There are numerous scriptures that speak to the iniquity of the fathers, but I have chosen to share one that is in the first listing of the Ten Commandments. This pillar is found listed second in Exodus 20:4-6:

"You shall not make for yourself a carved image—any likeness of anything that is in heaven above, or that is in the earth beneath, or that is in the water under the earth; you shall not bow down to them nor serve them. For I, the Lord your God, am a jealous God, **visiting the iniquity of the fathers upon the children to the third and fourth generations** *of those who hate Me, but showing mercy to thousands, to those who love Me and keep My commandments."*

We see here that God's promise of visiting the iniquity of the fathers down upon the children to the third and fourth generation is part of the second commandment. The commandments are not going to go away, folks! The thing that we need to understand about the iniquity of the fathers is the proper definition of the word "iniquity," which extends beyond the meaning of "sin." For iniquity actually means, **"any lifestyle lived outside the will of God and His authority."** In essence, any lifestyle that is chosen to be lived without any repentance for it. We see that God has promised in this second commandment that He is going to **visit the iniquity of the fathers** upon the children unto the third and fourth generation of them that hate Him. It is essential that we understand that iniquity extends beyond sin, for it is a **chosen** lifestyle lived outside God's will. And we need to understand, that iniquity can pass down in two major ways. In studying this subject, the word "visits" stands out. While God hates iniquity, we find that in His mercy He "visits" the persons connected to that iniquity. **I find it refreshing that some of the descriptions the English dictionary gives for "visits" are "come and see; a meeting; an official call for inspection or supervision!" God most definitely is "an official" and how merciful that the purpose of His visit—His inspection—is not only to inspect, but to give instructions about how to clean up the mess and get things running properly!**

INIQUITY CAN PASS DOWN THROUGH LEARNED BEHAVIOR

Iniquity can most definitely pass down through **learned behavior**. Here are some examples: If parents are screamers while rearing their children, then when their children become parents, they more than likely choose to correct their children in either of two extreme ways. They will either be screamers like their parents or go to the opposite end of the spectrum and be passive. Those who choose to be passive typically don't want to see any wrong their children are doing, for in their hearts, they readily succumb to being "taken on a guilt trip"—feeling condemned when they consider speaking to their children about their misbehavior issues. They fear if they correct their children, it would lead to screaming at them—just like their parents screamed at them. Therefore, they become dysfunctional as a parent by ignoring the issue. So we see that iniquity passes from parents to children by way of their negative learned behavior.

INIQUITY IS NOT CAUSED BY "GENES"

As you look at secular psychology and secular counseling, you find terms describing a variety of conditions, all of which entail problems that hinder them in one way or another from functioning in a healthy, normal way socially. They are labeled as having "social behavioral disorders" and/or "mental disorders." Some such labels are: bipolar, bipolar manic, manic-depressive, chronic fatigue syndrome, schizophrenia, homosexuality, attention deficit disorder, and attention deficit hyperactivity disorder. Sadly enough, "new disorders" continue to lengthen the list! Tragically, a grievously high percentage of these precious souls have been falsely tagged "incurable!" It has also been declared, "it must be in the genes" or "it's a chemical problem in the person's body!" Extensive research continues to go on, and on, and on, trying to figure out how to counteract the "gene" that "makes" someone schizophrenic, bipolar, bipolar manic and such. Of course, while the search goes on for the cure—many precious victims are given coping-medications that carry harmful side affects—including "depression with possible suicidal thoughts!" As if this "terrible affliction" isn't bad enough for the person, what about his children? What about his future generations? Will they also be born with this gene plague?

If a person cannot be "re-gened" and has been diagnosed as "incurable," neither he nor his family are given any hope for a happy life! Some have been quite wrongfully told by counselors, "God made you that way, so you can't help it!" I so long for all of these precious people to be told that their Creator did not make them that way and that He is a God of Hope and that He can cure them of those "disorders!" So, dear ministers and counselors, I ask that you please, prayerfully examine the "symptoms" of these "disorders," which I explain in the next chapter, "Victory Over Addictions and Behavioral Disorders." I believe as you study them from God's viewpoint, you will see much hope for your counselees who have been diagnosed with such!

In truth, when there is something going on within a person's emotions that hinder him from communicating normally with others—it is a direct result of "sin" at some point in his life, either passed down through "iniquity" or through giving into temptation and choosing to walk in a sinful lifestyle. From the biblical perspective, persons with these "disorders" are given a great deal of hope for escape from them! For these are actually spiritual conditions rather than physical conditions!

I believe you will agree that God does not fashion a person in such a way that he is incapable of interacting with people! I find no where in the Bible where He makes a person with such severe "disorders" that he is hindered from getting saved and living out the Christian life that God intended for him! What I do find in the Bible is hope for him recorded in God's Word! In Genesis 18:14a, we read: ***"Is anything too hard for the Lord?"*** And in Luke 1:37, we are told: ***"...with God nothing will be impossible."*** We find evidence of such in the story told in Mark 5:1-20, of a man diagnosed as having "an unsound mind" and being "demon possessed," and we read that he was set free of those "disorders" in verse 15, *"Then they came to Jesus and saw the **one who had been demon possessed and had the legion, sitting and clothed and in his right mind**...."* (Also see: II Timothy 1:7; Philippians 4:13; Romans 12:1-2; II Timothy 3:16-17) Indeed, he was "in his right mind"—he no longer had "a mental disorder" for he ran to Jesus and worshiped Him!

B. THE ANCESTRAL DEMON PILLAR

What an encouragement to have discovered the cancerous culprit behind **the ancestral demon pillar**. In Mark 9:14-32, as you read, you will notice that we have an overflow from Pillar Number One, for it had to do with the iniquity of the fathers, but it's talking about how it can pass down through learned behavior and ancestral demons.

INIQUITY CAN PASS DOWN THROUGH ANCESTRAL DEMONS

While the teachings of those who say such behavioral problems are in the genes give no hope since one cannot be "re-gened," our hope is enlarged in biblical studies as we learn about the cause and the cure behind the iniquity of the fathers! As I previously shared, **learned behavior** is one of the major ways that the iniquity of a father can be passed down to his children—to the third and fourth generations! And an **ancestral demon** will be passed down at the conception of a child. An ancestral demon may be passed down to the first child, yet not in the others. Then there may be an ancestral demon found in another of the father's children rather than the first for various reasons.

As I work with folks, we must come to an agreement that the truth is that iniquity can continue to pass down in generations in this twenty-first century. And, if this is true, we have already determined that they pass down through learned behavior and ancestral demons, who amplify such behavior. If the counselee and counselor cannot agree upon this pillar number one, then counseling will not be successful—thus I will not counsel this person. If he later contacts me and says that he has come to embrace these truths and is truly desperate, then I will schedule another time for him.

Now I am going to teach about the iniquity of a father passing down an ancestral demon to his son by using the story of the father with the demonic young son which is found in Matthew 17:14-21; Mark 9:14-29; Luke 9:37-42. However, I think it wise to set the scene of where the disciples were in their understanding of this matter at that point in time, for there is an important lesson to be learned for the benefit of all Christians!

In Mark 9 I'm going to point out some critical issues pertaining to **"progressive revelation"** in the midst of the first thirteen verses. At that point in time, Jesus, The Living Word, made some statements that the disciples did not understand. However, as time went on—after His death, burial, and resurrection—they came to understand what He said and told them to remember! For example, let us begin reading in Mark 9:1:

> *"And He [Jesus] said unto them, 'Assuredly, I say to you that there are some standing here who will not taste death till they see the kingdom of God present with power.'"*

I submit to you that Jesus' apostles had no idea what He was telling them, but then we begin to see things materialize when we read Mark 9:2-6:

80

> *"Now after six days Jesus took Peter, James, and John, and led them up on a high mountain apart by themselves; and He was transfigured before them. His clothes became shining, exceedingly white, like snow, such as no launderer on earth can whiten them. And Elijah appeared to them with Moses, and they were talking with Jesus. Then Peter answered and said to Jesus, "Rabbi, it is good for us to be here; and let us make three tabernacles: one for You, one for Moses, and one for Elijah"— because he did not know what to say, for they were greatly afraid."*

Concerning what Peter said in the midst of this awesome scene, while I've been preaching or speaking at a workshop, I've often used it to make some applications to present-day people. Since I was saved at age ten and became a member of a Baptist Church, I have been a member of a number of Baptist churches—for sixty-three years now. And over the years I have declared, "Now, Peter must have been a Baptist, for over so many years, during business meetings, I have seen all too many Baptist church members who have reacted like Peter! They were distracted from critical spiritual matters and chose to just focus on physical matters—neglecting to prayerfully seek God's wisdom and will!" I have gone on to explain that James and John were quietly observing, but Peter was not! **Rather than Peter being in an attitude of seeking to understand why Jesus was showing them this astonishing scene, Peter thought he just had to say something, so he just jumped right in on the conversation between Elijah, Moses, and Jesus!** As we read Peter's words, we see that he wasn't comfortable with speaking out—he was fearful (like James and John)—yet we find him blurting out a physical idea that popped into his head, which clearly revealed that he was taking a physical approach to a spiritual matter, as we read Mark 9:5b-6:

> *"'...Rabbi, it is good for us to be here; and let us make three tabernacles: one for You, one for Moses, and one for Elijah'—because he did not know what to say, for they were greatly afraid.'"*

As I read of Peter's idea to build tabernacles for the three of them (Jesus, Moses, and Elijah), I was reminded of how many times large amounts of funds had come into many different churches over the years and the vote always carried to build a new building, remodel one, or add another building to the present one. Votes typically carried to hire a new staff member to take the load off the present staff. Now let me be quick to say that I am most definitely not against constructing buildings from which God's Word is preached and taught—and where God's people can congregate for fellowship! But what I am saying is that after having built so many buildings, how many of them have heard in those walls a vote that carried to hire Godly biblical counselors who are sound in doctrine and include spiritual warfare in their counseling sessions? How many such counselors are there in comparison to other full-time, salaried staff members? And why are there volunteer counselors in some churches who go without being paid a just salary to provide their needs while they make certain there is godly counsel readily available for hurting souls?

Now I am well aware of some church members being guilty of wrongfully thinking that part of the pastor's job description includes counseling all the members—along with preaching, teaching, going to all the functions, visiting all the members, visiting the sick, conducting weddings and funerals, etc.—plus being on call 24/7! I know there are some biblical counselors salaried in some churches—but I also know that far too many of them stop short of spiritual warfare counseling. Over and over again, news has come to me that they have fallen short of getting to the root causes of dear souls being held tightly in Satan's strongholds! Some such counselors have even revealed that they are afraid to deal with the demons! And of course, the demons are delighted to be able to keep their ground!

I am also aware that some churches that provide counselors place limitations on counselees with critical problems—if they haven't completed their counseling within a predetermined amount of time, they are referred out to secular counselors. So it is out of a grieved heart, I ask, how many church members are taking time to seriously acknowledge the spiritual needs of many people within those church walls? How many members would willingly take on the responsibility to build up the spiritual health of the Church family? It is my heart's desire that today's churches—whether Baptist denomination or other Christ-based denominations—would not be afraid to take a spiritual view of the people both inside and outside the church walls. For, there is a dire need to focus on the war that Satan is so deceitfully raging against God's children! Oh, that Christian soldiers would take a brave stand for them and make it a priority to build the Kingdom of God!

After Peter made his pitch to build a tabernacle, we then see the next thing that transpired on the mountain, in Mark 9:7-10:

> *"And a cloud came and overshadowed them; and a voice [our heavenly Father's] came out of the cloud, saying, 'This is My beloved Son. Hear Him!' Suddenly, when they had looked around, they saw no one anymore, but only Jesus with themselves. Now as they came down from the mountain, He commanded them that they should tell no one the things that they had seen, till the Son of Man had risen from the dead. So they kept this word to themselves, questioning what the rising from the dead meant."*

Now folks, **I do not believe in "experiential theology!" I do not believe that you experience things, then write theology**. But, what I do believe is that **when you experience theology, you understand theology better**! What am I saying? A couple of days after Jesus and the disciples had come down from the mountain, note what Jesus told the disciples in Mark 9:30-32:

> *"Then they departed from there and passed through Galilee, and He did not want anyone to know it. For He taught His disciples and said to them, 'The Son of man is being betrayed into the hands of men, and they will kill Him. And after He is killed, He will rise the third day.' But they did not understand this saying, and were afraid to ask Him."*

We see that even though they received this message from God, from Jesus Himself, it did not mean that they understood at that point in time. And, of course, Jesus knew they didn't understand it; thus, He also knew that if they shared this news with others, neither would they understand. The instructions were clear, for them to keep silent until He arose from the dead, until they experienced what He said would come to pass—His death, burial and resurrection on the third day. Until then, they would not understand. This is **"progressive revelation,"** which I was taught years ago while in seminary. **I do not believe in any "new revelation to the Church,"** for I believe that God, from Genesis through Revelation has already told the Church, His believing people, everything that He is going to tell them. Now let me be quick to say that **I do believe in "the type of revelation pertaining to God's will for our lives," such as His giving His "wisdom and direction as we live our daily lives."** He calls everyone according to His specific purposes in this life. He wants each Christian to listen to and obey Him as he lives on His earthly mission field. Again, concerning the overall "revelation" to the Church and its functions, God has said all that He's going to say about it, from the book of Genesis through the book of Revelation—and as you know there is plenty to share without an extra word being added to it!

LESSON ABOUT AN ANCESTRAL DEMON IN THE BIBLE

So it's important for people to understand that **what I'm teaching and dealing with is not a new revelation. It's not new theology!** Folks, when I got so desperate to learn more about how to help people with critical issues, and listened intently for Him to teach me, He opened up my heart to His truths that were already written in His Word! **He just enabled me to walk deeper into His Word and learn more!** Now keep all of this in mind as we take a deeper look in the story of the father with the demonic son, through which the iniquity of the father and the ancestral demon will be taught!

The day after Jesus and the disciples were on the mountain, we see the story of the father and his demonic son begin to unfold as Jesus approaches the scene, in Mark 9:14-16:

> *"And when He came to the disciples, He saw a great multitude around them, and scribes disputing with them. Immediately, when they saw Him, all the people were greatly amazed, and running to Him, greeted Him. And He asked the scribes, 'What are you discussing with them?'"*

Now let's examine the crowd for a moment. **The scribes—keepers of the Law—were arguing with the disciples.** Some were mocking the disciples because of their failure to succeed in casting a demon out of a little boy. Now these scribes believed in Jehovah, and while they respected Jesus as a "prophet"—they had not yet recognized and embraced Jesus as the Messiah! They were some of whom the scripture spoke about in John 1:11-12:

> *"He came unto His own, and His own received Him not. But as many as received Him, to them gave He power to become the sons of God, even to them that believe on His name."*

Now, let's go back a little in time to examine the disciples. Jesus had gone upon a mountain and called unto Himself twelve disciples, appointing them to preach, to heal the sick and to cast out demons. For we see evidence of that in various passages of scripture. We read in Mark 3:14-15:

> *"Then He appointed twelve, that they might be with Him and that He might send them out to preach, and to have power to heal sicknesses and to cast out demons."*

We read a bit further that they were certainly obeying Him, in Mark 6:12-13:

> *"So they went out and preached that people should repent. And they cast out many demons, and anointed with oil many who were sick, and healed them."*

The number of disciples had multiplied and they were also preaching repentance and healing the sick and casting out demons! But do you recall what seventy disciples that the Lord had sent out reported upon their return visit to Him? We read their report in Luke 10:17:

> *"Then the seventy returned with joy, saying, Lord, even the demons are subject to us in Your name."*

While the disciples were understandably very excited about the new converts and those who had been healed and set free from demons, Jesus was deeply concerned as He wisely detected an underlying, negative issue! This negative issue applied not only to those disciples of yesteryear, but when He warned them, He was warning all servants of the Lord today concerning "their own" Christian accomplishments! For, **we should look closely at Jesus' words of warning concerning the "evil spiritual realm"** in Luke 10:18-20:

> *"And He said to them, 'I saw Satan fall like lightning from heaven. Behold, I give you the authority to trample on serpents and scorpions, and over the power of the enemy, and nothing shall by any means hurt you. Nevertheless **do not rejoice in this**, that the spirits are subject to you, but **rather rejoice because your name is written in heaven.**'"*

Indeed, we must stay keenly alert to resist the temptation to become prideful concerning who we are in Christ—that we have authority in Christ—but rather, be humbly grateful! We can do all things in Christ who strengthens us—but we should acknowledge that such work is only accomplished because He is working through us to accomplish His will! What a privilege it is to be used of the Lord! What joy to know that we do not have to fear the demons yet at the same time, not be prideful and boast of Jesus doing this work through us!

Most surely the disciples' missions had been very successful—until the day we find them in the midst of that multitude of people where they are unable to free a man's demonic little boy—and they were being mocked for their failure! Then we read what happened after Jesus had asked (for our learning) what the commotion was all about in Mark 9:17-18:

> *"Then one of the crowd answered and said, 'Teacher, I brought You my son, who has **a mute spirit**. And wherever it **seizes him**, it **throws him down; he foams at the mouth, gnashes his teeth, and becomes rigid**. So I spoke to Your disciples, that they should cast it out but they could not."*

Matthew 17:15 states that the father also appealed with these words: *"Lord, have mercy on my son, for **he is an epileptic and suffers severely**; for he often falls into the fire and often into the water."*

Luke 9:38-39, reported that the father was crying out: *"...saying, Teacher, I implore You, look on my son, for he is my only child. And behold **a spirit seizes him, and he suddenly cries out; it convulses him** so that **he foams at the mouth**; and it departs from him with **great difficulty, bruising him**."*

Other translations show that the father reports that his son **pineth away** and that the mute spirit **teareth** the boy.

Let us take a moment to go deeper by learning from the original Greek language, the meaning of the words that the father used to describe the boy's behavior when the "mute spirit" took control of him:

1. The Greek word for **"mute spirit"** is **"alalon,"** which means **"one who cannot speak"**.

2. The Greek word for **"seize"** is **"katalambanō,"** meaning **"to take hold of, to pull down, to take possession of."**

3. As we read **"it throws him down,"** in Greek we find the word **"katalepsy"** which compares **"behavior like unto one throwing a fit."** And, we also find that the Greek word for **"to throw"** is **"ballō"** which confirms to us that the boy was not clumsy—not prone to tripping and falling—nor was his body chemistry off balance. Because that word actually reflects the true severity of the boy's condition—**"suicidal mania induced by a demonic being."**

4. As we read that **"he foams at the mouth, gnashes his teeth,** and **becomes rigid,"** the Greek word **"rēgnumi"** describes **"one suffering a convulsion; a seizure that is caused by a demonic spirit."**

5. The word **"pineth"** [1085] that was translated from the Greek word **"xērainō"** literally means **"a drying up, withering up, shriveling up,"** so his father is telling Jesus in essence that the demon is causing the very life to be sucked out of his son.

6. The Greek word for **"teareth"** is **"rēgnumi,"** which means **"distortion, convulsions as in one demonically possessed."**

(Those Greek words and definitions were taken from Word Studies in the Greek New Testament, Vol. 1, pages 180-187, by Kenneth S. Wuest, William B. Eerdsman Publishing Company, Grand Rapids, MI 49502.)

Now that we have a deeper understanding of the boy's spiritual bondage—that it was truly a spiritual condition, the controlling of a person by demonic forces, let us now focus on his father, from whom he acquired that ancestral demon!

In Mark 9:17 (and in Luke 9:38), when the father began his appeal to Jesus to help his son, and described his condition, he respectfully addressed Jesus as **"Teacher"—like Rabbi**.

Then we find Jesus responding to the man, but as He does, He is also addressing the "great multitude" observing Him, which we read in Mark 9:19a:

> *"He answered him and said, '**O faithless** generation, how long shall I be with you? How long shall I bear with you?...."*

However, it's important to note that Jesus used an additional word besides "faithless" to describe that generation, which is recorded in both Matthew 17:17 and in Luke 9:41:

> *"Then Jesus answered and said, '**O faithless and perverse** generation, how long shall I be with you? How long shall I bear with you?...."*

As we look at the word **"faithless"** that Jesus used in speaking to that generation, in the original Greek language, we see that the Greek word **"apistos"** [571] stands for **"disbelieving, without faith, untrustworthy."** The Greek word for **"perverse"** is **"diastrĕphō"** [1294] meaning, **"to distort, misinterpret, corrupt, turn away."** (The New Strong's Exhaustive Concordance of the Bible; James Strong, LL.D., S.T.D.; Thomas Nelson Publishers, Nashville, Camden, Kansas City)

Then we read of Jesus' action and what happened to the little boy in Mark 9:19b-20:

> *"'...Bring him to Me.' Then they brought him to Him. And when he [the mute spirit; ancestral demon] saw Him, immediately the spirit convulsed him, and he fell on the ground and wallowed, foaming at the mouth."*

The demon within that precious little boy most surely displayed that **he had legal rights** to him, which he certainly did not want to give up! While Jesus certainly knew everything about this man and his son, **"as with other examples in His Word—He asked a question for our learning!"** We read of Jesus' question and the father's reply in Mark 9:21: *"'...**How long has this been happening to him?'** And he said, 'From **childhood.'"***

In the father's reply, he actually used the Greek word, **"paidiothen"** [3812] literally meaning **"from infancy."** Now prayerfully ponder this question: How did this **"infant"** acquire a demon spirit? Did this baby deliberately choose to establish a sinful lifestyle? Of course not! Now there are four ways a person can invite demons into his life, and they are based on **(1)** what you do, **(2)** who you do it with, **(3)** where you go, and **(4)** what you join. Now surely you would agree that none of these apply to a baby, do they? So, none of these applied to the little boy, for he was not yet accountable for his behavior! Therefore, the only other explanation is that **(5)** he acquired the "mute spirit" by way of—the iniquity of his father passing down to him! As you will soon see, this is revealed to us in scripture!

Note carefully the crucial change in how that the father continues his appeal, in Mark 9:22:

> *"And often he has thrown him both into the fire and into the water to destroy him. But if You can do anything, have compassion on us and help us.'"*

Do you see a difference in the father's attitude toward Jesus? Did you notice that **when he first appealed to Jesus, he was focusing on his son**—please fix **him**! Now, we see that he is appealing to Jesus, the Teacher to **"help us!" He had become conscience of a "connection" between himself and his son!** Does this not reveal that the father had come under conviction not only for his lack of faith—his weakness of faith—but for the fact that he was directly responsible for his son's condition? Indeed, for what does Jesus say next?

> *"If you can believe, all things are possible to him who believes."*

Now it's important to notice how the father responds—including calling Jesus by **"another name"** as he tearfully repents of his lack of faith and expresses his desire to trust him more.

> *"Immediately the father cried out and said with tears, 'Lord, I believe; help my unbelief!'"* (Mark 9:24)

As we read of the story told in Matthew 17:14-15, we see that the father had not only begun calling Jesus **"Lord,"** but by his actions he confirmed a heart-change in his view of Jesus:

> *"And when they had come to the multitude, a man came to Him, kneeling down to Him and saying, 'Lord....'"*

At that point the man who chose to take responsibility for his son's spiritual condition and for his own sin, was humble and of a repentant heart! Do you also see by his switching from simply calling Jesus whom he had respected as a wise Master Teacher—a Rabbi—that his eyes were open and he saw Jesus on a much higher plateau—**as one in high, Godly authority?** Indeed, this dear man chose to believe that Jesus, the Master Teacher, Rabbi of all rabbis, was the promised Messiah!

Now it's vital that we acknowledge **at this point, that the man's son is still legally bounded up by the demonic "mute spirit!"** It is **after** the father cried out, confessing his own sins and accepting responsibility for his son's spiritual bondage that we see Jesus—the Lord, the Messiah—healing the man's son. Jesus knew the demonic program within the young boy! Do you see God's truth revealed to help us understand that the ancestral demon had legal claim to the boy **by the father's sin of unbelief?** His iniquity had passed down to his precious son. Thus, **the ancestral demon had legal claim through the father "turning a deaf ear" to acknowledging Jesus as the**

promised Messiah! It was only after the father repented that the ground was claimed back from the ancestral demon! What joy it is to then read of the boy's freedom!

> In Matthew 17:18 it's reported: *"...Jesus rebuked the demon, and it came out of him; and the child was cured that very hour."*

> In Mark 9:25-27 we're told: *"...He rebuked the unclean spirit, saying to it:* ***'Deaf and dumb spirit, I command you, come out of him and enter him no more!"*** *"Then the spirit cried out, convulsed him greatly, and came out of him. And he became as one dead so that many said, 'He is dead.' But Jesus took him by the hand and lifted him up, and he arose."*

How thankful I am for the lesson the Lord revealed through this father and his little boy. **However, this is not the end of the lesson Jesus revealed to us through this father and son**! Let's look carefully at the rest of the story! We see that the disciples were puzzled about why they had not been able to cast the demon out of the little boy as we read their question and Jesus' answer to them in Mark 9:28-29:

> *"And when He had come into the house, His disciples asked Him privately, 'Why could we not cast it out?' And He said to them,* ***'This kind can come out by nothing but prayer and fasting.'"***

With the disciples waiting until they were alone with Jesus may indicate that they were embarrassed that they were not able to cast the demon out of the little boy. But they also showed an interest in learning why they had failed. For one thing, let us remember that the disciples believed Jesus was the Messiah and they had a good track record for casting out demons. Let us also remember that they were present when Jesus declared, "O faithless and perverse generation!" We could ponder various reasons for their "failure." Had doubt set in, wavering and weakening their faith because this case was perhaps a bit different from the others? Or, having set so many demonic persons free, had they become cocky or perhaps even mechanical? Were they just going through the motions, forgetting they were not the power source, but merely instruments of God with the privilege of using God's weapons of war—their God-given power and authority? While it could have been a combination of reasons, there is another reason which Jesus revealed when He declared, *"this kind can come out by nothing but prayer and fasting."* There are three words that we should take a close look at in Jesus' statement—one of which I assure you will teach us a lesson about an amazing truth concerning the father and his son—and the ancestral demon! **Let us note that concerning the word "fasting," some of the earlier manuscripts do not include the word "fasting"; however, it does serve a goodly purpose to encourage people to "fast from" anything that hinders them from spending quality time with the Lord, while seeking His wisdom concerning a matter.**

Now concerning the word **"prayer,"** it's important to remember that at this point in time, Jesus was nearing His crucifixion! Therefore, He knew that after His death, burial and resurrection, He would soon return in the form of the Holy Spirit to live in the hearts of all believers. Residing in their hearts, He would be their Master Teacher and Counselor who would give them wisdom as they grew still and listened to Him. The disciples would begin to understand things after Jesus' crucifixion and resurrection!

Let us remember that at this point in time, the disciples were doing all that Jesus had taught them to do. He was teaching them something for the future—and is telling us today, that after we have done all the practical things, yet have no results, take time to draw aside from distractions to listen for Him to give us wisdom. We have Him—the Living Word—in our hearts, and we also have the privilege of His written Word to study. Therefore, let us take a moment to investigate that third word in the passage **"kind."** **What did Jesus mean when He said "this kind?"**

As we look up the word **"kind" in the original Greek language, we find the Greek word, "genos" [1085] and are amazed at its meaning. It means, "offspring, born, kin, family, stock, a nation, breed."** Just as we came to understand that the father was responsible for the stronghold that the demonic, mute spirit had on his son—**we now have even more confirmation that it was "ancestral!"** The word **"genos"** is connected to another Greek word, **"ginomai" [1096]** meaning **"to cause to come into being; become; be brought to pass."** Because Jesus was doing what the Father was telling Him to do—He knew **the program within the father and son!** He was able to address and teach us that **generational demons—the links between father, son and the ancestral demon—are blocks and programs that legally claim precious souls—until Jesus, the Son sets them free!** Folks, what I want so badly for you to hear and understand is that **we are talking about programs.** We are talking about **duplexes (flip-sides), fragmented personalities (wounded personalities/parts of the soul), lifestyle and ancestral demons—plus specialized, customized demon-clones!** God warned us that Satan has tactics that he uses in this world to try to render God's Christians inoperative so they cannot fulfill God's purpose for them. We can truly see this in Ephesians 6:11: *"...put on the whole armor of God, that you may be able to stand against **the wiles of the Devil**."* The word **"wiles" in the Greek is "methodeia" [3180]** which means to slyly trick, deceive, beguile, and use cunning strategies.

THE AGE OF ACCOUNTABILITY—TODAY

Before we move to the third pillar, let us take a moment to compare a lesson about a subject that was involved in the case of the father and son that applies to this present day—**"the age of accountability."** While we do not find an age of accountability stated in the New Testament, upon reading Jesus' words in Matthew 5:17-18: *"Do not think that I came to destroy the Law or the Prophets. I did not come to destroy but to fulfill. For assuredly, I say to you, till heaven and earth pass away, one jot or one title will by no means pass from the law till all is fulfilled."* Knowing that Hebrews 13:8 says, *"Jesus Christ is the same yesterday, today, and forever,"* while I have no written evidence, I believe this subject matter in the Old Testament, by the mercy of God, applies to New Testament times—and our times.

Upon looking in the Old Testament, we find God stating that He was going to walk the children of Israel to death in the wilderness for disobeying Him when He told them to go in and claim the land of Canaan. **God said everyone of that generation would die in the wilderness except for Joshua, Caleb, all of the children under the age of 20 living at that time, plus all of those who were born during the forty years of wandering in the wilderness**. God considered children age 19 and younger as not fully understanding sin and the consequences of it, thus, until they reached age twenty, they were not held accountable.

It is also important to note that **if they were age 20 or older, they could serve in Israel's army and were treated as adults**. This logically aligns with the fact that when a person chooses to accept the Lord as his Savior, he becomes a Christian soldier in God's army fighting against the enemy, Satan. So while studying the fact that God stated that those who were 19 years and younger would go into the promised land, I am led to believe that if a child age 19 dies before he comes to believe on the Lord Jesus Christ as his personal Savior—he is mercifully taken to heaven.

> *"Then they brought little children to Him, that He might touch them; but the disciples rebuked those who brought them. But when Jesus saw it, He was greatly displeased and said to them, 'Let the little children come to Me, and do not forbid them; for of such is the kingdom of God. Assuredly, I say to you, whoever does not receive the kingdom of God as a little child will by no means enter it.' And He took them up in His arms, laid His hands on them, and blessed them."* (Mark 10:13-16)

It truly grieves me when some Christians (including parents and those in ministry) go to either of two extremes when it comes to witnessing to children. Some fail to keep in mind that some children mature faster than others. Some people are prone to think that children reach the age of accountability long before the age of 19—that they should at least be saved by 10, 11 or 12, if not younger. Some even become worried when children show no guilt at all when they have sinned, and they are only sorry that they got caught in the act of sinning and have very unpleasant consequences to pay! This troubles the Christian adults for they view the children's rebellious behavior as an indication that they do not view themselves as sinners in need of a Savior! Out of worry, some parents and spiritual leaders get ahead of the Holy Spirit and manipulate and press children to "make a decision to follow Christ." All too often, children go forward to please their parents or spiritual leaders and "go through the motions," but in doing so, they are left with a dangerous false sense of security that "membership in the church" gets them to heaven—that they are saved! Now you can imagine how the enemy delights in that!

Now let me be quick to say that over many years of ministry, I have known a goodly number of children who were saved at young ages, but I have also known far too many who were not saved! Of course, to the other extreme, some children receive little or no witnessing of salvation's plan—an attitude that they will "come around when they're ready to do so." Of course, we know that the Lord most surely convicts them and woos them unto Himself, but He also wants them to hear God's Word and testimonies of His people to encourage them! It is my hope that all parents and spiritual leaders would obey Jesus' words: "...*Let the little children come to Me, and do not forbid them; for of such is the kingdom of God.*"

90

YESTERYEARS' SPIRITUAL CONDITIONS ARE THE SAME TODAY

We learned other things in the story of the father with the son suffering demonic seizures. Had the little boy lived today, counselors in the secular mental health institutions would have more than likely listed in their diagnosis of the little boy: "agoraphobic," one having a fear phobia, and obsessive compulsive behavior disorder. Can you imagine every time that dear young boy moved from point A to B, no matter where he was, without warning the demon would seize whatever opportunity he saw to throw the boy down and inflict harm upon him. If there were rocks on the pathway, a cliff close at hand, a fire burning, or a pool of water, don't you believe that this young boy was filled with such great fear—a phobic fear—as he anticipated that a demonic seizure would take control of him, once again bringing him painful scrapes, bruises, burns, and possible drowning? Unless we have experienced such, we cannot imagine how the boy must have felt. Perhaps when it was bitterly cold, in fear he withdrew to a corner, wrapped in a blanket rather than enjoying the warmth of a fire near his family. I've sometimes wondered if the boy was even reluctant to bathe for fear the demon would try to drown him. Perhaps if he could avoid his parents' instructions to bathe, he preferred to stay dirty over the nice feeling being clean! Thinking about how our own children, their spouses, and our grandchildren enjoy swimming, I've wondered how the boy must have longed to go to a lake and enjoy swimming with his family, but of course the danger of drowning surely must have put a damper on the occasion or totally restricted him from such fun.

Most definitely, this boy could not lead a normal lifestyle like other children. I have found myself wondering about his social life, too, had he lived today. I would more than likely be correct in saying that as he displayed his "social behavioral disorders" in his daily life, he would suffer rejection by most children—robbed of playing with them. Perhaps he would even be jealous of other "normal" children. Surely he would be very troubled in his heart—not understanding the "whys"—confused, and perhaps be withdrawn, resentful, depressed, and angry about life in general. Were he living today, I wonder when secular labels were placed on him how his heart ached upon hearing the cruel sentence passed upon him—"no cure!" But my hope for him would surely be that his father and mother would desperately seek biblical counseling that included spiritual warfare—freedom through Jesus Christ. My hope is the same for children of today!

I believe part of the reason why such a large percentage of church members, including those in leadership, don't want to discuss the subject of demons today, is that all too many have been led astray by the secular world's portrayal of the "evil world!" A fearful uneasiness comes to their minds when the word "demons" is spoken and they think of the "Hollywood demons." They recall the chain-saw massacres, "The Exorcist," "Friday 13th," and other weird movies with vampires, zombies. So they steer away from even considering studying about the biblical truths concerning the reality of demons. The secular world most surely deems them far more powerful than they should! If Christians—especially ministers and other leaders in the church—would come to properly understand the demonic, they could teach others this crucial, truthful information. In doing so, they would come to understand "dysfunctional" people! They would recognize the true culprits—the enemies, the demons behind the scenes, and learn that with the Lord Jesus, there is no reason to fear them! Like the father did with his little boy, they would learn not to fear the demonic and instead, take the problem to the Lord Jesus in whom they can completely trust!

If I learn that a counselee does not really agree that a person can really become demonic through negative-learned behavior, a sinful lifestyle, and/or through ancestral demons then there is no reason to continue with the counseling session. I tell such a person that it would be a waste of time for both of us. And, if he chooses not to embrace those teachings of the Lord, it would be just as difficult for him to embrace additional teachings that would perhaps also seem bizarre to him. Hopefully, though, my counselee will have chosen to accept all of God's truths, including the truths found in pillar number three.

C. THE DOUBLE-MINDED MAN PILLAR

Pillar number three is the double-minded man pillar, which is taken from two passages of scripture, one in James 1:2-8, and the second in James 4:1-10—with the two primary verses being verse 8 in both of them. As I explained in "Liberating the Bruised" (in Part I of Chapter Nine), it is crucial for one to know that **the book of James was written to Christians, thus this subject matter is actually talking about some Christians literally being double-souled!**

> Look at James 1:2-8: *"My brethren, count it all joy when you fall into various trials, knowing that the testing of your faith produces patience. But let patience have its perfect work, that ye may be perfect and complete, lacking nothing. If any of you lacks wisdom, let him ask of God, who gives to all liberally and without reproach, and it will be given to him. But let him ask in faith, with no doubting, for he who doubts [wavers] is like a wave of the sea, driven and tossed by the wind. For let not that man suppose that he will receive anything from the Lord;* **he is a double-minded man, unstable in all his ways.***"*

The Greek word **"dipsuchos"** (the "p" is silent) translates into English as **"double-minded."** This Greek word dipsuchos is used only twice in the New Testament, and both times, they are found in the book of James (which was written to Christians). It appears in James 1:8 and in 4:8 as well—where it is translated "double-minded." Now, let us look closely at James 4:1-10:

> *"Where do wars and fights come from among you? Do they not come from your desires for pleasure that war in your members? You lust and do not have. You murder and covet and cannot obtain. You fight and war. Yet you do not have because you do not ask. You ask and do not receive, because you ask amiss, that you may spend it on your pleasures. Adulterers and adulteresses! Do you not know that friendship with the world is enmity with God? Whoever therefore wants to be a friend of the world makes himself an enemy of God. Or do you think that the Scripture says in vain, 'The Spirit who dwells in us yearns jealously'? But He gives*

92

*more grace. Therefore He says: 'God resists the proud, but gives grace to the humble.' Therefore submit to God. Resist the devil and he will flee from you Cleanse your hands, you sinners; and **purify your hearts, you double-minded [you dipsuchos].** Lament and mourn and weep! Let your laughter be turned to mourning and your joy to gloom. Humble yourselves in the sight of the Lord, and He will lift you up."*

It is very sad that when the word **"dipsuchos"** was translated from Greek and Latin into English as "double-minded," the true meaning was diminished—watered down. For, when people hear of a person being described as **double-minded**, they typically assume that the person is simply wishy-washy and indecisive. That is not the correct translation of the word from the original Greek language. **In the Greek, double-minded literally means double-soul, two souls, split soul. In Latin, "dipsuchos" means "duplex."** Back in the "old days" duplexes were more common than today. While perhaps many of you know what a duplex is, for those who are not familiar with this type dwelling place, a duplex is a house with a single roof under which two dwelling places lie, with a wall in the middle, dividing one from the other. Two different families would be found living under one roof, like the Smiths on one side and the Jones family on the other.

As we consider the true meaning of the word double-minded in this scripture, it's especially interesting to know that this word is not found in other books, such as those holding the plan of salvation, but it is found in the book of James! Why? Is there a special reason God put this word in the book of James? Let me pose a question to you with a clue in it. If you and I were going soul winning together, we would not use the book of James, would we? Why? Because **the book of James is an instructional book for Christians**. Therefore, the matter concerning one being double-minded is written clearly in black and white for us to see. God chose to give us as Christians this awesome pillar number three in our book of James! **Clearly, the Lord has told us that not only can a lost person be a duplex, but Christians can also have a double-soul, two souls, a split soul—that a Christian can be a duplex!**

Rita and I have been to Switzerland twice where I counseled in workshops, once in 1999 and once in 2001, both times staying in the homes of precious Christians. Both times, we compared the English and German translations of various scriptures, and pertaining to the word "double-minded," their German Bibles said, "double-souled." After our last trip there, our understanding of a **"double-souled person"** was confirmed again—that it was much deeper than wishy-washy, indecisive thinking! Some time after we returned home, we received an e-mail from the dear lady we stayed with. She was so excited about what she had read in her new German Bible that was of an even more accurate translation than her old one. She stated that this translation said, **"zwiegeseelte"** which translates to literally say, **"the soul was parted into two parts."** She added that she was so happy that Christians could now better understand that there really are Christians who are **parted into two parts—duplexes!** Through this, we have more biblical evidence yet to share with Christians who are tormented duplexes. I know first hand that Christians can be duplexes, for I was one! What sweet relief when the Lord taught me how to go about liberating the

93

bruised, for He enabled me to deal with my issues, tear down the wall that divided me, claim back ground from the enemy and find freedom! Thus, I was spiritually healthy to help others with clarity of mind!

In order to liberate these duplex Christians, it's necessary to know how to go about it. It just continues to grieve me to know of various leaders in ministries who continually practice "casting out demons," declaring the persons to be free—yet, the persons return again, voicing their same bondage. It's crucial to understand that it is very typical of demons to hide while well-meaning people are attempting to cast them out. I have also learned while counseling persons who have experienced such counsel that each of the ancestral demons let one of their **less important demon-workers** leave in order to fool ministers/counselors. They enjoy playing cruel games! Some counselees who have been told that they are free are intimidated and too embarrassed to say that they don't feel free. Some such counselees have reported that they even experienced a temporary peace which later proved to be a false peace—and the torments resumed. Why? Because, these well-meaning ministers and counselors are not addressing the root cause of the counselee's problems—the duplex!

Therefore, it is crucial for you to understand that if you do not deal with the duplex, you can attempt to throw out demons until hell freezes over—which you know will not happen—and your counselee will remain in bondage. The demons may get quiet for a brief period, but you can be assured, they will resume their work "when the coast is clear!" Some counselees have reported having the same demon cast out of them over and over again, and from this they have become so discouraged, that they have succumbed to deep depression. So often, then, they are prime targets for thoughts of suicide. The people declare that if this is the way they're going to have to live the rest of their lives, they would rather just die, for they know they have the promise of living in heaven with Jesus. The Devil and his demons continue to bombard them with thoughts that suicide is the only way to escape their problems!

Take note that some people have the misconception that a person who commits suicide goes to hell "because there is no opportunity for him to repent for murdering himself." That such a person will go to hell is **a lie and the Bible stands to prove it a lie**. We see several of God's people in the Bible who committed suicide. One is a person in the Old Testament who is even listed in the "hall of faith" in Hebrews 11:32—Samson! So, fear tactics such as, "You'll go to hell if you kill yourself!" that some counselors use in an effort to prevent a Christian from considering the option of suicide, is clearly stated in error! It saddens me that some counselors even go to the extent of having their counselees sign a contract that they are aware that they'll go to hell if they kill themselves.

While I'm certainly not by any means encouraging anyone to commit suicide, **Christians will not go to hell because they kill themselves**! I know that God wants us to tell them of His love and of His truths that can set them free to live with peace and joy in their hearts! Furthermore, He certainly wants us to tell them that they can be wonderful blessings to other duplex-Christians on their appointed mission fields on this earth as they tell of what the Lord Jesus has done for them!

Now, having embraced the biblical truth about the understanding of the **dipsuchos, the zwiegeseelte, the soul parted into two parts, the duplex**, we will move to the next pillar.

D. THE DISSOCIATION PILLAR

In the past, I have used the word "disassociation." While the words **"disassociation"** and **"dissociation"** mean the same thing, the latter has become the more commonly used term, which I will use henceforth.

> The definition of dissociation means: *the act of taking apart or dissociating; a state of disunion; separation; in psychology, the process in which a group of mental activities breaks away from the main stream of consciousness and functions as a separate unit; an intensified dissociation can lead to multiple personalities.* (Webster's New Twentieth Century Dictionary, Second Edition, Copyright © 1975 by William Collins+World Publishing Co., Inc.; page 532)

Grievously, all too many troubled souls today fit into this category, which I have chosen to entitle this as **The Dissociation Pillar**. We see people in the secular realm of counseling diagnosed with a wide variety of dissociation disorders, from DID (dissociation identity disorder) to MPD (multiple personality disorder), which by the way, isn't mentioned today as much as the less critical disorder, DID. And it is not uncommon today to hear people voice knowing someone who is bipolar.

As we prayerfully consider helping people in these wide ranges of disorders, I believe it is critical for all ministers and counselors to understand that it is very unwise to think it necessary to analyze their counselee and place him in a single, specific category as they begin counseling him. For in doing so, they can be deceived and hindered from finding some hidden issues in the person's life. Until they actually delve into the counseling procedures, they cannot know the amount of bondage the person is in. I have begun counseling persons whose counseling forms reflected little evidence of great strongholds, yet in the counseling process, major strongholds were discovered.

Therefore, I urge you to wisely view and counsel every counselee the same whether they have minor issues or major, for God's solutions cover them all. If I have learned that my counselee was an SRA victim—one who has been severely abused in satanic rituals—I would not counsel her any differently than any other counselee. The only difference would be that it would simply take a little longer to help her deal with all the issues. Yes, I said "a little longer," for as I've told people before, if my SRA victim is truly desperate about dealing with her issues, putting the past behind, and moving on with Jesus, her counseling would not drag out in agony for months and even years as so many other dear souls have sorrowfully endured. And before we embark on how to go about helping such precious souls, let us take time to further examine what the Mental Health section on WebMD has to say about DID and MPD:

"DISSOCIATIVE IDENTITY DISORDER (DID) this day in time often finds itself included with **MULTIPLE PERSONALITY DISORDER (MPD)** even though MPD is more severe than DID.

"What is Dissociative Identity Disorder? Most of us have experienced mild dissociation, which is like daydreaming or getting lost in the moment while working on a project. However, dissociative identity disorder is a severe form of dissociation, a mental process, which produces a lack of connection in a person's thoughts, memories, feelings, actions, or sense of identity. Dissociative identity disorder is thought to stem from trauma experienced by the person with the disorder. The dissociative aspect is thought to be a **coping mechanism** — the person literally dissociates himself from a situation or experience that's too violent, traumatic, or painful to assimilate with his conscious self.

"Is Dissociative Identity Disorder Real? You may wonder if dissociative identity disorder is real. After all, understanding the development of multiple personalities is difficult, even for highly trained experts. But dissociative identity disorder does exist. It is the most severe and chronic manifestation of the dissociative disorders that cause multiple personalities.

"Other types of dissociative disorders defined in the DSM-IV, the main psychiatry manual used to classify mental illnesses, include dissociative amnesia, dissociative fugue, and depersonalization disorder.

"What Are the Symptoms of Dissociative identity Disorder? Dissociative identity disorder is characterized by the presence of two or more distinct or split identities or personality states that continually have power over the person's behavior. With dissociative identity disorder, there's also an inability to recall key personal information that is too far-reaching to be explained as mere forgetfulness. With dissociative identity disorder, there are also highly distinct memory variations, which fluctuate with the person's split personality.

"The "alters" or different identities have their own age, sex, or race. Each has his or her own postures, gestures, and distinct way of talking. Sometimes the alters are imaginary people; sometimes they are animals. As each personality reveals itself and controls the individual's behavior and thoughts, it's called "switching." Switching can take seconds to minutes to days. When under hypnosis, the person's different "alters" or identities may be very responsive to the therapist's requests.

"Along with the dissociation and multiple or split personalities, people with dissociative disorders may experience any of the following symptoms: Depression, mood swings, suicidal tendencies, sleep disorders (insomnia, nigh terrors, and sleep walking), anxiety, panic attacks, and phobias (flashbacks, reactions to stimuli or "triggers"), alcohol and drug abuse, compulsions and rituals, psychotic-like symptoms (including auditory and visual hallucinations), and eating disorders.

As Christians, looking from our biblical viewpoint, we can well understand the hidden truth of the matter—the mystery of why and how this happened to such precious souls. And as we have read mental health's view and diagnosis of such tormented souls, with confidence and joy, we can offer God's truths, His solutions that offer sweet release from the "coping mechanisms" and all other torments. We can give them great hope by teaching them that, as Ephesians 6:2 says: ***"...we do not wrestle against flesh and blood, but against principalities, against powers, against rulers of the darkness of this age, against spiritual hosts of wickedness in heavenly places."*** We can teach them that through our Lord Jesus Christ and His teaching and counsel, they can be healed from DID and MPD. Victory can be theirs if they are desperate and trust the Lord to set them free. As I was reading Psalm 23, as I had done for many years, that day, the words *"...He restoreth my soul..."* stood out more boldly than ever before. **That is when I began calling the fragmented personalities "wounded parts of a person's soul"—wounded personalities which most surely our Lord says that He desires to restore!**

To learn more about how to help wounded souls, let us look further into our Lord's Word on which I base our next lessons.

> *"For though we walk in the flesh, we do not war according to the flesh. For the weapons of our warfare are not carnal but mighty in God for pulling down strongholds, casting down arguments [imaginations] and every high thing that exalts itself against the knowledge of God, bringing every thought into captivity to the obedience of Christ."* (II Corinthians 10:3-5)

You usually find that many members of a church where spiritual warfare is taught, have this scripture memorized. However, most do not see the very deep meaning within this scripture. As we begin looking at this scripture, we see that though we walk in the flesh, we do not war after the flesh, using tangible weapons of war. Instead, **the Christian is fully equipped—"mighty through God to the pulling down of strongholds, casting down arguments"—or as other translations say, "casting down imaginations."** When someone wants to disassociate from something traumatic that is going on in his life, he develops what the secular realm deems, Dissociation Identity Disorder. **He dissociates—separates himself from reality by imagining a more comfortable, safer place he'd rather be—a way of escape. The core personality, rather than seeking refuge with the Lord and rolling his terrible experience with all of its emotional fallout on the cross, as he gives way to imaginations unrestricted by reality—he doesn't realize the danger of what's happening. He is unaware that out of the wounds that he suffered in the traumatic experience he created a "wounded part of his soul"—an escape mechanism. He is not aware that the next time his surroundings become uncomfortable, when seeking refuge, he will once again return to that wounded part of his soul—that escape mechanism, rather than the Lord.**

These escape mechanisms of dissociation are called by a variety of names by other counselors as well as myself. Let's take a moment to simplify this matter, avoid confusion and help everyone relax more with the subject of these escape mechanisms. In "Liberating the Bruised," I referred to them as "fragmented personalities" but since then, I have also called

them other names. As you know, it is not uncommon for a person to be called by variety of names. Some may address a man by his first name while others by his second name or a combination of the two. He may be called by one or more nicknames while also being referred to by others as Dad, Grandpa, Uncle, Mister, or by titles denoting his vocation, but he is only one person.

Likewise, as my counselees and attendees of my workshops have learned, when I am referring to a "wounded part of a person's soul," instead of saying the whole name every time, I often refer to that particular part with a variety of names such as: fragmented part, fragmented personality, wounded part, and wounded personality. There are some counselors who refer to wounded parts as "alters," nevertheless, we are all talking about a "bruised, damaged part of a person's soul." It seems that at this point in time, it would be more confusing for us to take it upon ourselves to attempt to narrow the matter down by only using one name throughout this book to identify the "wounded part of the soul" rather than familiarizing everyone with all the identifying names that have already been so widely used by many to identify the "wounded parts of the soul"—that began as a way of escape but became controlling parts that failed to bring them the kind of peace and joy that they were seeking.

With the core having established a place of escape, when other upsetting, traumatic situations occur, he withdraws and allows that wounded personality to take the lead. It is like giving a "power of attorney" to that created, fragmented personality, thus, the core forfeits some of his control—hands over the keys to his vehicle and lets him do the driving. When the person experiences overwhelming negative feelings about something—such as lust, guilt, fear, anger, and rage—and he earnestly prays for the Lord to remove them, yet, the feelings remain, the person becomes confused and understandably upset! There are many people who have, when struck with overwhelming fear as they face unpleasant realties, prayed and declared the scripture, *"God hath not given us a spirit of fear...."* Yet, they found themselves unable to shake off the fear that gripped them—fears such as having to cross a bridge, fly in an airplane, or being in a close or dark place. Some become fearful even when a kind, good person approaches to give them a hug. They have sought God's forgiveness for letting the fear grip them, yet they simply cannot pray-away these tormenting thoughts. They don't understand why they feel so fearful but as they move through each day, they are reminded that they are being held in captivity—not in control of their lives, but being controlled. Particularly if the core personality is weak and passive, the strong-willed wounded personalities will more frequently be in control.

Let us look again more closely at the portion of II Corinthians 10:5 where the Lord makes it clear that we are to be ***"casting down imaginations, and every high thing that exalts itself against the knowledge of God...and bringing every thought into captivity to the obedience of Christ."*** He says that if a person creates a personality in his imagination, in his mind, he is exalting that personality above Christ—whether the person is lost or saved—he is looking to that personality to help him with his problems. While this is certainly not God's will, out of His merciful, permissive will, He allows him to have a "temporary place of escape" to get through difficult situations. God declares that the wounded part of the person's soul should surely be cast down, for the wounded personality not only has been exalted above Christ, it does not obey God and the principles and precepts of His Word! The wounded personality only obeys its own selfish desires.

This is why it's important that we address and deal directly with wounded parts. However, as I've explained in my book, "Liberating the Bruised," before we can help anyone, we must first make certain that the counselee is saved, that he knows the Lord Jesus as his personal Savior. God is the only authority on which a person can be set free from his bondage. So, this is why the fragmented personality must be brought to receive Christ in order to deal with his issues. When we find those— such as little boys, little girls, teenagers who were created through imaginations as a way of escape for the core personality—we take them to Jesus, lead the wounded personalities to accept Christ as the core did, and unload all their sin issues.

It has truly been a joy to see so many people set free through these procedures, and they don't have to spend years trying to unload such issues, little by little, as some counselors claim! If they look to the Lord Jesus with sincerity and desperation, freedom is near—not far away! Now, let me be quick to state, as I also did in my first book, that had that person—that core personality—died while still in bondage, he or she would still have gone to heaven—most surely without the fragmented personalities and demons! And, I believe as we continue this study, you will understand the necessity of bringing unity between the core personality and all his or her wounded parts.

THREE MAJOR STORAGE VAULTS

Within pillar number four, there are three major types of storage vaults that one can create to hold the wounded personalities of dissociation. When something is going on in a person's life that he doesn't want to accept, even though the person is not consciously selecting a particular place in which to keep them, I have always found them in one of three storage vaults. **As you look at them, please keep in mind that during the counseling sessions, the core personality is totally aware of all that is going on.**

When a person experiences a trauma in his life, it can create a storage vault that stores either the memories, the emotions, or both the memories and emotions together, which can affect him for years! The person can experience extreme up-and-down emotions in a wide variety of ways when he comes under stress. Various things can trigger it, such as hearing certain sounds or words, smelling various odors, seeing a person who reminds him of someone, or seeing an object or place that stirs up a memory. The triggering of such things is like unto someone punching a button in his building's elevator and taking him to a floor on which there is a connecting storage vault. The button is pushed, the elevator ascends or descends, the door opens, and the wounded personality storing that memory and/or emotions will begin acting out in the core personality. For instance, when he arrives on that floor and that vault opens before him, the core may suddenly display fear, anger, hatred, and rage. Most of the time—although not always—the core personality isn't even aware that he has taken a ride on his elevator and switched from one floor to another—switched from his core personality to a wounded one!

Then, when the pressure of whatever pushed his button subsides and the elevator door closes, the wounded personality is left in the vault again—and the core breathes a sigh of relief. However, with the counselee understanding that he does have spans of time in which he knows "something negative" happened, he stays in a continual state of worry that the intense emotions and/or memories that led to his negative behavior will return at any moment! He did exactly what he did not want to do and fears that he will be lured to do it again!

Our dear brother Paul even expressed experiencing such in Romans 7:15: ***"...For what I am doing, I do not understand. For what I will to do, that I do not practice; but what I hate, that I do."*** This is why some precious people who have serious battles going on within themselves, particularly those who have addictions and critical behavior problems, become so discouraged after having exhausted secular solutions that they sometime end up committing suicide. Now we will take a look at those storage vaults.

STORAGE VAULT #1: In storage vault # 1, a wounded personality is found that contains all the emotions and the memories connected with a particular experience, thus, leaving the core personality with amnesia pertaining to it. Example: the core personality simply doesn't recall a particular bad experience, and during a counseling session, is amazed to learn from one of his wounded parts that something terrible happened to him during his childhood. But he comes to the truthful realization that it did happen, that it was a very painful experience that he had rather it not had ever happened. And, that's why he stored it in storage vault # 1.

STORAGE VAULT #2: In storage vault # 2, a fragmented personality is found that retains the emotions of an experience, but is void of the memories connected to it. Examples: the core personality becomes angry very easily, but doesn't know why. He may be quick to go into a rage, triggered by something that's perceived as very trivial, and can't understand why he does this. Perhaps a person considers sex that's properly within a marriage as dirty, and doesn't know why. One may be afraid of sex and doesn't know why. Another may be afraid of men, but doesn't know why. One may be afraid of women, but doesn't know why. And, yet another experiences lustful thoughts and cannot understand why he can't stop it. It's because the memories of the experience itself, apart from the emotions, are stored away in storage vault # 2. The person is just experiencing the emotions.

STORAGE VAULT #3: In storage vault # 3, a wounded part is found that has all the memories, but tightly imprisons all of the emotions, shutting down the person's emotions. Example: Often times, we find when the core's emotions are so tightly squelched, he feels that if he expresses his emotions, he will make himself more vulnerable to verbal and/or physical abuse. He can tell you everything negative and horrible that has happened to him. While doing so, you will see no sorrowful facial expressions, no tears, and no body language whatsoever for the emotions he felt while experiencing anything negative. For "all the bad emotions" are locked away in the wounded

100

personality lacking emotions in storage vault #3. Emotionally, the person remains like stone, protecting himself from potential chances of being manipulated and abused.

IF THE COUNSELEE DOES NOT AGREE

Having explained to my counselee this study of the four pillars that hold up the platform of counseling the bruised, if the counselee does not agree and will not admit that these things can be the source of some of his problems, then he is not ready to work—he is not desperate enough. It's like when you are witnessing to someone, inviting him to accept the Lord as his Savior—if he is not ready, you cannot make him get saved. Most surely, you do not want to "bruise" him! **It's an invitation, not a law that you can enforce, and neither can you force him into the counseling ministry.** A person must be ready and willing to deal with his issues. To push the issues, you would only frustrate him. For one to receive counsel, he must be in agreement with the type counseling he is to receive, and be desperate for the Lord to liberate him. As I've stressed earlier, there must be unity between the counselor and the counselee, as Amos 3:3 says, *"Can two walk together, except they be agreed?"* At this point, if the counselee agrees with God's truths shared, we are ready to proceed to the next point.

IF THE COUNSELEE AGREES

It is crucial that the counselees believe in these teachings and that they know they have every right through their authority in Christ to deal with Satan's strongholds. Then we can confidently approach the time for counseling. For many counselees, the preparation procedure and some of the counseling procedures can feel like unto having physical surgery without the anesthetic! Because, most have very painful memories they must deal with. But for them to rid themselves of the pain permanently, things must be handled in the "counseling surgery room." However, with our Great Physician's truths, they are assured that their surgery will not be unbearable and will be successful! With this wonderful hope, it's usually very early on that "God's patients" begin to feel at ease with what they are facing. The more comforted they become with the truths of God, the more confident they become and surgery will go much more smoothly—and more quickly! They can even get excited about standing on their authority in Christ—our Great Physician—and their right to this spiritual surgery, their right to become spiritually healthy and fulfill the plan that the Lord intends for them!

Now would be a good time for us to take a close look at addictions and behavioral disorders so that we can better understand the truth that there is, indeed, victory in Jesus over them!

Chapter Three
VICTORY OVER ADDICTIONS
AND BEHAVIORAL DISORDERS

"...Brethren, stand fast and hold the traditions which you were taught, whether by word or our epistle. Now may our Lord Jesus Christ Himself, and our God and Father, who has loved us and given us everlasting consolation and good hope by grace, comfort your hearts and establish you in every good word and work."
(II Thess. 2:15-17)

We are living in an age when one can sit in the privacy of his home and peer at a television—like a window to the world—on a daily basis, watching stories unfold endlessly about people with "serious emotional problems." Grievously enough, children are included in that ever mounting number. Of course, that window to the world is not the only place that these sad stories are told, for newspapers and magazines tell of them also. Heartbreaking stories come flooding in by internet, emails and word-of-mouth. So many precious souls are longing for freedom, for hope to be given them—hope for a happy ending to their sad story!

Many dedicated servants in ministry and Christian counselors with sincere compassion to help souls overcome their serious behavioral disorders have sacrificed time and energy in attempting to bring their story to a happy ending. All too many have ended up discouraged upon stopping short of leading the person to the freedom for which he so desperately yearned. As I've shared before, the reason is that they did not go deeply enough, into the roots of spiritual warfare—the wounded parts, the flip-side, and the ancestral demon and his network. Please understand that I am truly grateful to these precious servants of the Lord who do care, and I know that they are trying very hard to help these hurting souls by applying what they have been taught thus far in attempting to help them! In recent times, I have become very encouraged that there is an increasing number of pastors, ministers and counselors who are now studying about God's teaching concerning spiritual warfare in order to have additional tools with which to help "repair" and restore such precious souls to lives of "normalcy"!

I pray that my intentions are understood concerning secular counselors, for I most certainly do not intend to discredit, or insult secular counselors and their methods of therapy—including the fact that they provide medications for some of their patients. I fully understand that some patients who arrive at their centers are in a state of "bouncing off the walls" and "threatening suicide." Therefore, I understand their giving medications to calm down their out-of-control patients. These medications bring the patient into a more tranquil state until the patient becomes more comfortable about talking with the counselor. In the process, they can begin lowering the dosage until they can eventually step them off of the medication completely—especially since so many medications have negative side-affects and especially when given over a lengthy period of time. I must add that I have been grieved to learn that some patients who are depressed and taking anti-depressants have only become more depressed—some even to the point of becoming suicidal—and committing suicide! You have probably even heard commercials, as I have, about prescriptions having "possible" negative side affects.

Over the years I have read many articles written by secular counselors concerning "mental health" explaining the various disorders of their patients and the type of help they offer them. I want secular counselors to understand that I am actually grateful for those who sincerely care about trying to help hurting souls overcome their debilitating conditions! I know many are compassionately applying what they have been taught in the secular mental health field—with sincere hope of their counselees living normal lives! I do wonder how many have become frustrated and even grieved that the "amount of hope" they are able to offer comes in smaller measures than is apparently needed for their critical patients. As I have read many of their articles, it appears they can only offer each patient the "hope of coping—along with the aid of medications and therapy the rest of his life." Not unlike pastors, ministers, and Christian counselors—I can well imagine how discouraged some secular counselors must be when they all too often fall short of accomplishing their goals of helping their patients reach the point of living "normal lives." I wonder if it is sorrowful to some who feel they are "spinning their wheels," and are robbed from experiencing the joy of watching their dysfunctional counselee transform into an emotionally healthy person. I wonder after they have counseled a number of patients for extended periods of time and they're not "all-better," if they are even concerned about their reputation as a "successful" counselor. This brings me to say that my heart's desire is that these precious, caring counselors would at least spend some time seriously considering God's wondrous teachings. Oh, that they would consider the hope that is in Him not only for salvation of souls, but also His teachings concerning spiritual warfare in the midst of the Holy War that surrounds us all! The number of godly laborers in God's spiritual-warfare counseling fields are still all too few! Oh, that these precious caring secular counselors would join God's army—join with us as Christian soldiers in this war against the enemy of God and His children!

I must inject at this point that both in the secular realm of counseling as well as the Christian realm of counseling, we all meet persons who choose of their own free will not to function normally in this life, nor to contribute any good works. They have, instead, chosen to focus on themselves and draw attention to themselves! They just seem to "enjoy" giving themselves "pity-me-parties!" As I mentioned earlier in this book, they want to keep telling their sad stories rather than putting the past behind and running life's race set before them! I call such people "professional counselees" and "time-zappers," who are probably mentioned in mental health journals—those who never overcome their behavioral disorders!

Then there are ever so many counselees who sincerely long for freedom from the torments of their behavioral disorders. Over the years, many precious counselees have come to me who had been diagnosed by secular counselors to have behavioral disorders. Most had been to both secular counselors as well as some Christian counselors but had not yet reached freedom from these tormenting strongholds on their life. They came to our home, desperate and still clinging tightly to hope that they could be set free through Christian counseling that included spiritual warfare. They were full of hope that the root cause of their problems could be uprooted so that they could walk a normal, victorious life! I am extremely grateful to tell you that upon these precious souls placing their **hope in the Lord Jesus Christ** and applying God's truths that can liberate the bruised, **they most surely found the freedom, the victory for which they longed to embrace!**

A. HURTING, TORMENTED SOULS HAVE HOPE IN JESUS CHRIST

How truly humbled I am that the Lord has seen fit to teach me how to help them, and He has given me the joy of leading them to the freedom in which they longed to walk! How grateful I am to be able to tell you that the Lord has "successfully" set souls such as these free! When each one chooses to seek the Lord with all his heart and embraces Him as his personal Savior, He fulfills his hope!

> *"...gird up the loins of your mind, be sober, and rest your hope fully upon the grace that is to be brought to you at the revelation of Jesus Christ; as obedient children, not conforming yourselves to the former lusts, as in your ignorance; but as He who called you is holy, you also be holy in all your conduct, because it is written, 'Be holy, for I am holy.'"* (I Peter 1:13-16)

Knowing these truths, there is no doubt in my mind that our Lord Jesus Christ will provide solutions for all the troubled souls who are tormented by the "serious emotional problems"—if they are willing to seek the Lord Jesus and let the hope that He gives lead them to His truths that can set them free! For the Lord tells them clearly in His Word that no matter what their emotional spiritual condition, nothing is too hard for Him to "fix"!

> *"**Ah, Lord God!** Behold, You have made the heavens and the earth by Your great power and outstretched arm. **There is nothing too hard for You**."* (Jeremiah 32:17)

The Lord tells each one that there is **no cause to worry, doubt or fear** as he moves forward **with his hope that lies in Jesus**!

> *"For God hath not given us a spirit of fear, but of **power** and of **love** and of **a sound mind**."* (II Timothy 1:7)

As I stated earlier in my book, the God does not speak to "mental health." He speaks only of organic and non-organic, which means that He speaks of "physical illnesses" and "sin." The Lord tells us that many things were written about people in the Bible as examples from which we are to learn lessons—from people who obeyed God and from people who disobeyed God. In order to gain a better understanding of "physical illnesses" and "sin," **let us take time to go back in time** to the Garden of Eden and look at the lesson.

105

On one point, when the serpent sinned in the garden, tempting and lying to Adam and Eve, God took away his privileges—cursed him. (Genesis 3:14) Adam and Eve both chose to disobey God's one-and-only loving, protective rule—not to eat of the Tree of Knowledge of Good and Evil—God had no other choice but to do something drastic! For their own good (in the long run), He had to send them out of the garden where they would have lived for eternity in their fallen state and corrupted the garden for their future offspring! Therefore, He had to cause them to live on the earth "only temporarily" until He transported them to heaven. Thus, it was appointed unto them once to die! (Heb. 9:27) They had to pass through His God-ordained, natural process of dying.

As a result of Adam and Eve's sin, God said,

> *"...**Cursed is the ground for your sake**; in toil you shall eat of it all the days of your life. Both thorns and thistles it shall bring forth for you, and you shall eat the herb of the field. In the sweat of your face you shall eat bread till you return to the ground, for out of it you were taken; for dust you are, and to dust you shall return."* (Genesis 3:17b-19)

We also read evidence in the New Testament that **all creation was caused to suffer the fallout right along with all the humans!**

> *"For we know that **the whole creation groans** and labors with birth pangs together until now. Not only that, but **we also who have the first fruits of the Spirit even we ourselves groan within ourselves**, eagerly waiting for the adoption, the redemption of our body."* (Romans 8:22-23)

Each one of us should not be quick to criticize Adam and Eve, for had any of us been in that garden, we, too, would have fallen. We read proof of that in Romans 3:23: *"...**all have sinned and fall short of the glory of God.**"*

Let us also take great care to understand that **God is by no means being cruel in cursing the ground!** Did you notice that He said, *"Cursed is the ground **for your sake**"*? Those who deem God cruel are entertaining human reasoning and Satan's reasoning rather than comprehending the amazing wisdom of God in the matter. The better we get to know God—our Creator—the better we can understand His all-wise reasoning! The first thing we need to know about Him is that He is in totality, "Love"—**God is love—God is motivated by LOVE!**

> *"Beloved, let us love one another, for **love is of God**; and everyone who loves is born of God and knows God. He who does not love does not know God, for **God is love**."* (I John 4:7-8)

Along with our choosing to love the Lord—our heavenly Father—with all our hearts we need to **trust** that He has His own good, all-wise, loving Godly reasons for doing various things that we may or may not understand! **The important thing is that we trust our heavenly Father no matter what!**

*"Trust in the LORD with all your heart, and **lean not to your own understanding**."*
(Proverbs 3:5)

When our heavenly Father says in His written words, "don't do this-that-or-the other"—it is because He knows this-that-or-the-other can do harm to us and/or others! The situation is like parents training up young children in the way that they **should** go. Children would do themselves a great favor if they would trust their parents and obey without question! And since God is a loving God, He deserves for all His children to trust Him without question even when obeying Him comes with what may be deemed as "unpleasant duties!" Our Lord, God Almighty invites us to remember that He is the Parent, we are His children—His creation:

> *"...Who has made man's mouth? Or who makes the mute, the deaf, the seeing, or the blind? Have not I, the Lord?"* (Exodus 4:11)

> *"...Indeed, O man, who are you to reply against God? Will the thing formed say to him who formed it, 'Why have You made me like this?' Does not the potter have power over the clay, from the same lump to make one vessel for honor and another for dishonor?"* (Romans 9:20-21)

As a wonderful, good parent, our Potter, our heavenly Father is. He invites, He calls us to communicate with Him! His rule is **surely not** that "children should be seen and not heard!" **He calls us to come and reason with Him**: *"'Come now, and **let us reason together**,' says the Lord."* (Isaiah 1:18a)

Out of God's love for all of His clay vessels, He has provided protective love-rules and longs for every person to abide by these love-rules for his own sake as well as for the sake of others. However, as you well know, **God does not violate our freedom of choice! Otherwise, we'd all be robots!** Due to a vast number of people choosing to reject and disobey God, **we find ourselves in the midst of a Holy War—good against evil—until the day the Lord Himself puts an end to this world as we know it!** As you know, because all human beings have the choice to behave "good" or "bad" during their walk on earth, their behavior affects many other people. Therefore, those who choose to be "bad" most surely can cause sorrow and pain to fall upon those who choose to be "good." In the midst of this good-against-evil setting, sorrow and pain is certain to come to a large majority of us, no matter how much we love the Lord and desire to please Him. While the Lord may or may not tell us exactly "why" some unpleasant things happen, He does invite us to take time to let Him give us wisdom concerning things. He stands ready to give instructions on how to deal with any situation that comes our way, and strength as well!

> *"**If any of you lack wisdom**, let him **ask of God, who gives to all liberally** and without reproach, and it will be given him."* (James 1:5)

107

Due to the curse that came upon mankind and the earth as a result of sin in the Garden of Eden, it's very clear that humans "naturally" suffer the consequences of sin—which **includes a very wide scope of out-of-kilter nature!** Along with our Lord's commandments for our behavior, God very wisely told us in His Word about foods that are good for us and foods that are bad for us—so that we could try to take good care of the clay vessels we're temporarily housed in, until His appointed time for us to die. As we attempt to eat as He would have us eat, let us remember that due to mankind's fall, the earth and our environment sometimes even harms the "good" foods. Down through the ages humans have taken various things from God's creation to create products intended to both help the earth and help humans—only later to discover that they had harmful side affects! Various physical defects in humans have been the results. As a result people have suffered physical harm. Some babies have even been born with various physical deformities, handicaps, blindness, deafness, defects in their brain, down syndrome, etc.

Some humans have taken God's "products" and created things for pleasure—drugs—that also have very destructive side affects. So, all of these things contribute to the process of the state of deterioration of mankind—that started at the fall in the Garden of Eden. Combining those truths with the fact that humans war against one another, enables us to better understand why our Lord said He would surely come before mankind literally destroys himself, as we read in Mark 13:20: *"...unless the Lord had shortened those days, no flesh would be saved; but for the elect's sake, whom He chose, He shortened the days."*

Let me make it clear that when people suffer "bad things"—suffer minor to major physical problems—it does not necessarily mean that they are in sin! It does not mean if parents have a child born with deformities, or down syndrome, they are in sin! It does not mean when people develop Alzheimer's disease, suffer strokes, or have cancer—or are involved in an "accident"—that they are in sin! As I covered this subject in the previous chapter, this can happen to many people due to the condition of this cursed earth—this cursed environment—whether they are right with the Lord or stubbornly walking in sinful lifestyles! God allowed these things for whatever His all-wise, holy reasons are!

There are **various sicknesses and diseases**, for which God has mercifully given mankind wisdom to know how to treat. As you recall, our brother Luke in the New Testament was a "doctor!" You are well acquainted with people in the world today who have created helpful medications. Helps have been created from God's creation, plant life, animal life, from His fresh and saltwater creatures, and from minerals in the earth—"dust" from which He created our ancestor, Adam! Of course, with humans not always hearing and following God's instructions, some are harmful rather than helpful!

Then, there are other conditions that have especially become "widespread" in recent times, that some people have placed in the same category as "sicknesses," which are now more commonly called **"addictions"** and **"behavioral disorders."** However, based on God's biblical teachings, I firmly believe that these are **completely different from the more common "afflictions," "sicknesses" and "diseases!"** Therefore, I believe God teaches us that these "addictions" and "behavioral disorders" are to be treated differently from the others if they are going be rescued from these conditions! Now, let us spend some very serious time, prayerfully examining the categories of "addictions" and "behavioral disorders." We will start with alcoholism.

B. ALCOHOLISM

It is common knowledge that drinking alcohol can alter one's thinking and behavior. So, it comes as no surprise upon prayerfully studying our God's Word on the subject, we will understand that it is most surely not a "sickness." On the contrary, our heavenly Father deems it a choice to "sin." A person who has come down with the flu can truthfully declare that he is "sick"—he caught the "bug" from someone or from "a virus in the air!" Some have mistakenly said of the alcoholic, "Bless his heart, he can't help it—it's a sickness." That is a lie! You cannot "catch alcoholism!" God's Word is full of warnings against drinking "wine that stirs within itself" (fermented), which shows that the person has freedom of choice to obey the Lord in the matter, or disobey Him and suffer consequences. **This is one amongst many of our loving, merciful, all-wise heavenly Father's protective love-rules!**

> *"Who has woe? Who has sorrow? Who has contentions? Who has complaints? Who has wounds without cause? Who has redness of eyes? Those who linger long at the wine; those who go in search of mixed wine. Do not look on the wine when it is red, when it sparkles in the cup, when it swirls around smoothly; at the last it bites like a serpent, and stings like a viper. Your eyes will see strange things, and your heart will utter perverse things. Yes, you will be like one who lies down in the midst of the sea, or like one who lies at the top of the mast, saying: 'They have struck me, but I was not hurt; they have beaten me, but I did not feel it. When shall I awake, that I may seek another drink?"* (Proverbs 23:29-35)

As you read, our Father does not declare that an alcoholic is sick! And He most surely would not create someone to be "prone to seek another drink" that bites like a serpent and brings sorrow to the individual and to his family and friends! How critical is this matter to God? In the Bible, we read the example of some God-fearing, loving parents grievously reporting to God-ordained elders the "sin" of their son who was a stumbling block to others. God deemed the matter so serious that the unrepentant person was even to be put to death, as we read in Deuteronomy 21:20b-21:

> *"'This son of ours is **stubborn** and **rebellious**; he will not obey our voice; he is **a glutton and a drunkard.'** Then all the men of the city shall stone him to death with stones; so you shall put away the evil from among you...."*

While the Lord says the spiritual condition of alcoholics is "unrighteousness"—not a sickness—at the same time He mercifully gives freedom from it if the alcoholic repents:

*"Do you not know that the **unrighteous** will not inherit the kingdom of God? Do not be deceived. Neither fornicators, nor idolaters, nor adulterers, nor homosexuals, nor sodomites, nor thieves, nor covetous, **nor drunkards**, nor revilers, nor extortioners will inherit the kingdom of God. And **such were some of you**. **But you were washed**, but you were **sanctified**, but you were **justified in the name of the Lord Jesus** and **by the Spirit of our God**."* (I Corinthians 6:9-11)

Clearly we see that the drunkards spoken of in this verse were not "sick," but rather had a choice to make to remain "in sin," "in a self-destruct mode," or to repent and have their sins washed away, be sanctified, and justified by their trust, their belief, in the Lord Jesus Christ as their personal Savior! Out of God's love, we find many other scriptures in the Bible that says the drinking of fermented beverages is a sin. Of course with alcohol causing negative alterations of one's mind and judgment—thus being a sin—the same protective love-rule applies to all other "drugs!" Persons using these are not only chemically abusing themselves—but other people on their pathway often suffer dire consequences, even death, as a result of their out-of-control behavior! **Here is a question to ask yourself: Were a list made comparing the "good" that alcohol and drugs bring forth with the "bad" that they bring, which do you believe would be the longer list of the two?**

As you have probably read my testimony, I speak from experience, for I, Joe Allbright, was a drunkard for over five years! A miserable struggle, a battle was going on within me, and my core personality was most certainly losing the battle! But, upon my precious Savior's being on my side, continuing to convict my heart of sin, lovingly ministering to me, and even spanking me, I finally chose to cry out to Him! I called my behavior "sin" and repented of it! And, oh, how I thank the Lord for delivering me! From that point on, I no longer desired to run from His will, nor to have alcohol touch my lips! He rescued me, for which I am eternally grateful—as is my precious family! The battle was won through Jesus!

Oh that we will purpose in our hearts to help rescue precious alcoholics from Satan's grasp, so they can learn that they can overcome the addiction and their negative-learned behavior patterns! What a blessing we can be when we teach them that God loves them so much that He generously sprinkled into His Word very clear warnings about Satan's traps of alcohol and its addictive stronghold! Let's take time to examine a few of them before moving on.

When a person gets saved—becomes a Christian—our Lord declares to them: ***"...you are a chosen generation, a royal priesthood, an holy nation, a people of His own, that ye should show forth the praises of Him who hath called you out of darkness into His marvelous light; who once were not a people but are now the people of God, who had not obtained mercy but now have obtained mercy. Beloved, I beg you as sojourners and pilgrims, abstain from fleshly lusts which war against the soul, having your conduct honorable among the Gentiles, that when they speak against you as evildoers, they may, by your good works which they observe, glorify God on the day of visitation."*** (I Peter 2:9-12) And look at the instructions that God issues to His priests pertaining to wine and strong drink: ***"Do not drink wine or intoxicating drink, you, nor your sons*** *with you, when you go into the tabernacle of meeting, lest you die. It shall be a statute forever* **throughout your generations, that you may distinguish between holy and unholy, and between unclean and clean,** *and that you may teach the children of Israel all the statutes which the LORD has spoken to them by the hand of Moses."* (Leviticus 10:9-11) **Did you notice that He was not talking on behalf of that individual only, but on behalf of his future generations?**

Is it any wonder that He warns us to strive to be holy—to be clean—to teach our children His statutes? For He declares: **"Wine is a mocker, strong drink is a brawler, and whoever is led astray by it is not wise."** (Proverbs 20:1) We find more of His loving warnings as we read: **"Hear, my son, and be wise, and guide your heart in the way. Do not mix with winebibbers, or with gluttonous eaters of meat; for the drunkard and the glutton will come to poverty, and drowsiness will clothe a man with rags."** (Proverbs 23:19-21; also see I Corinthians 5:11)

Especially when hard times come—strong temptation points to the bottle as a means of escape rather than seeking the Lord for guidance! While a Christian may not be held in captivity physically like the Israelites were—our heavenly Father's warning to them still applies to His present day people. For we are clearly warned in the following verse that if we consistently give into temptation—to the bottle—Satan can most surely take us into captivity and govern our behavior as well! The verse is found in Isaiah: *"Woe unto them who rise early in the morning, that they may* **follow intoxicating drink; who continue until night, till wine inflames them!** *The harp and the strings, the tambourine and flute, and wine are in their feasts; but* **they do not regard the work of the Lord, nor consider the operation of His hands. Therefore my people have gone into captivity...."** (Isaiah 5:11-13a.)

Before we move on, let us read the marvelous story of victory when God's children obey Him in spite of being held captive against their will in extremely unpleasant surroundings! This powerful story is found in the first chapter of the book of Daniel—a man full of faith and love for His God. We find him in the palace of Nebuchadnezzar, where **Daniel "...purposed in his heart that he would not defile himself with the portion of the king's delicacies, nor with the wine which he drank; therefore he requested of the chief of the eunuchs that he might not defile himself."** (Daniel 1:8) Also with Daniel were Hananiah, Mishael, and Azariah who also purposed in their hearts that they would do the same as Daniel. After comparing them to others who ate the same as the king, Nebuchadnezzar declared: **"...among them all none was found like Daniel, Hananiah, Mishael, and Azariah; therefore they served before the king. And in all matters of wisdom and understanding about which the king examined them, he found them ten times better than all the magicians and astrologers who were in all his realm."** (Daniel 1:19-20) What beautiful testimonies!

RABBITS THAT RUN

In our ministry, in dealing with a lot of persons who are held in Satan's trap of alcohol and/or drugs (prescription or illegal), their chemical abuse is just "a rabbit that runs"—it takes them away from the real reason that they drink and/or use drugs. The chemical substance is not the root cause of their "emotional" condition. While some have become "hooked on drugs" through peer pressure—wanting to be accepted—or "just looking for a good time"—others use alcohol and/or drugs as a hiding place from hurts and painful memories—or circumstances they fear. They just want to escape from unpleasant memories, realities, or from responsibilities that overwhelm them! In stepping into the chemical territory, they have become trapped, addicted to the liquor or drug. No matter what the reasons—**addiction is born of a choice to sin!** A substance was sought after to escape their problem rather than seeking after the Lord to solve the problem. There is no doubt that they, not unlike myself in times passed, have a struggle, a battle going on within themselves!

The alcohol and drugs are not the root cause of a person's problem. The "root" is whatever causes the person to "run like a rabbit"—seeking after something to transform "his world" into a more pleasant surrounding for himself. Until that "root" is pulled up, examined, and removed from that person's life, he will continue to yield to the "manipulation of the root" in his life, thus continuing to search for escape routes. When he becomes desperate for freedom, seeks the Lord Jesus Christ with all his heart and submits to sound biblical warfare counseling, freedom is close at hand! Of course, if a person's condition is "critical" due to the excessive use of the chemical, he may have to admit himself into an alcohol/drug treatment hospital for physical aid. As his body goes through detoxification, his vital signs may need to be monitored and treated until he is stabilized. Then, upon being eager for sound biblical counseling, once those root causes have been dealt with that are holding the alcoholic or drug addict tightly in the clutches of the enemy—ancestral demons, lifestyle demons and wounded personalities—victory is his to claim!

C. IS THERE NO HOPE FOR VICTORY OVER BEHAVIORAL DISORDERS?

I am extremely grateful to be able to share that over many years with many souls who came to me for counseling who had been diagnosed with a variety of behavioral disorders—and having spent years in both secular and Christian counseling, plus having taken medications—found plenty of hope and complete victory through our Lord Jesus Christ! So many had heard that they were "incurable—hopeless cases!" What joy it always is to see such persons achieve total release and freedom from their debilitating condition. Not unlike the alcoholic and the drug-addict, they too had struggles and battles going on within themselves. They learned that, indeed, nothing is impossible with our Lord Jesus when souls turn to and depend on Him to deal with the root causes of their behavioral disorders—the roots to which Satan clings ever so tightly!

UNDERSTANDING AND SEEING HOPE FOR BEHAVIORAL DISORDERS

As you prayerfully read about some of the behavioral disorders, I believe you will agree that these "roots" are not at all too hard for our Potter—our heavenly Father—to snatch out and retrain the person in positive behavior patterns! He is our hope—our salvation—our shield! I believe as you review these behavioral disorders that you will understand how a person who is desperate to win the battle within himself can most surely rely on the Lord to snatch out the roots and win the battle in their behalf!

I believe as you prayerfully read the following behavioral disorders, you will agree that none of these battles is too hard for our Lord to win! His truths can indeed set such captives free!

ANHEDONIA is a disorder affecting a person's ability to experience or show "joy." **It's as if he is emotionally frozen**, and in the midst of this lack of joy a door of invitation swings open for depression. With secular counseling and medication, symptoms come and go.

ANXIETY DISORDER is that of a person who reflects the **inability to concentrate and focus on daily responsibilities**, which hinders him from performing his job correctly. His **mind races "here and there" as he worries, doubts, and fears—imagining worst case scenarios!** His constant state of worry can result in headaches, muscle tension, sweating, and fatigue. He can become extremely irritable–and may be so tense and upset that he cannot swallow. Anxiety disorder can be divided up into five categories: **(1)** general anxiety disorders; **(2)** obsessive compulsive disorder (OCD); **(3)** panic or anxiety attacks or disorders; **(4)** post traumatic stress disorder or syndrome; and **(5)** social phobia.

ATTENTION DEFICIT HYPERACTIVITY DISORDER (ADHD) AND ATTENTION DEFICIT DISORDER WITHOUT HYPERACTIVITY (ADD)

The two above disorders are reported to affect approximately 5 percent of children in the United States. It affects more children than adults; however, more adults are being diagnosed on a daily basis! The disorder seems to affect more boys than girls, and **the common symptoms are short attention spans, low concentration levels, low comprehension levels, and indecisiveness.** So you can well understand why it has been noted that people with these disorders often have little or no organizational skills.

My heart has been so very grieved to see too many children diagnosed with the two "disorders" stated above, with parents being given no hope for their being healed; thus, counselors prescribe medication to put them in a tranquil state so that they are less prone to disturb others—along with urging the parents to avoid giving their children beverages and foods containing caffeine and sugar (which contribute to feelings of nervousness and being on an uncontrollable high). In my opinion, it's like putting a band-aid on a cancer! It only covers up, conceals the root problem and does not treat it properly or successfully! Not only that, medications such as Ritalin are known to have negative side affects. Recent studies have revealed that it may even be causing cancer in some children. I am very troubled over these children taking medications.

OUR POTTER HAS A BETTER WAY

Over the years, I have observed a number of Christian parents with children who have been diagnosed with these same symptoms, but rather than take the secular route, they ministered to their children according to biblical teachings. They refused to succumb to the pressures of school teachers and tranquilize their children. Instead, they sought God's solutions. They kept everything in proper balance, which included doing the "practical things." They took precautions to limit the amount of beverages and foods with caffeine and sugar in their children's diets. They made sure there was a goodly measure of both physical activities and activities in a relaxed setting—and times for rest. They took time to get to know where their children's strengths and weaknesses were, and their God-given talents as well. Our Potter forms every person with different abilities and talents for different purposes in life, and the Lord says: *"Train up a child in the way he should go, and when he is old [mature in the Lord], he will not depart from it."* (Proverbs 22:6) Knowing this, these parents approached the problem from a spiritual standpoint—Christians versus the enemy, Satan.

These parents took most seriously the importance of making certain that their own lives were clean before the Lord—that the enemy had no ground in their precious lives! In doing this, they could be assured that they could set the Godly examples before their children that they needed to see on a daily basis! They were dedicated to training up their children in God's ways. These parents remained sensitive to their children's level of understanding of what "sin" is and that Jesus paid the debt for their sin. If the children were mature enough to fully understand, they gave them opportunity to invite the Lord Jesus into their hearts—and they were saved! Now they could do all things through Christ who strengthens them—who would also continue to train them up in the way that they should go. Indeed, there is victory for those precious parents and their children with ADHD and ADD. I gratefully report that I've known many of these children not only to win the battle, but they have gone on to excel in their "social skills" and in their schooling as well! So, for the precious children who have battles going on within themselves, there is, indeed, victory in Jesus, our Hope!

AGORAPHOBIA describes persons who **have great fear**. They **suffer panic attacks for various reasons**. Some persons fear things such as public places, being trapped, being in close spaces, and crowded places, such as malls. They may fear walking or riding over bridges, riding in elevators, and flying in airplanes.

AUTISM—A NEURODEVELOPMENTAL DISORDER—is when a person is **hindered from communicating socially with others**. It has been reported to show up in ages as young as about three years old. The person is usually not diagnosed, however, until he approaches school age. It has been reported that treatment at very early age can help him live a near normal life. In our ministry, we have dealt with two counselees with autism and are so very grateful to report that they are walking in victory today with the Lord Jesus!

BIPOLAR DISORDER I AND II: **(1) episodes of mania and major depression** is found in persons with bipolar number one, while, **(2) major depression but with a lesser number of episodes of mania**, is bipolar disorder number two, which is called **hypo-mania**.

The bipolar disorder in a person's life reflects highs and lows. Bipolar is the medical term that is also known as manic depression. A person in this state tends to be irritable, overly excited, withdrawn, and even suicidal at any given moment. A person who has been diagnosed as bipolar has difficulty controlling his emotions—which of course can cause his social behavioral problems with people. He can also do the opposite—isolate himself from people, even those who are naturally closest to him!

Bipolar disorder affects approximately 5.7 million adult Americans, and about 2.6% of adult Americans age 18 and older every year. Bipolar disorder is more likely to affect children whose parents have the disorder. If one parent has the disorder, there is 15% to 30% chance that the children will be affected. The percentage increases 50% to 75% for children when both parents have the disorder.

It's reported that the disorder can start early in childhood or as late as middle age. More than two-thirds of people with bipolar disorder have at least one close relative with the "illness" or with "major depression." Studies of this bipolar disorder reflect that one out of five patients commit suicide. (Information from the National Institute of Mental Health) It is my deep conviction that this disorder is a very serious spiritual condition—a battle with the enemy, with ancestral ramifications!

CHRONIC FATIGUE SYNDROME (CFS) is a disorder which is characterized by **extreme fatigue that does not seem to diminish with bed rest**, and it can worsen with physical or mental activities. The "Chronic Fatigue Study Group" reported that some people who suffer with this condition recover completely while others grow progressively worse. They also said that it can have symptoms like the flu but can linger for months or even years, and there are very few treatment options available.

CLINICAL DEPRESSION is a mood disorder in a person which reflects **extreme moodiness, sadness, no desire to participate in any activities, and difficulty in focusing and concentrating. He desires to just stay in bed and sleep. He isolates himself and has very little or no appetite, and seriously entertains suicidal thoughts, and obsesses about ways he might succeed in doing it.**

DISSOCIATIVE IDENTITY DISORDER (DID) this day in time often finds itself included with **MULTIPLE PERSONALITY DISORDER (MPD)** even though MPD is more severe than DID. Let's take time to further examine what the Mental Health section on WebMD has to say about DID and MPD:

> **"DISSOCIATIVE IDENTITY DISORDER (MULTIPLE PERSONALITY DISORDER)** dissociative disorder identity disorder (previously known as multiple personality disorder) is a fairly common effect of severe trauma during early childhood, usually extreme, repetitive physical, sexual, and/or emotional abuse.

> **"What is Dissociative Identity Disorder?** Most of us have experienced mild dissociation, which is like daydreaming or getting lost in the moment while working on a project. However, dissociative identity disorder is a severe form of dissociation, a mental process, which produces a lack of connection in a person's thoughts, memories, feelings, actions, or sense of identity. Dissociative identity disorder is thought to stem from trauma experienced by the person with the disorder.

115

The dissociative aspect is thought to be a **coping mechanism** — the person literally dissociates himself from a situation or experience that's too violent, traumatic, or painful to assimilate with his conscious self.

"Is Dissociative Identity Disorder Real? You may wonder if dissociative identity disorder is real. After all, understanding the development of multiple personalities is difficult, even for highly trained experts. But dissociative identity disorder does exist. It is the most severe and chronic manifestation of the dissociative disorders that cause multiple personalities.

"Other types of dissociative disorders defined in the DSM-IV, the main psychiatry manual used to classify mental illnesses, include <u>dissociative amnesia</u>, dissociative fugue, and depersonalization disorder.

"What Are the Symptoms of Dissociative identity Disorder? Dissociative identity disorder is characterized by the presence of two or more distinct or split identities or personality states that continually have power over the person's behavior. With dissociative identity disorder, there's also an inability to recall key personal information that is too far-reaching to be explained as mere forgetfulness. With dissociative identity disorder, there are also highly distinct memory variations, which fluctuate with the person's split personality.

"The "alters" or different identities have their own age, sex, or race. Each has his or her own postures, gestures, and distinct way of talking. Sometimes the alters are imaginary people; sometimes they are animals. As each personality reveals itself and controls the individual's behavior and thoughts, it's called "switching." Switching can take seconds to minutes to days. When under hypnosis, the person's different "alters" or identities may be very responsive to the therapist's requests.

"Along with the dissociation and multiple or split personalities, people with dissociative disorders may experience any of the following symptoms: Depression, mood swings, suicidal tendencies, sleep disorders (insomnia, nigh terrors, and sleep walking), anxiety, panic attacks, and phobias (flashbacks, reactions to stimuli or "triggers"), alcohol and drug abuse, compulsions and rituals, psychotic-like symptoms (including auditory and visual hallucinations), and eating disorders.

It seems we all agree that these conditions are **"coping mechanisms"** that are typically found in a person who has been traumatized through extreme, repetitive physical, sexual and or verbal abuse. These **coping mechanisms are created places within himself to which he retreats—hiding places where he is surrounded by a state of denial**. When he experienced stress and trauma, he emotionally created "wounded personalities" without his even realizing he was doing it!

One day, I was reading Psalms 23, as I had done for many years. But that day, the words *"...He restoreth my soul...."* stood out more boldly than ever before. And, that is when I began calling the fragment personalities "wounded parts of a person's soul"—wounded personalities, which most surely our Lord says He desires to and can restore!

EATING DISORDERS ARE DIVIDED INTO THREE TYPES

1. ANOREXIA is an **eating disorder that causes dangerous and extreme weight loss through persons literally starving themselves**. It also became classified as a "mental disorder"—obsessing over being fat, fear of food making them fat. When eating with other people, they cunningly hide their food elsewhere so that people think that they are eating it. Of course they suffer malnutrition and soon their general health breaks down causing all sorts of health problems! They choose not to eat as a means of "controlling their weight" and without actually realizing it they are, instead, "literally starving themselves to death"!

2. BULIMIA is an **eating disorder that is just as dangerous to one's health as Anorexia. Persons with this disorder practice "binge eating and purging."** They have an obsessive need to control their weight but they overeat. Then, they excuse themselves "to the restroom" where, in secret, they cause themselves to throw up all the food they have just binged on. And, of course, this will cause all sorts of health problems with their getting so little nourishment, too. Their body steadily deteriorates and death approaches.

3. GLUTTONY is an **eating disorder that leads to obesity.** While they eat an abundance of food, it typically does not consist of a healthy diet, thus they suffer malnutrition and soon their general health breaks down causing many health problems.

FIBROMYALGIA means **pain in the muscles, ligaments, and tendons, and is accompanied by fatigue**. It has been considered possibly to be an arthritis-related condition, but at this time, **the medical field reports that they do not know for certain—have no proof—what causes this condition.**

HOMOSEXUALITY AND LESBIANISM DISORDER, ALSO SODOMY

Before I cover this crucial subject, let me first say that God loves all homosexuals, and Rita and I do as well! It grieves us very deeply to hear of how ministers, Christian counselors and other Christians shyly and/or fearfully tip-toe around this critical subject as if these precious homosexual souls are playing a harmless game! Because God lovingly shares in His Word, the contrary—it is **"a very dangerous lifestyle game to play."** **Their aggressive enemy-opponent, the Devil, is determined to bring them down by seeking to steal their God-created natural strengths and**

gifts of masculinity and femininity that will ultimately weaken, disease, cripple and destroy them. Indeed, as John 10:10 says of our evil opponent and of our loving Lord, the Captain of our team: *"The thief does not come except to steal, to kill, and to destroy. I have come that they many have life, and that they may have it more abundantly."* We are extremely grateful and happy to say that all of the homosexuals and lesbians, plus men and women who were involved in other sexual activities—fornication, adultery, bestiality, etc—who came to our home for counseling with great hope and desperation for the Lord to free them, indeed, found freedom, peace and joy! **They won the game!**

God had love-laws in heaven and in the Garden of Eden for everyone's protection, and from those examples, we should embrace the realization that if we do not obey His rules, His very strong warnings, then extremely serious consequences will come! Just as God's rules were not to deprive Adam and Eve from pleasures and blessings, neither are His commandments and statutes set to deprive us, as Satan would have us believe! As we read earlier of the Lord's love-laws concerning the importance of not drinking fermented, alcoholic beverages, He lovingly warns us all about **"sexual sins,"** sins that He knew full well would bring disease, suffering, and death to His precious children! It is for these reasons that we look back to Old Testament times. He even laid down the law that people who engaged in sexual sins were to actually be put to death! Why? Because He knew—and knows—full well that not only would the people who sinned become diseased and suffer sorely, but they would even pass it on to innocent victims, including precious little children! This brings us to **another sexual sin** named by mental health as **"pedophilia."** Let's look at their diagnosis:

PEDOPHILIA DISORDER is typically defined by mental health professionals as a psychiatric illness, behavioral disorder in adults or late adolescents (persons age 16 and older), characterized by a primary or exclusive sexual interest in children age 13 or younger. A pedophile typically prefers a child as a sexual partner. Persons with this "disorder" are thought to have very likely experienced trauma or abuse themselves as children. Some are found to be driven by anger or need for power and control (e.g., violent/sadistic offenders). Treatments recommended are medications including chemical and surgical castration, private and group therapy, but no hope is given for them to be cured. Pedophiles rarely seek help voluntarily from mental health professionals.

Once again, it is extremely grievous to know that sentences are being pronounced on precious souls, announcing their doom to never be set free from the tormenting stronghold on them—no hope for them ever knowing the joy of living a normal, healthy, happy lifestyle!

One would have to be totally in denial today not to acknowledge that the devastating diseases birthed from sexual acts have mounted to enormous numbers of both guilty and innocent "victims of the enemy" all over the world! Is it any wonder that humans in these present days have become so "germ" conscience? Great numbers of products have been manufactured, advertised, and sold that sanitize—anti-bacterial this, that, and the other. How very tragic that many humans aren't as equally attentive to their Creator's warnings—His instructions about cleanliness in these specific areas! We find God's love-laws in these matters in both the New and Old Testaments. **Oh, that**

more of God's people would become diligent about offering God's truths in love on this subject—share His appeals and warnings concerning all sorts of "sexual sins," which we read in His Word:

In Deuteronomy 23:17, of male or female prostitution God says: *"There shall be no ritual harlot of the daughters of Israel, or a perverted one of the sons of Israel."*

In Leviticus 20:7-8; 10-22, we find that God went into great detail to lovingly and sternly warn us all about this subject, from which I dare not leave out one word: ***"Consecrate yourselves therefore, and be holy, for I am the LORD Your God.*** *And you shall keep My statutes, and perform them: I am the LORD who sanctifies you...the man who commits adultery with another man's wife, he who commits adultery with his neighbor's wife, the adulterer and the adulteress, shall surely be put to death. The man who lies with his father's wife has uncovered his father's nakedness; both of them shall surely be put to death. Their blood shall be upon them. If a man lies with his daughter-in-law, both of them shall surely be put to death. They have committed perversion. Their blood shall be upon them. If a man lies with a male as he lies with a woman, both of them have committed an abomination. They shall surely be put to death. Their blood shall be upon them. If a man marries a woman and her mother, it is wickedness. They shall be burned with fire, both he and they, that there may be no wickedness among you. If a man mates with an animal, he shall surely be put to death, and you shall kill the animal. If a woman approaches any animal and mates with it, you shall kill the woman and the animal. They shall surely be put to death. Their blood is upon them.. If a man takes his sister, his father's daughter or his mother's daughter, and sees her nakedness and she sees his nakedness, it is a wicked thing. And they shall be cut off in the sight of their people. He has uncovered his sister's nakedness. He shall bear his guilt. If a man lies with a woman during her sickness and uncovers her nakedness, he has exposed her flow, and she has uncovered the flow of her blood. Both of them shall be cut off from their people. You shall not uncover the nakedness of your mother's sister nor of your father's sister, for that would uncover his near of kin. They shall bear their guilt. If a man lies with his uncle's wife, he has uncovered his uncle's nakedness. They shall bear their sin: they shall die childless. If a man takes his brother's wife, it is an unclean thing. He has uncovered his brother's nakedness. They shall be childless. You shall therefore keep all My statutes and all My judgments, and perform them...."*

Now as we read the Lord's warning against sexual sins again in the New Testament, we will notice that one detail is different—the death penalty is withheld during this "grace period"—with much hope that these precious souls will choose to come to repentance and find their salvation in Jesus Christ! However, it's important that we see that there are still serious consequences on earth for those who choose not to repent and continue to disobey and walk in their own rebellious way.

We read confirmation of this in Romans 1:26-29a, *"For this reason God gave them up to vile passions. For even their women exchanged the natural use for what is against nature. Likewise also the men, leaving the natural use of the woman, burned in their lust for one another, men with men committing what is shameful, and receiving in themselves the penalty of their error which was due. And even as they did not like to retain God in their knowledge, God gave them over to a debased mind, to do those things which are not fitting; being filled with all unrighteousness, sexual immorality, wickedness...."*

Oh that all the precious people who are involved in such sins would embrace the fact that God told them not to do these things because He loves them! Oh, that ministers would not tip-toe around the subject but in loving boldness take the opportunity to share the love of God concerning it with the wonderful news that He can help them overcome! How very grateful that we have had the privilege in our ministry of seeing a number of homosexuals and lesbians come to repent and receive the Lord as their Savior, and find freedom from Satan's stronghold! We've also had the privilege of seeing ones who were already saved, repent of their sexual lifestyle and find joyful freedom through Christ!

You see in the following verse in the New Testament that our Creator, our heavenly Father, is merciful and forgiving when His precious children choose to repent and turn from their wicked, self-destructive ways:

I Corinthians 6:9-20 speaks so beautifully of God's forgiveness: *"Do you not know that the **unrighteous** will not inherit the kingdom of God? Do not be deceived. **Neither fornicators**, or idolaters, nor **adulterers, nor homosexuals, nor sodomites**, nor thieves, nor covetous, nor drunkards, nor revilers, nor extortioners will inherit the kingdom of God. **And such were some of you. But you were washed, but you were sanctified, but you were justified in the name of the Lord Jesus and by the Spirit of our God.** All things are lawful for me, but all things are not helpful. All things are lawful for me, but I will not be brought under the power of any. Foods for the stomach and the stomach for foods, but God will destroy both it and them. **Now the body is not for sexual immorality but for the Lord, and the Lord for the body.** And God both raised up the Lord and will also raise us up by His power. **Do you not know that your bodies are members of Christ?** Shall I then take the members of Christ and make them members of a harlot? Certainly not! Or do you not know that he who is joined to a harlot is one body with her? For 'the two,' He says, 'shall become one flesh.' But he who is joined to the Lord is one spirit with Him. **Flee sexual immorality. Every sin that a man does is outside the body, but he who commits sexual immorality sins against his own body.** Or do you not know that **your body is the temple of the Holy Spirit who is in you**, whom you have from God, and **you are not your own?** For **you were bought at a price; therefore glorify God in your body and in your spirit, which are God's."*

We praise the Lord for His mercy and grace—the power and authority to deal with the flip-side personalities and wounded personalities of these precious people! We thank Him for leading us on to victory over the evil one—Satan, the ancestral demons and all their networks!

OBSESSIVE COMPULSIVE DISORDER (OCD) is a disorder that is reflected in a person by his seeming **inability to stop his repetitive, ritualistic behavior that displays anxiety, panic, etc.** He **appears to be programmed to be obsessive and compulsive.** In my ministry, I have found precious people with this disorder to have a family history of ancestral strongholds! I thank the Lord for setting them free!

PANIC DISORDER is an **anxiety disorder that brings on recurrent panic attacks in a person at any given time.** A person will display an **uneasiness, nervousness, and shortness of breath.** When this happens, it is common for such a person to worry that he might be having a heart attack, especially since chest pains and sometimes pain down the left arm can accompany the panic attack! A person experiencing this may have the feeling that he is actually going to die. Medical studies show that this panic disorder is one of the most common mental disorders in the U.S.A. today! Most definitely, the culprit is hidden in spiritual warfare, from which our Lord can set the victim free!

PERSONALITY DISORDER is made up of a number of **different social behavioral disorders,** all of which I have also found in counselees as I worked with them:

1. **ANTISOCIAL** describes persons who have **no regard for the rights, feelings and safety of others.**

2. **AVOIDANT** describes persons who are **very self-conscious to the point of removing themselves from social interaction.**

3. **BORDERLINE** describes persons whose behavior reflects **constant instability in their mood and self-esteem and interpersonal relationships.**

4. **DEPENDENT** describes persons whom I see as **"very needy!"** They **display a constant dependence on other people to nurture them and to be assured of their approval, as well.**

5. **NARCISSISTIC** describes a person who **lives his life as if he is the most important person in all the world. "It's all about ME!"** He is **obsessed with himself, feeling no real emotions concerning others**—or what's going on in his life!

6. **SCHIZOTYPAL** describes persons who live lives of **social isolation with very irrational reasoning with all sorts of bizarre behavior.**

POST TRAUMATIC STRESS DISORDER (PTSD) occurs in **persons who have undergone horrific traumatic experiences**—such as soldiers on the battlefront of war. Another good example is that of first-responders to terrible natural disasters, including the first-responders to the terrorists' attack on 9/11. All such people are certainly vulnerable to suffer traumatic stress! Some of them **find the horrible memories playing over and over in their minds**. This causes attacks of **excessive feelings of helplessness** in their lives which cause them to **feel vulnerable**. They become so stressed that they become irritable and paranoid as flashbacks, highlights of the trauma, bombard them from time to time.

SCHIZOPHRENIA is typically known as a psychotic break or disorder that makes persons void of most of life's normal activities because of their **disarranged, fluctuating perception of thoughts, behavior, plus delusions and hallucinations**. From my own observations—apart from counseling—in the people I have learned about who have been diagnosed with schizophrenia, most did not know the Lord Jesus as their personal Savior. They had been institutionalized numerous times, some having had shock treatments, in addition to taking some very powerful drugs. Many who have taken strong medications and have had shock treatments have found great difficulty in remembering some things as well as difficulty in being able to stay alert and focused. They find it hard to concentrate, so they are hindered from making rational decisions pertaining to any form of counseling. I am so very grieved to say that I have learned of some of these who became so overwhelmed with the battle that in the depth of their depression they committed suicide.

However, the ones with the various behavioral disorders as mentioned above, who knew the Lord Jesus as their Savior and came to our home in desperation, seeking counseling, when they filled the requirements of reading "Liberating the Bruised" and filling out the counseling form, they found victory over the battle within them through Jesus Christ! I have worked with only a small number of people diagnosed with schizophrenia, but all of them had previously been institutionalized and had family histories of relatives who had "serious mental disorders." I found all of them to have ancestral demons. What joy it has been for me to see precious souls who have had behavioral disorders deal with their issues, confront the enemy and take back the ground from him, and walk away in freedom to live normal lives! Indeed, there is hope and victory in Jesus Christ!

TOURETTE'S SYNDROME is a diagnosis given to persons having **constant involuntary "tics" or "twitching of the face and head" plus "body dysfunctions" such as "jerking about."** When this happens, they also give forth various outbursts such as grunting, cursing, and screaming out obscenities. Tourette's syndrome usually starts in childhood and sometimes occurs less often and becomes milder once they are younger adults. Secular counselors usually offer therapy by urging their patient to vocalize their problems, work on their stress levels, and encourage them to focus on relaxation. When counseling children with this behavioral disorder, I have always found ancestral demons connected to their "nervous system".

TRICHATILLOMANIA is a **"need" or "an urge" within a person to pull out body hair**. Persons who have this form of impulsive control disorder pull out their scalp hair, eyebrows and/or eyelashes hair. Some also even pull out their pubic hair. This condition can possibly move into a more severe disorder of self mutilation that can cause major bodily injury! They **can venture into hard pinching, cutting, and burning themselves—various ways of mutilating their own bodies**.

SATANIC RITUAL ABUSE (SRA) victims who have **suffered ritual abuse during worship rituals to Satan.** They have suffered horrific experiences, physically, mentally, emotionally, sexually—some even to the point of being made to kill babies, young people, and adults! Some young girls have been dedicated as Satan's bride, impregnated by a high priest, and made to give birth to babies, then kill them on an altar as a sacrifice to Satan. Because of the horror they have endured and the traumatic affects that it has had on them, they are usually diagnosed by secular counselors as DID and MPD and other such mental and emotional disorders. Most definitely I always find ancestral demons in such abused victims!

D. GOD'S HOPE AND HELP AWAITS ALL

Upon embarking on helping someone with any of the preceding behavioral disorders, two main issues should always be prayerfully considered as possibilities: **(1)** it could be something ancestral/generational, or **(2)** it could be that somewhere back in the individual's life, he was emotionally, physically, mentally, and/or sexually abused. If that proves to be the case, then everything I taught in "Liberating the Bruised" and now in this book can certainly be applied to the precious person's case. I will most surely deal with wounded parts of the person's soul as well as demonic networks connected to the behavioral disorder.

How very grateful Rita and I are that God's solutions—biblical counseling—taught in my first book and in this book has proven over and over again to have helped many people! Precious persons with the previously mentioned addictions and/or behavior disorders who became sick and tired of being sick and tired of living dysfunctional, tormented lives that were void of peace and joy found victory! Many have come who were only clinging to a thread of hope, many even saying, "You're my last hope!" We have had quite a number of counselees say after reading my book and applying God's truths to their lives, "The biblical teachings in 'Liberating the Bruised' saved my life—I was hopeless and suicidal!" What joy to know that many others have embraced the same freedom that the teachings and the case studies reflect—and many others in the future can as well! The choice is theirs!

Because our hearts are so burdened, we have found ourselves unable to move on to the next chapter until we have addressed some of our great concerns pertaining to "mental disorders"—under the care of both non-Christian and Christian counselors. For a moment, let's step aside to consider how persons in those categories view "physical healing," which comes and cannot be attributed to anything humans have done—it just happens. For instance, in hospitals, both non-Christians and Christians have seen patients "on their death beds" surprise everyone by "pulling through" and going on to live longer. **(1)** Some non-Christians have stated that they are left to give credit only to

"God"— "a higher power," and (2) the Christians declare without doubt that God—their Creator—chose to perform a miracle and heal them. Most surely, our Lord has chosen to do that in the past and continues to do so today and in the future according to His will.

Keeping that in mind, let's step back over into the realm of secular counseling—**non-Christian counseling** pertaining to "mental health issues—mental disorders." As we said earlier, we appreciate the fact that there are so many men and women in the secular counseling fields who truly care about others and desire to help them deal with the torments in their minds! God bless them for caring! After examining their methods of counseling, though, knowing they have to see many of their patients year after year after year without leading them to total freedom and normality, we wonder if it troubles their hearts. There is all too large a number of these counselors, however, who continue to insist that their methods are "the only way" to help these "victims of mental disorders." Sadly, with the Creator left out of the equation, and their methods founded on "human reasoning" along with "prescriptions that provide a therapeutic effect," they fall short of achieving their goal of helping their patients find emotional bliss. We are saddened that so many keep using their same methods and medicines over many years, never having the joy of seeing their patients healed and happy! Oh that they would at least consider that perhaps what so many Christians say—that our Lord Jesus can heal people of all kinds of afflictions, including mental disorders—is true!

Other extremely great concerns fall into these three categories of counseling offered by well-meaning Christian ministers and Christian counselors, whether their sessions do or don't include dealing with "addictions" and "mental disorders": (1) Secular methods blended in with "some" biblical counseling, but no dealings with root causes attributed to the demonic. (2) While excluding all secular methods, they offer biblical solutions but also exclude any dealings with the root causes connected to the demonic. (3) Sound biblical counseling including dealing with the demonic, yet failing to go deeply enough to get to the root causes connected to the flip-side, wounded personalities, and the ancestral demon and his network. **Oh, that all Christian ministers and counselors would embrace and thoroughly apply all of God's truths as they deal with all root causes, including those of "addictions" and "mental disorders" connected to the demonic. For, in doing so, the world would have a better opportunity to see that Jesus is the Great Physician!**

Now we repeat, when a person is not yet crying out to the Lord in desperation for help, it is sometimes a last resort to administer medication to a patient who is "bouncing off the wall" while he is being demonically controlled and/or until alcohol or illegal drugs are out of his system. But it troubles us greatly that after he is calmed down and is being ministered to by the Word of God that is so full of hope—why is he, like so many other souls, told that his measure of hope for good mental health is limited for him? God says that if His Son sets you free—you are free, indeed! Grievously, all too many Christians who give counsel to their brothers and sisters have taken away a very large portion of their hope. They have done this by breaking the sorrowful news to them that while they walk with the Lord in His will for their precious lives, they are "still being held by a disorder," thus they must also take drugs for the rest of their live! It has been sorrowful for us to also hear of some family members and friends of these "victims of mental disorders" join the counselors in agreeing with them—that there is no hope for complete freedom from their disorder or the medications that hold serious side affects.

How grievous it is to think of how many tragic stories we have heard of precious souls like him—**Christians—who have been pronounced "doomed to endless counseling sessions and swallowing pills with life-threatening side effects."** The very thing that is a destructive part of their "mental disorder" is "depression"—one of the side affects warned with such prescriptions—along with "suicidal thoughts!" Many such precious souls have cried out, "The voices are still there! They won't leave me alone! They are tormenting me!"—and in their exhaustion, weary of fighting against them with so little hope for freedom given them—they do what the voices are telling them to do and end it all by committing suicide! Of the cases in which we came to learn more details about, we are grateful to say that the demons lost in the end, for those precious souls were Christians and are residing in heaven today!

We should take care not to steal hope from God's precious children. In Hebrews 6:17-20, we read these **powerful promises from God—assuring us that He does not change, is not a liar, and He—Jesus—is our hope—an anchor for our souls**! *"Thus God, determining to show more abundantly to the heirs of promise the immutability of His counsel, confirmed it by an oath, that by two immutable things, in which it is impossible for God to lie, we might have strong consolation, who have fled for refuge to lay hold of the hope set before us. This hope we have as an anchor of the souls, both sure, and steadfast, and which enters the Presence behind the veil, where the forerunner has entered for us, even Jesus, having become High Priest forever according to the order of Melchizedek."*

As you can understand, we find it very difficult to understand why some Christians blend human reasoning in so generously with their faith in God. For many declare with great faith that Jesus is the Great Physician! Their Great Physician sometimes heals people without their even asking Him! He gives humans much wisdom and abilities to know how to "repair" so many physical ailments and injuries! But "Hold on a minute! When it comes to healing 'mental disorders', that's a different realm!" Upon their declaring that God is limited in that "department," we are convinced that the "limitation" is most surely not on God's part, but rather, on the part of the doubting ministers and counselors. Their limited faith in the realm of "mental disorders" is connected with their limited faith concerning the reality of "the demonic—spiritual warfare!" There is also another factor connected to this though, for **some Christians are more afraid of demons than they trust God!** Oh how our hearts long for these precious Christians to reconsider and prayerfully gain wisdom—and courage—on this critical subject from the Great Physician—the One who finds nothing too hard for Him to do! We're told that with God, nothing is impossible that falls into the realm of His will! He surely desires for His people to be set free! Therefore, it concerns us when ministers and counselors reflect their lack of faith to their counselees—they are guilty of causing them to have less faith, less trust in the Lord!

We find ourselves wondering what measure of trust some ministers and counselors would have if they could step back in time and ride in the boat with Jesus and the disciples as they *"...came to the other side of the sea, to the country of the Gadarenes, and when He had come out of the boat, immediately there met Him out of the tombs a man with an unclean spirit, who had his dwelling among the tombs; and no one could bind him, not even with chains, because he had often been bound with shackles and chains. And the chains had been pulled apart by him, and the shackles broken in pieces; neither could anyone tame him. And always, night and day, he was in the mountains, and in the tombs, crying out and cutting himself with stones. When **he saw Jesus from afar, he ran and worshiped him**."* (Mark 5:1-6) The amazing grace of God allowed that poor, needy demonic man—wrongfully declared by the people to be hopelessly crazy, mentally deranged—to recognize Jesus as Lord, the Great Physician who could totally heal him!

As we seek God's truth in the matter, we see evidence of what would nowadays be wrongfully diagnosed as "an incurable mental disorder" instead of it being "a demon problem!" Because just as the man recognized who Jesus was, the demon inside him did also! The demon *"...cried out with a loud voice and said, 'What have I to do with You, Jesus, Son of the Most High God? I implore You by God that You do not torment me.' For He said to him, 'Come out of the man, you unclean spirit!' Then, He asked him, **'What is your name?'** And he answered, saying, **'My name is Legion; for we are many.'"*** (Mark 5:7-9)

While Jesus knew full well what the demon's name was, for the sake of our learning something He asked, *"What is your name?"* **On future pages, as you examine the counseling procedures that the Lord has given me, you will see that I ask what names the flip-sides, wounded personalities, and demons carry, for their names hold meanings that reveal the work they do in the core personalities lives. In answer to Jesus, when the demon answered that his name was "Legion," it told us (for our learning) that there was an army of demons tormenting and seeking to kill the dear man. For a Roman Legion consisted of 6,826 soldiers. This man was truly severely tormented by this unclean spirit and the thousands of demons in his charge!**

As we continue reading in Mark, chapter 5, the demons begged Jesus to let them go into a herd of about 2,000 swine, which He did—but then the swine ran into the sea and drowned. (By the way, our all-wise God actually did not let them have their way—for in the end, they lost their physical housing!) When the people tending the swine saw what happened, they ran and spread the news in the country and in the city. A large crowd returned to the scene. **Were they happy for the man whom they had seen for so long, crying and cutting himself amongst the tombs, who was now miraculously healed and "sitting, clothed, and in his right mind"?** What were their thoughts? Their greed and self-centeredness had surfaced as they considered their priorities—their financial losses when those approximately 2,000 swine went running wildly into the sea and drowned! **Being greatly concerned about their pocket books, they begged Jesus to get out of their country!**

If present-day counselors were able to go back in time and observe what took place that day, have the privilege of seeing that dear man "sitting, clothed and in his right mind," we wonder how each would have reacted. Would all of them immediately acknowledge that **"...God has not given us a spirit of fear, but of power and of love and of a sound mind"**? (II Timothy 1:7) Would all rejoice and thank the Lord for setting the man totally free from all the demons? Or would some doubt that he would remain free and believe that such a horribly tormented man must really be "incurable"—and "just to be on the safe side," shouldn't he be chained up again? And would some determine that he must be on medications for the rest of his life? How many would think that even though he seemed alright "for the moment," surely time would prove that he could not function "normally" in the world? What did happen to this dear soul with the severe mental disorder? We are blessed to be able to read what happened to him in Mark 5:18-20: **"And when He [Jesus] got into the boat, he who had been demon-possessed begged Him that he might be with Him. However, Jesus did not permit him, but said to him, 'Go home to your friends, and tell them what great things the Lord has done for you, and how He has had compassion on you. And he departed and began to proclaim in Decapolis all that Jesus had done for him; and all marveled."** Not only was he able to function normally—out of his love for and gratitude to the Lord, with joy he willingly surrendered to his home mission field—and people came to believe on the Lord Jesus Christ!**

Oh that all Christians would prayerfully take time to get alone with the Lord and allow Him to impart His wisdom concerning the fact that He has not given His people a spirit of fear, but of power and of love and of a sound mind! He truthfully declared that if the Son sets one free, he is free, indeed!

Now we will move on to the next chapter of this book, which we pray is a truly helpful chapter to help you better understand core personalities, broken parts of the core, flip-side personalities, wounded parts of the soul, and various categories of demons, including demon-clones and mind-sets.

More Tools *for Liberating the* Bruised

Chapter Four
UNDERSTANDING THE CORE, FLIP-SIDE, WOUNDED PERSONALITIES AND CATEGORIES OF DEMONS

"Hear, my children, the instruction of a father, and give attention to know understanding; for I give you good doctrine: Do not forsake my law...Get wisdom! Get understanding! Do not forget, nor turn away from the words of my mouth. Do not forsake her, and she will preserve you; love her, and she will keep you. Wisdom is the principal thing; therefore get wisdom. And in all your getting, get understanding." (Proverbs 4:1-2; 5-7)

A. CORE PERSONALITY

The core personality is the person that God created from the foundations of the world. For we read in Psalm 139:13-16: *"For You formed my inward parts; You covered me in my mother's womb. I will praise You, for I am fearfully and wonderfully made; Marvelous are Your works, and that my soul knows very well. My frame was not hidden from You, when I was made in secret, and skillfully wrought in the lowest parts of the earth. Your eyes saw my substance, being yet unformed, and in Your book they all were written, the days fashioned for me, when as yet there were none of them."*

We also read that our Creator knows everything about every person He created! For we read in Psalm 139:1-4: *"O LORD, You have searched me and known me. You know my sitting down and my rising up; You understand my thought afar off. You comprehend my path and my lying down, and are acquainted with all my ways. For there is not a word on my tongue, but behold, O LORD, You know it altogether."*

Our Creator knows us all well—"inside and out!" We also read in Ephesians 1:4: *"...He chose us in Him before the foundation of the world, that we should be holy and without blame before Him in love."* He wants every soul—for our own sake— to choose to place our trust in Him and follow Him all the days of our lives.

Our Creator creates each core personality with the freedom of choice to reject or accept the Lord Jesus as his Savior! If he chooses to accept the Lord, then, when he dies, he can indeed stand "holy and without blame before Him!" **When a Christian is being held captive by the strongholds of Satan, God mercifully gives that Christian the authority to be "boss" over the entire inner** system. You've heard the saying, "the buck stops passing here." That certainly applies to the core personality's authority and responsibility in the system. Throughout the counseling time, how much progress is made toward victory depends on the core and his choices! It is essential (1) that the core knows who he is in Jesus Christ—that he is secure in Him—and (2) participates throughout the counseling procedures! For, he alone can determine the outcome—defeat or victory!

The core need not fear but trust that the Lord will enable him to deal successfully with the flip-side personality, all the wounded personalities, and the ancestral demon and his network. The flip-side is established in a person when "iniquities of the fathers" are passed down to him. The ancestral demon is on the "dark-side" of the duplex but the core is on the "safe-side" where he can hear the Lord convicting his heart, wooing him unto Himself, giving opportunity to be saved. When the core gets saved, then the "safe-side" of the duplex is then called the "saved-side" of the duplex. Most definitely, the core then has full authority and power through his Lord Jesus Christ to "pull down strongholds, to cast down arguments—imaginations—and every high thing that exalts itself against the knowledge of God! Every thought is then brought into captivity to the obedience of Christ!" He can do all things through Christ who strengthens him! (Philippians 4:13)

THE IMPORTANCE OF USING A PERSON'S TRUE FORMAL NAME

Throughout counseling, it is extremely important to use the true formal (or full) name of each counselee that is shown on his or her birth certificate. For when you are dealing with the ancestral demon carrying the person's formal name, if you have not stated the true name, it gives opportunity for the ancestral demon to claim that you did not deal with the person appropriately or accurately; therefore, he "has the right" to hold onto his "merchandise!" From experience, I know this to be a critical issue, so you will see in the counseling procedures how I take care to state the "official" name, the "formal" name of the person I'm counseling throughout all the counseling procedures. You may find it monotonous and wearisome, but please believe me, it is crucial! After a time, you will get used to it and it will flow naturally for you.

When counseling a woman concerning her "core personality's formal name": (1) If she has never been married, I use her full birth name when addressing her core personality. (2) If she is married, I use her maiden name coupled with her married name at the end. (3) If she is divorced but kept her married name, I include her married name. Otherwise, the previous married name is not included. (4) Concerning the ancestral demon of both men and women, I address him as, "Ancestral Demon core personality's formal name."

Concerning the formal name of an adopted person, while counseling in specific areas when you need to state the "legal" birth name: (1) Use the "name that is written on his official birth certificate." (2) If there was no birth certificate and he has no knowledge of his biological family, just adoption papers, use "his given name plus the names that God knows." The reason I do this is because of the necessity to stay as close to the legal names as possible because of the demons being legalistic and possibly having legal rights to claim. Another reason to do this is because if the child was conceived by an unknown father, all the bases are covered.

B. BROKEN PART OF THE CORE

It is rare for a person to have a broken part of his core, and it is also quite rare for one to have more than one broken part of his core. However, while counseling severely abused persons, such as victims of Satanic Ritualistic Abuse, I will certainly stay on the alert for this possibility. Like a splintered bone, **a broken part of the core is a wounded personality on the safe side of the house which has been created by the core himself before salvation.** This splintering occurred due to a very significant trauma and this part will hold either memories or emotions, or both, as a result of the traumatic event. Broken parts are very different from "wounded personalities" for I have found the "broken part" missing, lost, or hidden from the rest of the system. Sometimes the broken part that has been taken away or shielded does not know what has happened in the system after his age. For example, if he is two years old, he will not know anything about the core past age three. Such personalities are usually very young in age. Most of the time you will not find a true broken part past the age of nine or ten. It's typical for a broken part to say they are lost, alone, or confused, and not know why they exist.

Very often a broken part of the core will not even know about God or Jesus Christ. Since a broken part is hidden from the salvation experience, he has not trusted Jesus Christ as his Lord and Savior. Therefore, the broken part is tremendous ground for the ancestral demon to operate from, causing interference and confusion for the core. This is especially true if the counselee was a victim of Satanic Ritualistic Abuse (SRA) early in his life, who is more susceptible to such broken parts on the safe side of the duplex. This is due to such extreme evil activities such as the core as a child being dedicated to Satan, his family members or other care-givers involved in major sorcery, and curses having come down to him due to the sorcery in the family. The ancestral demon carrying the full name can most definitely use the broken part as a gateway to go back and forth from the "safe side" to the "dark side" of the duplex and wreak havoc! Therefore, the ancestral demon will most surely try very hard to hide the broken part of the core!

C. FLIP-SIDE PERSONALITY

I explained the flip-side personality at length in my book, Liberating the Bruised. And, I shared in Part I of Chapter Nine that I derived the term "flip-side personality" from James 1:8 and James 4:8, which refers to some people being a **dipsuchos** and literally means **two-souled or split-souled.** I also mentioned that it is very important for us to keep in mind that **the book of James was written to Christians!** In James 1:8, the Lord is actually saying that **Christians can be two-souled or split-souled, "unstable in all their ways".**

A flip-side personality is always found to be manipulated by the ancestral demon carrying the full, formal name of the core personality. Through iniquity, the ancestral demon gained permission—the right—to operate on the "dark-side" of the duplex in the core personality's life. The core lives on the "safe" side while the opposite side is the flip-side, living on the "dark" side of the duplex. It is on the dark side that the ancestral demon plus his network manipulates and operates. When a core personality gets saved, the flip-side, deceived by the ancestral demon in charge, does not choose to get saved. Therefore, in order for the core personality to achieve freedom, broken parts of the core, the flip-side, and the wounded personalities must all be led to the Lord and saved. You can well understand that the ancestral demon carrying the full name will try every way possible to keep this from happening.

D. WOUNDED PERSONALITIES/WOUNDED PARTS OF THE SOUL

Wounded personalities, also called wounded parts of the soul, are fragmented pieces from the core personality, who live on the dark side of the duplex. The wounded parts are mechanisms of dissociation, housed in different personalities (Part II of Chapter Nine) in "Liberating the Bruised"). Each wounded personalities has been brought into existence through a deep wound in the core—a trauma, repeated abuse whether physical, verbal or emotional, or the continuation of a sinful lifestyle. The wounded personalities are **coping mechanisms. And the ancestral demon views the first wounded part as his "first fruit," his offspring!** Each wounded personality has been created by the core to perform certain tasks that the core finds unpleasant, and each one serves a particular purpose and has its own set of thinking and emotions. Many severely fragmented counselees typically have many wounded personalities who are designated to perform specific chores. For instance, a wife married to a very verbally abusive man may create a "wife personality" to tolerate having sex with her unkind, unloving husband while she—her core personality—escapes into denial.

Remember to treat all the wounded parts with as much care and compassion as you show the core because they are like little fractures of the core's personality.

When a core personality with a flip-side **consistently gives way to temptation and dwells on sinful thoughts, he becomes vulnerable to his ancestral demon's being able to manipulate another wounded personality into being** who will take on the behavior related to the sinful thoughts. As a result, the stronghold increases in power—more ground is claimed!

Wounded personalities will not go away until they have been led to willingly deal with their issues, repent and be healed through the mercy and grace of Jesus Christ. Until they do this, they continue to elevate themselves above Christ's throne and authority. They represent sinful thinking which behavior patterns will reflect through the core's life. This thinking is contrary to God's truth declared in His Word, therefore, that is why scripture explains the need for these sin issues to be "cast down." (II Corinthians 10:3-6) Most certainly, until they are dealt with, the core will not have peace! Only through **willingly applying the Lord's biblical principles** can these wounded personalities be brought into submission of the Lordship of Jesus. The excuses for sin, lack of confession and repentance, lack of unforgiveness, and doubts about God, self and life are the strongholds the ancestral demon carrying the full name is amplifying and magnifying in the core's life. **Until these sins are dealt with, the demons have legal rights to hold onto their ground!**

E. POWER DEMONS, DIFFERENT TYPES: ANCESTRAL AND LIFESTYLE

If I do not find the power demon to be an ancestral demon—no flip-side—in the person's life who has clearly reflected that he is being manipulated by the demonic, I will find a different type of "power demon." I will find that at a particular time in the core personality's life he consistently yielded to a certain sin, and therefore, Satan was given an open invitation to claim ground in the person's life. A **"power demon"** moved in and eagerly looked forward to luring the core more deeply into sinful behavior by which he could build his network of demons! **This type of power demon is a lifestyle demon.** Early on in the counseling procedure though, I will be able to establish whether or not the person has an ancestral demon or a lifestyle power demon. **There will only be one power demon—one demon over all the other demons.** Note the difference between the two types of power demons: **(1) The ancestral demon will carry the core personality's formal name and there will be a flip-side and wounded personalities. (2) The lifestyle power demon will carry a name that simply reflects the ground to which he laid claim in the beginning.** I will, however, deal with this power demon in the same way concerning the wounded personalities. **It's important that we share with the counselee that if he does not deal with his power demon that was invited in by "his own iniquity," his iniquity can be passed down to his descendants in the form of an ancestral demon with a flip-side!**

SINFUL LIFESTYLES—INIQUITIES—INVITE POWER DEMONS IN

The Tempter so delights when a person yields to his temptations—especially God's children! He is so proud of himself when they have followed him into a sinful lifestyle! How grievous it has been to see ministers of the Gospel yield to temptation and give the enemy ground in their precious lives which destroys their personal testimonies before others, as well as their ministries! Through a consistent walk in sin, a demon is invited to move in, claim ground, and becomes a **"power demon"** who readily lures his victim even deeper and deeper into sin. With his victim having chosen to walk in a sinful lifestyle, he has allowed "iniquity" to take up residence in his heart—and this power demon transforms into an ancestral demon for the next generation—this person's children and future generations until he is dealt with! As you can see, it is most critical, as Ephesians 6:10-18 teaches, that Christians take great care to keep their armor on—keep their lives clean before the Lord—clean before the demons! I feel impressed that I should share two examples of persons who allowed power demons to take up residence in their lives. As you can understand, I will use fictitious names.

EXAMPLE #1 - CAIN WITH A POWER DEMON OF SEXUAL PERVERSION

A man was referred to me by his pastor who knew my ministry dealt with the demonic and that I was certain that Christians could be demonically controlled. The man, who was in his late forties and was a salesman, taught a men's Sunday morning bible study class at his church. The pastor told me that this gentleman—I'll call Cain—was a great Christian, but he had gotten into a sinful situation while out of town for a week at a sales conference. One night after a long day, some of the other salesmen attending the conference talked Cain into going out for a few drinks. In this particular city, it was known that entertainment of the sexual nature is brought to some such conventions! Prostitutes come from miles around to offer their "services"—for a fee! Sad to say, after this man had a few drinks, he had dropped his "shield of faith" and accepted "a date" with one of the prostitutes. The next day he awoke in the world of reality—hung-over and overwhelmed with guilt and grief! He was so angry with himself for what he had done and he cried out to the Lord for forgiveness. When he got back home, he could not shake the guilt away nor the memory of what he had done.

For several weeks, he found himself buried so deeply in self-condemnation and remorse for his sins, he couldn't keep it to himself any longer! He went to his pastor and shared his problem. The pastor prayed with him and even though the two felt God had forgiven him, they agreed that it may be best for him to take a break from teaching the men's class—but just for a while.

Much to this dear man's discouragement—things grew worse rather than better. He found himself drawn to adult bookstores and adult xxx-rated movies and strip joints. With all of this happening, he went back to see his pastor. After once again praying together about the situation, the two decided that he should be open with his precious Christian wife and tell her of his horrible situation. While sobbing in deep remorse, Cain confessed everything to his wife and sought her forgiveness. She forgave him, they prayed together—and hoped all would be settled. Nevertheless, Cain continued to find himself being pulled into the enemy's sinful places. He told his wife how tormented he was and they went together to see the pastor again. After praying and seeking God's wisdom, they all agreed that something extremely evil was controlling Cain. It was then that my ministry came to the pastor's mind and he gave the Cain my contact information.

Now the reason I felt it important for you to read Cain's story is that his counseling sessions did not turn out to follow the typical counseling procedures. Nevertheless, with him being desperate for freedom and me being desperate for wisdom to help him, the Lord mercifully allowed us to turn the tables on the enemy and Cain was set free! Because of this Cain became a valuable teaching tool for ministers and counselors. When Cain arrived, I began applying the teachings that you are reading about in this book of tools. I looked for a flip-side—a duplex—and an ancestral demon but found none. I also searched for a wounded personality because of all of the guilt, sadness, shame and the recurring sins in the adult bookstores, adult xxx-rated movies, and strip joints, but I found nothing!

As I was earnestly praying, seeking God's wisdom concerning Cain's life, **I felt strongly impressed to see if ground had been legally claimed by "a power demon of sexual perversion" when Cain yielded himself—at the start—"to become one with the prostitute through the sexual act."** He had joined himself to a person with **"a power demon of sexual perversion"**—and thus, like the prostitute, was being controlled by this **"power demon of sexual perversion!"** I asked the Holy Spirit, through the power of Jesus' blood and the word of Cain's testimony and my testimony, to bring the power demon in charge of all the sexual perversion up to talk with me. Immediately, that power demon was up, and his name was "sexual perversion" and proudly declared that he had come into Cain's life when he had sex with the prostitute at the sales convention. We learned that the power demon, in only a few months, had not wasted any time building his network—masturbation, bisexuality, homosexuality, and pornography—and self-hatred! One can see, Cain's life, as well as his wife's was about to be turned upside down and be destroyed!

> Cain prayed, confessing and repenting and acknowledging God's convicting truths in His Word in I Corinthians 6:13-20: *"Foods for the stomach and the stomach for foods, but God will destroy both it and them. Now **the body is not for sexual immorality but for the Lord, and the Lord for the body**. And, God both raised up the Lord and will also raise us up by His power. Do you not know that **your bodies are members of Christ**? Shall I then take the members of Christ and make them members of a harlot? Certainly not! Or do you not know that **he who is joined to a harlot is one body with her**? For 'the two,' He says, shall become one flesh. Flee sexual immorality. Every sin that a man does is outside the body, but **he who commits sexual immorality sins against his own body**. Or do you not know that **your body is the temple of the Holy Spirit who is in you, whom you have from God, and you are not your own**? For **you were bought at a price; therefore glorify God in your body and in your spirit, which are God's.**"*

After Cain and I prayed, we asked the Lord Jesus to bring the power demon of sexual perversion to attention and commanded him to attach all his network to him—masturbation, bisexuality, homosexuality, pornography and self-hatred. We asked the Lord Jesus to blood-link them to the power demon with blood-links that could not be broken, made of the blood Jesus shed on Calvary, and send them all to the Abyss, including the demons that had transferred to his wife, which the Lord did! Then I led Cain to pray that the Lord Jesus would take His powerful blood and literally saturate his being from the top of his head to the soles of his feet, every crack and crevice of his life, body, soul, spirit, mind, and emotions. I prayed that the Lord would bring His Shekinah glory and light up his entire life, and fill all the vacancies that were left by the demons who were sent to the Abyss. Then Cain said that he immediately felt a peace sweep over him. What joy to know that he and his wife were able to heal and get on with living the lives that the Lord intended them to live! Through this entire ordeal, Cain's pastor had learned and gathered these counseling tools for his own tool box—which he would use to help others in his own ministry!

135

EXAMPLE #2 - MIRIAM WITH A POWER DEMON "CONTROL"

A delightful college student I'll call Miriam, whom we'd known since she was a young child, came to our home for counseling after she had been date-raped by one of her college friends. She said that for a long time, she told no one about the rape because she felt so unclean, grieved, and even had thoughts of feeling guilty—that it was somehow her fault for not being able to prevent the act! (Eventually, however, to protect others from him, she did report the date-rape to necessary school officials—who did nothing about it.) She confessed to me that at times she felt so despondent that she had been entertaining thoughts of suicide, and now she said that she was having additional thoughts—self-hatred. She added to her sad story that she also had feelings like the rape was still going on inside her almost nonstop. She was now at the point of isolating herself from people more and more. When I'm pressing some people to tell me the truth, I'll say, "Now, look right here in my blue eyes—tell me the truth!" After Miriam shared that she was not only withdrawing even from her closest friends—she was also withdrawing from having sweet conversations with her Lord Jesus, she suddenly leaned forward and drew her face closer and looked right into my blue eyes in such a way as if to say, "Listen to me—I'm telling you the truth!" as she declared, "I know the Lord Jesus told me to come and tell you what happened to me!"

As I worked with Miriam, what I did not find was a flip-side—a duplex—or an ancestral demon carrying her formal name. What I did find was a power demon that came in and claimed ground when she was raped and his name was "Control" who had immediately begun setting up his network. In that network, I found demons of isolation; dirty and unclean; guilty; it's your fault; self-hatred; and suicide. I also found a demon-produced personality of her rapist carrying his formal name—and his job was to make her feel as if he were raping her repeatedly. This Demon-Produced personality carrying the rapist's name was controlled by his boss, the power demon, "Control".

Miriam and I prayed and she forgave her college friend who date-raped her and she gave him over to the Lord—for Him to handle! Then we went through the procedure of asking the Lord Jesus to bring up the power demon that came in during the rape and having all his network, including the Demon-Produced personality of her rapist, attached to the power demon with blood-links that could not be broken, made of the blood Jesus shed on Calvary, and sent them to the Abyss. And, after doing so, like Cain, precious Miriam declared that she immediately felt an awesome peace from the Lord embrace her!

Over the years, I have dealt with numerous counselees who rather than having ancestral demons, they had "power demons" that were either connected to lifestyles or traumatic experiences like the previous two examples. How very grateful I am that the Lord so patiently taught me about these tools so that more of Satan's captives can be liberated!

F. ANCESTRAL DEMON AND HIS NETWORK ON FLIP-SIDE/DARK SIDE

For a thorough discussion on the iniquity of the fathers and the ancestral demon carrying a person's full, formal name, please see Chapter Nine of "Liberating the Bruised."

When there is an **ancestral demon carrying the formal name of the core personality**, he is considered the **power demon** over the system—his network of demons. Having moved in legally by way of the iniquities of the fathers, he operates—manipulates and controls—the flip-side in the life of the core personality. The ancestral demon's network consists of a number of demons which he appoints to do various jobs for him. There is **typically a gatekeeper within the ancestral demon's** network. He gets his orders from the ancestral demon, and one of his jobs is to open and close the gate, letting demons in and out. Another part of his job is to attract other people who are demonic, so that the core is vulnerable to more temptation which will allow the ancestral demon to obtain even more ground in his life. There can **also be more than one gatekeeper in a person's life.** There can also be **a lifestyle gatekeeper** as a result of a person's stepping into a sinful lifestyle—such as being involved in pornography, prostitution, etc.

While the ancestral demon and his network are powerful, the Christian's core personality has authority through Jesus Christ over them to resist and overcome if he chooses to do so! While acting as a territorial demon in the core's life, the ancestral demon has authority over his own demonic network, but he does not have authority over the core who is "saved and sealed with the blood of Jesus!" He may "call the shots" for the demons under his command standing on the flip-side, but he cannot go against the will of the core when the core chooses to exercise his authority in Christ! The ancestral demon can seize opportunities only to do his dirty work when they are given to him—by iniquity flowing down through the core's generations, or through ground the core has given him through sinful choices.

When the core gives the ancestral demon opportunity to manipulate his life, the ancestral demon is able to amplify and magnify particular memories and connected emotions of the wounded personalities. He is, in other words, permitted to "influence" and "use" the wounded personalities who are operating in the core—and cast imaginations his way! This is why it is so vital that the core has sincerely confessed all known sins in his life before he begins counseling! The way the core responds to the difficulties of life has a great impact on the amount of manipulation the ancestral demon is allowed to have over the core. If the core personality is to have freedom, he must choose to take the Lord at His Word and believe and trust that through Him he can defeat the enemy!

The Lord's Word says in Romans 10:17: *"So then faith comes by hearing and hearing by the word of God."* In Romans 14:23b, we read: *"...whatever is not from faith is sin."* Hebrews 11:6 tells us: *"...without faith, it is impossible to please Him."*

Keep the wonderful truth in mind, that the ancestral demon carrying the full name of the core was not strong enough to keep the core from salvation in Jesus Christ! Neither can he keep the flip-side from salvation after the core is saved! The scriptures say when Christ is lifted up before man, men are drawn to Him. Therefore, a legitimate flip-side will be drawn to the Lord just like the core was. God wants unity in the counselee's life. **God will draw the flip-side unto Himself, bring healing to the core, flip-side, and wounded personalities—make them whole— and dissolve the dividing wall!** If the core is desperate to have this done, he must determine to work toward that end, for Paul said in Philippians 2:12b-13: *"...work out your own salvation with fear and trembling, for it is God who works in your both to will and to do for His good pleasure."* How marvelous to know that our merciful Lord finds pleasure in setting Satan's captives free!

G. DEMON-PRODUCED PERSONALITIES, DEMON-CLONES, MIND-SETS

EXAMPLE #1 - DEMON-PRODUCED PERSONALITIES OF A REAL PERSON

Demon-produced personalities are demonic reproductions of a real person: They can be a copy of any human—and can come from family bloodlines as well. They can spring forth anywhere from what one might call a minor circumstance to a major evil setting—but in either case, it has a strong, evil grip on the core personality! **The demon-produced personality carries the name and age of another real person other than the core personality.** The Demon-Produced personality acts like the other person—reflecting all the weaknesses, negativeness, pessimism, and evil in that person's life. It may be a demon-produced personality of an abuser such as a domineering, controlling parent or spouse. It may be a reproduction of a sexually abusive husband—or sexual partner—or rapist. In spite of the core's hating that particular behavior, the Demon-Produced personality indwelling that person acts out that same abusive lifestyle toward other people!

Example of a demon-produced personality—a reproduction of a real person: I'll call the dear lady Sue who was age 27. She had come to me for counseling and I had to give her shorter appointment times and space them farther apart because she was going to college part-time and working full-time. Before her next appointment, she called me, crying while explaining that she and her professor had had a major argument over a final exam that she had taken. She admitted that she very rudely confronted him about his marking a couple of her answers as "wrong"—and he failed her. She continued crying as she shared with me that what upset her the most was the fact that while she was treating the professor so rudely, she was strongly conscious of the fact that she sounded exactly like her mother! She felt as if her Mother was inside of her! I encouraged her, saying that when she came for her next appointment, we would trust the Lord to reveal the problem and solve it for us.

At our next appointment, I asked the Lord to bring up the personality or demon that was so rude to the professor—and up came a "haughty woman" who said her name was "Jane" and she was 52 years old. Since Sue was only 27 years old, I knew it had to be a demon. I asked, "Demon, what are you doing in Sue's life?" The demon-woman, Jane, answered, "I am not a demon! I'm Sue's mother!" I asked again, "What is your purpose in Sue's life?" "Jane" answered, "I am here to protect her! She's a weak person and I am strong! I won't put up with any man who is like her professor!"

Over the years, I have dealt with numerous demon-produced personalities in the lives of counselees.

DEMON-CLONES OF CORE, FLIP-SIDE, OR WOUNDED PERSONALITIES

Demon-clones are **demons fashioned by the ancestral demon as clones—copies—of the core, flip-side, or wounded personalities**, which as you can imagine, can cause much confusion! **Keep in mind that the ancestral demon can even clone himself!** The demon-clone typically either works for the ancestral demon or another demon in his network, on the dark side of the duplex. These clones hide behind masks of deception! A demon-clone typically speaks as if he really thinks he is a personality—the real wounded personality of which he is an actual copy. Demon-clones have been programmed by the ancestral demon to really think they are personalities. In reality, they have been programmed like a robot!

Perhaps we can clarify further what a demon-clone is by illustrating him as a "file folder." Let us say that a child wanted to have friends very badly but repeatedly was rejected, thus a wounded part named "Lonely Wounded Personality" was created on the dark-side. Then, as time went on, when the core suffered rejection by another person, the power demon—the boss in the system—formed a **"file folder with a tab titled "Demon-Lonely-Clone."** Then, as time marched on, each time the person suffered another painful rejection and another wounded personality was created, and not unlike using a copy machine—a copy was made of that additional wounded personality and was placed inside the Demon-Lonely-Clone's file folder. This single Demon-Lonely-Clone can have a large number of copies inside his file, and there can be other demon-clones—file folders—carrying other negatives, such as "fear".

While demon-clones can come about through the core's experiencing various painful experiences, they can also be welcomed in by the core's dabbling in occult practices and/or his ancestral demon holding generational iniquity connected to the occult and sorcery. In such cases, there may be a file folder with the title on the tab reading, "Demon-clone Rituals." If the core or someone in his direct family line made a pact with Satan there is a good chance a demon-produced personality (or demon-clone) will be there, for it can flow down generationally as a curse. As I shared before, it has the legal right to do this if the core or family members gave them ground by practicing witchcraft, divination or any occult rituals. This demon will be very powerful and will seek to block progress by casting doubt at the core or wounded personalities concerning the truth of God's Word. Without a doubt, deception against God's truths is a tool that demon-produced personalities and demon-clones use against the core.

With hope of lessening the chances of being discovered, some demon-clones portray themselves as "one of the good guys." These demons cannot be saved, for they already had their chance to choose to be on the Lord's side while dwelling in heaven! Without a doubt, we will never find one displaying any repentance! **You can be sure that during counseling the Lord will expose the truth about demon-produced personalities and demon-clones, so there is no reason to be discouraged or fearful concerning them! The Lord will provide!**

SPECIALIZED, CUSTOMIZED DEMON-CLONES
FOR FUTURE DEVELOPMENT

Specialized, customized, demon-clones for future development are different. In the year 2005, I had my first encounter with a "specialized" or "customized" demon-clone. I learned that the ancestral demon forms this type of clone very early in a core personality's life but keeps it a secret for years—hidden away for very special assignments in the future. When the Lord exposed this truth to me and taught me how to deal with them, I realized that I had encountered such before. The Lord had shown mercy to the counselee and me by allowing us to attach the specialized, customized demon-clones to the ancestral demon with blood-links that could not be broken, made of the blood Jesus shed on Calvary, and send them out! After learning of them, I began discovering more of them and more readily recognized them.

Without a doubt, the evil demonic beings can certainly be enormous hindrances in various ways in this life, but we cannot point our fingers at them and declare, "The Devil made me do it!" The problem lies with people choosing of their own accord to listen to and heed the Devil's suggestions! Therefore, they are hindered by their own wrongful choices. We can certainly attest to the fact that in the midst of counseling, some counselees can make some wrong choices that hinder the counseling procedures! Let me be quick to say that for some counselees who have suffered severe abuse—their battle is not only with external temptation, with which everyone contends, but the enemy has a stronghold that battles with them internally—luring them away from God's will. **This brings me to share an example of a precious counselee who had an ancestral demon with a customized demon-clone programmed for future development—with a special assignment—in his network:**

EXAMPLE #2 - DEMON-CLONE OF THE OPPOSITE SEX

A very precious brother-in-Christ who was a senior pastor of a church had suddenly found himself stepping into an arena of temptation and sin, which actually came as a great shock to him! Like so many other Christians, he was surely not a perfect man or pastor, but he did love the Lord and desired to walk in His will. **It was if he was seeking to stay on the straight and narrow path and suddenly tripped over a big, invisible log!** While counseling him, I learned that this **big, invisible log** was a **specialized, customized demon-clone that was programmed for future development!** The "log" turned out to be that of the opposite sex—a **"woman-demon-clone carrying a family name."** When the woman-demon-clone told me the human name she called herself, it was the name of a relative of this man—an ancestor! However, I have chosen to use the name "woman-demon-clone" which will serve better to teach you the difference between other demon-clones, such as "a demon-clone of a real person" and other "demon-clones that do not stay hidden until a specific point in time." This dear brother reported during counseling that over the course of a year, the woman-demon-clone had been tormenting him—clearly desiring control of his life as she kept pointing out good looking men to him. The battle had intensified to such heights of torment that he longed to be able to talk with some Christian brothers who might be able to help him, but he didn't have confidence that any Christian brothers he knew—nor his friends—would understand and be able to help him. Bombarded constantly with the tempting torments of the "woman-demon-clone," his flesh and spiritual strength declined to such a degree that he "tripped over that invisible log"—and found himself snared—in a police sting operation! The woman-demon-clone did not succeed in leading him to actually become involved with a man, but she certainly succeeded in laying across the pathway like a log and causing him to fall into a trap!

I am so very happy to be able to share that when my dear brother was brought before the magistrates, he heard the wonderful words, "No bill!" Grievously, however, he was not forgiven—not found as a "No bill!"—by a very large number of his Christian brothers and sisters. A happy ending came to his story in spite of that! What saved him from self-destructing was knowing that God loved him (and his dear wife), and out of his sincere love for God, he didn't hide and he didn't run! Instead, he snuggled up to Jesus, trusting that He would provide help in his time of need. The Lord did, indeed, provide all of his needs. For when he came to me for counseling, he was soon released from the trap inspired many years before by Satan! When this dear man was nine years old, he was molested by a male cousin. And, I discovered a nine-year-old "little girl." She reported that she saw herself as a girl—felt like a gentle, small little girl. She said she was very lonely and wanted somebody to like her.

As it turned out, this **"little-girl-demon-clone"** stayed in the background as the man grew to manhood, but in the mean time, she was aging also—thus, grew up to be the **"woman-demon-clone"**—who had suddenly become aggressive, desiring to control the core's life. She reported that she just wanted to be a part of the core's life but that he steadily fought against her. She said that she kept telling him that she could make him happy—while pointing out very handsome, masculine men. She was clearly very determined, yet said that she could wait. Indeed she had already demonstrated that when she waited "for a more opportune time!" **Upon interrogating the ancestral demon, he confessed that the "woman-demon-clone" was "a specialized, customized demon-clone programmed for future development!"**

While the "woman-demon-clone" did not achieve all the goals that she anticipated, she did manage to serve as that log! She even declared that she was happy about the police sting operation for she felt a little freedom in the midst of that experience! Her freedom was short lived though! What joy it is to know that the Lord set our precious brother free and not only restored his soul, but the Lord restored his hope—his self-worth in Christ that he was most surely not a throwaway! Indeed, the Lord is using him in awesome ways through his God-given talent of writing, as well as teaching God's Living Word and ministering to others out on the highways and byways of life—leading them to walk upon our Lord's straight and narrow pathway!

Now, I will share a testimony from a dear lady whom I counseled who also had a demon-clone, programmed for future development—a special assignment.

EXAMPLE #3 - TESTIMONY OF A CRYING CLONE

"After working with someone else who used the methods Dr. Joe Allbright taught in his book, *'Liberating the Bruised,'* off and on for about six years, the Lord did much healing and deliverance during that time, restoring my soul in stages. Later, I went to Dr. Allbright's May 2006 workshop, during which the Lord showed me that there were still some problems in my life that needed to be addressed. The Lord did more of His mighty work when I went to Dr. Allbright in November 2006 and I was finally delivered of the ancestral demon that bore my full formal name. Other things were dealt with as well, including a 37-year period of off-and-on depression which led to suicidal ideation, medication, and one hospitalization with a suicide watch. I was able to go off—and stay off—the antidepressant I had been on (and unable to successfully stop despite numerous attempts) the past three and a half years, and which I once took every fall for seasonal affective disorder depression. I went home and did my once a week, 6-week phone follow-up with Dr. Allbright.

"Even though I knew I was no longer depressed, there were times when I suddenly would be overcome with a feeling of deep, tremendous sadness that caused me to cry over and over for long periods of time. There was never any rhyme or reason to it. It very frequently was not related to anything in particular, coming out of nowhere, even in the midst of being happy over something. It was happening quite often, and I was even thinking about going back on my antidepressant even though I knew I wasn't depressed. I just didn't know what else to do because I'd cried out to the Lord and the problem wasn't going away."

"I'd mentioned this problem to my pastor and to my prayer partner, telling them that I was absolutely sick to death of crying like this because it had gone on for more years than I could remember. Both of them said, "Well, you know tears are cleansing," not knowing what else to say besides that they would pray for me. I'd heard that for years—and even said it to others when they would cry. I angrily replied to them both, 'I am so sick of hearing that! I don't ever want to hear that again or to say that again to anyone who is in this type of pain and crying like this!'"

"Right before the 6-week follow-up period was over, I mentioned the long-term problem to Dr. Allbright that I'd been having, which we thought had been dealt with in our counseling sessions together. As he asked me questions, I revealed to him that I'd been crying like this since I went into my first major depression at age 15 when I'd left my 'first love' and had to move away because my father came back from Vietnam and we got relocated. The Lord had revealed during one of my sessions with the other counselor that I had fragmented at that time. The Lord dealt with that fragment during that time."

"Dr. Allbright had gone through all his usual procedures, but he then instructed me to ask the Lord about there possibly being a special demon-clone assigned to me at that fragmentation time of 15 years old, which was doing all the crying, holding all my tears. He also taught me how to deal with it in prayer with the Lord. I did as Dr. Allbright instructed. It only took a few minutes. I didn't "feel" anything or hear anything from the Lord at that time, but I just went about my day after that as I'd planned. Later on that afternoon, I felt that sadness coming on again, but I took my authority in Christ and shut it down. That was the last time I even remotely felt it. It has never returned. I have since cried over other things. But, my crying now is "normal" crying, short-lived and always related to a particular present-tense event—unlike the "clone" crying which was so deep, gut wrenching, and often unrelated to anything."

"I am so grateful to the Lord for bringing the people into my life through which He was able to restore my soul! I am so grateful to Dr. Allbright and those others for their obedience and availability to the Lord! I continue to be amazed at how quickly I have grown and changed since the Lord did the work of getting rid of the birth ancestral demon. **I truly am that metamorphosed butterfly who will NEVER be the same!**"

Now I am going to share an example of a demon-produced or demon-clone personality which reflects a portion of a counseling format:

EXAMPLE #4 - DEMON-PRODUCED OR CLONED PERSONALITY
DEE INFINITY, AGE 2 TO 54

Joe: Lord Jesus, I want to talk with the wounded or cloned personality who calls herself "Dee Infinity" and says she is age 2 to 54, and also claims to be connected with sexual experiences and actual sexual acts that occurred at approximately 2:00 and 4:00 a.m. each morning—which are caused by demons or Satan himself. Lord Jesus, I want this one to come up and talk to me.

Dee: I second guess everything I do. I'm full of guilt, inadequacy, inferiority, insecurity, and I can't do it right. I'm all the different kinds of mothers to all my children. I am unclean feelings, dirty feelings—have the need to please men. I carry the program of sexual desire and lead her to feel she must let men manipulate her.

Joe: What else do you do or carry in the core personality's life?

Dee: I knock her out. (It literally makes her pass out.) I'm her cause to fear men, fear failure! I cause her to get lost and to lose her stuff. I speak to her mind and I tell her things.

Joe: What things do you tell her?

Dee: I remind her of her past. I tell her that everybody is sick of her. I keep the wounded parts from integrating. She goes to get help and it doesn't help because I won't let her believe that it helped and she believes me because I am in her. She looks like an idiot. Everybody thinks she's a crazy woman and that she must love this state of mind.

143

Joe: What is your right or authority to hold her?

Dee: Fear. I give her the thoughts and feelings that she will never be better. I make men attracted to her and she really gets scared. I play with her mind. She says that she is not sexual, but I make her sexual. I tell her that there is no person without sexual desires unless they are perverts like her. I flash thoughts in her mind and make her think that they are her own thoughts.

Joe: When did you start all this… in her childhood… When?

Dee: At her age two. I messed up her children, too! I cursed them with despair, depression, rage and anger.   I am her life. I know how to make her emotions. I cause her to think she is losing it. I am her mind that causes her to self-destruct. I give her thoughts in her mind that are based on truth and she believes they are her own thoughts. I am the ground that allows all her demons to stay like it's real wounded ground. I give all the ground for Satan and his demons to have sex with her.

Joe: What is your connection with Dee and where she lives?

Dee: I don't care where she lives. I will be there wherever she lives.

Joe: What is your ground or authority to stay in Dee's life?

Dee: Because that is who she is! Confusion…losing things…getting tossed in all directions. I tell her she can't handle it or deal with it. And, she's confident that she doesn't have anybody and everybody is sick of her! I isolate her because I don't want to make Satan or his demons mad!

Joe: By the authority of Jesus Christ and His blood, I command Ancestral Demon Dee Sue Harris to stand before the eternal throne of the Lord Jesus Christ where only truth can stand and tell me what this Dee Infinity, age 2-to-54 years old, Dee Infinity is.

AD: Dee Infinity is a cloned personality that is programmed for future development but it stands like human wounded ground. It provides the ground for me to stand on and stay on, and I am going nowhere!

We are ever so happy and grateful to be able to say that this precious sister in the Lord was set free and is now a very strong, beautiful instrument of the Lord whom she so dearly loves. Clearly, out of her great love, gratitude and trust, she serves her Jesus consistently in willing obedience! She's a wonderful missionary in God's fields!

EXAMPLE #5, DEMON-CLONE WITH MIND-SET AND INHERITED CURSE

A very delightful Christian lady came for counseling. She was married to a dear Christian man and they had several precious teenagers. It didn't take us long at all to learn that this sweet lady was very intelligent—and she was a very pretty lady who most definitely did not have a weight problem at all! However, as I use this particular portion of her counseling experience as a good illustration of a demon-clone with a mind-set, you will soon learn that the enemy had certainly aggressively attained ground and continually fed her lies and controlled her thoughts! I have changed all the names to protect this precious sister, and I will call her "Jodie Irene (Ignoramus) Walker".

When I contacted a demon-clone, she said, "My name is Penny! I'm a shiny penny! I want to be noticed!" While interviewing her, she reported that a lot of bad stuff flowed down on the father's side of the core's family. She boasted, "I'm a demon-clone with a mind-set that came in through Oscar and Jessie." I learned that she did not like the family name—her maiden name "Ignoramus"—because it implied ignorance. I also found that the core had changed her name to Monroe—an alias. She shared that she changed her name to fictitious ones a number of times. This provided a clue and I soon learned that "Oscar Ignoramus" was where the family curse began and had been passed down through the family. He had most surely taken up residence in this precious lady's life and carried her formal name "Jodie Irene (Ignoramus) Walker".

Penny then sadly added that after Jodie accepted the Lord as her Savior when she was in her twenties, it had become harder for her to control Jodie's thoughts, for she had begun arguing with her—thoughts between the two were clashing! Penny added that she did enjoy getting Jodie to argue with her children—making her feel that she had to be right, not them! Penny continued to reveal how strong her control was over Jodie's thought processes! **Jodie reflected her mind-set when she said:** *"I am complicated and so messed up that no one can figure me out. I can't do anything well. I have no gifts or talents. I am not smart. I am always falling down because I am accident prone. I am lazy and selfish. I am fat and ugly. People don't like me. I am alone. I am a prisoner in my own house. People don't respect me, especially my children. I carry sickness and migraine headaches. I am not a sexual person—I don't need sex. I don't like sex. If I were smart, God would be using me to minister somewhere. I will embarrass myself if I talk in a group. People are rolling their eyes behind my back, and no one takes me seriously. The demons will leave everyone else but me and I am passing them on to my children. The demons have left and come back so many times now that I don't know what is true anymore."*

Jodie had learned of biblical teachings about spiritual warfare—that through Jesus Christ, she could receive victory over this wicked, condemning mind-set. She became determined to trust the Lord that He would enable her to defeat the thoughts that were so aggressively condemning her. When I was dealing with the ancestral demon carrying her formal name, he boasted, "Jodie wants to be free but you can't get rid of me or the demon-clone mind-set Penny, because Jodie is so visual that she sees our roots go down deeply inside her and when efforts are made to pull us out, she always sees the roots snapping off!"

We are so happy, knowing the ancestral demon and his network, including Penny, the demon-clone with the mind-set, were pulled out by the roots by our Lord Jesus Christ! Our precious sister Jodie Irene walks in victory with *"power, love and a sound mind."* She is a beautiful instrument of the Lord, telling others that He definitely sets Satan's captives free!

Please note that in future chapters, I will share counseling procedures concerning the core, flip-side, wounded parts, and categories of demons, including demon-clones and mind-sets. Pertaining to mind-sets, sometimes they can be detected through reviewing the counseling form, during the first counseling session, or while interrogating the ancestral demon before sending him out. Concerning the demon-clones, while you may find them while working, it's more typical to find them upon the ancestral demon's refusing to leave, which exposes his ground by way of the clone!

In the next chapter, you will find some helpful, practical tools that have helped me immensely in ministering to counselees, and I hope they help you as well!

Chapter Five
REQUIRED TOOLS OF PRACTICALITY

Upon learning the requirements I ask of a counselee before I agree to counsel him, some ministers and counselors have told me that they think the preparation time spent to lay so much ground work takes too long for both the counselor and the counselee. They've asked: "Why don't you meet with the counselee and just ask God to direct you while you're moving along during the sessions?" Dear ones, I am now 74 in this year 2010, and over the many years, the Lord has grown me up from a spiritual babe to maturity, teaching me rich lessons as I cried out in desperation to learn from Him in order to help people. I believe with all my heart that the "preparation lessons" He taught me have proven to more wisely use God's time and eliminate much confusion. Two things that the Lord has taught me, which we should all remember, is the fact that our Lord is both **a God of miracles** and **a God of practicality**! There were times when He deemed it right to **work a miracle**, and other times when He displayed plain and simple—**practicality**! **God has not changed!**

The Lord has shown me that what's **missing in the lives of all too many Christians today is "practicality"—they just want miracles!** They lack patience and want everything to come quick and easy! Many even command God, "by faith," in Jesus' name to just zap everything instantly into being okay, for themselves as well as on behalf of others! While that sounds nice and easy—I've seen proven so many times that our all-wise, practical heavenly Father does not zap everything all-better upon command of His children! We live in a world full of people, including all too many Christians, with "I want it now!" attitudes! They are in high gear and most surely don't want to sacrifice time and energy—especially concerning helping a counselee face and deal with some past, painful ordeals in his life. Some counselors, in hopes of "getting the job done quickly," have fallen into error by "naming and claiming" while using "selective choices of scripture." Too many have deliberately selected the passage found in John 14:14: *"If you ask anything in My name, I will do it."* They have asked and declared: "By faith, be free! Be healed!" They error by skipping over verse 13, which reads: *"...whatever you ask in My name, that I will do, **that the Father may be glorified in the Son."*** In doing so, they are a stumbling block to souls, hindering their achievement of freedom. We further read of how we are to desire that God's will be done, as we read I John 5:14-15, which clearly states: *"Now this is the confidence that we have in Him, that if we ask anything **according to His will**, He hears us. And if we know that He hears us, whatever we ask, we know that we have the petitions that we have asked of Him."* We should take great care to fully trust that He has pure, good reason for not giving us "what we <u>want</u> because <u>we</u> think its right!" It brings glory to the heavenly Father when His child seeks and willingly submits to His will. All too often well-meaning Christians ask for "favors" that are truly not in the will of God. **Oh that all Christians would willingly pray to Him, "Thy will be done, precious Lord!"**

How wonderful it would be if all God's precious children would realize and accept the fact that He most surely deems it necessary for each individual to "be practical" and to "be real" with Him! **"Honesty's the best policy!"** He urges souls to come before Him honestly and deal with their sins—including forgiving those who have trespassed against them! He deems it necessary that they spend time with Him, deal with the "known" sins in their lives, and repent. Only then can they find complete freedom from the unknowns that cunningly manipulate and control them from within. **Just as you cannot get saved for another person, neither can you claim his freedom for him from the enemy.** How thankful I am that He gives wisdom to willing servants in ministry, counselors and others, so that they can lead souls to Him, and to their freedom! It is without doubt that I know this tool is a very practical tool to use in that endeavor. **I know that it was given to me by my practical Creator—our Master Carpenter! He indeed, shares the best tools!**

I am very happy to say that a goodly number of counselees have shared that while they were taking time to fulfill my requirements, their hearts were blessed when "known" sins were brought to the forefront, and that they were able to deal with them! They found help as they read in "Liberating the Bruised," the fifth chapter, "Restoring True Worship," which thoroughly addresses the issue of known sins. As the readers faced these realities, they came under conviction that they needed to confess their sins before the Lord, and then they were even more encouraged and desperate to get on with dealing with the unknowns that were hindering them from having peace and joy. They began to eagerly look forward to finding God's way of escape from the stronghold and torments of the enemy!

There have even been some people who worked through their "unknown issues" privately and found freedom—just between the Lord and them! They did not even have to come for counseling! What joy it is to know that precious souls can work through this practical process and learn that they can stand strong in their Savior, resist the devil and make him flee! Most assuredly, souls can find freedom, peace and joy through Jesus Christ!

When Jesus had a boat, He rode in it. When He didn't, He walked on the water. When there were multitudes of hungry people, He used what was available—He multiplied a small amount of bread and fishes and provided food for them all! The Lord repeatedly shows us that He is a very practical God. He so often requires that we look around and use what's available to us. You remember reading when Jesus was being pressed by a large crowd, He stepped into Peter's fishing boat and told Peter to go out a little distance from shore so He could use the boat as a podium from which to preach. He actually could have just walked out on the water and stood there. He didn't have to use a fishing boat, which probably had the strong smell of fish, but He chose to use it! How grateful I am that the Lord gave me wonderful, practical tools so I don't have to "fly by the seat of my pants" to accomplish His will! I do know without doubt that the Lord blessed me with these tools which have proven over and over again to be power-tools! I would shudder to think of counseling without them! I'm happy to be able to share the following practical tools in hopes of helping your counseling sessions go more smoothly as you experience the joy of helping counselees obtain their freedom!

A.   TOOL #1: RECOGNITION OF BEING CONSISTENTLY INCONSISTENT

One of the questions that come up so often in workshops is, "When does a person need this type of counseling?"   One of my answers is that **when a person recognizes that he is consistently inconsistent.** I ask the person seeking counseling if he realizes that no matter how much he reads God's Word, goes for traditional Christian counseling, and tries to obey Him, something from within hinders him from consistently obeying the Lord. I ask him if he gets up in the morning with every intention of pleasing the Lord, yet he feels anxiousness inside, driving him, like "a dog that is always very eager to go hunting!"   When he acknowledges that his urges are like that—urges so strong that he feels he must charge on in spite of wanting to stop, and when he adds that he can't stop in spite of knowing that he, and perhaps others, will suffer consequences at the end of the run, then it is evident that he needs and is ready for this type of counseling!

B.   TOOL #2: DESPERATION FOR GOD TO RESCUE AND CHANGE THEM

It is wonderful when a person has faced the reality that he is **consistently inconsistent** and he has become sick and tired of his present state and longs for and agrees to receive biblical counseling that includes spiritual warfare!   **The greatest attitude a person in bondage can have is that of desperation for God to rescue him from his inconsistencies, from Satan's strongholds!**

C.   TOOL #3: REQUIREMENTS BEFORE RECEIVING COUNSELING

In order to be very wise with the counselor and counselee's time, the counselee must be willing to study God's teachings concerning spiritual warfare which reflect the type of counseling he will be receiving. He must fulfill the following before receiving counseling:

1.   Read Joe E. Allbright's book, "Liberating the Bruised."
2.   In addition to reading "Liberating the Bruised," do **one** of the following:
    a)   Listen to the set of five "Counseling the Bruised" CDs of Joe talking about additional helps that the Lord taught him after writing "Liberating the Bruised," while reviewing the syllabus containing materials and illustrations discussed on the CDs.
    b)   Read "More Tools for Liberating the Bruised."

D.   TOOL #4: AGREE WITH AND SIGN MINISTRY'S COVER PAGE

After the counselee has (1) read my ministry's cover page, he must sign it, stating that he is fully aware of and agrees with the type of counseling he is to receive from my ministry. And (2) he must fill out my counseling form to give me detailed background information about himself and his family so that I am better equipped to help him. I encourage him to answer the questions like he would answer God—be honest for his own sake! I explain that with his filling out the form ahead of time, it will spare us both from having to spend an enormous amount of face-to-face time to gather the information directly from him. I explain to him that I will spend much time reviewing his form and making notations so that I can determine how much one-on-one time I will need to schedule for him. I assure you that by having this accomplished ahead of time, in the majority of cases the average individual is led to freedom within two days of counseling 9:00 a.m. to 6:00 p.m. each day! Those who have been severely abused, such as victims of Satanic Ritual Abuse, take longer, but for those who are desperate, total freedom can be theirs also!

Now I will share a copy of the **cover page** and the **counseling form** that I use. You are welcome to use the cover page as a guide to customize and set for your own ministry, and you may also use the information on the counseling form to create your own.

SAMPLE COPY OF OUR MINISTRY'S COVER PAGE

INSTRUCTIONS FOR FILLING OUT THE CONFIDENTIAL PERSONAL INVENTORY

1. **As you share your heart on the following pages, the "Joe E. Allbright Evangelistic Assoc., Inc." assures you of confidentiality**—both with this inventory form and all the information that you share during your counseling sessions—unless, however, you indicate clearly to us that the state you are in is a serious threat to your own life or the lives of others. Following your last session, after you have reported in to Joe once a week for six weeks and he sees that you are still walking in complete freedom, this inventory form and all notes taken in your sessions will be destroyed to protect your reputation.

2. **This is a Christian ministry.** Joe is an ordained minister, with his doctorate in biblical counseling, and he is also a Certified Christian Counselor and Certified Clinical Therapist. He is not a psychologist or psychiatrist, and does not use hypnosis. Counseling sessions are usually scheduled for two full days per person, from 9 a.m. to 6 p.m. each day. When Joe is counseling a woman, it is our strict rule that Joe's wife, Rita, will be present in our home/office, to protect everyone's reputation—our "good names." Love offerings are what supports this ministry and make it available at no charge. While love offerings are very gratefully accepted, they are not required for your counseling sessions.

3. If you are a married woman, we prefer that you have your husband's approval and blessing for Joe to counsel you. If you are still living at home under your parent's authority, we require their approval and blessing for us to minister to you.

4. **For your own sake, we request full disclosure and complete honesty as you fill out this inventory form.** Be sure to note all incidents from your past that have produced trauma, great disappointment, or hurt. If we are unable to deal with situations in detail, and with

complete honesty, the results will not be satisfactory and will be harmful in the long run. So, please do your best to answer each question that applies to you. **Please take care to fill out the form legibly in black ink and in your own handwriting. This is very important, for even changes in one's handwriting at times can prove to be very helpful during counseling.**

5. Jesus Christ gave His life on Calvary for our freedom! However, our ability to walk in the freedom He intended, and have peace and joy in our hearts, depends on our willingness to surrender every area of our life to Him (including wounds from the past). **True freedom** is not the freedom to do what we want, when we want. **True Freedom** is the ability to bring every area of our life under the direction and control of Jesus Christ. **The purpose of this questionnaire is to help you identify unsurrendered areas of your life that are keeping you from walking in the freedom that God has intended for you.**

6. **Satan is the common enemy of God and His children, and Christians are not exempt from his abuse.** Satan and his demons oppose Christians' freedom to walk in God's will for their lives. Satan will not easily give up any strongholds or areas of oppression that he claims in your life. Since the garden of Eden, Satan has been attacking mankind in an attempt to "get back at" God for kicking him out of heaven when he chose to rebel. Therefore, he tries to fill you with doubt and confusion about gaining freedom from your bondage. However, Joel 2:32 promises that **Christ is our Deliverer,** *"And it shall come to pass, that whosoever shall call on the name of the Lord shall be delivered.* Throughout your counseling time, you must depend on Christ as your Deliverer and recognize that He is the only One who can help you. Your counseling time with Joe requires Christ alone working through us, to set you free.

7. Because of the enemy's opposition to your complete freedom, ask yourself this question, **"Am I really desperate to be free?"** Experience has proven that liberation is for the desperate! Therefore, if you are not desperate, it would be a waste of your precious time and the person's time who is counseling with you. If you truly want freedom, you must predetermine that you will do whatever it takes and stick with the discipleship required until you have the complete freedom that God intends for you. **We urge you not to stop halfway with your counseling, for if you do, that will allow the enemy to increase your bondage. You will be worse off than before. (Luke 11:26)**

8. Since **forgiveness of those who have sinned against you is one of the greatest weapons in bringing about liberation**, we ask that you be willing to let the Lord enable you to forgive those who have wronged you. The purpose of forgiveness is to remove Satan's right to justly accuse and oppress you in these areas.

9. **For your own sake, there are three essential requirements for you to fill before your first counseling session: 1)** Fill out this form thoroughly and return it to Joe as soon as possible so that he can review it and determine if you need 2, 3, or 4 days of counseling.

After he receives your form and reviews it, he will telephone you to schedule your appointments. **2)** In order to be wise with time, please read Joe's book, "Liberating the Bruised." **3)** In addition to that, please, **either** read that book's partnering book "More Tools for Liberating the Bruised" which shares additional biblical helps that the Lord has taught him since writing the first book. The new book contains extensive counseling procedures, sample prayers for various subjects and many related biblically founded studies. **Or** in addition to reading the first book, you may listen to his set of five "Counseling the Bruised" CDs and review the accompanying syllabus with materials and illustrations which contain highlights of "More Tools for Liberating the Bruised." As you prayerfully study these materials, ask the Lord to help you work on as many things as possible before you come. You are encouraged to deal with as many of the "known" issues that you are aware of before your first counseling session. This will leave us more time to deal specifically with the "unknowns".

10. **Please pray** while filling out this form, asking the Holy Spirit to guide you and bring key things to your mind. He is your Helper, "<u>The</u> Wonderful Counselor," and will help you expose the darkness with His truth. For your own sake, please answer these questions as you would answer God Himself! And, on the last page, please add any pertinent information about your background and problems that you think might be helpful. **Please pray** for the Lord to give Joe and you wisdom during your sessions, to bring about your freedom from Satan's bondage.

I have read the above instructions and agree to fully comply:

          (Name)   (Date)

E.   TOOL #5: FILL OUT THE "CONFIDENTIAL PERSONAL INVENTORY"

The counselee must filled out the **"Confidential Personal Inventory" form. In the interested of time, I usually refer to it as the "counseling form" or the "inventory form" while some people call it the "CPI."** This marvelous tool will give me an enormous amount of vital information. While I have included it in this book, in order to wisely utilize space, it will not include all of the many lines and spaces that appear in it (18 legal size pages with very small print). I believe as you study the various critical details, you will agree that it will be of great help to you in your ministry! Most surely, for me, it has proven to be a powerful, God-given tool in achieving the freedom God desires for His people!

CONFIDENTIAL PERSONAL INVENTORY

PERSONAL INFORMATION

Please print your full name as shown on birth certificate, and if you are a married or divorced woman, add married name, please.

Date of birth: _____ Place of birth: _____
Mailing address: _____ Telephone(s): _____ Email Address: _____
Referred by: _____
Church affiliation (present; past): _____
Vocation: _____ Place of employment: _____
Education:
 From elementary through high school, highest grade completed: _____
 College education; degrees: _____ Other education/job training: _____
Please check marital status: Single _____ Married _____ Divorced _____
Spouse's name (if married, spouse's full name; if spouse is the wife, please include her
 Maiden name): _____
Date of marriage: _____
Contact info for spouse if different from yours; their work phone; place of employment: _____
If you are divorced, state number of times divorced: _____
Pertaining to your ex-spouse/s, please list their names, date of marriage and date of divorce, and
 please include maiden name/s of wife/wives:
Children: (Please print full names on birth certificates and birth dates, and indicate if adopted and if
yes please give biological name of father and mother if possible): _____

FAMILY TREE

(Please print your full name **again** as shown on birth certificate, and if you are a married or divorced woman, add married name.) _____

To your knowledge were you a "planned" child? _____
Were you conceived out of wedlock? _____
Are you adopted? _____ If yes, please fill out the following information based on your biological
 parents if possible.
To your knowledge, did you have a difficult, complicated, or traumatic birth? _____ If yes, explain:

SIBLINGS

List all of your siblings in the order of their birth, including their birth dates.

BIOLOGICAL PARENTS

INFORMATION ON BIOLOGICAL FATHER'S SIDE Father's full name	**INFORMATION ON BIOLOGICAL MOTHER'S SIDE** Mother's full name
GRANDPARENTS Grandfather's full name Grandmother's full name	**GRANDPARENTS** Grandfather's full name Grandmother's full name
GREAT-GRANDPARENTS Great-grandfather's full name Great-grandmother's full name	**GREAT-GRANDPARENTS** Great-grandfather's full name Great-grandmother's full name
GRANDMOTHER'S PARENTS Great-grandfather's full name Great-grandmother's full name	**GRANDMOTHER'S PARENTS** Great-grandfather's full name Great-grandmother's full name

Below, please list any of the above persons who have/had any negative character traits, or harmful, sinful lifestyle patterns (i.e., independence from or indifference toward God; idolatry, witchcraft, Satanism, immorality, sexual sins, perversions, greed, anger, jealousy, drunkenness, addictions, abusive speech, gossip, bitterness, unforgiveness, etc.). Such information might be helpful in pointing out possible strongholds that could have been passed down in your family as iniquity to the third and fourth generations.

INFORMATION ON FAMILY MEMBERS

1. Is your father living?
2. Is your mother living?
3. Are your parents presently married or divorced? _____ Briefly explain the attitude of their relationship:
4. Was your father clearly the head of the home, or was there a role reversal in which your mother ruled the home? _____ Please explain:
5. Do you have any step-brothers: _____ Do you have any step-sisters? _____ If yes, what was your relationship with them while growing up, and what is your relationship with them now? _____ Please explain:
6. During the first 12 years of your life, was there a sense of security and harmony or insecurity and disharmony in your home? _____ Please explain:
7. Were there any particular problems with your father? _____ With your mother? _____ With your brother/s and sister/s? _____ If yes, please explain:

8. Below, please check the appropriate rating for the moral atmosphere in which you were raised during the first 18 years of your life:

	Overly Permissive	Permissive	Average	Strict	Overly Strict
Clothing					
Sex					
Dating					
Movies					
Music					
Literature					
Freewill					
Drinking					.
Smoking					
Church Attendance					

9. How does/did your father treat your mother?
10. How does/did your mother treat your father?
11. Would you consider your father as passive, strong and manipulative, or neither?
12. Would you consider your father to be a perfectionist? Did he seek perfectionism from you?
13. Do you struggle with honoring your father? _____ If yes, why?
14. Would you consider your father to be your friend?
15. Briefly describe your relationship with your father:
16. Would you consider your mother as passive, strong and manipulative, or neither?
17. Would you consider your mother to be a perfectionist? _____ Did your mother seek perfectionism from you?
18. Do you struggle with honoring your mother? _____ If yes, why?
19. Would you consider your mother to be your friend?
20. Briefly describe your relationship with your mother:
21. How would you describe your family's financial situation when you were a child?
    Poor _____ Slight financial struggles _____ Moderate income _____ Affluent _____
22. Briefly explain whether or not your parents are Christians and, if yes, whether or not their lifestyles measured up to Christ-like behaviors:

FAMILY AND PERSONAL HEALTH

1.   Are there any addictive problems in your family (alcohol, drugs, etc.)? ____ If yes, please explain:

2.   Is there any history of mental illness in your family? ___ If yes, please explain:

3.   If there is any history of the following ailments in your family, please place a check beside the ailment:

_____	Tuberculosis (TB)	_____	Heart disease	_____	Diabetes
_____	Glandular problems	_____	Cancer	_____	Ulcers
_____	Thyroid	_____	List others:		

4.   Please describe your parents' concern for the following:
      a. Diet _____   b. Exercise _____   C. Rest _____

5.   Describe your eating habits (i.e. junk food addict, eat fairly regularly or sporadically, balanced diet, serious disorders, etc.):

6.   Do you have any addictions or cravings that you find difficult to control (tobacco, drugs, alcohol, sweets, food in general, etc.)? _____ If yes, please explain:

7.   Are you presently taking any kind of medication for physical and/or psychological reasons? If yes, please list each medication and explain its purpose:

8.   Do you have any problem sleeping? _____ Are you having nightmares or disturbances? If yes, please explain:

9.   Does your present schedule allow for regular periods of rest and relaxation? _____ Please explain:

RELATIONSHIP WITH SPOUSE

1.   If married, do you love your spouse?

2.   If a husband, do you demonstrate your love for your wife with kind deeds and loving her sacrificially like Christ loves the Church? (Ephesians 5:21-33; I Corinthians 13)

3.   If a wife, do you demonstrate your love for him with kind deeds, and showing him respect, obedience, and submission? (I Peter 3:1-6; Ephesians 5:21-33; I Corinthians 13)

4.   Please share how you get along with your spouse:

5.   Is your spouse a Christian?

6.   Do you and your spouse have a good, healthy sexual relationship together?

EMOTIONS

1.   Do you have trouble giving and receiving love?

2.   **State** below, under **"Earliest Age"** the **earliest age** you remember experiencing difficulty in **controlling any of the following emotions** and **check** under **"Present"** if you still struggle with controlling those emotions:

156

	Earliest Age / Present		Earliest Age / Present
Frustration	/	Bitterness	/
Anger	/	Depression	/
Anxiety	/	Fear of Losing your mind	/
Loneliness	/	Fear Committing Suicide	/
Worthlessness	/	Fear Hurting Loved Ones	/
Hatred (for self)	/	Fear of Death	/
Hatred (for others)	/	Fear of _____	/

3. Name the above emotions that you feel are sinful and explain why:

4. Have you ever thought that perhaps you were "cracking up"? _____ If yes, have you feared "cracking up"—"going crazy"—recently? _____ Please explain:

5. Concerning your emotions, whether positive or negative, check those that best describe you:
    _____ Readily express my emotions
    _____ Express some of my emotions, but not all
    _____ Readily acknowledge my emotions' presence, but l am reserved in expressing them
    _____ Tendency to suppress my emotions
    _____ Feel it is safer not to express how I feel emotionally
    _____ Tendency to disregard how I feel emotionally since I don't trust my feelings
    _____ Consciously or subconsciously deny my emotions; it's too painful to deal with them

6. Do you presently know someone with whom you could be emotionally honest (i.e., you could tell this person exactly how you feel about yourself, life, and other people)? Please explain:

7. How important is it that you are emotionally honest before God? _____ Do you feel that you are always honest with God? _____ Explain:

MENTAL HEALTH

1. Have you ever been diagnosed with any emotional and behavioral disorders? _____ If yes, please list the clinical terms and your age when each was diagnosed:

2. Have you ever had psychiatric counseling? _____ If yes, were you hospitalized? _____ If yes, for how long?

3. Have you ever had any shock treatments? _____ If yes, how many?

4. Have you ever been psychoanalyzed? _____ If you have had any other clinical counseling and treatments, please explain:

5. Have you ever had anyone lay hands on you pertaining to spiritual and/or physical healing? If yes, please explain:

6. Have you ever wished to die? _____ If yes, please explain:

7. Have you ever entertained thoughts of suicide? _____ If yes, please explain:

8. Have you ever attempted suicide? _____ If yes, by what method and why?

9. Think back to your earliest memory and briefly describe it:

10.   Within the following ages, how many actual memories do you have? _____ (Not memories based on pictures someone has shown you or what someone has told you about the past.)
       Age 0 to 5: _____   Age 6 to 12: _____

11.   Do you suffer from lapses of memory or time? _____ If yes, please give an example:

12.   Do you spend time wishing you were someone else or fantasizing that you are a different person? _____ Do you imagine yourself living in a different time, in a different place, or in different circumstances? _____ Please explain:

13.   Please **state** below, under **"Earliest Age"** the **earliest age you struggled** with any of these subjects, and **check** under **"Present"** if you **still struggle** with any of them:

	Earliest Age / Present		Earliest Age / Present
Daydreaming	/	Lustful Thoughts	/
Thoughts of Inferiority	/	Thoughts of Inadequacy	/
Worry	/	Doubts	/
Fantasizing	/	Obsessive Thoughts	/
Insecurity	/	Blasphemous Thoughts	/
Compulsive Thoughts	/	Dizziness	/
Headaches	/	Hardness in Emotions	/
Apathy	/	Skepticism	/

14.   Please **state** under **"Earliest Age,"** the **earliest age** you remember **strong, prolonged fear** to any of the following, and **check** under **"Present,"** if you **still do**:

	Earliest Age / Present		Earliest Age / Present
Failure	/	Inability to Cope	/
Authority Figures	/	The Dark	/
Rape	/	Violence	/
Satan & Evil Spirits	/	The Future	/
Crowds	/	Heights	/
Insanity	/	Public Speaking	/
Opinions of People	/	Old Age	/
Enclosed Spaces	/	Terminal Illness	/
Open Spaces	/	Spiders	/
Crossing Bridges	/	Animals	/
Insects	/	Loud Noises	/
Snakes	/	Grocery Stores/Malls	/
Pain	/	Death	/
Being Alone	/	Accidents	/
Women	/	Death or injury of loved ones	/
Men	/	Divorce/ Marriage Break up	/
Water/Swimming	/	Other	/
Flying in Airplane / Other	/		

15. Would you consider yourself to be an optimist, realist, or pessimist? _____ Please explain:

16. Please **state** under **"Earliest Age,"** the **earliest age** you remember having any **behavioral patterns** with the following subjects, and **check** under **"Present,"** if you **still do**:

	Earliest Age / Present		Earliest Age / Present
Impatience	/	Irritability	/
Temper	/	Racial Prejudice	/
Legalism	/	Moodiness	/
Rebellion	/	Violence	/
Anti-Semitism	/	Religious Pride	/
Stubbornness	/	Grudge – Holder	/
Vengeance	/	Intimidator	/
Manipulation	/	Self - Centered	/

17. Do you readily engage in gossip, slandering a person? If yes, who do you gossip about?

18. Do you struggle with covetousness (i.e. desiring others possessions, position, spouse, etc.)? If yes, please explain:

19. Do you struggle with modern idolatry (i.e., materialism, being a workaholic, sports addict, addiction to any **consuming** lifestyle or interest that deters you from God's will)? _____ If yes, please explain:

20. Please check if you have acted out, verbally or in your mind, the following in the past: Swearing? _____ Blasphemies? _____ Obscenities? _____

21. Check if you currently act out the following, verbally or mentally: Swearing? _____ Blasphemies? _____ Obscenities? _____

22. Do you readily engage in lying? _____ What are you more readily prone to lie about? ___

23. Do you have a problem with stealing? _____ If yes, please explain:

24. If you have stolen things, do you still have any of the items in your possession? _____ If yes, what are they and to whom do they belong? _____

25. Are there people in your life that you cannot stand to be around, or perhaps when you're around a certain person, you feel a relational wall of tension between the two of you? List any person/s with whom you experience the following emotions and explain why you feel the way you do about them:
     a. Unforgiveness
     b. Resentment
     c. Bitterness
     d. Hatred

26. Have you ever wished someone would die? _____ Have you ever entertained thoughts of how to go about murdering someone? _____ If you answer any of the above with "yes," please explain:

27. Have you ever murdered anyone? _____ If yes, who did you murder and why? _____

SPIRITUAL HISTORY

1. If you were to die right now, do you know, without doubt where you would spend eternity?
2. Suppose you die tonight and appear before God in heaven and He asks, "By what right should I allow you into My presence, to live in heaven for eternity?" _____ How would you answer Him?
3. I John 5:11, 12 says, "God has given us eternal life, and this life is in His Son. He who has the Son of God has life; he who **does not have** the Son of God does not have life," Do you have the Son of God in you? _____
4. When did you receive Christ as your Savior? (John 1:12)
5. How do you know for certain that you received Him?
6. Were you baptized as a believer? ____ Were you "christened" or "baptized" as an infant? If yes, please explain:
7. Are you plagued about doubts of your salvation?
8. In one word, who is Jesus to you?
9. What does the blood of Calvary mean to you?
10. Is repentance part of your Christian life?
11. Do you struggle and experience doubt and unbelief in attempting to live the Christian life daily? If yes, in what areas of your life?
12. Are you presently enjoying fellowship with other believers, and if yes, where and when?
13. Are you under the authority of a local church where the Bible is taught? _____ If yes, do you regularly support it with your time, talents, and tithes? _____ If not, why not?
14. Do you regularly read the Bible? _____ If yes, where, when, and to what extent?
15. Do you find prayer time with God difficult mentally? _____ If yes, please explain:
16. While attending church or other Christian ministries and functions, are you plagued with foul thoughts, jealousies, or other mental harassments? _____ If yes, please explain:
17. Do you feel like you have ever experienced a call from God to the Gospel ministry? _____ If yes, explain:
18. Have you had any spiritual experiences that you would consider as out of the ordinary? If yes, explain:

RELIGIOUS CULT HISTORY

1. Are/were your parents and/or grandparents superstitious? _____ Were you in the past? Are you now superstitious?
2. Have you ever worn or owned "lucky" charms, fetishes, amulets, or signs of the zodiac? If yes, do you still have any of those in your possession? _____ If yes, name them:
3. Do you have any witches, such as "good luck kitchen witches" in your home?
4. Do you own or have any symbols of idols or items used in spirit worship? Please check any of the following that you own: Buddha _____ Totem poles _____ Masks _____ Carvings _____ Dream catchers _____ Fetish objects / feathers _____ Native art _____ Pagan symbols _____ Statues of people (dead or alive) that you believe hold any special powers? _If yes, please explain your thoughts about them:

5.   Are you willing to rid your home of any object that is displeasing to the Lord (Deut. 7:26)? If not, please explain why:

6.   To your knowledge, have you or any of your relatives, (parents, grandparents, great-grandparents, etc), ever been involved in any of the **occult, cultic, or non-Christian "religious" experiences** below? _____ If yes, beside the activity in which you and/or they were involved, please initial where applicable as follows:

S = Self   F = Family member   S/F = Self and Family member

Astral projection		Incubi and Succubi (sexual spirits)		Greek Fraternity	
Ouija board		Fetishism		Daughter of the Nile	
Table lifting		Christian Science		Shriner	
Speaking in a trance		Unity		Job's Daughter	
Automatic writing		Scientology		Amaranth	
Visionary dreams		The Way International		Greek Sorority	
Telepathy		Unification Church		Zen Buddhism	
Ghosts		Church of the Living Word		Hare Krishna	
Materialization		Mormonism		Bahaism	
Clairvoyance		Jehovah's Witness		Rosicrucianism	
Fortune-telling		Children of God		Astrology	
Tarot cards		Swedenborgianism		H. W. Armstrong	
Science of Creative Intelligence		Transcendental Meditation (Worldwide Church of God)		Yoga	
Palm-reading		Unitarianism		Eckankar	
Rod and pendulum (dowsing)		New Age		Roy Master	
Amateur hypnosis		Silva Mind Control		Theosophical Society	
New Age medicines		Eastern Star		Father Dine	
Magic charming		Doe		Blood pacts	
Freemason		Mental suggestion (attempts to swap minds)		Other	
Elk		Black and White Magic		Other	
Islam		Demolay		Other	
Black Muslim		Rainbow Girl		Other	

7.   If yes, to what degree were you/they involved, and to what level did you/they climb in the organizations?

8.   Is there any Masonic regalia or memorabilia in your possession? _____ If yes, what is it?

9.   Have you ever been hypnotized, attended a "New Age" seminar, or participated in a séance? _____ If yes, please explain:

10. Have you ever been involved in any of the martial arts? _____ If yes, which ones and to what level have you advanced?

11. If you have been involved in martial arts, do you still practice it?

12.   Have you ever learned about or used any form of mind communication or mind control? If yes, explain:

13.   Have you ever taken a class or read books on parapsychology or witchcraft? _____ If yes, please explain:

14.   Do you have, or have you ever had, an imaginary friend or spirit guide offering you guidance or companionship? _____ If yes, please explain:

15.   Have you ever experienced what you would term as premonitions? _____ Deja vu? _____ Psychic sight? _____

16.   Have you ever been involved in fire-walking? _____ Voodoo? _____ Any other form of religious pagan ceremony? _____ If yes, please explain:

17.   Do you have any tattoos? _____ If yes, please describe, tell their meanings, and/or why you were tattooed:

18.   Do you have any body piercing or mutilations? _____ If yes, please describe, tell why you got them, and any meanings they may have:

19.   To your knowledge, has any curse been placed on you or members of your family? _____ If yes, please share who made it and why:

20.   Have you ever heard voices or emotional messages in your mind, had repeating and nagging thoughts that were foreign to what you believe, or felt like there was a dialogue going on in your head? _____ If yes, please explain:

21.   What experiences have you had that would be considered supernatural, out of the ordinary?

22.   Have you been involved in Satanic rituals of any form? _____ If yes, please explain:

23.   Have you ever made a pact with the Devil? _____ Was it a blood pact? _____ If either of your answers is "yes," please explain:

24.   Have you ever been emotionally and physically battered (excluding sexual abuse)? _____ If yes, please explain:

25.   Have you ever been sexually molested? _____ If yes, please explain:

26.   Have you ever been a victim of incest, sexually molested by a family member? _____

27.   Have you ever committed fornication (a sexual act by an unmarried person)? _____ If yes, about how many partners? _____ Are you currently having an affair with someone? _____

28.   If married, have you ever committed adultery (a sexual act by a married person, with someone other than your spouse)? _____ If yes, are you currently having an affair? _____ If you are, are you willing to break it off? _____ If not, why?

29.   Have you (man or woman) ever been raped? _____ If yes, how many times? _____ Please tell at what age/s you were raped:

30.   Have you ever molested and/or raped anyone?

31.   Have you ever been personally involved with a person who has had an abortion? _____ If yes, please explain:

32.   If a woman, have you ever had an abortion? _____ If yes, please tell how many abortions you have had and how old you were when the abortion/s took place:

33.   Have you ever had a baby or fathered a baby and adopted the baby out? _____ If yes, was the baby conceived out of wed-lock?

34.   Have you ever had a desire to have sex with a child? _____ If yes, occasionally or often?

35.   Have you ever fondled a child sexually? _____ Have you ever had sex with a child?

36. Have you ever committed incest?
37. Are you sexually frigid?
38. Have you practiced masturbation in the past? _____ Have you been practicing it recently?
39. Have you ever been attracted to pornography? _____ Did you become regularly involved in it? If yes, what is the earliest age you remember pursuing it? _____ And, how were you introduced to pornography? _____ Please explain:
40. Are you currently active in pornography? _____ If yes, do you desire to be free from it?
41. Have you ever had homosexual or lesbian thoughts and desires? _____ If yes, what is the earliest age you recall being attracted to a person who was the same sex as yourself? _____ Do you currently entertain those thoughts? _____ Have you been a cross-dresser in the past? _____ Have you been cross-dressing recently? _____ If yes, do you desire to cease dressing contrary to your sex?
42. Have you ever actually had a homosexual or lesbian experience? _____ If yes, did you become sexually involved in a steady relationship? _____ If yes, are you still in that relationship? _____ If yes, do you desire to be free from the relationship and homosexuality?
43. Approximately how many hours of TV do you watch per week? _____ List five of your favorite TV programs that you enjoy viewing:
44. Have you played demonic games such as Dungeons and Dragons? _____ Have you visited any demonic internet sites? _____ Have you watched any demonic films? _____ Explain:
45. Do you still participate in any of the above demonic activities now? _____ Are there other activities you are involved in that you would consider evil or demonic?
46. Approximately how many hours do you spend on the computer other than strictly mandatory work? _____ In what way do you use this time?
47. Approximately how many hours do you spend each week reading? _____ What do you read primarily (newspapers, magazines, secular books, religious book, the Bible, etc)?
48. Do you listen to music often? _____ What types of music do you enjoy the most?
49. What do you enjoy doing for recreation?
50. Do you have any hobbies, if yes, please list them:

Please remember to make sure you answer the following questions as if you are answering God.

51. What do you really think about yourself?
52. What do you really believe other people think about you?
53. What do you really believe God thinks about you?
54. Do you have any other problems, burdens, underlying or repetitive sin that you feel this questionnaire has not given opportunity to share? ___ Please pray and ask the Lord to bring to your mind any other relevant issues, while remembering that the enemy, Satan, has legal rights to stay and torment you until the root of each issue is dealt with. So, please try to pinpoint when each problem began and if they were connected to a traumatic experience or if Satan simply succeeded in snaring you and you gave in to him. Please do feel free to share any additional information that you believe may be helpful to your finding total freedom in Christ during your counseling sessions:

F.   TOOL #6: GATHER MISSING INFORMATION BEFORE COUNSELING

Please note that there are times, upon receiving a person's counseling form, that I find that he has failed to provide sufficient information on some points—especially about how old he was when various outstanding events took place. When this happens, I call him to talk and pray with him, asking the Lord to help him recall information that will reveal an approximate age. Most of the time, the Lord blesses by stirring a memory, such as the grade he was in at school. Having this information ahead of time spares us from having to spend time searching for it during his counseling appointments.

In the next chapter I will share more tools that are very useful to me as I glean information from the person's inventory form before scheduling his appointments. I've used these tools for many years and they have helped me to organize the information in such a way that the counseling procedure goes more smoothly. I do so hope that these tools likewise will be helpful in your ministry!

Chapter Six
TOOLS TO GLEAN INFORMATION
FROM COUNSELEE'S COUNSELING FORM

Noting that the person has signed my cover page explaining my ministry and requirements, I am left to believe that he understands and is in full agreement. Then go over his attached, 18 page "Confidential Personal Inventory" form that he filled out and returned to me. I believe as you studied the form in the previous chapter, you will readily agree with me that this is an immensely informative tool, for when the person enters my office; the counseling form has already told me volumes about his life.

Reviewing an average counseling form and taking notes usually takes me from four to six hours, unless a person has added additional pages of information. Page 18 of the actual form is a blank, lined page for additional information the person may want to share. Some people add very little or nothing at all, while others have added more like a book! I have had as many as 167 pages in addition to the form! I spent a large part of two days gleaning essential information from that particular inventory form! However, as you can imagine, it would have taken a great deal more one-on-one time to gather information from this person. Now, I must add, that while some people add unnecessary information, the Lord is always faithful to give wisdom to help me know "necessary" apart from "unnecessary!" So you see that the amount of time spent in reviewing a person's form definitely depends on how detailed the person is—and how many pages of additional information he shares. If the form is filled out correctly in detail, without extra pages, I believe it represents saving anywhere from 30 to 40 hours that would have been spent in asking the counselee questions and taking notes!

From page one, asking "Personal Information," I am able to gather name, address, and general information about the counselee and his family. **From pages two and three, asking for information concerning his "Family Tree" and "Information on Family Members,"** I will have gather information about his health, his lifestyle, and behavioral issues, as well as the same issues about his family. In also having information about his family history, his ancestors of both his father and mother, plus other family members—it will help me find any connecting demons and personalities. And this family history could be extremely helpful in his counseling since it can expose whether or not the "iniquity of the fathers" has passed down—if there is an ancestral demon and flip-side—a "duplex"—an opposite side of his core personality. While reviewing the person's inventory form, almost from the get-go I will be able to glean evidence of wounded personalities. I really can't stress enough that the form is extremely helpful—invaluable!

While I will share many details of my counseling procedures in future chapters, I believe it will be helpful for you to be at least become somewhat acquainted with things I will be looking for on the person's form—some questions that it would prompt me to ask them. I will look for answers to a number of questions, such as these:

- Is there a broken core?
- Is this person's life full of confusion?
- Are there some doubts concerning his salvation?
- Has this person made a deal or pact with Satan and his demons?
- Are there a lot of the same-type illnesses in the family, as in previous generations?
- Are there ancestral demons?
- Are there wounded personalities?
- Is there a flip-side to this person—will I be dealing with a duplex?
- Are there enough wounded parts to have required a caretaker?
- Is there a wounded part that is full of doubt and/or fear?
- Is there a major thread that runs through the counseling form that gives me a direction or clue about what is going on, such as any of the following?
  - Are there ritualistic tones in the counseling form?
  - Are there a lot of the same generational iniquities showing up in his ancestors?
  - Are there a lot of generational "mental health" problems?

After finding evidence on the form that certainly reveals that there is a flip-side and wounded personalities, plus an ancestral demon, there will be some specific questions that I will ask each of them. While I will get into extensive counseling procedures in future chapters, I thought it would be helpful for you to at least become acquainted with these basic questions, before I show you how I glean information from a person's counseling form.

When I contact the flip-side, I will ask these six questions:

1. Flip-side, why didn't you get saved at age _____ when the core personality got saved?
2. Based on the core's age which should match, I ask the flip-side, "Are you age _____ ?"
3. What is your name?
4. Will you tell me some things about yourself, please?
5. What do you do in the core personality's life when you are in charge?
6. What are the major emotions that motivate and manipulate your life?

The flip-side can answer in five ways, and during this time, the core and flip-side can be switching back and forth while communicating:

1. The flip-side will shove the core personality out of the way and talk to you.
2. The core personality will have to report what he <u>hears</u>.
3. The core personality will have to report what he <u>feels</u>.
4. The core personality will have to report what he <u>senses</u>.
5. The core personality will have to report what he <u>sees</u>.

166

When I contact a wounded part, I will ask these six questions:

1.   What brought you into being?
2.   What is your age?
3.   What is your name?
4.   Will you tell me about you?
5.   What do you do when you are up (in control) in the core's life?
6.   What are the major emotions that motivate and manipulate your life?

The wounded part can answer in five ways, and during this time, the core and the wounded part can be switching back and forth while sharing <u>helpful</u> information:

1.   The wounded part will shove the core personality out of the way and talk to you.
2.   The core personality will have to report what he <u>hears</u>.
3.   The core personality will have to report what he <u>feels</u>.
4.   The core personality will have to report what he <u>senses</u>.
5.   The core personality will have to report what he <u>sees</u>.

While I am interrogating the ancestral demon and demons, since the core personality is always well aware of what is going on during counseling, he is free to inject any <u>important</u> comments into the conversation between counselor and the ancestral demon.

In various places on the form, having asked people to the best of their ability to share what their age was when they experienced something in particular, I don't find it unusual for some not to have memories of their very early childhood. Some don't have any memories of the first five years, or even the first twelve years. The worst one I've had was one who was 37 years old and she had no memories during the first 27 years of her life. Having all the other information enabled me to have a basis from which I could start asking her questions—and of course, the Lord was our help—He enabled her to recall the additional necessary information from those lost years and she received freedom!

THREE NOTE PADS

Now I will share some practical, "organizational" tools that "work for me," tools that I use in gathering information from the counseling form that helps to retrieve truth about persons who are in bondage. I always use **THREE LETTER-SIZED, LINED NOTE PADS:**

A.   TOOL #1 NOTE PAD: INFORMATION GLEANED BEFORE SESSIONS

This note pad is for **recording crucial information gleaned from the counselee's form before they come for counseling. Later, I will add information to this same pad while going over the form with the counselee.**

167

B.   TOOL #2 NOTE PAD: INFORMATION GLEANED DURING SESSIONS

On the second note pad, I record **all the information that I gather while actually working with the counselee about the flip-side, wounded personalities, and the ancestral demons.**

C.   TOOL #3 NOTE PAD: JOTTING NOTES FOR FUTURE USE

My third note pad is **for jotting notes during counseling sessions, which I deem important but the subject is to be dealt with at a later time.** For instance, if I'm working with the flip-side and I learn some information about a wounded personality or a demon masquerading as a wounded personality, I will put it on my Tool # 3 Note Pad under the heading of the related subject. Then, as I work with the person and a related subject comes up, I will be able to easily refer to my **"Reserve for Future Use" note pad.** There is times when I make a notation of something that I'm not sure at that point how or where it fits in.

KEEP EXTRA PADS ON HAND

I always **keep many extra note pads on hand**, for often times I need two extra pads on which to record information on the flip-side, wounded personalities, and ancestral demons. For me, it's just an easy way to keep track of things.

Now, I'm going to take you through a completed form that I received from someone, and share how I took notes, which should give you some good examples. I have used a fictitious name and made a lot of changes to protect the person's identity. I will call this dear man, Mark Lewis Williams.

D. HOW TO RECORD INFORMATION ON TOOL #1 NOTE PAD

AT THE TOP OF NOTE PAD #1

At the top of my note pad, I wrote Mark's **present age** and the **age that he accepted the Lord Jesus Christ as his personal Savior**, and below that, I wrote **his full name**. (Be sure to note: If the person is a married woman, I always include her maiden plus her married name <u>unless</u> she is legally divorced.) Also, in the upper left hand corner of my note pad, I always make a notation of the name of the **person who referred them to me**.

LIST ALL NEGATIVE INFORMATION
EASILY GLEANED FROM COUNSELING FORM

I went through Mark's inventory form, recording all essential information that I would need during the sessions. In the far left, narrow column of the note pad, I listed the ages, while leaving the broad, right area for recording the information pertaining to each of the ages.

Referred by: Mr. & Mrs. Adam

Age 19, saved at age 13
Mark Lewis Williams

ANCESTRY — His family background revealed a great deal of ancestral iniquity had been readily available to pass down. I was so glad that Mark was still so young and that he came in desperation seeking help!

FIRST 12 YEARS — Mark said, "My life was filled with security and harmony, but sometimes disharmony because of my father's depression and anger. My mother never did or said anything about his anger. My mother even ignored me when I was suicidal. She required perfection out of me."

FIRST 18 YEARS — The moral atmosphere I was raised in was 50 percent average and the other 50 percent was strict or overly strict.

AGE 3 — I remember pulling a pan of hot cocoa off the stove onto myself.

AGE 5 — Stubbornness

AGE 6 — Loneliness; headaches; remembers Dad throwing a big potted-plant at me when he was very angry.

AGE 7 — Fear of flying in an airplane; etc.; lying about everything.

AGE 8 — Daydreaming; worry; fantasizing; fear of authority figures; fear of opinions of people; manipulation; lying about everything.

AGE 9 — Doubts about self, life, people, and God; fear of insects; impatience.

AGE 10 — Lustful thoughts; moodiness; worthlessness.

AGE 11 — Depression, thoughts of inadequacy; Mother was hard on me; masturbation; symptoms of bipolar.

AGE 12 — Masturbation; frustration; anger; anxiety; bitterness; thoughts of inferiority;

AGE 13
Hatred for self; hatred for others; obsessive thoughts; compulsive thoughts; religious pride; I got saved at church camp; I planned to kill kids in my school because they made fun of me, laughed at me and never made me feel like I fit in or was welcome; the pale face that talks to me without moving its mouth is connected with a pact with the Devil.

AGE 13-18
I feel like I don't belong and like God doesn't want me; bitterness and hatred for kids; fear of God.

AGE 14
Fear of open spaces; rebellion; tried to kill myself by closing the garage door, starting the car and letting it idle; the pale face talks to me without moving its mouth; kids never make me feel welcome; bitterness and hatred for kids in middle school.

AGE 14-16
I felt like God wanted me to be a pastor.

AGE 15
Fear of committing suicide; the pale face talks to me without moving its mouth; I started hearing voices saying: "You should be sorry." They make me feel scared, guilty and angry.

AGE 16
Intimidation; self-centered; prideful; irritability; I became regularly involved in pornography; hearing voices saying: "You should be sorry."

AGE 17
At a get-together I was hypnotized and I loss three hours of time period in my memory.

AGE 17-19
Addicted to alcohol; use alcohol sometimes to forget things; other times, I don't know why I drink and very rarely drink at social functions.

AGE 18
Skepticism, first sexual intercourse.

AGE 19
Feeling hopeless. Fear of losing my mind. Tried to kill myself by overdosing on my medication. Spiritual experience: when I tried to kill myself, God caused me to throw up all the pills. I struggle with playing video games and allowing them to deter me from God's will. Masturbating with addiction to pornography and I wanting to be free from it. The pale face that talks to me without moving its mouth is still talking to me. Body piercing is a way to express myself outwardly. A very soft voice says: "You're worthless," and repeats over and over again, "You can't get ahead! It's always going to be like this! You have failed God! He doesn't want you!"

FLIP-SIDE, WOUNDED PERSONALITIES, AND DEMONS
VS. CORE PERSONALITY

Having completed recording that information up to Mark's present age of 19, **on the next page of my note pad**, I did the following:

1. **I drew a vertical line in the center—from top to bottom, forming two columns.** At the **top, on the left side** I wrote, **"Flip-side, Wounded Personalities and Demons,"** and on the **right side**, I wrote, **"Core Personality"**.

2. **Under the title of "Flip-side, Wounded Personalities and Demons" I listed the negative subject matter that Mark declared as very obvious to him in his life.** Now keep in mind that Mark is a Christian who is very positive he got saved at age thirteen. Grievously, from his counseling form, I found evidence of these 62 negatives: stubbornness, loneliness; headaches; daydreaming and fantasizing; worry; fear of flying, etc.; fear of authority figures; fear of opinions of people; manipulation; lying about everything; doubts about self, life, people and God; fear of insects; impatience; lustful thoughts; moodiness; worthlessness; depression; thoughts of inadequacy; fear of Satan and evil spirits; masturbation; frustration; anger; anxiety; bitterness; thoughts of inferiority; insecurity; apathy; fear of failure; fear of being alone; temper; vengeance; violence; grudge-holder; bipolar; sexually attracted to same sex; wish I could die; hatred for others; wants to kill kids at school; unforgiveness toward mom; hatred for self; obsessive thoughts; compulsive thoughts; I don't belong, God doesn't want me; fear of open spaces; religious pride; rebellion; fear of committing suicide; wishes he could die; attempted suicide; intimidation; self-centered; prideful; irritability; addicted to pornography; hears voices condemning him; hypnotized, lost 3 hours of memory; addicted to alcohol; skepticism; hopelessness; fear of losing mind; addicted to video games.

3. Upon Mark arriving for his first session, we discussed a few things and we both prayed. **When I was certain I was talking to his core personality that the Lord created, I handed him the note pad opened to the page with the negatives listed on the left side** and asked him to **please list on the right, under "Core Personality" all the positives, the good things, even Godly things that he knew about himself.**

I feel that I have been blessed if I get a dozen things listed there, but most of the time, the counselees will only list from three to six positive things. Sometimes, with people who are in less critical condition, the list will be longer though. **After Mark listed the positive things about himself, I found that he had listed six things: (1)** I was saved at age thirteen; **(2)** I am compassionate about God; **(3)** I try to be honest with God; **(4)** I have the fruit of the Spirit; **(5)** I am not afraid to stand up for God; and **(6)** God has used me before.

This is how I listed all the information:

FLIP-SIDE, WOUNDED PERSONALITIES & DEMONS (The Dark Side)		CORE PERSONALITY (The Safe Side)
1 stubbornness	41 obsessive thoughts	1 I was saved at age 13
2 loneliness	42 compulsive thoughts	2 I am compassionate about God
3 headaches	43 I don't belong; God doesn't want me	3 I try to be honest with God.
4 daydreaming; fantasizing	44 fear of open spaces	4 I have the fruit of the Spirit
5 worry	45 religious pride	5 I am not afraid to stand up for God
6 fear of flying, etc.	46 rebellion	6 He has used me before.
7 fear of authority figures	47 fear of attempting suicide	
8 fear of opinions of people	48 wishes he could die	
9 manipulation	49 attempted suicide	
10 lying about everything	50 intimidation	
11 doubts about self, life, people, and God	51 self-centered	
12 fear of insects	52 vengeance	
13 impatience	53 prideful	
14 lustful thoughts	54 irritability	
15 moodiness	55 pornography	
16 worthlessness	56 hears voices condemning him	
17 depression	57 hypnotized, lost 3 hours	
18 thoughts of inadequacy	58 addicted to alcohol	
19 fear of Satan and evil spirits	59 skepticism	
20 masturbation	60 hopelessness	
21 frustration	61 fears of losing mind	
22 anger	62 addicted to video games	
23 anxiety		
24 bitterness		
25 thoughts of inferiority		
26 insecurity		
27 apathy		
28 fear of failure		
29 fear of being alone		
30 temper		
31 vengeance		
32 violence		
33 grudge-holder		
34 bipolar		
35 sexually attracted to same sex		
36 wish I could die		
37 hatred for others		
38 want to kill kids at school		
39 unforgiveness toward mom		
40 hatred for self		

There was no doubt in my mind that Mark had a duplex with **62 negatives** operating against his core personality, the personality that God thought up from the foundations of the world. The core is soft, pliable, reachable and teachable, apart from the mess inside him. Due to the iniquities of the fathers and sinful acts in Mark's life, all those negative things were a tremendous hindrance to his

172

core personality. Knowing all this, I knew the work was surely cut out for me to deal with the "dark side of the house"—the duplex and demons holding Mark in bondage. Judging from Mark's negative behavior patterns, his flip-side, his "dark side" had not accepted Christ as Savior when the core person did at age thirteen! As I began counseling, I drew a graphic similar to the one you see pictured below, to give Mark a visual of his core personality that the Lord created, plus the opposite side of the house where Satan was manipulating and controlling the core with the flip-side and wounded personalities.

CONCEPTION - "WILLIAM" (? SOUL)	CONCEPTION - "MARK LEWIS WILLIAM"
FLIP-SIDE & WOUNDED PERSONALITIES AD with formal name with demon network AD with family name with demon network AD Williams family name with demon network AD O'Mar family name with demon network AD with name of its works and network Demon-produced personality Demons masquerading as personalities Lifestyle demons and their networks Shared demons (1) those shared out and 　(2) those shared in from other networks Gatekeeper/s with other networks	CORE PERSONALITY SOFT, PLIABLE, REACHABLE AND TEACHABLE BEFORE SALVATION CALLED: THE SAFE SIDE OF THE DUPLEX OR THE LIGHT SIDE OF THE DUPLEX
"THE DARK SIDE OF THE DUPLEX" WOUNDED PERSONALITIES 　Age 8　　　　　　Age 11 & 12 "I Don't Have A Name"　"I Don't Have A Name" 　　　　　　　　　　(Bipolar)	AFTER SALVATION CALLED: THE SAVED SIDE OF THE DUPLEX SAVED AT AGE 13
Age 13 "Hatred That Made A Pact With The Devil"	MARK and JESUS
THREE DEMON PRODUCED PERSONALITIES CONNECTED TO SEXUAL PERVERSION Age 11, "No Name" Age 15, "No Name" Age 19, "No Name"	

Again, I want to remind you that if Mark Lewis Williams had died before being set free—he would have gone to heaven! But until he dealt with the other side of his duplex, he would not only be hindered from walking in God's will for his precious life, he would continue to be tormented with thoughts of suicide. When he got saved, the duplex did not automatically come over to the right side! People can disagree and debate this matter until they are blue in the face, but if they would prayerfully and thoroughly examine the scriptures, they would forfeit the debate. For, in James 1:8 and 4:8, which I talked about in detail earlier, God clearly stated that Christians can be duplexes.

Having read this precious young man's inventory form, correlated the ages, and gathered the necessary information, I was then ready to schedule Mark's counseling sessions and begin counseling. I am very grateful and happy to say that Mark most surely received freedom via the precious Lord Jesus—and the peace and joy that came with it! He is joyfully walking in God's will for his precious life today. What a marvelous testimony he has to share!

One would always hope that a counseling session would go smoothly from start to finish— with no snags whatsoever. However, the reality is that apart from the issues with the Devil and his demons, problems can arise—hindrances! Therefore, I believe it will be of help to you and your counselees if I share some of the hindrances that I have encountered over the years, plus some tips on how to deal with them. **I do hope that the next chapter about hindrances will be an encouragement and help to you.**

Chapter Seven
HINDRANCES TO GETTING WORK DONE

It delights the enemy when counselees and/or counselors allow various things to become hindrances to the counseling process! I have already stressed **the need for counselors to have clean hearts**— to be in right standing before the Lord—for as the Lord says: *"...there is no creature hidden from His sight, but all things are naked and open to the eyes of Him to whom we must give account."* (Hebrews 4:13) Every minister's and counselor's prayer should be as the one in Psalm 51:1-2; 6-8; 10:

> *"...Have mercy upon me, O God, according to Your loving kindness; according to the multitude of Your tender mercies, blot out my transgressions. Wash me thoroughly from my iniquity. And cleanse me from my sin...Behold, You desire truth in the inward parts, and in the hidden part You will make me to know wisdom. Purge me with hyssop, and I shall be clean; wash me, and I shall be whiter than snow. Make me hear joy and gladness...create in me a clean heart O God...."*

With your heart clean before the Lord, He says that *"...the effective, fervent prayer of a righteous man avails much."* (James 5:16b) You can hear God's voice within your heart more clearly, which will enable you to better lead hurting souls to find sweet release!

A.   HINDRANCES: COUNSELORS NEGLECTING TO KEEP BOUNDARIES

We caution ministers that they must, indeed, set and keep boundaries for their own sake, their family's sake, and their counselees' sakes as well! I have seen some ministers break down their health "running with their tongues hanging out" all the time, as if God's cheering them on! Some act as if they're on a mission to prove to themselves or to others how much they love God. Then there are others who allow the enemy, Satan, to put them on a guilt trip, accusing them of not caring enough to "sacrifice beyond the call of duty!" Such precious servants have fallen by the wayside having suffered burnout which is not an uncommon thing amongst ministers, counselors, missionaries, and other servants. Some reports once revealed that the average time for burnouts was seven years. Of course this delights the enemy!

Remember that one can be doing good things out of the will of God, which is actually sin! While doing "good things" they endanger their health while going above and beyond where God wants them to go, and they also endanger the relationship of their spouse and family! It's crucial for everyone to stay in the boundaries of God's calling—in family and ministry! **We stress again that ministers, missionaries, counselors and other servants of the Lord are NOT CARETAKERS**

that are held responsible 24/7 for every emotional need of their counselees! All too many counselors, especially those involved in spiritual warfare counseling, have suffered burnout within those seven years!

Rita and I have been in this counseling ministry for more than 30 years, and because we have stayed within the boundaries God set for us, we have not suffered burnout. When the Lord tells us to draw aside and take a break—rest—we choose to obey Him rather than the enemy! As I shared earlier in this book, God should come first, then family whom He established first, then church/ministry and the fields beyond on which He leads His people. I cannot stress enough the importance for ministers and counselors to stay snuggled up to the Lord, listening carefully to Him—letting Him establish His boundaries and His schedule for you!

B.   HINDRANCES: INSINCERE,   CO-DEPENDENT,   AND   PROFESSIONAL COUNSELEES

In God's counseling fields, it is sad to report that there are some hindrances pertaining to counselees, of whom ministers and counselors should be made aware, for their sakes as well as the counselees. I am grateful to say that I have had only a few counselees fall into the categories of being **(1) insincere, (2) co-dependent, and (3) professional counselees**. I hope that as I share about them, it will help you to be keenly alert so that you are spared from the enemy's zapping precious time that could otherwise be spent on counselees who sincerely desire help. **Upon understanding "where they are coming from," appeal to them to yield their hearts to the Lord. If they remain stubborn, explain that because of their choice, further counseling would be unfruitful, so you can no longer counsel them.**

INSINCERE COUNSELEES

The **"insincere counselees"** go from one counselor to another, over and over. Typically, they have very undisciplined lifestyles and don't like to follow orders issued by others. Some may appear to be sincere about wanting help, but if their counselors don't counsel them exactly the way that they think they should—or they don't give them enough attention and sympathy—they move on, trying other counselors. Some actually sound off to their counselors as if they think they know more than the counselors—with some even telling their counselors how they believe they should be counseled! Some clearly derive a sinful satisfaction from telling their sad stories over and over again, detail by detail, whether privately with a counselor or in group counseling. **They are insincere—not really desperate for the Lord to give them freedom and get on with their lives.** We are very grateful that we have seen only a very low number of insincere counselees!

CO-DEPENDENT COUNSELEES

After leading a person to freedom, and giving him instructions for how to begin establishing new, Christ-like behavior patterns and resisting temptation to walk in his old negative-learned behavior patterns, he may desire that you, as his "beloved counselor" be available to disciple him—very often and for a very long time to come! He may want you to be available to answer any question he may have—large or small—and advise and pray with him over various negative issues that pop up in his life. Upon our having known such co-dependent persons, we've found it typical of each one, that if he cannot reach his counselor, then he begins calling his friends until he reaches one who brings him satisfaction.

Such a co-dependent person is a prime target for Satan to keep pointing him to more peaceful settings where he would love to enjoy long, frequent visits—with you as his counselor or with his friends! Let me be clear that I am not saying that a counselor and the person's friends should not encourage him! Please understand that I am not talking about the average counselor-counselee situation, nor normal friend-relationships! I'm talking about a co-dependent person who totally depends on others to answer all his concerns, give him advice and solutions to all his problems— and comfort him by praying for him. If he can't reach any of these support-people—he gets very distraught—to tears!

All such co-dependent persons have actually allowed themselves to become addicted to time with their counselor and other people—they are co-dependent! Their behavior is not unlike a child becoming attached to his favorite "Teddy Bear!" Persons of this type may or may not have been brought up in a dysfunctional family setting; they may or may not be in the midst of a stormy time in their lives, such as marriage or family problems; they may just simply be a very immature Christian who needs to be redirected—from their negative-learned behavior patterns, to positive Christ-like ones! When a counselor or the person's friends allow themselves to become the person's Teddy Bear, they are doing the co-dependent person no favors! You see, the Lord should be their "Teddy Bear," the One they snuggle up to when life's storms are blowing about! The One who will talk to them if they will be still and listen! Therefore, if you fail to redirect them to spending time with the Lord, the Wonderful Counselor, the Master Teacher, you are **allowing yourself to take God's place in times when He wants to be alone with and talk to your counselee Himself!** Too many counselors have made the serious mistake of being available 24/7—or near that—every time their counselee needs them. When counselors yield to this temptation, they are not only sinning, they are aiding their counselees to sin. They are robbing them from the opportunity to hear from their Creator!

We must add that we are very sad to say—again—that we've witnessed **some counselors** who have heeded Satan's lie that they are being selfish if they aren't on duty 24/7—so **Satan has them traveling on a guilt trip.** Satan has managed to mislead **some counselors to be co-dependent upon their counselees needing them**—as it seems to serve to give the counselor more self-worth, self-edification. They have put themselves on a leash, giving their counselees their cell phones and hopping up in the midst of family times and meetings—or sleep—to answer their beacon call. When we think of such, it brings to mind how out-of-touch so many Christians are with God's timetable! We think of the story of Jesus arriving in Bethany "too late" according to Mary whose brother Lazarus had died and was already buried. For we see she's distraught, in John 11:32, falling at Jesus' feet, declaring, *"LORD if You had been here, my brother would not have died."* And other believers are seen, in verse 37, criticizing him: *"...Could not this man who opened the eyes of the blind, also have kept this man from dying?"* Of course as we read the account, we know Jesus was in tune to His Father's voice who had told Him exactly what time He was to arrive and that the timing held a specific purpose! For in verse 40, Jesus is found explaining His "misinterpreted tardiness" to Mary this way: *"...Did I not say to you that if you would believe you would see the glory of God?"*—God's will in the process of being accomplished! We hope that all ministers and counselors will remember Jesus' example for their sake, and for the sake of others!

Now we will share a great—but very sad—illustration that happened to us concerning a lady we easily spotted as **co-dependent**. A lady who had come here for counseling and found freedom, but like so many others, she had to learn to resist temptation to yield to her old, negative-learned behavior patterns. Now she had been instructed how to go about doing that and encouraged to "be still and know God" for He's available all the time! We assured her that when temptation came or a problem arose, that rather than immediately running to the phone to get advice from a person—as she had always done before she received freedom—if she would submit to the Lord, resist the devil—he would flee and she could be still and hear what God had to say to her. Well, our words of encouragement went unheeded, and she would call after office hours and on our days off, leaving messages on our "answering machine." She would even declare, "If you're there, pick up! Please, please pick up because I reeeeeally need to talk to you!"

Even if we were home, hearing her leaving her message in the other room, we refused to pick up, knowing that God was right there available to talk to her if she would hush and listen to Him. We knew in our hearts that we were to obey the Lord for her sake. Then, one day she called during office hours and when Joe answered, she said, "Thank you, Brother Joe, for not picking up when I called over the weekend! You see when you didn't pick up, I called each of my friends and could not reach one of them. In desperation, I decided to get still and snuggled up to Jesus like you told me to do. I submitted myself to the Lord and resisted the devil! I was so happy to find out that **I could hear God's voice inside, talking to me**! He gave me instruction and I had peace! Thank you! Thank you! Thank you!"

Our dear ministers and counselors, we encourage you not to yield to temptation to let down your guard or your boundaries—for in doing so; you will bless yourself, your family, and your counselee!

PROFESSIONAL COUNSELEES

There have been a number of occasions in which a person has come for counseling, has filled all the requirements, and he appears to be sincere about his desire to be helped. However, having used God's freedom tools, just as I think I'm getting very close to his receiving freedom, more issues pop up. The person weeps as he begins reporting that another, and another, and another horrible memory is flooding into his mind. Therefore, it appears that he will need more counseling. When this happens, I check out three possibilities: **(1)** I always go back to check the validity of their salvation. When I am satisfied that he is saved, then I ask the Lord for discernment concerning the other two possibilities: **(2)** if the person is truly being bombarded with some legitimate memories that we need to deal with, or **(3)** if the person is **"a professional counselee."** I recognize that I must take care not to endanger my counselee by falling into the **snares of impatience and assumption** that he **must** be **"a professional counselee."** Therefore, I stay prayerfully alert, seeking God's answer!

However, persons who have suffered extreme abuse by family members or close friends—and especially SRA victims—are very vulnerable to Satan's luring suggestions! With the severely abused counselee having been deprived of a loving family, he easily latches onto anyone offering a listening ear with a caring heart. Counselees such as this are especially drawn to those in the realm of counseling ministry—representatives of God's love—where they feel more safe, lest apt to suffer abuse. As I've stated before, the average counselee is free after two days of counseling, from 9:00 a.m. to 6:00 p.m., but severely abused persons such as the SRA victims take longer. Depending on each individual, victims can take anywhere from as little as four days to a dozen days! In spending more time with them and knowing they are "in a safe place now," they may very well start calling their counselors "dad" and "mom." We know this is true and have experienced it first hand. Some begin asking if they can get together with us on a casual basis—for personal special occasions, go places together. We are most surely not to reject our counselees who are our brothers and sisters in the Lord, part of the family of God! However, many do not perceive the fact that with having counseled so many people over the years, our "extended family" has grown into a crowd of enormous size! It is just impossible to spend personal time with all of them! Having so little time to spend with our immediate family—we should not feel guilty about not playing with all of our counselees even though we love them! We desire to always let the Lord direct hearts to when we can accept invitations to fellowship with our extended family members!

It is very critical that we guard against such counselees falsely assuming that we will serve as replacements for their parents. Rita and I speak of this from a very grievous experience we went through. God had given us both discernment that a person could be a "professional counselee." The person began calling us "dad" and "mom" in such a manner that we felt uneasy. It became evident that the person's emotions had taken her beyond the expressions of "spiritual parents, and brother and sister" and into the physical realm. We prayerfully proceeded, trusting that the Lord would soon reveal the truth and if we had no doubt that she was consumed with literally claiming us as her parents, and we would address the situation. In time, during conversations with the person, truth was revealed that she did want us for her parents! It had even become evident that she was quite jealous of our own children and would have nothing to do with them. Invitations to family gatherings were turned down. Hoping she would come to repentance, we lovingly explained to her about the grievous spiritual condition of "a professional counselee" into which she had allowed the enemy to lure her. Sadly, because she was not repentant, we had to cease being a part of her life. This precious lady ended up choosing to divorce her precious Christian husband who loved her so dearly. And upon her meeting an older woman, whose children would have little or nothing to do with her; she readily began viewing her as a mother-figure. And, the older woman longed to have someone to care for, a daughter who needed her. No doubt Satan was quite pleased, for the young lady was held in a "needy" snare while the older woman was held in a "needing-to-be-needed" snare. Both were robbed of walking in God's will for their precious lives. Please understand that we share this only to urge and encourage all Christians who have a heart for helping others, to seek God's wisdom for you to **establish boundaries, for your sake as well as for the sake of the "professional counselees"**.

C.   HINDRANCES: COUNSELEE'S LACK OF SALVATION, FEAR, TRUST, AND REPENTANCE

HINDRANCE OF A LACK OF TRUE SALVATION

As I touched on earlier in this book, **the most critical of all hindrances is for the core personality to lack true salvation**. Therefore, if the slightest hint of his doubt surrounding his salvation arises, it will be a waste of time to continue with further counseling until that matter is settled! While working with your saved core personality, you will find in working with the flip-side and wounded parts that it is necessary for all of them to also choose to join in with the core in believing in the Lord Jesus Christ as their personal Savior and Lord! Please take care to know that this is not to say that if the saved core had died before the flip-side and wounded personalities had placed their trust in the Lord Jesus Christ, the core would have been hindered from going to heaven! The core would have gone to heaven—and would have been made whole!

HINDRANCES OF FEAR AND LACK OF TRUST

Fear of the demonic and lack of trust that the work can be accomplished are common factors that go hand-in-hand in some counselees—but also in some flip-sides and wounded personalities! When a person has experienced abuse and/or traumatic experiences in the past, he harbors much fear and lack of trust, which are very typically embedded in wounded personalities. Sad to say, **there are all too many Christians who are more afraid of the demons than they trust the Lord**, which can be an enormous hindrance to making progress with your counselee! Therefore, take care to encourage your counselee by often sharing God's wondrous words of truth with him! Concerning fear, remind him that *"...God has not given us a spirit of fear, but of power and of love and of a sound mind."* (II Timothy 1:7) And, explain that it is the enemy who is declaring lies to him that he should be fearful, so that he will think Satan is more powerful than his Savior, Jesus Christ!

Explain to him that he is sinning by believing Satan's lie, and encourage him to confess his fear as sin, and then thank the Lord that through Him, he can do all things through Christ (Philippians 4:13), which includes winning the victory over the enemy! Furthermore, he needs to agree that the Lord is on his side and has a good plan for his precious life, for we read: *"...I know the thoughts I think toward you, says the LORD, thoughts of peace and not of evil, to give you a future and a hope."* (Jeremiah 29:11) *"And we know that all things work together for good to those who love God, to those who are the called according to His purpose."* (Romans 8:28) Therefore, if your counselee admits to being fearful and not trusting the Lord to provide victory over the enemy, lead him to pray, asking the Lord to forgive him for yielding to temptation to fear and failing to trust that He will enable him to deal with all the issues, claim back the ground from Satan, and have a victorious ending. You will also eventually lead the flip-side and wounded parts to claim victory over the enemy's fear and lack-of-trust tactics, too!

HINDRANCE OF UNCONFESSED KNOWN SINS, TINY OR HUGE!

Remember, dear servant of the Lord, as you work with your counselees do not neglect to use **God's Word, scripture, for it is a tremendous tool** as He directs your heart, for we're told that*"...the word of God is living and powerful, and sharper than a two-edged sword, piercing even to the division of soul and spirit, and of joints and marrow, and is a discerner of the thoughts and intents of the heart!"* (Hebrews 4:12) His Word convicts hearts, lovingly inviting them to repent and find peace through His forgiveness.

If while counseling there is a hindrance, a blockage of progression in counseling, then check to see if there are any known sins that the counselee has kept secret—**secret sins, hidden either out of embarrassment and shame or not wanting to give up a particular sin**!

Urge your counselee to deal with any **sin-hindrances that he just flat enjoys and doesn't want to give up**, remind him that the Lord says: *"If I regard iniquity in my heart, the Lord will not hear."* (Psalm 66:18) He cannot expect for the Lord to bless him in other ways! Explain that this does not mean that God cannot hear his voice, but rather that He will not communicate with him until he is repentant of these destructive hindrances. God desires for us all to deal with the sin-issues, right our hearts, be in unity with Him so that we can enjoy sweet fellowship, sweet communication with Him and know the joy of walking in His will! The very next verse after the one stating God will not hear those who stubbornly cling to iniquity, we read of God communicating with one who is repentant: *"But certainly God has heard me; He has attended to the voice of my prayer. Blessed be God, Who has not turned away my prayer, nor His mercy from me!"* (Psalm 66:19-20) **Therefore, if he stubbornly chooses not to repent, it would be useless to continue with his counseling sessions.**

It is also grievous for any Christian to believe that God views some sins to be greater than others—that it's okay to secretly harbor **"tiny sins"—"no big deal!"** Anyone believing this is believing a lie! **A very tiny sin is equal to that of a sin that is deemed by some as an enormously horrific sin**! Proof is found in God's Word when we read: *"For whoever shall keep the whole law, and yet stumble in one point, he is guilty of all."* (James 2:10) The fact is that Satan knows this, and when he's allowed to claim that "inch," he is all too eager to attempt to "take a mile"!

If you find that the core is too embarrassed to state what a particular known sin is that he considers "enormously horrific," encourage him by reminding him that all of us are equal, all of us have sinned as we read in God's Word: *"All have sinned and fall short of the glory of God."* (Romans 3:23).

181

You can share that our Lord also says: *"He who covers his sins will not prosper, But whoever confesses and forsakes them will have mercy."* (Proverbs 28:13) We also read in God's Word: *"...Every idle word men may speak; they will give account of it in the Day of Judgment. For by your words you will be justified, and by your word you will be condemned."* (Matthew 12:36-37) For the Christian, this has nothing to do with his salvation, for it is permanently secured—once saved, always saved—but he will be judged according to his works—either to receive or not receive rewards. There have been times when the core personality has wept with extreme embarrassment and shame about something he has said or done, that the Lord has given me a peace to allow him to pray silently, confessing that particular known sin and thanking the Lord for His mercy and grace upon them. And, I know as I move along with the counseling that if the person was not sincere—or if it's a matter I need to deal with—the Lord will bring it up during the counseling process.

Having a confidence that all the known sins have been dealt with, then the counselee and I can relax, knowing that as we proceed with the counseling, the Lord will uncover the unknown sins and bring healing to the core personality that He created from the foundations of the world! For, as I quoted earlier, He says in His Word: *"Confess your trespasses to one another, and pray for one another, that you may be healed. The effective, fervent prayer of a righteous man avails much."* (James 5:16)

While the saved counselee can most surely have power and authority through Jesus Christ to receive freedom from Satan's stronghold on his life, there are some other things that can either delay him from attaining it—or cause him to remain in bondage. Therefore, it is essential for the counselor to stay alert to the following possible hindrances in the process of counseling the core personality as well as the flip-side and wounded personalities! In our ministry, we have seen in counselees, the hindrances of **insincerity, co-dependency, and the professional counselee**. They vary in some ways, but nevertheless, it is clear that Satan stands ever ready to continue to deceive them and lure them away from God's will for their precious lives! **All three fall into one common category though—they've been in counseling too long!**

D. HINDRANCES: BAD BEHAVIOR AND DISHONESTY IN CORE, FLIP-SIDE AND WOUNDED PERSONALITIES

Whether you are counseling the core, flip-side, or a wounded personality, if he misbehaves and is dishonest, it is extremely important for you to remind him that Jesus loves him and died to pay his sin-debt on Calvary, and wants him to be free from Satan's stronghold. Remind him that *"Jesus said...I am the way, the truth, and the life. No one comes to the Father except through Me."* (John 14:6) Teach him that because Jesus is the truth and never lies, the enemy can't touch or capture Jesus. Stress that if he chooses to misbehave, be dishonest and be unrepentant, Satan will still have a foothold on him, so it's important for him to be truthful for Jesus says: *"And you shall know the truth and the truth shall make you free...therefore if the Son makes you free, you shall be free indeed."* (John 8:32, 36) By his honesty in telling the truth and repenting, he will be set free!

The majority of the time, when I contact a wounded personality to answer a question, I like to speak directly with him to gather information about behavior for which he's responsible rather than have the core relay the information to me. **I find it helpful to always remember that there is a wide range of types of wounded parts with whom I will be communicating.** So the responses will vary. Some are nice, some naughty, some shy, some friendly. Others are passive, while others aggressive. Some are very kindly while others are down right mean! And some shyly whisper while others are loud-mouths!

I may find one counselee with a very confident core, who is ready to get everything out in the open no matter what. I may find another counselee who is extremely reluctant for various reasons, to be open and completely honest in counseling. In putting limitations on sharing essential details, he hinders the progress from being made speedily! A flip-side of a counselee may be found who is more than happy to be up and "running the show" because the core is weak. Therefore, be prepared to meet a variety of personalities, each being capable of giving you a wide variety of information needed to lead the core personality to his freedom—but some more of a hindrance than a helper! **Be patient!**

There have been times when a personality (core, flip-side, or a wounded part), has been reluctant to share, and another personality suddenly spoke up and began to share some helpful information, and I allowed them to do so. Some have even interrupted with a tattletale attitude, but nevertheless, valuable information came forth. **However, I do strongly urge you not to allow personalities to rudely interrupt repeatedly! Let them all know that they will get their turn when the time is right. Be very mindful of the necessity to depend on the Lord to give you wisdom as to when to let each one speak, and understand that it's okay for the core and wounded personalities to take turns speaking from time to time in light of sharing helpful information! However, it is best to keep such at a minimum to cut down on confusion and gather the information separately from each personality. Things will flow much more smoothly!**

E. HINDRANCES: COUNSELEE EDITING INFORMATION IN SESSIONS

Sometimes even the core can be a hindrance, as well as the flip-side and wounded personalities! Remember that the core is always well aware of all that is going on. When I am asking the core's flip-side or wounded personality for information, **if the core is very controlling and prideful—or on the other hand, he's shy and embarrasses easily**—he can attempt to squelch information by interrupting before his flip-side or a wounded personality has a chance to speak! In either case, when I'm depending on the core to share what he hears, senses, feels, or sees, he may be prone to analyze things and select what he wants to edit out before relaying the other information to me! Therefore, I stress to the core personality that **(1) he is the chief reporter** on whom I'm depending to gather accurate information, while **(2) I am the chief editor** who is depending on God to help me figure out what it all means!

This is why I sometimes have to remind a counselee that he is doing himself more harm than good if he, as the core personality, is not relaying "the whole truth and nothing but the truth" to me! If I am dealing with a flip-side or wounded part who seems unable to speak, **I remind the core of how important it is for him to report exactly what he is hearing, feeling, sensing, or seeing. I also remind the core that Satan is pleased when he holds back information, for that just gives Satan more ammunition to use against him and prolongs his achieving freedom, peace and joy!**

HINDRANCE OF DEEMING SOMETHING "UNIMPORTANT"

Sometimes while dealing with the flip-side or wounded personalities, I have used all the information the core gave me concerning what he was hearing, feeling, sensing or seeing, yet the work could not be completed. So, I recognize that another **possible hindrance** could be that the **core was treating matters "carelessly"—not taking care to share details that he mistakenly thought "unimportant!"** While it may not have been deliberate on his part, nevertheless, he was still not being completely honest! So, I quiz him to see if he has, indeed, been careless by thinking it's not important! And, I remind him that we must know more of the details in order to complete the work and claim victory over the enemy!

While quizzing the flip-side and wounded parts, there are times when I find that it is they who are clinging stubbornly to their information about their roles and connecting emotions in the core's life—thus, withholding details from the core personality. The deliverance process can be hindered in these ways, but as I depend on the Lord to prod them along, I know I will eventually get the information from all of them.

Pertaining to the flip-side and wounded personalities, along with the information you are gathering, be alert to changes in **voice tones, body language, facial expressions, and tears, which can be very important helps. Use these changes as opportunities to help you gather more information.** For instance, if the wounded part you are communicating with becomes emotional and begins to cry you can say, **"I'm so sorry that you're sad. Why are you sad? How old are you?" These questions can lead you to find that wounded personality. Then, ask "What is your name?" and "Why are you crying?" and so on.** While there are some counselees who speak the entire time in their normal adult voice while speaking for a wounded personality, there have been scores of others of who actually sounded like very young children when their younger wounded parts spoke. Some have looked down and sucked their thumbs or fingers while twisting their hair, while some have also pulled their cuddly toy or their "blanket" from a bag they brought with them and clung to it through a large part of their counseling sessions.

On the other end of the spectrum, when interviewing flip-sides and wounded parts who are so full of anger and bitterness, they have raised their voices, shouted, and used bad language. While I allow them to voice their feelings, I take full authority through Jesus Christ not to allow any of them to become unruly! I have very seldom had wounded personalities, or demons for that matter, get beyond the point of "attempting" to be destructive. When I have, upon my commanding them through my authority in Jesus Christ for them to cease doing whatever they were doing, they immediately obeyed, settled back down and behaved themselves. There is no reason whatsoever to let any wounded part or demon get out of hand! Authority is had through our Redeemer, Jesus Christ!

F.   HINDRANCE: CORE/WOUNDED PART REFUSE TO FORGIVE SELF

In the midst of a Christian dealing with all his known sins, and then dealing with all his unknown sins when they are revealed during counseling, an enormous hindrance is sometimes found when the core personality deems his sins so great that even though he declares, "I know God has forgiven me!"—he says that he cannot forgive himself. Of course Satan is most certainly agreeing and reinforcing his thoughts—condemning him for the very sins Satan tempted the core to commit!

It is crucial to know that when the counselee and I believe that we have dealt with all of the strongholds in his life, yet the ancestral demons and his network won't leave, it is possible that **the core personality is harboring unforgiveness against himself**. If so, the demons still legally hold that piece of ground and do not have to leave! Sometimes while counseling such persons, upon commanding the demons to leave a person, the demons have boastfully declared their legal right to stay—based on the fact that the core personality has not forgiven himself! **How very grateful I have been when God has caused the demons to trip up, literally stumble over their own tongue!** Our evidence of that is found in Psalm 64:7-8b, 10: *"...but God shall shoot at them with an arrow; suddenly they shall be wounded. So **He will make them stumble over their own tongue**...the righteous shall be glad in the LORD, and trust in Him, and all the upright in heart shall glory."* Their tattling backfired on them! Their ground was revealed so that the core could deal with it and head on toward freedom! How happy the counselee and I have been when we have heard them slip up and in smart-aleck tones declare such things as "Our ground is his self-hatred!"

Before I check to see if the core personality is harboring unforgiveness toward him, I first check to see if there is a wounded personality connected to self-hatred, self-unforgiveness, self-condemnation, or self-idolatry. Whether I'm speaking with a wounded personality or the core personality, I warn him that the demons do not have to leave as long as he clings to these sins. Then I begin sharing God's truths about the "sin of not forgiving himself" to bring him under conviction of this sin—and to repentance.

I explain that with his choosing not to forgive himself, he is elevating himself as a judge above "The Judge above all judges"—our merciful, forgiving Judge who is the sovereign, Almighty God! I explain that it is not unlike self-idolatry, and that upon his not forgiving himself, he is implying that God is wrong to forgive him! I quote I John 1:9 to him: *"If we confess our sins, He is faithful and just to forgive us our sins and to cleanse us from all unrighteousness."* I also quote Romans 8:1: *"There is therefore now **no condemnation** to those who are in Christ Jesus, who do not walk*

185

according to the flesh, but according to the Spirit." **I remind him that while none of us deserve forgiveness, when we sincerely ask for forgiveness, through our merciful Savior, by His grace we are forgiven—we are justified—"just as if we never sinned!" "Amazing Grace, how sweet the sound that saved a wretch like me," indeed!**

G. HINDRANCES: ATTEMPTED BY DEMONS, BLOOD-LINKED BY JESUS

In Matthew 12:29, Jesus stated: *"...How can one enter a strong man's house and plunder his goods, unless he first binds the strong man? And then he will plunder his house."* We read in Matthew 26:28: *"For this is My blood of the new covenant, which is shed for the remission of sins."* Therefore, the truth is that the only power and authority we have over the enemy Satan and all his demons is through our Lord Jesus Christ who shed His blood in our behalf on the Cross. In willingly shedding His blood to pay the sin-debt of mankind, Jesus gave Christians the authority, the legal right to resist temptation and to claim back any ground given over to the enemy, Satan!

BLOOD-LINK THE DEMONS OF HINDRANCE

As you would guess, during counseling **the demons are not shy about trying to interfere, especially because they are subject to losing the ground that they've claimed!** They will try various ways to **distract, disturb, and cause confusion** with the personalities—including slyly masquerading as wounded personalities, or performing as clones of the core or flip-side. They will try to bring up subject matter that will lead you to only waste time "chasing rabbits"—getting you off the main subject at hand! **The ancestral demon will also try to slip out and/or send out some of his network so they can't be found.**

Through Jesus Christ, we can bind up our strong enemy and plunder his goods, reclaim what he has stolen from God's people! During counseling sessions, **I take great care to tell the ancestral demon, his network and other demons that I am not attempting to control and bind them up by my own power, but rather, by the power and authority given through Jesus Christ and His shed blood. Therefore, they must obey! As you saw in the examples I gave earlier, and as you will read in the counseling procedures that follow, I ask the Lord to blood-link them all together with blood-links that cannot be broken which are made of the blood Jesus shed on Calvary. This prevents the demons from being a hindrance during counseling.** If I discern that the ancestral demon has posed a hindrance by transferring out or has sent out some of his network in hopes of hiding, I command through Jesus' authority that they all come back. When I know they are back, I ask the Lord to bind up together, the ancestral demon and his network with blood-links that cannot be broken, made of the blood Jesus shed on Calvary, so that they cannot leave again. I stay on the alert until the core has dealt with all his issues, and we have finished dealing with the flip-side and all the wounded parts. Then, there is nothing left to delay the core personality from receiving his freedom, and peace and joy from the Lord Jesus. We then proceed with our God-given power and authority to deal with the ancestral demon and his network, plunder their house and sentence them to their doom. Since they are blood-linked together with God's chains made of Jesus' blood, and stripped of all their legal rights to ground in the counselee's life, then out they all must go from the core's life!

I hope that this chapter has provided information that you have found encouraging to you personally as a fellow servant and help in your ministry also! I will now take you into my counseling room and share the procedures that I am so very grateful that the Lord taught me so that I could lead precious souls in bondage to freedom through our Lord Jesus Christ!

Chapter Eight
TOOLS FOR BEFORE AND DURING FIRST COUNSELING SESSION

A.   PRAYER TOOLS FOR THE COUNSELEE

While the counselee is waiting for his appointments, in order to encourage and help him, I give him some tools to use—some prayer tools to pray sincerely! I urge him to stay snuggled up to the Lord with an attitude of trust and gratitude that the Lord will, indeed, provide the freedom, peace and joy for which he longs. **I always urge a counselee to pray these example prayers, because they actually serve to teach him during his time of waiting that his hope is in Jesus Christ!** The prayers are great helps for teaching him to gratefully voice to the Lord the truths He has spoken concerning His love and His authority over and protection from the enemy—and the promise that He will lead him to freedom in His perfect timing and ways! I believe you will find them to be immensely valuable tools for helping and encouraging all of your counselees while they await their freedom!

The following prayer is a short one that he can pray when he first awakes in the morning—it is especially good for mornings when he didn't get up early enough to have ample quiet time with the Lord—thus, is forced to rush about getting ready! Actually this is a good morning starter-prayer for every Christian—whether in bondage or free, for there are times when one is "providentially hindered"!

SAMPLE SHORT MORNING PRAYER

"Lord Jesus, I give You my will, rights, and control. I give You my life, family, ministry, finances, needs, desires, direction, and flesh. Search me and try me, see if there be any wicked way in me. Remove those things that need to be removed, and bring into my life what needs to be brought in. I confess that You are all I have, You are all I want, and You are all I need. I choose to put on the whole armor of God that I may be able to stand against the wiles of the devil stated in Ephesians 6:10-18.

"Lord Jesus, by the power of Your shed blood, I cancel, renounce, and sever from my life, family, ministry, job, all of my holdings, my pastor, and Church family, plus any and all words of witchcraft, sorceries, incantations, divinations, Voodoo, Masonry, Kung-Foo, Karate, New Age, Satanist curses and any other curses that have been sent against us. I want each and everything sent back to the senders a

189

thousand fold, not out of anger or bitterness but that they may see and know the power of God with hopes of their accepting, loving and following Him. I want to thank You and praise You for this, in Jesus' name."

This is another prayer—a longer prayer that I share with the person. This prayer voices the need for the counselee to let the Lord be in control of his personal life. And, it voices that in spite of Satan's having a stronghold on his life at this point, He is trusting that the Lord will enable him to resist giving in to the enemy's desires as he moves through the day.

LONGER SAMPLE PRAYER FOR COUNSELEE TO PRAY

"Lord Jesus, I ask You to allow my core personality that You love so much and thought up from the foundation of the world, that is soft and pliable, reachable and teachable, repentable and saveable, to be totally submitted to You in order that You may control my life. If I have a flip-side, I want You to take it and any wounded personalities and put them in a safe place with Jesus so that they cannot interfere with us nor be interfered with. I want a shield of Your blood separating my core personality from all the rest. Lord, I want to be totally yielded to You so that You may teach me Your truths and bring healing and restoration to my soul.

"Lord, if there is an ancestral demon, I ask You to take the ancestral demon that carries my full formal name (state first, middle, and last) and bind, gag, and render the ancestral demon inoperative, including all of his personal network, any other ancestral demons and their networks, lifestyle demons, demon-produced personalities, demon-clones, and any demons that masquerade as wounded personalities.

"Lord, I want only my core personality interacting with You, and I want only the core personality, under the leadership of the Lordship of Christ, governing my life. Heavenly Papa, I want Your precious Son's blood surrounding me and protecting me from all evil while I work with You. I want to thank You and praise You for doing this in order for me to be able to become who You created me to be. It is in the name of Jesus that I pray these things and thank You. Amen."

Another prayer is a marvelous "Warfare Prayer" graciously shared by a precious brother-in-the-Lord, Dr. Victor M. Matthews. It is made up of approximately 85% scripture. I encourage the counselee to pray this prayer first thing in the morning—unless providentially hindered—and just before he puts his head on his pillow. Plus, I encourage the counselee to carry this prayer with him at all times—keep it handy to lead him in prayer at any time during the day or night when he is bombarded with tormenting thoughts from the enemy! It takes about 10 minutes to pray brother Victor's warfare prayer.

I have daily prayed Dr. Victor M. Matthews' marvelous prayer with deep sincerity in my heart for more than 20 years. For, this prayer is truly saturated with God's wondrous truths about the legal rights we have through Jesus Christ to consistently stand strong against the enemy! Many counselees have told me that it has truly served as an enormous encouragement to them. I believe that all ministers and counselors will find our brother Victor's warfare prayer to be a blessing to them as well!

WARFARE PRAYER BY VICTOR M. MATTHEWS

"Heavenly Father, I bow in worship and praise before You. I cover myself with the blood of the Lord Jesus Christ as my protection. I surrender myself completely and unreservedly in every area of my life to You. I take a stand against all the workings of Satan that would hinder me in my prayer life. I address myself only to the True and Living God and refuse any involvement of Satan in my prayer.

"Satan, I command you, in the name of the Lord Jesus Christ, to leave my presence with all of your demons. I bring the blood of the Lord Jesus Christ between us.

"Heavenly Father, I worship You and give You praise. I recognize that You are worthy to receive all glory and honor and praise. I renew my allegiance to You and pray that the blessed Holy Spirit would enable me in this time of prayer. I am thankful, Heavenly Father, that You have loved me from past eternity and that You sent the Lord Jesus Christ into the world to die as my substitute. I am thankful that the Lord Jesus Christ came as my representative and that through Him You have completely forgiven me; You have adopted me into Your family; You have assumed all responsibility for me; You have given me eternal life; You have given me the perfect righteousness of the Lord Jesus Christ so I am now justified. I am thankful that in Him You have made me complete, and that You have offered Yourself to me to be my daily help and strength.

"Heavenly Father, open my eyes that I might see how great You are and how complete Your provision is for this day. I am thankful that the victory the Lord Jesus Christ won for me on the Cross and in His resurrection has been given to me and that I am seated with the Lord Jesus Christ in the heavenlies. I take my place with Him in the heavenlies and recognize by faith that all wicked spirits and Satan himself are under my feet. I declare, therefore, that Satan and his wicked spirits are subject to me in the Name of the Lord Jesus Christ.

"I am thankful for the Armor You have provided. I put on the Girdle of Truth, the Breastplate of Righteousness, the Sandals of Peace and the Helmet of Salvation. I lift up the Shield of Faith against all the fiery darts of the enemy; and I take in my hand the Sword of the Spirit, the Word of God. I choose to use Your Word against all the forces of evil in my life. I put on this Armor and live and pray in complete dependence upon You, blessed Holy Spirit.

"I am grateful, Heavenly Father that the Lord Jesus Christ spoiled all principalities and powers and made a show of them openly and triumphed over them in Himself. I claim all that victory for my life today. I reject all the insinuations, and accusations, and the temptations of Satan. I affirm that the Word of God is true and I choose to live today in the light of God's Word. I choose Heavenly Father, to live in obedience to You and in fellowship with Yourself. Open my eyes and show me the areas of my life that do not please You. Work in me to cleanse me from all ground that would give Satan a foothold against me. I do in every way stand into all that it means to be Your adopted child and I welcome all the ministry of the Holy Spirit.

"By faith and in dependence upon You, I put off the fleshly works of the old man and stand in all the victory of the crucifixion where the Lord Jesus Christ provided cleansing from the old nature. I put on the new man and stand in all the victory of the resurrection and the provision He has made for me to live above sin.

"Therefore, today, I put off all forms of selfishness and put on the new nature with its love. I put off all forms of fear and put on the new nature with its courage. I put off all forms of weakness and put on the new nature with its strength. I put off all forms of lust and put on the new nature with its righteousness, purity, and honesty. I trust You to show me how to make this practical in my daily life.

"In every way I stand in the victory of the ascension and glorification of the Lord Jesus Christ, whereby all the principalities and powers were made subject to Him. I claim my place in Christ as victorious with Him over all the enemies of my soul. Blessed Holy Spirit, I pray that You would fill me. Come into my life, break down every idol and cast out every foe.

"I am thankful, Heavenly Father, for the expression of Your will for my daily life as You have shown me in Your Word. I therefore claim all the will of God for today. I am thankful that You have blessed me with all spiritual blessings in heavenly places in Christ Jesus. I am thankful that You have begotten me unto a living hope by the resurrection of Jesus Christ from the dead. I am thankful that You have made a provision so that today I can live filled with the Spirit of God with love and joy and peace, with longsuffering, gentleness, and goodness, with meekness, faithfulness and self-control in my life. I recognize that this is Your will for me and I therefore reject and resist all the endeavors of Satan and his wicked spirits to rob me of the will of God. I refuse in this day to believe my feelings and I hold up the Shield of Faith against all the accusations and distortion and insinuations that Satan would put into my mind. I claim the fullness of the will of God for my life today.

"In the Name of the Lord Jesus Christ, I completely surrender myself to You, Heavenly Father, as a living sacrifice. I choose not to be conformed to this world. I choose to be transformed by the renewing of my mind, and I pray that You would show me Your will and enable me to walk in all the fullness of Your will today.

"I am thankful, Heavenly Father, that the weapons of our warfare are not carnal but mighty through God to the pulling down of strongholds, to the casting down of imaginations and every high thing that exalteth itself against the knowledge of God, and to bring every thought into obedience to the Lord Jesus Christ. Therefore, in my own life today, I tear down the strongholds of Satan and smash the plans of Satan that have been formed against me. I tear down the strongholds against my mind, and I surrender my mind to You, blessed Holy Spirit. I affirm, Heavenly Father, that You have not given me the spirit of fear, but of power and of love, and of a sound mind. I break and smash the strongholds of Satan formed against my emotions today and I give my emotions to You. I smash the strongholds of Satan formed against my will today, I give my will to You, and choose to make the right decisions of faith. I smash the strongholds of Satan formed against my body today. I give my body to You recognizing that I am Your temple. I rejoice in Your mercy and righteousness.

"Heavenly Father, I pray that now and through this day, You would strengthen and enlighten me, show me the way Satan is hindering and tempting and lying and distorting the truth in my life. Enable me to be the kind of person that would please You. Enable me to be aggressive in prayer and faith. Enable me to be aggressive mentally, to think about and practice Your Word, and to give You Your rightful place in my life.

"Again, I cover myself with the blood of the Lord Jesus Christ and pray that You, blessed Holy Spirit, would bring all the work of the crucifixion, all the work of the resurrection, all the work of the glorification, and all the work of Pentecost into my life today. I surrender myself to You. I refuse to be discouraged. You are the God of all hope. You have proven Your power by resurrecting Jesus Christ from the dead, and I claim in every way this victory over the satanic forces in my life. I pray in the Name of the Lord Jesus Christ with thanksgiving. Amen."

by Victor M. Matthews

SAMPLE, SHORT EVENING PRAYER

While I've given the counselee our brother Victor's prayer, and urged him to pray it sincerely before going to sleep, I also give Him a shorter prayer He can pray no matter how weary—no matter how exhausted—he is when he puts his head on the pillow! I have stressed the importance of at least taking time to pray this short evening prayer:

> "Lord Jesus, I ask You to build a hedge of Your blood around my body, soul, spirit, emotions, and mind—conscious and subconscious. Don't let one thing get to me that doesn't first come by way of the Cross and through the blood of Jesus. Protect me by Your love and grace throughout the dark hours of the night. I thank You for this, in Jesus' name."

PRAYING FOR A PERSON NEEDING BUT RESISTING COUNSEL

While on the subject of prayers, before we move forward to gather the tools for the first counseling session, there is another prayer I believe you will find helpful in your ministry. You may have experienced people approaching you, asking how they can pray for persons they care about who are badly in need of help—some needing salvation and/or some Christians who have become entangled in the Devil's snare. They have added that these persons are so unhappy, yet seem to stay on the defensive when they bring up the subject of possible help for them, especially when "God" is brought into the picture! I explain to them that it's important that we remember that such persons, ninety-nine point nine percent of the time have been hurt over things that have happened to them in the past. As it has been said, "They are wearing their feelings on their shirt sleeves!" As you know, with unforgiveness deeply embedded in their hearts, Satan has established ground! These persons may even be angry at God for letting those things happen! They may even lash out in anger—even when close friends or family members approach them in loving kindness, with good intentions. **When I was burdened myself for some people such as this, the Lord gave me wisdom how to pray for them before engaging in conversation with them.**

Now care should be taken to understand the purpose of the following prayer! **As you will see, this is a prayerful appeal to the Lord to enable the person needing help to have a clear mind and heart as "the caring person" is with them "for a period of time" during which they will engage in conversation together. This time is to be spent "ministering" unconditional love, and complimenting him on the positives seen in him—his God-given talents---encouraging him.** Later—after he becomes secure in the caring person's love for him, then he will be more prone to "let the person into his world" to minister by sharing God's truths about salvation and spiritual warfare!

Example: we'll say that a grown son of a Christian couple is in a sinful spiritual condition and he comes by to visit them one evening. The well-meaning parents, out of their love and deep concern, express how worried they are about **"the negatives that are going on in his life"—be that of**

typically getting fired from jobs, drinking, gambling or whatever. However, with their **pointing out his sins rather than the positives they see in him and offering encouragement— helpful truths—hope to be rescued**—he misinterprets their appeals as "words of condemnation" rather than words of encouragement and hope. **With their having first pointed out his sins**, then when they lovingly tell him that God loves him and will help him if he lets Him, their kind words are overshadowed by the negatives. He translates the positive words as critical and condemning, so he becomes angry with them. Whether lost or saved, the man is in bondage. He is in turmoil on the inside and Satan is most surely contributing to the misinterpretation of the parents' good intentions! Therefore, before such caring souls spend "a private period of time" talking "casually" with a person who is easily offended, not open to discuss what's going on in his life or anything about God, I suggest that they pray the prayer posted below. **Pray the prayer silently—so that the person cannot hear—before communicating with him**. However, please note that if a sin-bound person is comfortable with you, trusts you, and confesses to you that he needs help and believes God is the only one who can help him, then you can explain about spiritual warfare and victory in Jesus. If he says he believes that what you're saying is true, then **ask his permission to pray this prayer for him aloud before you converse with one another**.

PRAYER FOR A PERSON IN NEED OF COUNSELING

"Lord Jesus, I ask You to allow me to speak with <u>core personality's formal name</u> whom You love so much and thought up from the foundation of the world, that is soft and pliable, reachable and teachable, repentable and saveable. If there is a flip-side, I ask You to take it and any wounded personalities and put them in a safe place with Jesus so that they cannot interfere with us, nor can they be interfered with. I ask that You put a shield of Your blood separating the core personality from all the rest. Lord, I ask that You enable me to see this person with Your eyes, hear them with Your ears, and comprehend them with Your mind. Lord, I want to speak with Your mouth and love this precious person with Your heart, for I desire for them to be healed by Your loving hand.

"Lord, if there is an ancestral demon, I ask that You take the ancestral demon carrying <u>core personality's full formal name</u> and bind, gag, and render the ancestral demon inoperative, including all of his personal network, any other ancestral demons and their networks, lifestyle demons, demon-produced personalities, demon-clones, and any demons that masquerade as wounded personalities.

"Lord, I want only the core personality interacting with me, and I want only the core personality under the leadership of the Lordship of Christ governing this person's life. Heavenly Papa, we want Your precious Son's blood surrounding us and protecting us from all evil while we work. I want to thank You and praise You for doing this in order for me to be able to minister to this person, and it is in the name of Jesus that I pray this. Amen."

After praying the prayer, then **it is critical to be sensitive to the Lord's voice, asking Him to give you wisdom as you converse with the person.** Ask the Lord to put a watchman at your mouth and a guard at your tongue! Be keenly aware of God's timing as to "when"—now or at a more appropriate time—that He wants you to share God's plan of salvation and/or discuss the basic truths about spiritual warfare. For, as you communicate with a bound soul who has "a short fuse," you should remember that God says: ***"A soft answer turns away wrath, but a harsh word stirs up anger. The tongue of the wise uses knowledge rightly...."*** (Proverbs 15:1-2a)

If the person indicates that he doesn't want to engage in conversation about spiritual matters, it is crucial to respect his choice—and remember not to "nag" the person! The presentation of sharing truths about spiritual warfare as the Lord directs is no different than witnessing to a person. The Lord just wants us to "set the table with healthy, delicious spiritual food"—then, it's left strictly up to the person to choose whether or not to accept the invitation and "come and dine." We must respect his right to choose to eat or not to eat of what has been set before him—and not try to force-feed him. When he leaves the table—if he leaves still unsatisfied, trust that the Lord will remind him of those abundant truths that were spread before him! He did not leave the table alone, for Psalm 139 says that he cannot escape God's presence! The Lord will not leave or forsake him and will continue to pursue him—convicting his heart, ministering to him in His wise, unique and wonderful ways.

I hope that all of these prayers will be of help to you in your ministry, and to your counselees as well. And now, I will take you through the procedures that I typically follow when a counselee arrives for his first appointment with me:

B.   TOOLS FOR THE FIRST COUNSELING SESSION

Upon the counselee's arriving at our home for his first counseling session, he has been welcomed and we have taken a little time for some casual conversation to help put him at ease.

TOOL #1: COUNSELOR'S OPENING PRAYER

Then, I start our session by praying:

> "Lord Jesus, I want to praise and thank You for this opportunity to spend time with You and this precious person that You have brought into my life, core personality's formal name, age ___, saved at age ___.

> "Lord Jesus, I ask that Your blood would purge and cleanse the atmospheric conditions over this building and in every square foot inside and outside. We ask that You do this, for we want it to be holy ground and a safe place to work.

"Heavenly Father, I'm asking You to shut down by the blood of the Lord Jesus Christ, all principalities, powers, god-heads, and all territorial demons that have been operating around our lives since our conception. We ask that You do not allow them to send or receive messages or messengers. Shut it all down. Do not allow Satan to use any demons to send any reinforcements into the network of demons in the person I'm working with. Shut Satan down totally pertaining to this person. I don't want Satan and his demons that are on the outside to be able to do anything but wiggle and watch in silence while this precious person works toward and achieves his freedom!

"Lord Jesus, I yield my will, my rights, and my control completely over to You. Put a watchman at my mouth and a guard at my tongue! And, allow me to say nothing to this precious person I'm working with that will not bring praise and glory to Your name and bring help, encouragement and edification to them. And, I ask that You help the core personality, core personality's formal name, to relax so that You can do Your work."

TOOL #2: COUNSELEE'S OPENING PRAYER

With each counselee, I don't know what to expect. Since many counselees are nervous—or even scared, some crying—I ask them to simply pray, **"Lord Jesus, I give You my will, rights, and control," and I also instruct them to pray anything else that they would like to pray.** Sometimes the additional things that they pray give me very helpful information, and it also shows the counselee that I want him to feel free to pray whatever is on his heart.

TOOL #3: CHECK OUT THE COUNSELEE'S SALVATION

I then move to a very crucial point, by checking out the validity of my counselee's salvation! There are two times to check out the validity of the counselee's salvation:

1.   At the very beginning of his first counseling session
2.   When progress is being hindered during counseling.

The following are wonderful passages to read to the counselee to confirm that our salvation is only through Jesus Christ.

John 3:16: *"For God so loved the world, that He gave His only begotten Son, that whoever believes in Him should not perish but have everlasting life. For God sent not His Son into the world to condemn the world, but that the world through Him might be saved."*

Romans 8:16: *"The Spirit Himself bears witness with our spirit that we are children of God."*

197

> Romans 10:9-13: *"...if you confess with your mouth the Lord Jesus and believe in your heart that God has raised Him from the dead, you will be saved. For with the heart one believes unto righteousness, and with the mouth confession is made unto salvation. For the Scripture says, 'Whoever believes on Him will not be put to shame.' For there is no distinction between Jew and Greek, for the same Lord over all is rich to all who call upon Him. For 'whoever shall call upon the name of the Lord shall be saved.'"*

As you can well understand, it is extremely crucial that the counselee knows when he truly accepted the Lord as his Savior. He doesn't have to know the exact date, but he should have some knowledge as to his approximate age—such as about what grade he was in—or memory of where he was when he invited the Lord into his heart. If he is not sure, then you must take time to lead him to pray, asking the Lord to help him recall it. If you find that he is lost, then invite him to receive Jesus as his Lord and Savior at that time. **Unless you and the counselee are secure as to when he got saved, all counseling will be in vain, for that is the only way he can have authority, through Jesus Christ, to overcome the enemy and claim victory!**

Once you have established when he received salvation, then you can confidently counsel and offer liberation to the bruised! His soul can be restored to the way God thought it up. He can then function without the strongholds through the flip-side, wounded personalities, and ancestral demons, thus live the abundant life that the Lord intended him to live!

Being secure with the age of salvation that the counselee has given, and with his having read "Liberating the Bruised," plus **either** listened to the CDs and review the syllabus **or** read "More Tools for Liberating the Bruised," he is aware of the topics of the flip-side, wounded personalities, and ancestral demons and the general process of counseling. Then I can confidently begin working with the counselee.

TOOL #4: REVIEW THE COUNSELING FORM WITH COUNSELEE

At this point, I share with the counselee what I was able to glean from his counseling form. I show him my double-columned pad with the "Flip-side" on the left with the list of negatives written below, and "Core-Personality" on the right, left blank. (Illustrated in Chapter Six.)

TOOL #5: NEED TO DEAL WITH KNOWN AND UNKNOWN SINS

I know while the counselee was looking at the list of negatives in his life, the list could have served to trigger any known sins that he has not yet dealt with. Having all known sins confessed before dealing with the unknowns is crucial, so I take time to ask the counselee if any sins came to his mind while going over the list. **To show him the importance of seeking forgiveness and not grieving the Spirit of God, I quote Ephesians 4:26-27: *"...do not sin: do not let the sun go down on your wrath, nor give place to the devil."* I would add that we need to make certain that the**

devil has no ground on which to stand! If he shares something he hasn't repented of, I then give him opportunity to ask the Lord to deal with it and claim back the ground that he gave to the devil in that act! (For more details, see Chapter 5, "Restoring True Worship" in "Liberating the Bruised.")

TOOL #6: COUNSELEE LISTS POSITIVES IN HIS LIFE

Having made sure that all known sins are confessed, I then hand my note pad to the counselee and ask him to please list, on the right side of the page, under "Core Personality," all of the good things that he knows about himself. (Illustrated in Chapter Six.)

After he has made his list, then I explain that this illustrates that he is a duplex, that this is why he is so troubled. Some counselees have said that this explains why one moment they are able to behave well, like they want to, while at other times, they become extremely angry and lose their temper, lashing out at others. There are some who share that they may be functioning okay for a time, and then at other times, they withdraw from the world and just want to disappear.

With my counselee agreeing that he is a duplex, that he has wounded personalities, and a flip-side that is the same age he is, which began at conception, plus an ancestral demon, then he more assuredly recognizes that an ancestral demon is behind all the manipulation and he is eager to begin.

C. BRIEFLY REVIEW VAULTS AND ELEVATOR WITH COUNSELEE

VAULTS: I remind the counselee of the three vaults illustration in which we will search for ones holding amnesia, memory, and emotions:

> **VAULT #1** A wounded personality is found that contains all the emotions and the memories connected with a particular experience, thus, leaving the core personality with amnesia, a repressed memory pertaining to it. Emotions and memories are locked away together.

> **VAULT #2** A wounded personality is found that retains the emotions of an experience, but is void of the memories connected to it. Memories are locked away.

> **VAULT #3** A wounded personality is found that has all the memories, but tightly imprisons all the emotions, shutting down the person's emotions. Emotions are locked away.

ELEVATOR: Having explained the vaults to my counselee, I then use the elevator illustration to help him better visualize how I'm going to deal with the wounded parts, with the youngest one forward. I start by using my counselee's current age—for an example, I will use age 40. I ask the person to imagine that he is like a 40-story building with an elevator running from the top, 40th floor, all the way to lowest sub-level floor. It has 40 floors above ground and it can have a number of sub-level floors, with the **first sub-level floor** being **"conception in the womb to birth."** There can be trauma both in the womb, and during and after delivery. Traumas that occur after delivery, **from the time of a person's birth, during all the weeks/months between, and up to his first birthday, are found on the first floor of the person's building**. As each year passes, another floor is added on top of the previous one.

EXAMPLE OF TRAUMA IN A NEWBORN BABY

To bring about a better understanding of how a traumatic experience can affect persons at such extremely young ages, I think it very important for me to share an example of a counselee in whom I discovered a newborn baby "on the first floor of her building" who clearly held vivid memories and emotions! As I share this example, I hope it will cause any doubters to come to accept the truth that even new-born babies and very young babies have the ability within their little minds to store memories and the emotions attached to them, and the truth that these memories and emotions can stay there all their lives. Some can stay tucked away without negatively affecting a person, while others can affect a person all his life unless he receives appropriate counseling. Of course, anyone who has been around babies very much can clearly see that while they are not yet educated in a vocal language, their body language and facial expressions readily express their emotions—such as contentment, joy, discomfort, and pain. Equally true, what they experience can be stored in their feelings—their emotions, whether it seems feasible to our human reasoning or not! **Keep that in mind, as I share this from a true case:**

A precious lady (wife and mother) came to me for counseling, and one of her disturbing problems was that she always felt very cold, even in hot weather! When she came here, she was dressed in several layers of clothing, which she kept on the entire time even though my office was not at all cold! She shared that she could never get warm and that she had been that way all of her life! Of course, she desired that the temperature in the family's home was kept very warm, which made all the other family members miserable in their "hot house!" As you can imagine, this did not make for sweet fellowship in their home. She had gone to a number of doctors who ran a wide variety of tests, trying to pinpoint her problem, but all was for naught! In desperation, she came to me for counseling. As I began searching "the floors in her building," I found a little newborn baby girl who was shivering with cold and sobbing. As I interviewed her, she told me that when she was born, because her mother was experiencing some serious complications from giving birth, a nurse just hurriedly placed her on the weighing scale, which was metal and extremely cold. She reported that she was left there for a very long time, shivering and crying, without any clothes or blanket. I dealt with the little cold baby and then moved on to other floors in the lady's building. It wasn't too long before I noticed the lady remove her jacket and then her sweater! No doubt, all the lady's family

200

members were delighted when the air conditioning could at last be set at a normal temperature in the house! Without a doubt, some traumatic experiences that babies endure can surely affect their adulthood in a negative fashion!

TRAUMAS MAY OR MAY NOT RESULT IN WOUNDED PARTS

If a person experiences more than one trauma, each one falls into a **similar category**, but it does not mean that each time a trauma occurred, separate new wounded parts were created. Instead, after the first wounded part was created, with the additional traumas being in the same or similar categories, the additional ones were just connected with the first wounded personality. Example: if a woman has had three abortions, the first wounded part created can take responsibility for the additional ones. Also, sometimes **if the flip-side takes responsibility** for the abortions, **there will be no wounded parts**. I was once told by a flip-side that the core was responsible for the abortions because she loved having sex but she didn't want any stretch marks on her body, nor did she want any babies!

D.   COUNSELEE STARTS WHERE HE IS MOST COMFORTABLE

Being confident that my counselee understands the essential truths, we are ready to begin. I explain that after I pray for him in a few minutes, then I will want him to tell me at which of three starting points he thinks he would be most comfortable: **(1)** a wounded personality, **(2)** the flip-side, or **(3)** the ancestral demon.

I remind the counselee that the flip-side has always been there and holds 90% of the power— the ground on which the demons stand. If they leave the choice to me, the flip-side is definitely where I prefer to begin, for I've learned that the sooner you deal with the flip-side, the better!

I also remind him that as he read in chapter nine in my book, "Liberating the Bruised," that rather than starting with the flip-side, I used to start with the ancestral demon, insisting that he tell me about his entire network, about all the demons that worked under him, and gathered information about the person's wounded parts. While it is a sure thing that you can do it this way successfully, you must be on guard constantly because the ancestral demon will sometimes lie, so you have to double check his information to make sure it's truth. As you can imagine, he gets a thrill out of trying to collar the counselor, jerk his chain, and waste time! **As illustrated in my first book, while freedom for the counselee can surely be had while starting with the ancestral demon, I am so glad and grateful that the Lord has taught me a "shortcut," an easier, more practical way—by gathering the information from the inventory form, then starting with the flip-side and wounded personalities before confronting the ancestral demon.**

To encourage the counselee to be totally honest with me during counseling, I always remind him that the demons are not going to leave until all of his wounded parts are healed. Most surely you can order the demons to leave until you are "blue in the face" and they still won't go, for they have the legal right to stand on the ground where there are wounds where sin has not been confessed. **I tell the counselee not to worry when demons refuse to leave, for it can actually be a good thing! For it could quite possibly reveal that there is something lingering in the core personality's life that is hindering him from receiving freedom.** Therefore, we continue searching for the ground, something held in a wounded personality or other hiding places. I encourage him never to hesitate concerning dealing with sin issues, for when each sin issue connected to all the wounded parts is dealt with, he can then legally, through Jesus Christ, claim back his ground and kick all the demons out! **I add that in the end, no matter where he wants to begin, freedom lies ahead! Then I pray a three-part prayer for the counselee.**

E.   THREE-PART PRAYER FOR CATEGORIZING

In the three-part prayer, I ask the Lord to divide the person into three categories, **(1)** the core personality, **(2)** the flip-side and all the wounded personalities, and **(3)** the ancestral demon and all his network.

CATEGORY ONE PRAYER: FOR THE CORE PERSONALITY

"Dear Heavenly Father, I ask You to place in category one, <u>core's formal name</u>, age, saved at age _____, the core personality You thought up from the foundations of the world, seated in the heavens with the Lord Jesus. Place a hedge of Your blood surrounding, protecting, loving and caring for her."

CATEGORY TWO PRAYER: FOR FLIP-SIDE AND WOUNDED PARTS

I pray, "Lord Jesus, please place in category two all of <u>core's formal name's</u> wounded personalities and the flip-side, the opposite side of her.

CATEGORY THREE PRAYER: ABOUT ANCESTRAL DEMON/NETWORK

I then pray very specifically (covering all the bases): "Heavenly Father, please place in category three <u>Ancestral Demon core's formal name and his network</u>, with all other ancestral demons and their networks, plus all lifestyle demons and their networks, all demon-produced personalities, demon-clones, demons that masquerade as personalities, gatekeepers and their networks, and any shared demons (those that share between networks in this person as well as from other people in bondage).

"Lord, I ask You to call in all shared demons that belong in this network so that they, too, can be dealt with. Precious Lord Jesus, please bind, gag and render all of the demons in this category three inoperative so that they cannot interfere with the counseling. Dear Lord, I thank You that You will bind up all the demons so that there will be no confusion during our counseling sessions. However, dear Lord, we trust that if You want to use any demons to provide some information that we need to learn early on, we thank You that You will use them to expose it in order to help prevent precious time from being wasted."

COUNSELEE THEN CHOOSES A CATEGORY

At this point, I ask the core personality where he wants to begin—with the flip-side, a wounded part, or the ancestral demon. With my second note pad in hand, I'm ready to begin counseling.

Chapter Nine
TOOLS FOR COUNSELING CORE, BROKEN PART AND FLIP-SIDE

As you begin counseling, not only must you stand confidently in your authority in Christ, but you should continue to encourage your counselee that he, too has the authority in Christ to stand confidently against the enemy. When necessary, remind him of the scripture that proclaims that with the Lord Jesus residing in his heart who has Satan and the demons "under His feet"—under His authority—through Christ, he has the authority to stand in confidence: *"You have put all things in subjection under His feet. For in that He put all in subjection under Him, He left nothing that is not put under Him..."* (Hebrews 2:8) If Christ, in the form of the Holy Spirit, lives in a person's heart then he has the authority to stand in victory over the enemy! This scripture reminds me of a wonderful old hymn that well expresses this truth, "Standing on the Promises of God!" Without a doubt, with Jesus, we can stand on His promises and defeat the enemy!

A.   GOD'S POWER TOOL—PRAYER

God has given us a very unique, tremendously powerful tool! This tool is called, "prayer!" However, it must be used properly in order for the tool to be used the way the Lord intended! This marvelous tool comes in two parts with a powerful connecting part. While **one part of this prayer tool transports our words to God,** so often there is neglect and failure to use the other part of the tool enough—or very much at all! For, **the other part transports God's words to us. The connecting part between the two is the wisdom-and-will-of-God.** Thus, it is ever so important that we use God's prayer-tool properly, while remembering that **we are the clay and the Lord is the Potter.** With the privilege of having this communication tool, we should always take care to remember that there are times when God's ways are not at all like our ways! While we are pleased when He chooses to say "Yes!"—we don't always readily understand when He answers with a "wait a while" or a "No!" Nevertheless, we should fully trust our Potter to know best whatever His answer is! We should never forget that we have been told to believe this:

> *"Now this is the confidence that we have in Him, that **if we ask anything according to His will, He hears us**. And if we know that He hears us, whatever we ask, we know that we have the petitions that we have asked of Him."* (I John 5:14-15)

Along with trusting the Potter to answer righteously so, we make certain that we use this communications prayer-tool properly—hold it in a very unique way. While holding it with boldness as we stand in our authority in Christ Jesus, it must also be held with humility and gratitude—the

205

three blended as one attitude. In order to be God's successful craftsman/craftswoman in the counseling field, we must constantly stay in tune with the voice of our boss, listening closely for His wisdom to direct our hearts as we minister to broken hearts, broken people! We must never venture into the dangerous territory of the enemy by taking on attitudes of cockiness or self-righteousness! It is only by the grace of our Lord Jesus that we are saved, through whom we have the privilege of approaching His throne of grace! Therefore, we must take care to listen carefully for our Lord's voice to transport His wisdom, His instructions while counseling! Of course, we should take care to pray in His will—that His will be done, not ours! If God's words, will and wisdom are not connected to our part of the tool—with communications flowing without static and interruptions, our labors will be in vain—and sometimes we can do more damage than good!

B. USING MY GOD-GIVEN POWER TOOL—PRAYER

I believe with all my heart that the Lord has been able to use me in helping so many souls find freedom through the Lord because I have always realized that without having an open communication with my Potter, my Lord Jesus, I could do nothing to help tormented, desperate souls. I would shudder to think of not properly using this wonderful communication tool with which He has blessed me. What a privilege, indeed! Therefore, I never begin or end a counseling session without using my God-given prayer-tool. **I earnestly seek the Lord's wisdom and direction throughout sessions, for without Him I would be like one who "doesn't have sense enough to come in out of the rain"!**

While I am happy to share many lengthy prayers with you that the Lord has led me to pray for various subjects, I urge you not to treat the prayers like they are magic-tools, nor that you should memorize them word-for-word as if they're the ultimate prayers you must pray! I do believe that for a while it would be very wise and beneficial for you to thoroughly study and use the prayers often so that you become thoroughly familiar with the contents that apply to various issues. I encourage you to relax with the Lord and trust Him moment by moment to give you wisdom how to pray and lead your counselee to pray!

Now I do not hesitate to always pray the lengthy prayers to which I'm referring, because they are full of God's marvelous Gospel story—from the beginning to our Lord's declaring, "It is finished!" When you find that much of the prayers' general content is repeated numerous times, I hope you will understand their enormous value! For instance, while dealing and praying with flip-sides and wounded personalities about what Jesus did for them on Calvary's Cross, so many have come under heavy conviction, crying tears of repentance and gratitude to Jesus for what He endured on their behalf when He became their sin so they could become His righteousness! I hope you will come to benefit from using the prayers that contain salvation's wondrous message with all flip-sides and all the wounded personalities!

RESPONSIVE PRAYERS FOR THE COUNSELEE

I explain to the counselee that I will lead him in **"responsive prayers"** pertaining to various issues—that I will say a number of words, then pause and allow him to repeat the words with sincerity. Then, we continue in that fashion throughout his prayers. However, I further explain that since he does not know exactly what I am going to lead him to pray, should he disagree with something or become very confused, he is to tell me so we can take time to discuss it. This doesn't happen very often, but the counselee needs to be assured that he has that right—that freedom—and that he should pray only if he is sincere. As you do the same with your own counselees, I believe you will agree that this helps the counselee to relax more and that counseling will go more smoothly and successfully.

IMPORTANT NOTE: A NEW NAME IS TO BE GIVEN TO BROKEN PARTS, FLIP-SIDE AND WOUNDED PERSONALITIES

When I wrote "Liberating the Bruised," as the flip-side and fragmented personalities were healed, before fusing and integrating them with the core personality, I allowed them to replace their major negative name, by selecting a new, positive name. There was nothing wrong with allowing them to do this. However, the Lord began impressing my heart that since they have confessed all sins and "written a check on the core's salvation," then, why not allow them to simply "write a check on the core personality's name." After all, in assuming the core's formal name, it accents the fact that they are, indeed, now ONE. They, too are new creations in Jesus Christ. As you study the following counseling procedures, you will see the steps that I take to accomplish this.

C.   FIRST, CHECK FOR A BROKEN PART OF THE CORE PERSONALITY

Let's say that my counselee is eager to hasten the counseling process and in knowing that the flip-side personality actually influences 90 percent of what's going on in his life, he has chosen to start with the flip-side. Of course, as I've shared before, I prefer to start with the flip-side. However, I tell him that before we go to meet the flip-side, **I need to first check to see if he has a broken part of his core. Then we will proceed with the flip-side.** I explain that having a broken part of the core is like unto a baseball player with a broken, splintered arm, while he could still throw and catch a ball with the other hand, and run the bases, he could not bat easily or successfully! **It is necessary for the baseball player's arm to be fully healed before going up to home base to bat, hit the ball and run the bases with a goal of defeating the opposing team!** Now, while it is extremely rare to find more than one broken part of the core, I will stay alert should there be more, especially if my counselee has been severely abused. **I begin by asking him to simply pray the following:**

COUNSELEE PRAYS

"Lord Jesus, I give You my will, my rights, and my control,"—plus anything else that the person wants to pray.

After my counselee has prayed, willingly giving his will, rights, and control to the Lord Jesus Christ, we proceed to move toward attaining his freedom. Since he has given me, as his counselor, the authority to speak on his behalf, I become like his lawyer; thus I have the right, to gather any needed information. **The Lord Jesus Christ, my counselee, and I as his lawyer-counselor are a team, working together in unity!** I then confidently move forward as his lawyer, his ambassador! **The broken part of the core, the flip-side, all legitimate wounded personalities, as well as the ancestral demon and his network are subject to answer all questions and provide all necessary information.**

COUNSELOR'S PRAYER, A TOOL FOR A BROKEN CORE

With the Lord having taught me about the possibility of there being "a broken part of a core," even though it's "**rare**," I will ask the Lord to reveal a broken part of the core personality if there is one! As I explained in chapter four, a broken part of the core is one that splintered off from the core due to a traumatic experience very early in the core's life. **I cannot successfully complete counseling with the flip-side or wounded parts if there is a hindrance of a broken core. I begin by praying this for myself and the counselee:**

"Lord Jesus, I yield my will, my rights, and my control completely over to You. Put a watchman at my mouth and a guard at my tongue! Allow me to say nothing to this precious person I'm working with that will not bring praise and glory to Your name and bring help, encouragement and edification to him. And, I ask that You help the core personality, core's full formal name to relax so that You can do Your work. Lord Jesus, I want to praise and thank You again for the opportunity to spend time with You and this precious person that You have brought into my life, core's full formal name, age _____ , saved at the age of _____. Lord Jesus, I ask that Your blood would purge and cleanse the atmospheric conditions over this building, every square foot inside and outside. We ask that You do this, for we want it to be holy ground and a safe place to work.

"Heavenly Father, I'm asking You to shut down by the blood of the Lord Jesus Christ, all principalities, powers, god-heads, and all territorial areas that have been operating around our lives since our conception. We ask that You do not allow them to send or receive messages or messengers. Shut it all down, and do not allow Satan to use any demons to send any reinforcements into the network of demons in the person I'm working with. Shut Satan down totally pertaining to this person. I don't want Satan and his demons that are on the outside to be able to do anything but wiggle and watch in silence while this precious person works toward and achieves their freedom!

"Dear heavenly Father, I ask You to place in **category one**, the core personality, <u>core's full formal name</u>, age ___, saved at age ___, that You thought up from the foundations of the world and seated in the heavens with the Lord Jesus. If there is a broken part of the core, then please put him in a safe place near to the core personality. With Your hedge of blood surrounding, and protecting, I ask that You place all of the wounded personalities and the flip-side, **in category two**.

"Dear heavenly Father, please place in **category three**, the ancestral demon carrying the <u>core's formal name</u>, with all other ancestral demons and their networks, plus all lifestyle demons and their networks, all demon-produced personalities, demons that masquerade as wounded parts, gatekeepers and their networks, shared demons (those that share between networks in this person as well as from other people in bondage). And, Lord, I ask You to call in all shared demons that belong in this network so that they, too can be dealt with. Precious Lord Jesus, please bind, gag and render all of the demons in this category three inoperative and blood link them all together with blood-links that cannot be broken, made of the blood Jesus shed on Calvary, to the ancestral demon carrying the formal name of the core, so they cannot interfere or cause confusion during counseling. However, dear Lord, we trust that if You want to use any demon to provide some information that we need to learn early on, we thank You that You will use such a demon to expose it in order to prevent precious time from being wasted."

PRAYER CONTINUES FOR BROKEN PART OF THE CORE

"Lord Jesus, we now ask that if there is a broken part of the core, we thank You that You will bring it up so that we can communicate with it. Amen."

It would be of great benefit to have any and all broken parts of the core handled, right off the bat! Just remember that in attempting to speak with a **broken part of the person's core**, he could be very reluctant or even fearful about coming forth and revealing his existence.

I begin by asking: "If there is a broken part of the core personality, please come up and talk with me. I won't hurt you. I'm here to help you and the core personality." If he's silent, I patiently continue to plead with him, "You need not be afraid. Please come up and talk with me."

When a broken part of the core responds, I ask him: (1) What brought you into being? **(2)** What is your age? **(3)** What is your name? **(4)** Will you tell me something about yourself? **(5)** What do you do in the adult core's life? **(6)** What are the major emotions that motivate, manipulate, and run your life? (List each one separately, with the ones under his care beneath his name.)

The answers will typically reflect details of a traumatic experience he suffered which the ancestral demon manipulates, magnifies and amplifies in the broken part. As you would imagine, a broken part is full of worry, doubt and fear, and feels worthless and unwanted.

BROKEN PART OF THE CORE PRAYS FOR SALVATION AND HEALING

Being satisfied that the broken part has shared all the necessary information, **I then explain about how the Lord Jesus loves him and would like for him to be healed and become a part of the core. Upon his saying, "Yes," I offer to lead him in a prayer of repenting and accepting Christ as his Savior—"writing a check on the core's salvation"—becoming one with the core.** With his willingness to do so, I lead the broken part of the core to pray this:

> "Lord Jesus, I, <u>name of broken part of the core</u>, age ____, confess that You, Lord Jesus, are the Son of God who was willing to give up all the glory, safety, and praise of heaven. You wrapped Yourself in flesh and came to earth as the God-man. You walked among mankind, never sinning, never doing anything wrong. You just walked among Your people, loving and caring for them. You told them that You were the Son of God but they didn't believe You and they rejected You. They called You a liar, a blasphemer, and the prince of demons! They condemned You, saying You were deserving of death. They spat in Your face, they plucked out Your beard. They also blindfolded You and hit You in the face with the palms of their hands, saying, "Prophesy to us, Christ! Who is the one who hit You?" Then, they abandoned You to the Roman soldiers who stripped You naked, beat You with a whip, put a crown of thorns on Your head, struck You on the head with a reed. They put a royal purple robe on You, and then they kneeled and mockingly worshiped You, saying "Hail, King of the Jews!"

> "And, Lord Jesus, You loved them unconditionally, so much that You allowed them to take You outside the gates of Jerusalem and nail You to the tree. And, hanging on that tree, You became all their sins and evil. You became all the sin and evil of the world—past, present and future. You became all of what Satan and his demons do, what they do to mankind, and what they have caused mankind to do to one another. You did this so mankind would have the opportunity, the choice to become Your righteousness."

At this point in the prayer, I look at the items I have already listed on my note pad when the broken part of the core responded to my six questions. I call off each thing listed, and resume leading the broken part of the core in **a responsive prayer, claiming his responsibility, (1)** confessing each thing as <u>his</u> sin and **(2)** acknowledging that Jesus became that sin when He was crucified to pay <u>his</u> sin-debt:

"Jesus, You became me, <u>name of broken part of the core</u>, age ___, all that I stand for, all that my name means and all that my personality represents. Lord Jesus, You became my sins of <u>call off each of the sins for which he's responsible</u>, that I acted out in the life of the <u>core personality's formal name</u>, age ___. Jesus You became it all and it killed You, put You in the ground for three days and three nights. The power of God raised You from the grave, giving You power and victory over the grave and death and victory over all of mankind's sin and evil. God gave You power and victory over Satan and his demons, all that they do to mankind and what they cause mankind to do to one another!

"Lord Jesus, I confess that You are my only way to be saved, to be safe, free, secure, loved, accepted, and cared for. Lord Jesus, I confess that You are my only way to have all my wounds, emotions and memories cleansed and healed. Lord Jesus, I, <u>name of broken part of the core</u>, age ___, yield my control to You and give myself to You. I repent of everything I stand for that stands against You and Your will Lord Jesus in the life of <u>core personality's formal name</u>, which has been locked up in me and all that my name means and all that my personality represents. Lord Jesus, I invite You to come into my life, save and forgive me, cleanse and heal me, deliver me from my name and all that my name stands for. I want a new name, I want to be <u>core personality's formal name</u>, a new creation in Jesus Christ, fully submitted to Your Lordship, and filled with Your abundant life."

NOW-SAVED BROKEN PART PAUSES IN PRAYER TO SPEAK TO CORE

I lead the broken part of the core to make this appeal to the core to accept him:

"Core personality, <u>core personality's formal name</u>, age ___, saved at age ___, if you will have me, I will no longer act out in your life, my old name, <u>name of broken part of the core</u>, age ___, all that my name used to mean, all that my personality used to represent, but I will live out my new name, <u>core personality's formal name</u>, a new creation in Jesus Christ, fully submitted to the Lordship of Jesus Christ, and filled with His abundant life."

NOW-SAVED BROKEN PART RESUMES RESPONSIVE PRAYER

Next, I lead the **now-saved broken part of the core to pray, thanking the Lord**:

"And, Lord Jesus, by Your powerful blood, if the core will have me, make us one. And, Lord Jesus, now that You have healed me, made me a new creation, and took back the ground and saturated it with Your precious blood, I confess and thank You that the demons have no right, no authority to stand on this ground, because I no longer exist as a broken part of the core. Lord Jesus, I praise and thank You, that in the fullness of Your time, when all the wounded parts are healed in the core's life, You will send all the demons to the abyss or the lake of fire, or You will annihilate them with the breath of Your Holy mouth. With a childlike faith I thank You for doing this."

CORE RECEIVES THE BROKEN PART OF THE CORE

I then ask the counselee, "core personality's formal name, do you want to invite the broken part of your core to be made whole, fused and integrated with you by the power of our Lord Jesus?" **Upon his desire to do so, I lead him to pray the following prayer:**

"Broken part of my core, now that Jesus lives in your life you have a new name core's formal name. You are a new creation in Jesus Christ and are no longer going to act out your negatives in my life. So, I invite you to come and be a part of my life."

(If you have a severely abused counselee and have found and dealt with **more than one broken part**, having dealt with all of them, you can add "I want that statement to stand for all of the broken parts, state the names of each broken part, their ages, and their works.")

CORE'S PRAYER FOR GOD TO FUSE AND INTEGRATE THEM

"Lord Jesus, I, core personality, core personality's formal name, age ___, saved at the age of, confess that I am broken also, broken apart from this broken part of my core. I am missing the first part of my life which is the broken part of my core, age ___. Lord Jesus, by the power of Your blood, I ask You to fuse and integrate the broken part, now core personality's formal name, a new creation in Jesus Christ, fully submitted to His Lordship and filled with His abundant life. Make him one with me, core personality's formal name, age ___, saved at age ___. I confess that every demon spirit that stood on this ground no longer has the right, ground or authority to stand on it! And, in the fullness of Your time, I thank You that depending on their behavior, You will send the demons to the abyss or the lake of fire, or You will annihilate them with the breath of Your Holy mouth. With a childlike faith I thank You for doing this."

REMINDER FOR BROKEN PART OF THE CORE STILL HIDDEN

If there is a broken part of this person's core, yet it remained in hiding at this point, just trust that while you are dealing with the flip-side or wounded personalities, the Lord will raise a red flag for you, revealing that there is one. You may then ask the Lord to put the flip-side or wounded personality that you're dealing with in a safe place temporarily while you take time to deal with the broken part, as I explained earlier. Take time to assure the flip-side or wounded personality that you will not forget them, that you will come back to help them.

If you later find more than one broken part of the core, after leading them all to the Lord, then fuse and integrate them with the core. And, if the flip-side and all the wounded personalities are already healed and fused and integrated with the core personality, then, simply ask God to fuse and integrate the broken part of the core to the flip-side and wounded parts that are already fused and integrated to the core personality. **This is like gluing a china plate back together, and this must be done or the demons will hinder you from completing the work of making the core personality whole—and refuse to leave!**

D. COUNSELOR IS READY TO CONTACT THE FLIP-SIDE

Like a baseball player with his broken arm now mended and able to resume throwing the ball and batting, with our Lord having healed the core's broken part, fusing them back together as one, the core is now in far better condition to get back in the game! As you know quite well, we're not engaged in a "game" with the opposition. We are engaged in serious warfare against the enemy, Satan! We are Christian soldiers in combat, thus, it is crucial that our soldier, the core personality, has all broken parts mended in order to stand strong in the midst of this warfare! **We will now hasten to ask the Lord to enable us to contact the flip-side personality:**

"Lord Jesus, the core and I both continue to yield our will, our rights, and our control completely over to You. I ask that You continue to put a watchman at my mouth and a guard at my tongue! Please allow me to say nothing during this counseling session that would not bring praise and glory to Your name and help, encouragement and edification to the core personality. Lord Jesus, I do not have the power on my own to fix anything in this precious person's life. Without You, I don't even have sense enough to get in out of the rain! This person and I are depending totally upon You. Only You can liberate the bruised!

"Dear heavenly Father, the core and I now desire to contact and deal with the flip-side personality. So, I ask You to please, place the core personality, core personality's formal name, age _____, saved at age _____, that You thought up from the foundation of the world, in **category one**, seated in the heavenlies with the Lord Jesus. With a hedge of Your blood surrounding, protecting, loving and caring for him, I ask that You please place the flip-side, and wounded personalities in **category two**.

"Dear heavenly Father, please place in **category three**, Ancestral Demon core personality's formal name, with all other ancestral demons and their networks, plus all lifestyle demons and their networks, all demon-produced personalities, demons that masquerade as wounded personalities, gatekeepers and their networks and shared demons (those that share between networks in this person as well as from other people in bondage). And, Lord, I ask You to call in all shared demons that belong in this network so that they, too can be dealt with. Precious Lord Jesus, please bind, gag and render all of the demons in this category three inoperative and blood link them all together with <u>Ancestral Demon core personality's formal name</u>, with blood-links that cannot be broken, made of the blood Jesus shed on Calvary, so that they cannot interfere or cause confusion during counseling. However, dear Lord, we trust that if You want to use any demon to provide some information that we need to learn early on or at a particular point, we thank You that You will use that demon as You deem appropriate, to expose it, in order to help prevent precious time from being wasted.

"Lord Jesus, I thank You that You will prevent the enemy from muting, deafening, or hiding the flip-side from me as I begin to communicate with him. I ask You to take Your blood, like a surgical knife, and separate the flip-side from the rest of the duplex and bring him up to meet me. I ask You to enable us to find the one that is the <u>same age as the core</u>, which has been there <u>the same number of years that the core has existed</u>, and he did not get saved when the core accepted Christ as his Savior. I want to talk with the one that is operating much of the negative traits currently active in the core personality's life. Father, thank You for shutting down and rendering everything else totally inoperative in the system. Thank You for binding up all the demonic networks, muting and disarming them, including masqueraders. Thank You for putting all other wounded personalities in a safe place so that they cannot interfere, switch personalities, or bring up any counterfeits. And, we thank You, Lord, that You are now going to allow us to speak with the true flip-side."

WHAT TO EXPECT AS YOU MEET FLIP-SIDE PERSONALITIES

Having met a large number of flip-sides over the years, I have observed a wide range of "attitudes" and "behaviors" in them. **Some are very soft spoken**, **some speak in an average voice tone, while others yet are extraverts**! While neither the soft-spoken flip-sides, nor the average flip-sides would win Mister Congeniality of the Year contests, they are not difficult to deal with. Flip-sides who are way-out-front extraverts may, however, require a little more work and patience on the part of the counselor! For they are clearly without shyness! Some reveal sarcastically their impatience, anger, aggression, rudeness and even obnoxiousness! I've seen such flip-side extraverts become quite frustrated and angry when I've commanded through my authority in Christ for them to come up and talk with me! Some have mockingly called me bad names, attempting to make me angry. If this happens to you, take care not to let them get the best of you! Be patient, don't yield to temptation to become frustrated and angry at him! Remember that he is definitely hurting also and needs help! He is not a demon! Relax and yield yourself to the Lord while standing firmly in His authority. Calmly voice that you and the core do not have to put up with the bad language and misbehavior, and command through authority in Christ that he cease acting out in that manner.

When they blurt out foul language and their body language appears rigid, it just reveals that they are on the defensive for various reasons—and are prepared for a fight! Some flip-sides—not totally unlike demons—will not only attempt to spew foul language, some threaten to throw objects that are close by, or even get up from the chair and start throwing things around in the room. Upon first hearing and seeing such behavior, in one sense, this actually helps to reveal what the flip-side does in the core personality's life—how he manipulates and uses the core. **However, I do not tolerate any flip-sides voicing obscenities or behaving in mean, vulgar or destructive ways!** I command them through the core's authority in Christ, and mine, that they immediately sit down, and cease using filthy language and misbehaving! I always make notations of what transpired, for they contain clues as to the ground the flip-side has in the core's life—the ground the ancestral demon is holding!

Remember that at this point in counseling, the ancestral demon that manipulated him into being still has legal claim to him! **Until I have brought the flip-side to salvation, there is a battle yet to be won not only for the sake of the core, but for the flip-side's sake as well!** Until then, I will not be shocked to observe "attitudes" and "behaviors" that a rebellious lost person—or demon—would reflect! **I take great care to assure the flip-side that I actually love him and I'm here to help him, not to hurt him!**

MINISTERS AND COUNSELORS, WATCH OUT FOR TRAPS SET FOR YOU

I'm sad to say that some ministers/counselors have gotten snared by **Satan's trap that is hidden beneath the process of "gathering information,"** and some are trapped so tightly, they fall into temptation of "enjoying the entertainment" as they watch flip-sides and demons put on **X-rated shows!** Some have paid the consequences by suffering property damage, bodily harm, and destruction of their reputation and ministry! You and I should always take care to remember that if we allow a flip-side and/or demon to get out of hand, we would actually be permitting him to use and abuse God's precious core personality! We would be putting ourselves and our ministries at risk also! God forbid!

Again, I encourage you to remember that upon first meeting some flip-sides (and wounded personalities), if they speak out some obscenities and misbehave somewhat in various ways, make notations of these things that serve to reflect how they operate in the core's life. Remember that your intentions are to gather necessary information to bring this sinful flip-side to Christ. Remind him again that you are there to help him, and proceed to interview him to gather helpful information, plus witness to him. As I ask a flip-side the following questions, I record his answers and other comments he makes on my note pad:

E.   QUESTIONS TO ASK THE FLIP-SIDE

1.   **"Flip-side, I would like to speak with you. Do you hear the sound of my voice?"** If he hesitates answering, I get a little more firm with him and declare, **"In the name of Jesus, you must come up here and talk with me. Are you there?"** The majority will respond in a regular tone of voice—but without an air of friendliness and patience! Typically they will say, "Yes, I hear you. I'm here!"

2.   I then ask, **"Why didn't you get saved at (age of core's salvation) when (core personality's formal name, age ____ , saved at age ____) did?** Now keep in mind that I know why the flip-side didn't get saved. Because, he is the opposing side of the core that was established through the "iniquities of the fathers" being passed down, the "dark side" of the duplex where the ancestral demon has staked his claim. From that iniquity, the ancestral demon was able to manipulate and control the flip-side. But it's important that I ask the flip-side why he didn't get saved because **his answers will reflect his perception of himself and what he stands for in the core's life**. He may say that he didn't want to get saved because he enjoys doing what he does—his lifestyle. On the other hand, he may say very pridefully that he just didn't want to give up his control!

3.   I then question him, **"Are you the same age as the core personality? Have you been there the same number of years that the core has been here?"** If it is the flip-side, he will answer, "Yes".

4.   My next question is, **"What is your name?" The flip-side seldom says his name is the same as the core's. Instead, he typically answers with a very negative name.** Some may carry names such as "Depression," "Anger," "Bitterness," while others may give names such as, "No Name," "I Don't Have A Name," "I Don't Know My Name," "I Don't Need A Name," etc.

5.   Addressing him by his name, I'll ask, **"I Don't Have A Name," will you tell me about yourself?** This allows him to relax more with you, as you are showing an interest in him—a sincere concern for him. There are times when a flip-side only shares a little about his opinion of himself while others will share a lot.

6.   I then get more specific and ask him, **"What do you do in the core's life when you are allowed to be in charge?"** Often, flip-sides are prideful about what they do in the core's life, while others reflect resentment for "having to be in charge".

7.   I ask the flip-side, **"What are the major emotions that motivate your behavior that manipulates and runs the core personality's life?** Upon discussing the flip-side's major emotions, you learn not only how he feels personally, but what he thinks of the core personality. His true feelings surface, revealing **(1)** if he really enjoys being in control and

takes advantage of the core every chance he gets to "do his own thing," or **(2)** if he views the core as a weak person, "a wimp" and he is angry and fed up with having to take care of the core by performing necessary, daily chores.

8. It is at this point that I take the **negative check list** and go down through it, reading them to the flip-side, asking him, one by one, whether or not each negative item belongs to him. For instance, "Flip-side, does 'hate' belong to you?" I **check off** the ones he says belongs to him, and I **highlight** the ones he says belongs to someone else. When he doesn't claim one, I also ask if he knows whom they belong to in the system. He may be able to give me additional information apart from himself and tell me which negative items belong to various wounded parts. I'll be ready to make side-notes for them if he does, **while keeping in mind that the same negative emotions that he admits to being his may very well be shared by wounded personalities, and neither may know about the other!**

9. When I have finished going through the negative check list, I then ask the flip-side if he knows any of the wound personalities in the system. **It is at this point I can find out if he is a caretaker over any wounded parts.**

10. I then ask the flip-side **if he helped the core personality fill out any of the counseling form**. If so, I ask what parts, which gives me additional information.

11. Being satisfied that I have retrieved all the information needed from the flip-side, then I ask him, **"Flip-side, his name, would it be correct to say that 'all of the above' represents what you do in the core's life? Are there any other things that we need to add to the list?"** List any additional information, then being at peace with the progress made, proceed to the next step with the flip-side.

12. At this point, knowing the Lord has been convicting him of his sins during our conversations together, **I ask the flip-side if he is sick and tired of living in a struggle with the core and not having any peace or joy**. If he says, "No," I quiz him about it to see why and discuss the matter with him, encouraging him to decide to repent and find peace and joy. It is rare for one not to come under conviction of the Holy Spirit wooing him unto Himself, and admitting that they're very unhappy though and desiring to change. (However, there have been a few very grievous occasions in which I had to deal with an extremely rebellious, unrepentant, obstinate flip-side, which I will address at the close of this chapter.)

LEADING THE FLIP-SIDE TO PRAY FOR HEALING AND SALVATION

I then offer to lead the flip-side in a prayer to repent and accepting Jesus as his Savior— "writing a check" on the core's salvation—and becoming one with the core. With his willingness to do so, I then lead the flip-side to pray for salvation as follows:

"I, flip-side, <u>his name</u>, confess that, You, Lord Jesus, are the Son of God who was willing to give up all the glory, safety, and praise of heaven. You wrapped Yourself in flesh and came to earth as the God-man. You walked among mankind, never sinning, never doing anything wrong. You just walked among Your people, loving and caring for them. You told them that You were the Son of God but they didn't believe You and they rejected You. They called You a liar, a blasphemer, and the prince of demons! They condemned You, saying You were deserving of death. They spat in Your face, they plucked out Your beard. They also blindfolded You and hit You in the face with the palms of their hands, saying, "Prophesy to us, Christ! Who is the one who hit You?" Then, they abandoned You to the Roman soldiers who stripped You naked, beat You with a whip, put a crown of thorns on Your head, struck You on the head with a reed. They put a royal purple robe on You, and then they kneeled and mockingly worshiped You, saying "Hail, King of the Jews!"

"Lord Jesus, You loved them unconditionally, so much that You allowed them to take You outside the gates of Jerusalem and nail You to a tree. And, hanging on that tree, You became all their sins and evil. You became all the sin and evil of the world—past, present and future. You became all of what Satan and his demons do, what they do to mankind, and what they have caused mankind to do to one another. You did this so mankind would have the opportunity, the choice to become Your righteousness.

"Lord Jesus, You became all of my sin. You became all of me, flip-side his name, everything that my name means, everything that my personality represents, and the sin of those that have hurt me, and those that I have hurt. You became...."

At this point in the prayer, I look at the negative check list, and each item that I have checked indicating responsibility of the flip-side, I read each one off, allowing the flip-side to claim his responsibility by confessing each one as his sin plus acknowledging that Jesus became that sin when He was crucified to pay our sin-debt. I would **lead him in a "responsive prayer," praying about things such as**:

"Lord Jesus, You became all of the above, plus my sin of hatred. You became my sin of fantasizing. You became my sin of obsessive, compulsive behavior," and so on. Having covered all the negatives he claimed, I would continue leading him to pray, "Lord Jesus You became it all and it killed You, put You in the ground for three days and three nights. The power of God raised You from the grave, giving You power and victory over the grave and death, and victory over all of mankind's sin and evil. God gave You power and victory over Satan and his demons, and all that they do to mankind and what they cause mankind to do to one another!

"I confess that the Lord Jesus had victory over all of my sin and evil, and that He is my only way to be saved. He is my only way to be safe, free, and secure. He is my only way to be loved, accepted, and cared for. Because of all of this, Lord Jesus, I give myself to You! I repent of everything that I stand for that stood against You that has been locked up in me, the flip-side, <u>flip-side's name</u>, all that my name stood for.

"Lord Jesus, I invite You into my life and I want to write a check on the core personality's salvation account, when he got saved at <u>age</u>. I ask You to come into my life, save me, forgive me, change me, cleanse and heal me. Please give me a brand new name. I no longer want to be called "Flip-side, <u>his name</u>." I want a new name. I want to be <u>core personality's formal name</u>," a "new creation in Jesus Christ," fully submitted to His Lordship, and filled with His abundant life. And, Lord Jesus, I thank You that the ancestral demon no longer has any ground in or claim on my life! And, I thank You, Lord Jesus, for saving me!"

Now, I lead the now-saved flip-side with his new name, to speak to the core personality:

"<u>Core personality's full name</u> , if you will have me, I will no longer live in your life as the flip-side carrying my old name with all that the name stood for. I will live as one with the core, fully submitted to the Lordship of Jesus Christ, and filled with His abundant life."

While proceeding with counseling connected with the flip-side, **I trust that the Lord will give me wisdom when I am to fuse and integrate the core and the new-named flip-side together as one.** But for now, I will see if the flip-side can help me to contact some of the wounded parts. **I begin by asking the Lord Jesus to hedge the flip-side about with His blood and keep him safe.**

SAVED FLIP-SIDE—A HELPFUL TOOL BEFORE FUSING TO THE CORE

As I've mentioned before, **usually the flip-side does not know about other wounded parts in the system unless he is a caretaker.** The flip-side usually knows only about the core and that he is to "control the core" according to the "program" within himself! **However, if the flip-side is a "control freak," "protector" of "his property," he will aggressively control as much as he can get by with in the core's life, so he will know about some, if not all, of the wounded personalities.** Such a flip-side will be revealed as he claims a good number of subjects on the negative check list.

So, before fusing and integrating the now-saved flip-side, new creation, to the core, I ask him if he will help me by answering some questions for me. Flip-sides usually always agree to do so, and this is the way I make my appeal:

219

"Flip-side, now <u>core's formal name</u>, a new creation in Jesus Christ, before I fuse and integrate you to the core, I would really appreciate it if you could help me by answering some questions. I am going to ask the Lord to put you up high so you can get a good view of the wounded personalities in the system so that you can report what you see to me. Will you, please do that for me?"

Upon his agreeing, I pray:

"Lord Jesus, I want You to take flip-side, now <u>core's formal name</u>, a new creation in Jesus Christ, and place him on a riser, podium, or stage so he can stand up and see. I ask that You allow him to see with Your eyes, to hear with Your ears, feel with Your heart, and have Your mind as he and I work together as we go to meet the wounded parts remaining in the core's life. And, we thank You for doing this."

A REMINDER FOR YOU

Remember to keep your **Tool # 3 Note Pad handy for your "reserve for future use" notes! Having an extra note pad or two on hand would not be a bad idea either!**

F. STAY ALERT TO TEST FOR TRUE OR FALSE WOUNDED PERSONALITIES

WHILE INTERVIEWING BOTH THE FLIP-SIDE AND CARETAKER WOUNDED PERSONALITIES, it is essential for you to **stay on the alert for any demons posing as wounded personalities**. If the flip-side or caretaker reports one or more wounded personalities, but while gathering information about the wounded personalities things just don't seem to add up— if you have a "check in your spirit"—the Lord is impressing you to check to see whether or not you are either dealing with **(1)** one or more genuine wounded personalities **(2)** or one or more demonic beings. **Therefore, it's essential for you to test the spirits, test for true or false wounded personalities.** Do not be reluctant to obey the Lord's command to test the spirit to see if they are of light or darkness. Trust your heavenly Father to reveal truth, to confirm whether they are genuine wounded personalities or masquerading demon-produced personalities or demon-clones. **(3)** It's important to remember that some demon-produced personalities and demon-clones may actually believe that they are genuine wounded personalities.

TEST FOR TRUE AND FALSE BY PRAYING: "Lord Jesus, as the flip-side (or caretaker wounded personality) looks at the group under his charge, I ask that You put chains on any that are actually demon-produced personalities, demons masquerading as personalities, demon-clones or just demons trying to mess with us."

UPON FLIP-SIDE OR CARETAKER WOUNDED PERSONALITY REPORTING SOME IN CHAINS, PRAY: "Lord Jesus, I ask You to please remove all beings that have chains on them and blood-link them with blood-links that cannot be broken, made of the blood Jesus shed on Calvary, to the Ancestral demon that carries the formal name of the core."

Then, we would resume gathering information from the flip-side or caretaker wounded personality about the wounded personalities. And now, I will show you how I go about interviewing the flip-side about wounded parts under his care.

G.   INTERVIEWING NOW-SAVED FLIP-SIDE ABOUT WOUNDED PARTS

I begin asking the now-saved flip-side, the following questions, taking care to make notations as he answers them:

1.   "Flip-side, now <u>core personality's formal name</u>, a new creation in Jesus Christ, do you see any wounded personalities there on the dark side of the house?"

2.   If he does, I ask, "How many wounded personalities are there?" **Let's say that he answers "twelve".**

Upon learning how many wounded personalities he sees, I want to **make sure that all of them are truly wounded personalities and not demons masquerading as personalities. So, I pray:**

"Lord Jesus, I ask that You put chains on any that are actually demon-produced personalities, demons masquerading as personalities, demon-clones, or just demons trying to mess with me."

3.   I ask, **"Flip-side, do you see any wounded personalities that are bound in chains?"** If he says, "Yes," I ask the Lord to remove all beings with chains on them and blood-link them with blood-links that cannot be broken, made of the blood Jesus shed on Calvary, to the Ancestral demon that carries the formal name of the core. Then I ask the flip-side whether those with chains are gone and if they are, I proceed. If those with chains are still present, I ask the Lord to give me wisdom as to what's going on. **Let's say that five were in chains, and the Lord has removed them, so the flip-side sees "seven" true wounded personalities.**

4.   I then ask the flip-side, **"Are you the caretaker of these 'seven' wounded personalities?"** When he assures me that he is their caretaker, I move on to the next step.

5. Then, I ask the flip-side, **"Can you ask each of them six major questions and share the answers with me, please?"** Upon the flip-side caretaker's agreeing to question the individual wounded personalities, **I write the flip-side caretaker's name down, and below it, list each wounded personality's name and age and the information each one gives him as he asks these questions:** **(1)** What brought you into being? **(2)** What is your age? **(3)** What is your name? **(4)** Will you tell me something about yourself? **(5)** What do you do in the adult core's life? **(6)** What are the major emotions that motivate, manipulate, and run your life?

6. Then I tell the newly-named flip-side that before I fuse and integrate him with the core: **"I would appreciate a little more help. I'm going to call out some of the things listed on the negative check list to which no one has laid claim, and I would like for you to tell me whether or not you know if any of the seven wounded parts are connected to them."** I call them off, make my list, and indicate on my check list that they have been claimed. As I've said before, usually a flip-side knows no wounded personalities unless he is a caretaker.

Being satisfied that I have gathered all the information from this flip-side that I can about the wounded personalities, I now proceed by asking **one more favor of the flip-side and that is for him to serve as proxy in praying for healing and salvation on behalf of the wounded parts in his care**.

SAVED FLIP-SIDE CARETAKER
PRAYS AS PROXY FOR WOUNDED PARTS

In cases where a flip-side has assumed the responsibility to protect and care for a number of weaker wounded personalities who are repentant of their sins, they are usually very willing to give their caretaker legal authority to be their spokesperson to voice their prayers for them. I then lead them to pray. **This is the prayer I would lead the flip-side caretaker to pray as the wounded personalities' proxy—with each of them praying silently but sincerely along with the flip-side:**

"Lord Jesus, I, now-saved flip-side, <u>core personality's formal name</u>, a new creation in Jesus Christ, fully submitted to Your Lordship and filled with Your abundant life, am going to be the prayer spokesperson for <u>names, ages of wounded parts; all that their names mean; all that each personality represents</u>.

"Lord Jesus, all of us <u>names, ages of wounded parts; all that their names mean; all that their personalities represent</u> confess that, You, Lord Jesus, are the Son of God who was willing to give up all the glory, safety, and praise of heaven. You wrapped Yourself in flesh and came to earth as the God-man. You walked among mankind, never sinning, never doing anything wrong. You just walked among Your people, loving and caring for them. You told them that You were the Son of God but they didn't believe You and they rejected You. They called You a liar, a blasphemer, and the prince of demons! They condemned You, saying You were deserving of death. They spat in Your face and they plucked out Your beard. They also blindfolded You and hit You in the face with the palms of their hands, saying, "Prophesy to us, Christ! Who is the one who hit You?" Then, they abandoned You to the Roman soldiers who stripped You naked, beat You with a whip, put a crown of thorns on Your head, struck You on the head with a reed. They put a royal purple robe on You, then they kneeled and mockingly worshiped You, saying "Hail, King of the Jews!"

"Lord Jesus You loved them so unconditionally, that You allowed them to take You outside the gates of Jerusalem and nail You to a tree. On that tree, You became all their sin and all their evil so they would have the opportunity and the choice to become Your righteousness. You became all the sin and evil of the world, past, present and future. You became all of what Satan and his demons do, what they do to mankind, what they cause mankind to do to each other so mankind would have the opportunity and the choice to become Your righteousness.

"Lord Jesus, You became our sins, what brought us into being, <u>names, ages of wounded parts; all that their names mean; all that their personalities represent</u>, that we acted out in the life of the <u>core personality's formal name and age</u>. We acknowledge that our sins killed You and put You in the grave for three days and three nights and the power of God raised You up from the grave. You had the victory over us and all that we stand for, all that our name means and all that our personalities represent. And Lord Jesus, we confess that You are our only way to be saved, to be safe, free, secure, loved, accepted, and cared for. Lord Jesus, we confess that You are our only way to have all our wounds, emotions and memories cleansed and healed, including <u>call off all negative acts claimed by each wounded part</u>.

"So, Lord Jesus, we, <u>names, ages of wounded part</u>, yield our control to You and give ourselves to You. We repent of everything we stand for that stands against You and Your will Lord Jesus in the life of <u>core personality's formal name</u>, which has been locked up in me and all that our names mean and all that our personalities represent.

"Lord Jesus, we invite You to come into our lives, save and forgive us, cleanse and heal us, deliver us from our names and all that our names stand for. We want new names. We want to be <u>core personality's formal name</u>, a new creation in Jesus Christ, fully submitted to Your Lordship, and filled with Your abundant life.

"Core personality, <u>core personality's formal name</u>, <u>age</u>, saved at <u>age</u>, if you will have us, we will no longer act out in your life, acting out our old names, <u>name and age of each wounded part</u>, all that our names used to mean, all that our personality used to represent, but we will live out our new name, <u>core personality's formal name</u>, a new creation in Jesus Christ, fully submitted to the Lordship of Jesus Christ, and filled with His abundant life. Lord Jesus, by Your powerful blood, if the core will have us, at the right time, make us one.

"Lord Jesus, we confess and thank You that the demons have no right, no authority to stand on this ground, because we no longer exist as we used to because You have healed us, made us new creations, and have retaken that ground, and then saturated and permeated that ground with Your precious blood. And Lord Jesus, we praise and thank You, that in Your time, when everything is healed in the core's life, that You are going to throw the demons out. You are our sovereign God and You will show us what You want done with the demons, depending on their behavior, whether You want to send them to the abyss or to the lake of fire, or to annihilate them with the breath of Your Holy mouth. And with a childlike faith we thank You for doing this."

COUNSELOR PRAYS TO PUT WOUNDED PARTS IN A SAFE PLACE

I thank the now-saved flip-side for helping me with the wounded parts who were once under his care. Then I pray the following:

"Lord Jesus, I ask You now to put a hedge of Your blood around all <u>"seven"</u> wounded personalities that were once under the care of the flip-side. They are <u>call out list names and ages of each wounded part</u> who are now <u>core's formal name</u>, new creations in Jesus Christ, fully submitted to Your Lordship, and filled with Your abundant life and I ask that You keep them safe until I can contact them later to work with them. I thank You for doing this."

CAUTION: Take care to remember to never fuse and integrate any wounded personalities from the dark side of the duplex to the core until you have brought the flip-side to salvation and fused and integrated him to the core personality!

H.   TIME TO FUSE AND INTEGRATE THE FLIP-SIDE WITH THE CORE

After I have a peace that I have gleaned all the information that the new-named flip-side is able to give me, then I proceed to fuse and integrate him with the core. Pray, asking the Lord to put the flip-side in a safe place with His blood hedging about him.

Then I ask the Lord to allow the core personality, core's formal name, age, who was saved at age, to speak with me. Knowing the core has heard and been a part of the entire session, I ask the core if he is ready to invite the new-name flip-side to be fused and integrated with him. I ask in this way:

> "Core personality, core personality's formal name, age, who was saved at age, please talk to me. Do I have core personality's formal name? Now that old name of flip-side has acknowledged and renounced his old name and all that the name meant and all that the old name represented, and has asked Jesus Christ to be his Lord and Savior, and is now core personality's formal name, a new creation, fully submitted to the Lordship of Jesus Christ, and filled with Jesus' abundant life, are you ready to have the flip-side fused and integrated with you?"

CORE CONFESSES SINS, RECEIVES THE FLIP-SIDE, AND PRAYS

It is an encouragement to the core to know that the flip-side who was operating his life has confessed his sins before the Lord, "wrote a check" on his salvation, and has a new name! Now the core will also go before the Lord and confess all sinful thoughts and behavior connected to the flip-side. The core ultimately is in control of his life, so they must accept responsibility!

Upon learning from the core that he is willing and ready to invite the new-named flip-side to be fused and integrated as one with him, I proceed to lead him to begin by first addressing the newly-named flip-side, carrying his own full name:

> "New creation in Christ, core personality's full name, age ____, who used to be flip-side his old name, now that Jesus Christ lives in your life, now that you no longer make a duplex in my life, and that your new name represents the righteousness and nature of Christ, I invite you to become a part of my life."

Then, I lead the core personality to pray this:

> "Lord Jesus I, core personality core personality's formal name, age _____, saved at age _____, I believe You are who You say you are. I confess that all my sin killed you. And, rather than roll all the hurt done to me onto You, I allowed the flip-side on the other side of the duplex where all my negative behavior, my hurts, pain, memories and emotions were stored, to control a large part of my life. I take full responsibility for all that is connected to the flip-side, all that his name means and his personality represents. I call it my sin. I ask You to cleanse me, forgive me, totally restore me.

225

"Heavenly Father, I confess the demons that stood on flip-side's ground have no right; no authority because flip-side, a new creation in Christ, who used to be <u>flip-side's old name</u> no longer exists! They have no ground to harass me mentally, physically, spiritually, or emotionally any longer! They have no right to stand on the ground that was ninety percent of the stronghold that was in my life! It has been removed by our Lord Jesus Christ!

"Father, when You are ready, in Your perfect timing, I trust that You will send the ancestral demon carrying the full name and his entire network to the abyss of God, the lake of fire, or annihilate him with the breath of Your Holy mouth—depending on how he responds. And, with a childlike faith I confess it as done because You are the eternal God and I see it as finished. And, Lord, I ask by Your powerful blood to seal all of the doorways to my mind and heal all of the parts of my damaged soul. I want to praise and thank You for this in the Name of Jesus.

"And, now, heavenly Father, I ask You, by the power of Your blood, to fuse and integrate <u>core personality's full name</u>, a new creation in Christ, who used to be "Flip-side, <u>his old name</u>, age of ____, with me, <u>core personality's full name</u> and make us one. Fill us with Your abundant life. And, I thank You that it's done."

TEST TO MAKE SURE CORE AND FLIP-SIDE WERE FUSED AND INTEGRATED

I ask the core:

1. "Please tell me, without editing, what you **hear, feel, sense** or **see**, if anything."
2. "What's going on inside right now?"

If the core answers that he feels something is wrong—such as hearing negative words, feeling a heaviness, sensing confusion, or feeling insecure or fearful, then it could be that the work is not quite done. Therefore, we need to find out why. I test by asking the Lord to bring up the flip-side so we can talk to him again. I begin by praying:

"Heavenly Father, I ask that You continue to bind, gag and render inoperative any and all demons, ancestral demons, lifestyle demons, power demons, demons masquerading as wounded parts, territorial demons, demons shared in and demons shared out, demon-produced personalities, demon-clones, demons masquerading as wounded personalities, and all of their personal networks so they cannot interfere with us or answer me.

"Heavenly Father, if the flip-side was not fully integrated, please make him come up and answer me when I call him. If any demon or demons are interfering in anyway, I ask that You shut them down."

Then I say, flip-side, if you are still there, please come up and talk with me. I am not going to hurt you. I just need your help so we can find out what's going on.

If the flip-side answers, "yes," then the flip-side was not integrated. So, I ask the following questions of him:

1.   "Why are you still there?"
2.   "Do you want to be integrated with the core?"
3.   "Did you mean what you said as you prayed along with me?"

Upon learning why he was still there and dealing with the issues, lead the flip-side to pray again and have the core pray again to receive him, as I explained earlier. When you are certain that the flip-side is integrated with the core, before moving on to deal with the wounded personalities, pray the following prayer:

> "Father, I want the core personality of <u>core personality's formal name</u>, who is age , saved at age _____ and is now one with the now-saved flip-side, placed in a safe place with the Lord Jesus with the blood of the Lord Jesus hedged about him, separating everything else from him so that we can find and meet whomever we need to work with today. I ask that You allow the core personality to hear all that goes on, but do not allow the core personality to interfere in any way, especially by squelching or preventing a wounded personality from coming up.

> "Heavenly Father, unless You wish to teach us something, I ask You to continue to bind, gag, and render inoperative Satan and all his demonic beings, including <u>Ancestral Demon core personality's formal name</u>, and all other ancestral demons, whether they be ancestral demons of works or of family names, lifestyle demons, power demons, demons that desire to be shared in and those which desire to be shared out, demon-produced personalities, demons that masquerade as wounded parts, and demon-clones including all their personal networks. I pray that they cannot render any wounded parts mute or deaf, that they cannot cause any confusion, chaos or misunderstanding. I pray that they are kept from pretending to be the core, the flip-side that no longer exists, or wounded personalities. I pray that they cannot misappropriate and block any truths from being shared, nor otherwise interfere or mess with us as we work."

At this point, with the core and newly-named flip-side fused and integrated, we are ready to move on and deal with the wounded personalities (in the next chapter). However, before doing that, as I said earlier, I will now share some information about how one must deal with an extremely rebellious, unrepentant, and obstinate flip-side.

I. DEALING WITH AN OBSTINATE, REBELLIOUS FLIP-SIDE

If you begin with the flip-side mentioned earlier in this chapter, asking the Lord to place the core personality into the three categories, and you find the flip-side to be uncooperative, you may have an obstinate, rebellious one. Make sure after he has identified himself as the flip-side, living on the dark side of the duplex, that he is not a demon masquerading as the flip-side or a clone of the flip-side. Ask him if it stands as truth before the eternal throne of Jesus Christ that he is, indeed, the flip-side. Ask the Lord to bind up all the demonic forces to the ancestral demon with blood-links that cannot be broken, made of the blood Jesus shed on Calvary, and render them inoperative, unable to interfere. Ask the flip-side to speak to you and identify himself.   Once you've established that he is, indeed, the flip-side personality, the same age of the core, then proceed to "minister" to him!

You should witness to the flip-side as you would any other wounded personality with the hope of their choosing to repent and right themselves with the Lord. Patiently, yet firmly appeal to him, explaining that God loves him and wants him to get rid of all the junk in his life that is not only hindering him from having peace, joy and a good life, but is literally destroying him. Encourage him that if he will accept the Lord Jesus as his Savior like the core did, that He will transform him into a new creation, fully submitted to Lordship of Jesus and filled with His abundant life.

Remind him that God thought up the whole soul, not a duplex. We read in Matthew 12:25: *"...Jesus knew their thoughts, and said to them: 'Every kingdom divided against itself is brought to desolation, and every city or house divided against itself will not stand."* **The Lord says where there is unity, He commands a blessing!** (Psalm 133:1-3)

Further explain to him: "You, Flip-side, have been fooled by the ancestral demon who manipulates and controls you. Without Jesus in your life, one day you will go to the lake of fire, right along with the ancestral demon and his network!" Let the flip-side know that he is like a puppet that is owned by the ancestral demon. He's like a marionette on the ancestral demon's strings—being manipulated as the ancestral demon pleases for his own evil works! Stress to the flip-side that the ancestral demon has deceived him into thinking that he is in control of the core, instead, it is the ancestral demon using him as his marionette on strings to manipulate the core! Declare to him that if he chooses to remain divided from the core, it will destroy him! Explain that when some of the core's ancestors chose to rebel against God and lived sinful lifestyles, their iniquities passed down to the next generations and the ancestral demon took advantage of his core personality and staked his claim on him on that "dark side of the duplex." Further explain that if the ancestral demon destroys the core, he destroys the flip-side right along with the core! You want to explain this to him because some flip-sides have been deceived into thinking that if they can get rid of the core personality by his dying, they as the flip-side will continue to live on!   Question him as to whether he believes this lie or not. If he thinks that it's a lie, repeat that the truth is, the ancestral demon is continuing to try to trick him with more of his lies.

You can share the example of God's not condoning "sin among His body of believers." In I Corinthians 5:1-13, we find that a Christian man in the Church is unrepentant of "sexual immorality"—*"that a man has his father's wife!"* (verse 1). The other Church members know of this, yet ignore it, so they're condoning it, and in doing so, they are allowing him to be a stumbling block to others! Paul preaches the truth that it is a very critical issue, and while he acknowledges that the man is saved and will go to heaven when he dies, while on earth, unless he repents, he cannot be permitted to associate with the other members. Furthermore, in verses 4-6, he declares: *"In the name of our Lord Jesus Christ, when you are gathered together, along with my spirit, with the power of our Lord Jesus Christ, deliver such a one to Satan for the destruction of the flesh that his spirit may be saved in the day of the Lord Jesus. Your glorying is not good. Do you not know that a little leaven leavens the whole lump?"* This man had a flip-side that was rebellious and unrepentant. Paul showed that the man needed to obey the Lord in this matter in order to help bring the man under conviction through their not allowing him to fellowship with the Church family. He would be brought to understand he could not fellowship with them until he came to repentance, and as long as he was unrepentant, Satan was free to do as he pleased with him.

Now as you think on this, take care to remember that in our counseling, the core personality has come in desperation to be set free from all that hinders him from walking in God's will and having peace and joy through Jesus Christ. Through the ancestral demon, a flip-side that is extremely rebellious and unrepentant, has established that duplex, allowing him to have some control over the core personality! The core has the same power and authority that Paul and the Church members had through Jesus Christ to turn the man out from their company. **Remember, the core can, likewise, turn his rebellious, unrepentant flip-side out to be in the company of Satan and his demons!**

If the flip-side continues to be rebellious and unrepentant, then announce to him what's going to happen to him! Explain that the core would be far better off without him and could operate just fine without him! This can be made possible by asking the Lord Jesus to amputate him from the core and attach him to the ancestral demon and his network—who will soon be sent to the abyss, the lake of fire, or be annihilated!

Quote God's words found in Matthew 5:29-30 to him, which gives the core personality the right to ask God to amputate him: *"If your right eye causes you to sin, pluck it out and cast it from you; for it is more profitable for you that one of your members perish, than for your whole body to be cast into hell. And if your right hand causes you to sin, cut if off and cast it from you; for it is more profitable for you that one of your members perish, than for your whole body to be cast into hell."*

When you have witnessed to the flip-side and you have reached the point of having a peace that you have said all that God wanted you to say, yet he still remains arrogantly rebellious and refuses to repent and accept the Lord as his Savior, you're left with only one alternative. You must take a very unpleasant but necessary action to permanently amputate him from the core personality! Once the Lord has convinced your heart that the flip-side is on the ancestral demon's side, willingly submitted to him, then it's time to let God Himself do major surgery on him to cut him away from the precious core personality.

Once again, I appeal, asking the flip-side if he has decided to choose to be amputated from the core. There have been times after I have shared these truths with a quite obstinate flip-side that he has suddenly broken down, sobbing and saying, "No, no, no! I am sorry! I will pray with you!"

There have been a few times when the "obstinate flip-side" was actually a demon-clone of the flip-side or a demon-produced personality just trying to fool me and get me off track. I'm grateful to say that this is far from the typical.

I am grateful to say that I recall dealing with only two obstinate, unrepentant flip-sides. I dealt with them by asking our Great Physician, to amputate the flip-side from the core, as I prayed the following short prayer:

> *"Lord Jesus by the power of Your blood, I ask You to attach the flip-side to the ancestral demon and his network, never to torment the core again! I thank You for doing this!"*

As I said before, encountering an unrepentant, obstinate flip-side is truly a rarity, for which I am extremely grateful to the Lord!

Now at this point, we thank the Lord for giving us wisdom in bringing a broken part of a core to salvation, healing and integration with the core! We also thank Him for giving us wisdom how to witness and minister to the flip-side of the core personality, and for bringing him to salvation and healing, plus fusing and integrating him with the core. Thanks be to our Lord! For in His doing so, 90 percent of the battle was won over the enemy—the ancestral demon and his network!

We will now march on to engage in the next battle which will be conquering the other ten percent of the ground the enemy managed to claim in the precious core's life! As we follow the Lord, our King of king's instructions, He will provide the tools of war that we need to use in rescuing the wounded personalities from captivity! Our King will most surely enable us to lead them to healing and salvation, and unite them with the core personality! So, let us move on now to the battle field where we will find the core and his wounded parts waiting for help!

Chapter Ten
TOOLS FOR COUNSELING CORE AND WOUNDED PERSONALITIES

How comforting to know that we made an enormous amount of headway in chapter nine! We know that the saved counselee has confessed all known sins at the very beginning, and those "unknown" sins that were uncovered which were connected to the flip-side. And at this point, we also know that the counselee's broken part of his core is healed, and that the flip-side came to repentance, received Christ as his Savior (wrote a check on the counselee's salvation), and was fused and integrated as one with the core. Now, we are ready to use the tools God has provided for us to deal with the wounded personalities in the core's life. **What joy to know that when the flip-side was dealt with and received salvation, 90 percent of the ground belonging to the ancestral demon carrying the formal name of the core personality was legally removed from him, through the core's power and authority in Jesus Christ! The ancestral demon is left with only 10 percent claim on the dark-side of the duplex.** His claim is only through wounded personalities living on the dark-side of the house—**five percent in the "first fruit"** and the other **5 percent in the remaining wounded personalities**. You can imagine how encouraged the counselee is to know how much victory has already been won and that total victory is not too far ahead!

You can well imagine that the ancestral demon is deeply agitated at this point with having lost 90 percent of his holdings that were in the flip-side and being left with only 10 percent holdings on the dark-side of the duplex! **However, until every wounded part is dealt with and led to salvation in Christ Jesus, then fused and integrated to the core, that ancestral demon has legal rights to stay put!** And, while he has the right to stand on his ground, you can be assured that he will do all that is within his power to keep what's left of his claim! In fact, he will try all the more to interfere and manipulate the wounded parts, as well as use his demon network to aid him in his evil cause!

We must understand that each of the wounded parts in the counselee's life was brought about when something traumatic happened in the core's life. Such traumas can stem from a wide range of causes. They may range from a major, horrific experience which some people may deem "minor," yet nevertheless, the "minor" was perceived by the core as "major!" The wounded parts have typically been created out of repeated abuse that occurred—verbally, physically, sexually—or through frightening or painful, traumatic events. Whatever the reason or reasons, wounded parts were created in the core as "coping mechanisms," with each individual wounded part having his own set of attitudes, emotions, and opinions, while dwelling on the "dark-side" of the duplex. From time to time, wounded parts alternate with the core and with one another, each surfacing to perform certain tasks the core allows them to perform when he chooses to "step out of the picture" for undetermined amounts of time! Counselors should take much care to remember to treat all the wounded personalities with respect and love, with the intent of helping them and bringing them to salvation, freedom, peace and joy—and oneness with the core!

A.   CORE REPORTS WHAT HE HEARS, FEELS, SENSES, OR SEES

Remember that through the saved core's power and authority through Jesus Christ, he is the "boss" over the system within himself, including the ancestral demon and his network! As you've probably heard it said of a boss, **"The buck stops passing with him!"** Like working with the core at the beginning of the counseling session to make sure that he is saved and has confessed all known sins, it is essential to make sure that all of the wounded personalities repent and receive salvation. A counseling session with a fragmented person is much like having the core sit in a room with a group of other people, and with the counselor interviewing each one individually. Each one is real—and is a reflection of the core's thoughts and emotions during various traumatic times in his past. Our counseling session is unique in that when I'm interviewing a particular wounded part if they do not choose to speak up and talk with me, I can then depend on the core to assist me. How? **With our unique blessing "in this room, in the group" the core is capable of hearing, feeling, sensing, and seeing what the wounded parts are saying and what their emotions are! Thus, the core, like unto an interpreter of languages, can pass on the information to me, as his counselor.**

WOUNDED PERSONALITIES TELL THEIR STORY

When the wounded personalities are willing and ready to tell their stories, then **the core personality will just "quietly sit back as an observer, listening, and refraining from interfering" unless a crucial matter arises and I need his assistance. However, as I stated before, the core is also free to share anything with me that he believes would be very important.** I will ask other wounded parts to come forth and communicate with me, and as each one comes forth, I will observe a variety of personalities, which are sometimes reflected in the core personality's countenance. Each one will reflect his individual personality and emotions, through facial expressions, gestures, and tone of voice. While you may have some that just tell their stories matter-of-fact—with no changes seen in the core's countenance—others will show more physical evidence of "who" they are. For instance, it's like seeing imitators—comedians—role-playing, switching their facial expression, body language, and voice tone to that of little babies or young children. Their vocabulary will match—just simplistic—even "baby-talk!" You may very well see this reflected from the core when you're dealing with younger ages. While I've met some wounded teenage personalities who have just reflected sadness through the cores' facial expressions and body language—there have been a number who behaved like a smart aleck! When counseling wounded parts, these things will be confirmed as each one tells his age, name and the story of how he came into being. In truth, God is miraculously taking you back in time with the counselee when he was that age— when he was upset and in pain emotionally and/or physically.

What a humbling privilege to be a part of the healing process of counseling! I will take a moment to share an example: I have had some very "prim and proper" ladies come for counseling, and when their young infant personalities came forth to talk to me, their facial expressions and body language switched to that of very young children. They sucked their thumbs, curled up in the chair and covered themselves completely with an afghan that was in my office. Some have gotten up and hidden behind the chair until I had convinced them that they were in a safe place. After being assured they were in a safe place, these precious "wounded personality toddlers" became very eager to tell their story and wanted to be free of the memories that tormented them. "Amazing grace—how sweet the sound!"

It is also possible that a **wounded personality can be brought into existence by the manipulation of the ancestral demon carrying the formal name and his network in the core's life**. For instance, the core with an ancestral demon may not be at all interested or active in a particular negative behavior such as pornography, nor be interested in persons of the same sex. However, a wounded part that came about through sexual abuse may cause the core personality to be drawn to it while not understanding why, and he is actually shocked and appalled by what he is feeling inside! He simply finds himself being drawn toward pornography materials, website porn, and experiencing feelings of attraction to the same sex. And, of course if he yields to the emotions he is feeling, Satan can more easily lure him to his perverted-sex trap and snare him.

Severely wounded parts can harbor "anger," "hatred" and "vengeance" for one or more persons who abused the core personality. Therefore, when something happens that upsets the core, the ancestral demon amplifies and magnifies the anger, hatred, and vengeance, causing the wounded parts to be so enraged that they drive the core personality to react wherever they are—perhaps shouting angrily and abusively at someone, physically hurting someone, or even murdering a person! I have interviewed wounded parts carrying "vengeance" who verbalized, "I'd like to murder someone, but the core won't let me do it!" Any core personality who has a lot of anger, hatred, and vengeance imbedded on the "dark-side" of his duplex is tormented with the battle going on inside him and usually longs for that battle to end. And, a person in this emotional state can become so weary of this battle, that he may come to also hate himself, thus the ancestral demon's suggestions that he kill himself does not sound like a bad idea at all—in fact, it sounds like a sweet release. Even though in counseling you may find a person who is full of extreme anger, bitterness, hatred, and vengeance toward others, take care to remember that he may very well feel the same about himself, thus he may be entertaining ways to commit suicide! Until the wounded parts are dealt with by the counselee exercising his authority in Christ and "casting down imaginations," he will continue to battle against the wounded personalities who act contrary to God's will.

When meeting a wounded part who comes forth but answers you with too few words to supply sufficient information, patiently encourage him. Assure him that he is in a safe place, that you will not hurt him and that God wants to help him and that you do also. Then, tell him that you would really appreciate his answering some questions so that you can help him. They usually start relaxing and answering with more information. When he shares the reason he came about, it will give you a clue. When he states what his emotion is, you'll better understand why he was so hesitate to talk about it. Perhaps his emotion is "pain," reflecting that it was too painful for him to readily say what happened to him, which brought him about. Perhaps he was a victim of an act, or acts, of sodomy by way of a close relative or close friend. Take care to be merciful to him and explain that you only need a little more information so you can take his case to the Lord, our wonderful Judge who can take away his pain forever and give him peace and joy. Add that he will no longer have to remember his pain, talk about it, or to be tormented by it! Encourage him with truth that if he will go to the Lord Jesus, He will take away all the "junk" and pain, He will heal, cleanse and restore him. Add that Jesus will unite him with the core, making them one.

TAKE ACCURATE, DETAILED NOTES

Always remember and trust that you and the core personality are certainly not left in the counseling room alone to handle the counseling, for the Lord Himself is present. And through His sweet Holy Spirit, He will nudge each wounded part to share necessary information! **As you take notes, be certain to write down <u>exactly</u> what the wounded part says even if you don't think it's that important at the time! Don't be impatient, don't rush, for if you do, you may miss some vital information and have to take time to backtrack for it!** Should you have to stop for any reason—including the possibility of being interrupted by another wounded personality or a demon wanting to put his two cents in—you will be able to go back to your notes and resume counseling where you left off! It is vital for you to have all the information down, easily accessible, when leading the wounded part to take all his "junk" to the Cross of Jesus! **Things will flow more rapidly and smoothly, I assure you! You do not want to leave anything out, to which the ancestral demon can still cling and try to manipulate and zap your time!**

WHEN DNA DOESN'T MATCH WOUNDED PERSONALITY

Another reason for taking accurate notes with a wounded personality is that **you may learn later that you were not actually dealing with a wounded personality but instead, a very clever demon masquerading as a wounded personality! When you run into difficulty later, trying to fuse and integrate one of the wounded personalities and discover it was a demon, you will have its DNA recorded!** You can quickly take away his right to stay in the core's life, and by your authority in Jesus Christ, sentence him to spend his life in the lake of fire!

Also, when interviewing a wounded part who has told you that his name is of a mystical nature, an evil supernatural connotation, stay on heightened alert for the Lord to let you know if it is a wounded personality who is connected to the occult, or if it is a demon-produced personality or a demon-clone!

Now we will go through the counseling procedures pertaining to the core personality and his wounded personalities.

B.   TRUST THE LORD TO CHOOSE FIRST WOUNDED PERSONALITY

In searching for the first wounded personality for us to meet, I always pray the following prayer, trusting that my all-wise Lord knows best!

> "Dear heavenly Father, I ask You to continually keep core personality, <u>core personality's formal name</u>, age ____, saved at age ____, **divided into the three categories**. The core seated in the heavenlies with the Lord Jesus in **category one**, all the wounded parts in **category two**, and in **category three**, the ancestral demon with the formal name, blood-linked together by Jesus' blood with all his demon network. And now, I would like for You to bring forward the first wounded part that You want me to meet, whether it is the "first fruit," a "wounded part who oversees a number of the other wounded personalities," or a wounded personality through whom You want to give me some important information at the beginning of our session. I trust You to control this counseling session as You deem best! I thank You ahead of time for doing it!"

C.   INTERVIEWING WOUNDED PERSONALITIES

A "FIRST FRUIT" WOUNDED PERSONALITY

The Lord may bring up the first wounded personality that fragmented from the core to meet me. This would be the youngest personality. **When this wounded personality fragmented on the dark-side of the duplex, which the ancestral demon established through iniquities of the fathers with the flip-side, he considered that wounded personality as his "first fruit" to use in securing his stronghold, his powerhouse, in the core's life. That "first fruit" contains 5 percent of the control and all the other wounded personalities are his other 5 percent.**

Since the "first fruit" usually knows a lot of the other wounded personalities, I may be able to gather a lot of information from him, if not all. **If the "first fruit" is willing to share, it will be of great benefit, for he can tell me about the other personalities and even act as spokesman for each one.** I will ask him to look in the system and see if he sees any wounded personalities younger than himself, and then ask him to look the other way and tell me about any others that he sees who are older than himself. I then ask him to give me information about each one. If I can deal with all of the wounded parts through him, then the ancestral demon's 10 percent powerhouse could be legally claimed from him in one conquering swoop! This would be my preference if I am not able to achieve this through the flip-side! This is how I pray when seeking the first fruit:

> "Heavenly Father, I ask You to continually keep the core personality divided up into three categories, the core seated in the heavenlies with the Lord Jesus, all the wounded personalities in category two, and the ancestral demon carrying the core's

235

formal name in category three, blood-linked together with all his demon network by the blood of Jesus. And, Lord Jesus, I'm looking for the "first fruit," the first wounded part on the dark-side of the house of <u>core's formal name</u>, age ____, born again at age ____. It could be somewhere from conception through age five, and I'm asking You to please bring that one up to meet me. And, I thank You, Lord, for doing it."

On the other hand, because the ancestral demon knows that his "first fruit" holds so much information, he may have manipulated and intimidated him into a state of hiding in a dark place, causing the "first fruit" to even think he is dead and in a grave. Therefore, the "first fruit" may hold excessive fear and will take more gentle coaxing before he will speak. **If this turns out to be the case, then a more "trustworthy" wounded personality is needed from whom I can gather information!**

A "TRUSTWORTHY" WOUNDED PERSONALITY

It would be rare not to find, amongst the variety of wounded personalities, at least one who is extremely reluctant to speak because he fears that if he talks he will get hurt in some way. Such a one may have come about when the core personality was told repeatedly as a child that he "should be seen and not heard!" You would not be surprised that this weak and fearful wounded one would carry a name such as "deaf and dumb personality" or "muted personality," and thus, would not be a good provider of information! So, I would need to find one who is not shy about sharing information about himself and telling me about others he knows about. Therefore, I would ask the Lord to help me find such a **"trustworthy"** one by praying the following prayer:

"Lord Jesus, since I was not able to gather any information from the "first fruit" about other wounded personalities, I ask You to please bring up a **"trustworthy" wounded personality** who can give me some information about those living on the dark-side of the duplex, one who controls or oversees a number of wounded personalities. I thank You for bringing up the one up in the system of core personality, <u>core personality's formal name</u>, age ____, saved at age ____, whom You know I can trust. I confess that in the name of Jesus, he cannot stay hidden, nor be hidden by anything in the system. He cannot be muted or deafened and will obey You and speak with me. I thank You that You will allow the core personality to be totally aware of all that is going on, and just sit calmly observing without interfering as I work with the wounded parts. I thank You, Lord, for doing this."

The **"trustworthy" wounded personality** that the Lord brings forth may be one who is very outspoken, strong, and readily plays the role of a **"caretaker"** or **"protector."** While he would be able to tell me a great deal of information, he may, however, be prone to hide information "to protect weaker" wounded personalities! He may not even want to cooperate at first for fear of losing his "place of authority," so he would take action to intimidate the one he thinks might be a "blabbermouth" who would reveal information he doesn't want to be told! Therefore, I would seek to reassure this caretaker, protector wounded personality that my intentions are to help, not hurt him or any of the wounded personalities! I would assure him that God loves him and all the wounded parts and that I do as well! In addition, I would assure him that God has solutions to help and heal all the wounded parts and remove their pain. Such appeals usually win caretakers over fairly quickly. I've had some caretakers and protectors even tell me later that they were weary of having to take care of the others! **Caretakers, even though some are reluctant at first, are usually very helpful to share information about themselves plus details about the wounded parts under their care. Locating caretakers cuts your time down considerably by not having to search out each wounded part! It spares the wounded ones from having to tell their painful, sad story! When such a short cut can be taken, the counselee walks away just as healed as he would have in working through every single issue!**

However, remember that you cannot trust the answer of a wounded personality about other wounded personalities until he has prayed to become a new creation. Without the mind of Christ, a wounded personality will be subject to confusion, thus he may not know a true wounded personality from a demonic being. For the enemy may bring up false personalities—demons masquerading as personalities and demon-clones that have been programmed to believe they are human. So, in order to be an accurate reporter, a genuine wounded personality needs to be healed by being saved. But, once the wounded part is saved, he can have the mind of Christ and be used by the Holy Spirit.

Upon a wounded personality coming up to talk to me, I always thank him for coming forth, and I then tell him that I am very glad to meet him, and that it is an honor to meet him. **Showing such courtesy reduces feelings of intimidation and helps him relax!** I reassure him further by telling him that he is safe in talking with me, that I do not intend to do anything that will embarrass him and I will not be mean to him. I urge the wounded personality to let me know if he experiences any type of harassment in the system while I'm communicating with him. I tell him that if the demons try to mess with him while we are talking together, I will make them stop.

REMINDER: TEST FOR TRUE OR FALSE WOUNDED PERSONALITIES

As I cautioned you while dealing with the flip-side who had wounded personalities under his care, likewise, it is crucial for you to **remain alert to true or false wounded personalities**. For, if something the wounded personality says just doesn't seem to add up, then the Lord is impressing you to check things out to see if you are either **(1)** dealing with a genuine wounded personality or **(2)** dealing with a demonic being. **Therefore, it is necessary for you to test the spirits as I explained earlier.** Do not be reluctant to obey the Lord's command to test the spirit to see if he is of light or darkness. Trust the heavenly Father to reveal truth, to confirm whether he is a genuine wounded personality or a masquerading demon-produced personality or a demon-clone. Then **(3)** in the process, it is important to remember that some demon-produced personalities and demon-clones may actually believe that they are genuine wounded personalities, and what they are saying is actually true.

First, remember that you may be talking with a true wounded part, so continue to be courteous, patient, and kind—unless you have seen or heard some things that have confirmed to you that you are definitely dealing with a demonic being! If while you are seeking to contact a wounded personality and it seems that "perhaps" a demon has rudely come forward claiming to be a wounded personality, upon quizzing him, you can always determine if he is lying by asking, **"Are you telling a truth that will stand before the eternal throne of Jesus Christ where only truth will stand?" He must answer this truthfully.** Sometimes, by simply asking such a one how old he is, uncovers his identity when he carelessly boasts, **"I'm as old as dirt!"** For certain, he's not a wounded part! Therefore, you must pray, asking the Lord to blood-link him by Jesus' blood to the ancestral demon carrying the core personality's formal name, with blood-links that cannot be broken.

Secondly, as you then ask to speak to a **"trustworthy" wounded personality** who could serve as a spokesman and one comes forward, thank him for coming up to speak with you. Ask him, **"What is your name and age?"** Then explain that **what you are about to pray concerning him is for his sake** and that you do not intend to offend or insult him, but since you know that even Satan himself can appear as an angel of light, you must continue to be on the safe side and check things out. Further explain, if he is a genuine wounded personality, nothing is going to happen to him, he will not be hurt and he will be able to continue working with you so he can be healed. But, if he is not a genuine wounded personality, then he will have to be shut down, blood-linked by Jesus blood to the ancestral demon carrying the formal name of the core, and dealt with in the near future.

Thirdly, as he agrees to the test, pray as follows to discover the truth:

"Heavenly Father, I want to test to see if name of wounded personality, age_____ , is a genuine wounded personality or if it is a demon masquerading as a wounded personality, a demon-produced personality, or a demon-clone customized/specialized for future development. I ask You, in the name and authority of Your Son, the Lord Jesus, that **if I am dealing with something demonic instead of a genuine wounded personality, to shut it down, bind its mouth shut so it cannot speak, and blood-link it with blood-links that cannot be broken, made of Your Son's precious blood, to the ancestral demon that carries the formal name of the core. Keep it from answering me as I ask some questions.**

"Dear Lord, I want to talk with whom I have been dealing who has identified himself as <u>name given to you</u>, age____. **(If he has not identified himself by name yet, refer to him as "whomever answered me when I called up a wounded personality who could serve as a spokesperson for other wounded personalities.")** Are you still here, can you hear the sound of my voice? If you are still here, please answer me.

1. If he does <u>not</u> answer: you can be assured that it was demonic and that the Lord shut it down and blood-linked by Jesus' blood to the ancestral demon. You can then move forward by asking the Lord to bring up the wounded personality you need to meet.

2. If he does answer: he is **a genuine wounded personality**, then you can continue with your interview with the wounded part.

3. Now take care to remember that a genuine wounded personality can be on either side of the duplex after the age of salvation! So, the next thing to do is to ask: **"Are you on the saved-side of the house or on the dark-side of the house in the core's life?"** **Please note** that you must handle things **differently** with those on the **saved-side of the house** than you do with those on the **dark-side of the house. The appropriate procedures for both saved-side and dark-side now follow:**

D.   QUESTION WOUNDED PERSONALITIES ON SAVED-SIDE OF DUPLEX

If the wounded personality answers that he is on the saved-side of the house, **then** you do not lead the wounded personality in a prayer of salvation. **After you have gathered all the information from him, you will lead him in "a prayer of repentance, seeking forgiveness for the sins that were committed".**

I begin ministering to the **wounded personality on the saved-side of the house** by asking the following questions—taking care to list all of his answers on my note pad:

1.   **Why did the core personality create you?** (His answer will reveal what was going on in the core's life when this wounded personality was created.)
2.   **How old are you?**
3.   **What is your name?**
4.   **Will you please tell me about yourself?**
5.   **What do you do in the core personality's life when the elevator stops on your floor?**
6.   **What are the major emotions that run, motivate or manipulate your life?**

The counselor must keep in mind that he must lead both the wounded personality on the saved side as well as the core personality to repentance. Whether the core was fully aware of the serious ramifications that could result in his sinful act or not, he chose to sin against God when he created the wounded part for the purpose of putting the trauma, the sin in him rather than rolling all his emotions—such as fear—over onto the Lord Jesus! He also sinned against the wounded personality. There is no room for excuses, for the core personality was saved when the wounded personality was created—he had the Holy Spirit living within his heart warning and convicting his heart not to yield to temptation! Out of his love for the Lord Jesus, he should have chosen to turn to the Lord to give him wisdom and strength to resist the temptation!

When the saved core creates wounded parts on the saved-side of the duplex, **the demons are most surely thrilled, for this gives them a legal right to go back and forth, from the dark-side to the saved-side of the duplex!** When this happens in the core's life, the peace of God that he had before this happened is diminished—surrendered to the demons, giving them more freedom to tempt further and manipulate. If a core personality continues to yield to temptation, he can create additional wounded personalities on the saved-side, thus, squelching his peace more and more. Typically, the core eventually becomes overwhelmed with depression. This most definitely can be one of the reasons why such a Christian ends up having "psychotic breakdowns" or he becomes "schizophrenic!" For the enemy has manipulated and deceived the precious Christian into thinking that all hope is gone, thus he is robbed of rest and peace! Of course being in such critical spiritual condition, he is bombarded with suicidal thoughts! I shudder to think of how the remainder of such a Christian's life will be spent if he does not find Godly counsel pertaining to the generational duplex—the ground on which the ancestral demon boldly stands. I encourage all pastors and counselors to keep in mind that wounded parts can be on both the saved side of the duplex as well as on the dark-side of the duplex.

REPENTANCE PRAYER
FOR WOUNDED PERSONALITIES ON SAVED-SIDE OF DUPLEX

Upon finding a wounded personality on the saved-side of the core's duplex, and learning that he is truly sorry for his sins and desires to confess them and ask the Lord to forgive him, it would be time to lead him in a prayer. In the following sample prayer, I will use the example of a core personality, age 40, who committed adultery and rather than seeking God's forgiveness, he yielded to temptation and created and stored all his guilt and memories of that sin in a wounded personality on the saved-side of his duplex:

> "Lord Jesus, I, <u>age 40</u>, <u>wounded personality Adultery on the saved side of the duplex</u>, confess that You became all the sin and evil of the world, past, present, and future. When You became it all, it killed You and put you in the ground for three days and three nights and God raised You up, giving You victory over all of mankind's sin and evil—past, present, and future. God also gave You victory over Satan and his demons—what they do to mankind and what they cause mankind to do to each other.

> "Lord Jesus, You had victory over the core's sin of adultery and his creating me to roll all his adultery junk into rather than rolling it over on You and Your Cross. Lord, I ask You not to lay this charge against the core—forgive him for he really didn't know what he was doing. Lord Jesus, I forgive the core for creating me— whether he knew he was doing it or not."

At this point, I pause the prayer and direct the wounded personality Adultery, age 40, to take time to speak to the core personality in this way:

> "Core personality, <u>core personality's formal name</u>, age ___, saved at age ___, I want you to know that I forgive you for creating me."

Then, I resume leading wounded personality Adultery, age 40, in the responsive prayer:

> "And, Lord Jesus, I want you to know that I am calling me, <u>wounded personality Adultery, age 40</u>, sin—all that my name means and all that my personality represents. I was created to carry the guilt, shame, rebellion, lust, adultery, worthlessness, uncleanliness, self-centeredness, sadness, and failure in the Christian core personality's life. I acknowledge that I do all these things in the core's life, plus I remind him that he is no good—that life's all about him—self. I never let him rest. Every time he has tried to pray and read and study the Bible, plus when he went to church, I bombard him with these things that are stored in me, hoping it would bring him to kill himself! Lord Jesus, I repent of all of this and I ask Your forgiveness.

> "Lord Jesus, I dump all of me, <u>wounded personality Adultery, age 40</u>, on the saved-side of the duplex—all that my name means, all that my personality represents—on Your Cross. I call it all my sin and I ask You to forgive me and I receive Your forgiveness."

At this point, I take a moment to lead the wounded personality on the saved-side to address Satan and the ancestral demon carrying the core's formal name in this way:

> "Now, Satan, you and <u>Ancestral Demon core personality's formal name</u>, I command you in the name of the Lord Jesus Christ that you give back all of the ground that the core surrendered up to you when he created me rather than rolling it all over on the Cross of Jesus!"

I then lead him to resume praying to the Lord Jesus in this matter:

> "Lord Jesus, saturate all that ground with Your blood. Heal, cleanse and totally restore it. Heal my mind, body, soul, spirit, emotions and memories. I don't want any of these memories or their negatives affecting me—presently or in the future! The demons no longer have any legal right to the ground on which they motivated or manipulated my being.

> "Lord Jesus, since I am forgiven now, I ask You to seal off that door that gave the demons the right to go back and forth. Seal off those negative emotions. Heal my damaged emotions and restore that torn part of the core's soul that I represented by giving me a new name. I no longer want to be <u>wounded personality Adultery, age 40</u>. I want a brand new name. I want my name to be the core personality's name, <u>core personality's formal name who has been totally forgiven and fully cleansed and washed by the blood of the Lord Jesus Christ</u>.

"Lord Jesus, since the demons no longer have any right, authority, or ground to stand on, I thank You that in the fullness of Your time You will put them in the abyss or the lake of fire, or you will annihilate them with the breath of Your Holy mouth. And, Lord, if the core will have me, make us one."

CORE'S PRAYER FOR NOW-FORGIVEN SAVED-SIDE PERSONALITY

Now it is time to lead the core personality to pray the following prayer concerning everything connected to the now-forgiven personality on the saved side of the duplex, that was once <u>wounded personality Adultery, age 40</u>.

"Lord Jesus, I core personality, <u>core personality's formal name</u>, age _____, saved at the age of ____ take full responsibility for my adulterous affair, and call it my sin for creating <u>wounded personality Adultery on the saved side, age 40</u> in which I hid the adultery—my guilt, shame, rebellion, lust, worthlessness, uncleanliness, self-centeredness, sadness, and failure. Whether I realized that I was actually doing that or not, I call it my sin and I ask You to forgive me. Lord Jesus, even though I later did repent and asked Your forgiveness for committing adultery, I did not realize that in spite of my repenting, the wounded personality and all the connecting negatives remained because the ancestral demon had claimed that ground for his own. So, Lord Jesus I take full responsibility for <u>wounded personality Adultery on the saved side of the duplex, age 40</u>, all that the name means, all that the personality represents, and everything that was stored in him. I call it all my sin and I repent and ask You to forgive me for the adulterous affair and all that was connected to it. I receive Your forgiveness and I dump it all on Your Cross with all its emotional fallout."

CORE ASKS NOW-FORGIVEN PERSONALITY FOR FORGIVENESS

I then instruct the core personality to ask: "<u>Now-forgiven personality Adultery on the saved side, age 40</u>, will you please forgive me for creating you rather than rolling it over on Jesus?"

Upon now-forgiven Adultery acknowledging that she forgives the core personality, I then take time to lead the core personality to confront and reclaim ground from Satan and the ancestral demon carrying the core's formal name in this way:

"Satan, you and <u>Ancestral Demon core personality's formal name</u>, I command you in the name of the Lord Jesus Christ that you give back all of the ground that the core surrendered up to you when he committed the adulterous affair and then created me, <u>wounded personality Adultery on the saved side, age 40</u>, rather than rolling it all over on the Cross of Jesus!"

I resume leading the core personality in the responsive prayer:

"Lord Jesus, saturate all of that ground with Your blood. Heal, cleanse and totally restore it. Heal my mind, body, soul, and spirit, plus all my memories connected to it and all the negative fallout. I don't want any of these negative memories affecting my life or my marriage, present or in the future. I do not want them interfering with my fellowship with You, dear Jesus! The demons have no right, authority, or ground because my sin has been dealt with! Lord Jesus, take Your blood and seal all those memories and their negative affects. Heal my damaged emotions and restore that torn part of my soul by fusing and integrating core personality's formal name, age 40, who has been totally forgiven, washed and cleansed by the blood of the Lord Jesus Christ who used to be wounded personality Adultery on the saved side, age 40. Make him one with me, core personality, core personality's formal name, age ____, saved at age ____. Lord Jesus, I confess that the demons have no right, no authority, and no ground on which to stand, and in the fullness of Your time, You will send the ancestral demon carrying the core's formal name and his entire network to the abyss or the lake of fire, or You will annihilate him with the breath of Your Holy mouth. And I thank you so much for doing this!"

MORE THAN ONE WOUNDED PERSONALITY ON THE SAVED-SIDE

If you have more than one wounded personality on the saved side of the duplex, **(1)** you can deal with each one separately, or **(2)** sometimes you can gather all the information concerning all of them, then find one who can serve as proxy for all of them if all are in agreement. The ones who have agreed to appoint a proxy will pray silently in unity along with the proxy. It simply depends on the attitude of each one of the wounded parts on the saved-side of the duplex. Often, I have found one that feels so overwhelmed with remorse that he wants the counselor to deal with him individually concerning his own sin-issues rather than having a proxy pray on his behalf. So you will find a mixture of decisions with wounded personalities on the saved-side of the duplex.

E.   QUESTION WOUNDED PERSONALITIES ON DARK-SIDE OF DUPLEX

After contacting a wounded personality and asking him if he is on the "saved-side of the duplex" or the "dark-side of the duplex," if he answers, "The dark-side," then I ask him the following questions, taking care to list his answers on my note pad:

1.   **What brought you into being?** (This will tell what was going on in the core's life when this personality was created.)

2.   **What is your age?**

3. **What is your <u>name</u>?** (Most of the time, but not always, the wounded personality is connected to what brought him into being—such as anger, desire to hide, or protect the core. However, the ancestral demon may have given him a name, such as Fouler that's connected to a program he wants played out in the core's life. Therefore, if the wounded personality gives you a name that does not reflect a connection to his family's names, a nickname, or other familiar names, then I quiz the wounded personality for more information.)

4. **What can you <u>tell me about yourself</u>?**

5. **What do you <u>do</u> in the adult core's life when the elevator stops on your floor and you come out and act up for a while?**

   a) **Would it be safe to say, "All of the above"?**

   b) **Do we need to add anything else about you?**

6. **What are the <u>major</u> <u>emotions</u> that motivate, manipulate, and run your life?**

   a) **Would it be safe to say, "All of the above"?**

   b) **Are there any other major emotions that you need to tell me about that are not listed above?** (Example: "I want to murder someone but the core won't allow it!")

ADDITIONAL QUESTIONS FOR DARK-SIDE WOUNDED PERSONALITY

1. **Are you willing to ask God to take out of you everything that goes against His will?**

2. **Are you ready to give all those hurts, wounds and all the junk to Jesus and ask Him to forgive and cleanse you, and then you can become one with the core personality?**

When the **dark-side wounded personality** is ready to give all his wounds to Jesus, repent and become one with the core personality, **pray, asking the Lord to keep all the demonic beings shut down so they cannot interfere in any way, unless He wants to teach us something**. Then lead the dark-side wounded personality to pray:

> "Lord Jesus, I, <u>name of wounded personality on the dark-side of the duplex</u>, age____, confess that, You, Lord Jesus, are the Son of God who was willing to give up all the glory, safety, and praise of heaven. You wrapped yourself in flesh and came to earth as the God-man. You walked among mankind, never sinning, never doing anything wrong. You just walked among Your people, loving and caring for them. You told them that you were the Son of God but they didn't believe You and they rejected You. They called you a liar, a blasphemer, and the prince of demons! They condemned You, saying You were deserving of death. They spat in Your face, they plucked out Your beard. They also blindfolded You and hit You in the face with the palms of their hands, saying, "Prophesy to us, Christ! Who is the one that hit You?" Then, they abandoned You to the Roman soldiers who stripped You

naked, beat You with a whip, put a crown of thorns on Your head, struck You on the head with a reed. They put a royal purple robe on You, and then they kneeled and mockingly worshiped You, saying "Hail, King of the Jews!"

"Lord Jesus, You loved them unconditionally, so much that You allowed them to take You outside the gates of Jerusalem and nail You to a tree. Hanging on that tree, You became all of their sin and evil. You became all the sin and evil of the world—past, present and future. You became all of what Satan and his demons do, what they do to mankind, and what they have caused mankind to do to one another. You did this so mankind would have the opportunity, the choice to become Your righteousness."

"Jesus, You became me, <u>name of wounded personality on the dark-side</u>, age _____, all that I stand for, all that my name means and all that my personality represents. Lord Jesus, You became my sins of <u>call off each of the sins for which he's responsible</u>, that I acted out in the life of <u>core personality's formal name</u>, age saved at age _____. Jesus You became it all and it killed You, put you in the ground for three days and three nights. The power of God raised You from the grave, giving You power and victory over the grave and death, and victory over all of mankind's sin and evil. God gave You power and victory over Satan and his demons, all that they do to mankind and what they cause mankind to do to one another! You had victory over me, <u>name of wounded personality on the dark-side of the duplex</u>, age , and all that I stand for, all that my name means, and all that my personality represents.

"Lord Jesus, I confess that You are my only way to be saved, to be safe, free, secure, loved, accepted, and cared for. Lord Jesus, I confess that You are my only way to have all my wounds, emotions and memories cleansed and healed. Lord Jesus, I, <u>name of wounded personality on the dark-side</u>, age _____, yield my control to You and give myself to You. I repent of everything I stand for that stands against You and Your will Lord Jesus in the life of <u>core personality's formal name</u>, age _____, saved at age _____, which has been locked up in me and all that my name means and all that my personality represents. Lord Jesus, I invite You to come into my life, save and forgive me, cleanse and heal me, deliver me from my name and all that my name stands for. I want a new name, I want to be <u>core personality's formal name</u>, a new creation in Jesus Christ, fully submitted to Your Lordship, and filled with Your abundant life."

NOW-SAVED, ONCE-WOUNDED PERSONALITY
PAUSES IN PRAYER TO SPEAK TO CORE

I now take time to lead the now-saved wounded personality to make an appeal, asking the core personality if he will consider accepting him:

> "Core personality, <u>core personality's formal name</u>, age ___, saved at age ___, if you will have me, I will no longer act out in your life, my old name of wounded personality on the dark-side, age _____, all that my name used to mean, all that my personality used to represent, but I will live out my new name, <u>core personality's formal name</u>, a new creation in Jesus Christ, fully submitted to the Lordship of Jesus Christ, and filled with His abundant life."

NOW-SAVED, ONCE-WOUNDED PERSONALITY
RESUMES RESPONSIVE PRAYER

Then, I resume leading the now-saved, once-wounded personality on the dark-side in this prayer of thanks to the Lord:

> "Lord Jesus, by Your powerful blood, if the core will have me, please make us one. Lord Jesus, now that You have healed me, made me a new creation, and have taken back the ground and saturated it with Your precious blood, I confess and thank You that the demons have no right, no authority to stand on this ground, because I no longer exist as a wounded part. Lord Jesus, I praise and thank You, that in the fullness of Your time, when all the wounds are healed in the core personality's life, You will send all the demons to the abyss or the lake of fire, or You will annihilate them with the breath of Your Holy mouth. With a childlike faith I thank You for doing this."

CORE WILLING TO ACCEPT
THE NOW-SAVED, ONCE-WOUNDED PERSONALITY

I then ask the core if he wants to invite the now-saved, once-wounded personality to be made whole, fused and integrated with him by the power of our Lord Jesus. Upon his desire to do so, I lead him to pray the following prayer:

> "<u>Old name of wounded personality on the dark-side</u>, now that Jesus lives in your life you have a new name <u>core personality's formal name</u>. You are a new creation in Jesus Christ and are no longer going to act out your negatives in my life. I invite you to come and be a part of my life."

CHOICE TO FUSE AND INTEGRATE
OR WAIT FOR MORE APPROPRIATE TIME

While the core has agreed to accept the once-wounded but now-saved and healed personality who was on the dark-side of the duplex so I could go ahead and fuse and integrate them, it's wise for me to be sensitive to God's will as to whether or not to fuse and integrate now or at a more appropriate time later. For there are some very important reasons to postpone the fusing and integrating!

I will surely explain how to go about fusing and integrating them later in this chapter, but I believe at this point, it would be very helpful to you if I first explain **reasons you should prayerfully seek God's will concerning appropriate times to fuse and integrate.**

F.   GOOD REASONS TO POSTPONE FUSING AND INTEGRATING

There are two good reasons to postpone fusing and integrating a wounded personality that is saved and healed with the core: **(1) A wounded personality may be found who can act as a caretaker or good reporter. After he is saved and healed, he can speak on behalf of some or all of the other wounded personalities in the system. It is critical that you do not fuse and integrate <u>a potential spokesperson</u> with the core because you will no longer be able to communicate with that individual personality who may hold a great deal of information! (2)** It is wise to delay fusing and integrating each wounded personality as they are healed <u>**simply in order to save time**</u> because you can fuse and integrate a goodly number of them all at one time.

WHILE PRAYERFULLY CAUTIOUS
FUSE AND INTEGRATE ONLY A CERTAIN FEW TO ENCOURAGE

Encouragement for the core in light of delays in counseling can be given through fusing and integrating a "certain few": If a minister/counselor's counseling schedule (or a counselee's schedule) allows the counselee only short counseling sessions that must be spread out over a period of time, causing the counselee to become discouraged when progress is slow, there is one thing you can do to encourage the counselee.

In such drawn-out cases, as long as you have already brought the flip-side to salvation and fused and integrated him to the core personality, you can fuse and integrate **certain wounded personalities that have been saved and healed** as an encouragement to the core. However, take care if you do any fusing and integrating that you **do not fuse and integrate the ones you believe would be most helpful to you!**

PUTTING A ONCE-WOUNDED, NOW-SAVED PERSONALITY
IN A SAFE PLACE

When I wait until a better time to fuse and integrate the once wounded but now-saved, new-name personality with the core personality, I explain to the now-saved personality that I'm going to pray, asking the Lord to put him in a safe place until a better time to fuse and integrate him with the core personality. I further explain that I'm going to search for more wounded personalities that are hurting and wanting help like he did. **Then I assure him that I will not forget him and that I will come back for him**! I then pray this:

> "Lord Jesus, I ask You to put a hedge of protection consisting of Your blood around this healed personality that used to be <u>old name wounded personality</u>, age <u>   </u>, who is now called <u>core personality's formal name</u>, a new creation in Jesus Christ, fully submitted to Your Lordship, and filled with Your abundant life, and I ask that You place him in a safe place until we need to meet him again. I thank You for doing it."

G.   WOUNDED PERSONALITY CARETAKER/REPORTER HELPS

We will assume that as I continue my search for more wounded personalities, a wounded personality who is a **caretaker** or one who would be a **good reporter, or spokesperson** will be found. **After I have led him to salvation and healing, I then show him the courtesy of asking him if he is willing to serve as such**. I add that the core and I would really appreciate his help, in order for the other wounded personalities to become new creations in Jesus Christ just like he is now. If a healed personality is a **caretaker**, he will already know the names and ages of those wounded personalities that he cared for. In that case, he may also know of others in the system, even ones that were not under his care!

I explain to the healed personality caretaker/reporter that I would very much appreciate it if he will **(1) identify those who are under his care** and **(2) share information about other wounded personalities** he may know of who are not directly under his care. I will encourage him by saying:

> "Based on the Word of God, it says we can do all things through the strength of Christ Jesus and He can accomplish His will through us if we allow Him to do so! Therefore, since you are a new creation in Christ Jesus, you can work with God's power now. You can see with the eyes of Christ, hear with His ears, feel with His heart, and comprehend with the mind of Christ. Is that not exciting?

> "Are you ready to go to work with me now as a team, so that we can see what's going on and meet the other wounded personalities who are hurting as you used to be, so they can become new creations in Jesus Christ just like you are now? I really appreciate your allowing me to meet the other wounded personalities. When we are

finished gathering the information, if you are comfortable, and they are as well, I would appreciate your praying aloud on their behalf, as their proxy, while they pray silently but sincerely in agreement, to receive Christ as their Lord and Savior. Would you like to be used by the Lord Jesus like that, too?"

If the <u>healed caretaker/reporter personality</u> agrees to do so, then I pray as follows:

"Lord Jesus, I ask You to put a hedge of protection consisting of Your blood around this healed personality that used to be <u>wounded personality's old name</u>, age ___, who is now <u>core personality's formal name</u>, a new creation in Jesus Christ, fully submitted to Your Lordship, and filled with Your abundant life, and I ask that You keep him safe as we work together to meet the other wounded personalities in the core's life that You would have us meet. Lord Jesus, place him on a riser, podium, or stage so he can stand up and see. I ask that You allow him to see with Your eyes, to hear with Your ears and to have Your mind as he and I work together to meet wounded personalities remaining in the core's life. We thank You for doing this."

Then, I ask this of the <u>healed caretaker personality who is acting as my reporter</u>:

"Since you have a new mind in Christ, do you see anyone in there who is still wounded like you used to be?"

CARETAKER/REPORTER'S TWO CHOICES

The reporter may answer that he sees or senses several at one time, or one or two at a time. Once the healed personality has identified all the wounded personalities that he is aware of, then I ask him to tell me what he knows about the wounded personalities. He may choose to handle the wounded personalities in either of these two ways:

1.   **If a caretaker/reporter is comfortable with gathering information from some or all of the wounded personalities under his care and is willing to share it:**
a) If the caretaker/reporter questions the wounded personalities under his care: I ask him to tell the wounded personalities for me that I appreciate their cooperation in sharing information. I ask him to assure them that my intention is to help them, not to embarrass or be mean to them. I ask him to also tell the wounded personalities if they experience any interference or harassment while communicating with the caretaker/reporter, to let him know so that he can tell me. I ask him to also assure the wounded personalities that I will not let the demons mess with them while I am conversing with the caretaker/reporter.
b) It is not necessary for me to go through the negative list of emotions, characteristics, behaviors with each one. I only need to ask the caretaker/reporter to tell me what emotions,

characteristics, and behaviors each one holds. **However, I can use my list of the ages that I obtained from the counseling form to ask the reporter if the wounded personalities hold the things listed for those particular ages.**

2.   **If the reporter prefers that I gather the information from some or all of the wounded personalities, then I proceed to meet and question those wounded personalities individually:**

   a) When asking a wounded personality questions, I thank him for coming up to talk with me and let him know what an honor it is to meet him. I reassure him that he is safe in talking with me and that I don't intend to do anything that will embarrass him or be mean to him. I also urge the wounded personality to let me know if he experiences any interference or harassment while communicating with me. I assure him that I will not let the demons mess with him while I am conversing with him.

H.   SIX MAIN QUESTIONS FOR CARETAKER/REPORTER OR YOURSELF TO ASK THE WOUNDED PERSONALITIES

Whatever the caretaker/reporter's choice was, it is needful that information is gathered about the wounded personalities which is covered by the following **six main questions (which lead into additional questions):**

1.   **What brought you into being?** (This will tell what was going on in the core's life when this personality was created.)
2.   **What is your age?**
3.   **What is your name?** (Most of the time, but not always, the wounded personality is connected to what brought him into being—such as anger, desire to hide, or protect the core. However, the ancestral demon may have given him a name, such as Fouler that's connected to a program he wants played out in the core's life. Therefore, if the wounded personality gives you a name that does not reflect a connection to his family's names, a nickname, or other familiar names, then I quiz the wounded personality for more information.
4.   **What can you tell me about yourself?**
5.   **What do you do in the adult core's life when the elevator stops on your floor and you come out and act up for a while?**
   a)   **Would it be safe to say, "All of the above"?**
   b)   **Do we need to add anything else about you?**
6.   **What are the major emotions that motivate, manipulate, and run your life?**
   a)   **Would it be safe to say, "All of the above"?**
   b)   **Are there any other major emotions that you need to tell me about that are not listed above?** (Example: "I want to murder someone but the core won't allow it!")

Once I have all the information concerning the wounded personalities connected to the healed caretaker, then I would **ask him if he knows of any other caretakers like himself that have other wounded personalities for which they are responsible, or other wounded personalities that have not been identified yet.**

If the healed caretaker/reporter identifies another caretaker and/or wounded personalities, I seek God's wisdom to see if He wants me to do either of the following: (1) Wait until later to contact the newly found caretaker and/or wounded personalities and go ahead and lead the healed caretaker/reporter personality to pray as proxy with the wounded personalities. Or (2) I explain to the healed caretaker/reporter and wounded personalities that I need to take a little time to search for some other wounded personalities. I also explain that I am going to ask the Lord to put them in a safe place and assure them that I will come back to pray with them and fuse and integrate them with the core personality. When they've been put in a safe place, I then ask to speak to the newly found caretaker/reporter and/or wounded personalities, and interview each one as I ask the six main questions previously listed. In the process, I would also ask the Lord to help me be alert to any stray wounded personalities that are hidden away. If I found any stray wounded personalities I would do the following:

TAKE TIME TO SEARCH FOR STRAY WOUNDED PERSONALITIES

To search for strays, look to see if there are any negative things left on the check list that have not been claimed. If so, it is important that you seek out any wounded parts who have escaped being discovered. Example, when gathering information from the counseling form, you see that it reflects a lot of trauma in the core's life around the age of five, yet no wounded personalities have been discovered at that age. If this is the case, pray this:

> "Heavenly Father, as I seek to meet with the various wounded personalities in core personality <u>core's formal name</u>, age ___, saved at age ___, that I have not met yet, I ask in the name of Jesus, that if there are demon-produced personalities, demons masquerading as personalities or demon-clones customized for future development involved in the life of <u>core personality's formal name</u>, who think they are human, I ask that they not be allowed to answer or otherwise interfere, unless You wish to teach us something or use them to accomplish Your will concerning these matters.

> "Lord Jesus, please allow us to speak with any wounded personality or wounded personalities that are approximately ___ years of age. Lord Jesus, please take the wounded personality that You know we need to meet by the hand, let him know that You are not going to allow any demonic being to hurt him or to be mean to him, and let him know that neither am I going to hurt or embarrass him when they come up to meet me.

"Dear Lord, if a wounded personality whom You know we need to meet at this time doesn't want to come up for whatever reason and is in hiding, I thank You that You will bring him forward. And, if he is mute or deaf, I trust You to not allow him to be silenced by intimidation or harassment. I thank You for doing this."

INTERVIEWING STRAY WOUNDED PERSONALITIES

I proceed to contact a stray wounded personality by saying:

"I am looking for a wounded personality that is approximately age ___. I just want to ask you a few simple questions, please. I want to assure you that you are in a safe place and that I do not intend to do anything that will embarrass you, nor will I harm you in any way. By the authority of the Lord Jesus, I am not going to allow any human or demon to hurt you or abuse you when you come up to talk with me. So please come up and talk with me."

When the wounded personality comes forward, I thank him for coming up to talk with me and tell him what an honor it is to meet him. I add that I want him to tell me if he experiences any type of harassment while communicating with me and that I'll not let the demons bother him!

Don't be discouraged if a wounded personality doesn't answer you, for if there are wounded personalities in the life of the core that have not been found and identified yet, the Lord will expose them in His perfect timing and way! For Jesus' said: *"...there is nothing covered that will not be revealed, and hidden that will not be known. Whatever I tell you in the dark, speak in the light; and what you hear, preach on the housetops."* (Matthew 10:26b-27)

Once you are confident you are working with a genuine wounded personality, seek to lead him to the Lord. Many times it may be as simple as asking a stray if he would like to know the Jesus whom the core and the healed personality know, and give all the pain, wounds and memories that he carries to Jesus, and become one with the core so that the core becomes complete for the first time in his or her life.

Having the stray wounded personalities handled, then you can contact the caretaker/reporter and wounded personalities connected to him, and let them appoint him as their proxy.

WOUNDED PARTS CHOOSE CARETAKER/REPORTER TO SERVE AS PROXY

Once all the wounded personalities that you have met so far express their desire to be saved and healed, then ask each one if he is comfortable with allowing the healed personality caretaker/reporter to pray aloud on his behalf while he prays silently along with the healed, caretaker/reporter personality. If one (or more) of the wounded personalities do not feel comfortable with allowing the reporter to pray with him as his proxy, then **(1)** offer to let him select another wounded personality with whom he is comfortable enough to let him pray as proxy in his behalf, or **(2)** he can choose to allow you to lead him in prayer.

To all of the wounded personalities explain the concept of one healed personality praying as a spokesperson on behalf of a group of others as follows:

> "If you are comfortable with it, you may give your proxy to <u>now-saved, once-wounded part with core's name</u>, a new creation in Christ Jesus who used to be <u>old name of wounded part</u>, age ____, which used to be just like you, to pray verbally on your behalf while you pray silently. Giving a proxy to someone is the legal process where one person, called a principal, gives another person, called an agent or attorney-in-fact, the legal right to act on his behalf just as if the principal were acting. The agent may bind the principal in a transaction just as if the principal himself had appeared and agreed to all the terms of the transaction. If you give your proxy to <u>now-saved, once-wounded part with core's name</u>, a new creation in Christ Jesus who used to be <u>old name of wounded part</u>, age ____, and used to be just like you, he will pray on your behalf. Please understand that even though you will not be praying aloud, you will be praying along with the agent, silently but in full agreement."

I then instruct the caretaker/reporter to ask each individual wounded personality under his care: "Are you comfortable giving your proxy—your legal right—to me, <u>now-saved, once-wounded personality with core personality's name</u>, a new creation in Christ Jesus who used to be <u>old name of wounded personality</u>, age ___, and used to be just like you? If so, as I pray aloud on your behalf, please, pray silently along with me."

HEALED CARETAKER/REPORTER PRAYS AS PROXY FOR WOUNDED PARTS

For the wounded parts that choose to let the caretaker/reporter serve as their proxy, I lead them to pray the following:

> "Lord Jesus, I am <u>name of healed personality (who is the caretaker/reporter)</u>, a new creation in Jesus Christ, fully submitted to Your Lordship and filled with Your abundant life, and I have been asked to be the prayer spokesperson for <u>list age/s and name/s of wounded part/s</u>, and <u>all that each one stands for and all that their names mean and that their personalities represent</u>. All <u>number of wounded part/s</u> of us confess that, You, Lord Jesus, are the Son of God who was willing to give up all the glory, safety, and praise of heaven. You wrapped Yourself in flesh and came to earth as the God-man. You walked among mankind, never sinning, never doing anything wrong. You just walked among Your people, loving and caring for them. You told them You were the Son of God but they didn't believe You and they rejected You.

253

"They called You a liar, a blasphemer, and the prince of demons! They condemned You, saying You were deserving of death. They spat in Your face, they plucked out Your beard. They also blindfolded You and hit You in the face with the palms of their hands, saying, "Prophesy to us, Christ! Who is the one who hit You?" They abandoned You to the Roman soldiers who stripped You naked, beat You with a whip, put a crown of thorns on Your head and struck You on the head with a reed. They put a royal purple robe on You, and then they kneeled and mockingly worshiped You, saying "Hail, King of the Jews!"

"And, Lord Jesus, You loved them unconditionally, so much that You allowed them to take You outside the gates of Jerusalem and nail You to the tree. And, hanging on that tree, You became all of their sin and evil. You became all the sin and evil of the world—past, present and future. You became all of what Satan and his demons do, what they do to mankind, and what they have caused mankind to do to one another. You did this so mankind would have the opportunity, the choice to become Your righteousness.

"Lord Jesus, You became all of our sin, everything that our names mean, everything that our personalities represent, beginning with <u>call off ages and names of each wounded personality</u> and <u>what brought each one into being</u>.

"We acknowledge that our sin killed You and put You in the grave for three days and three nights and the power of God raised You up from the grave. Jesus, You became all the <u>read off all negatives connect to part/s</u> that <u>core's formal name</u> feels and experiences when we act out badly. Jesus, You became <u>list ages and names of wounded parts</u>, and all that each one stands for, all that their names mean, and all that their personalities represent. Lord Jesus, You had the victory over all <u>the total number</u> of us, all that we stand for, all that our names mean, and all that our personalities represent.

"Lord Jesus, all <u>the total number</u> of us confess that You are our only way to be saved, to be safe, free, secure, loved, accepted, and cared for. Lord Jesus, all <u>the total number</u> of us confess that You are our only way to have all our wounds, emotions and memories cleansed and healed, including <u>read off list of negative emotions, behaviors, characteristics claimed by all the wounded personalities</u>. Lord Jesus, all <u>the total number</u> of us give ourselves to You. We repent of everything we stand for that stands against You and Your will, Lord Jesus, in the core's life that has been locked up in <u>list ages and names of wounded parts</u>, all that each one stands for, all that our names mean, and all that our personalities represent.

"Lord Jesus, all <u>the total number</u> of us invite You to come into our lives, save and forgive us, cleanse and heal us, deliver us from our names and all that they stand for. All <u>the total number</u> of us want a new name, we want to be <u>core's formal name</u>, a new creation in Jesus Christ, fully submitted to Your Lordship, and filled with Your abundant life.

NOW-SAVED, ONCE-WOUNDED PERSONALITIES PAUSE IN PRAYER TO SPEAK TO CORE

Lead the now-saved, once-wounded personalities to make an appeal to the core personality to accept them:

"Core personality, <u>core's formal name</u>, age ___, saved at age ___, if you will have us we will no longer act out in your life. We will no longer act out our old names of <u>list ages and names of wounded parts</u>, all that our names used to mean, all that our personalities used to represent, but we will live out our new names of <u>core's formal name</u>, a new creation in Christ, fully submitted to the Lordship of Christ, and filled with His abundant life. And Lord Jesus, by Your powerful blood, if the core will have us, make us one.

NOW-SAVED, ONCE-WOUNDED PERSONALITIES RESUME PRAYING

Resume leading the now-saved, once-wounded personalities to pray this:

"Lord Jesus, all of us, <u>call of names and ages of all the now-saved, once-wounded parts</u>, confess and thank You that the demons have no right, no ground, no authority to stand on this ground, because we no longer exist as we used to because You have healed us, made us new creations, and have retaken all that ground, and then saturated and permeated that ground with Your precious blood.

"Lord Jesus, we praise and thank You, that in Your time, when everything is healed in the core's life, that You are going to throw the demons out. You are our sovereign God and You will show us what You want done with the demons, depending on their behavior, whether You want to send them to the abyss, the lake of fire, or to annihilate them with the breath of Your Holy mouth. With a childlike faith, we thank You for doing this."

COUNSELOR PRAYS TO KEEP
ONCE-WOUNDED, NOW-SAVED PERSONALITIES SAFE WHILE WORKING

"Lord Jesus, I ask You to put a hedge of Your blood around all the total number of these now-healed, once-wounded personalities of core personality's formal name's soul that we have called out to You, call out list of names and ages of each wounded part who are now core personality's formal name, new creations in Jesus Christ, fully submitted to Your Lordship, and filled with Your abundant life and I ask that You keep them safe as we work together to meet the other wounded personalities in the core's life that You would have us meet."

SAVED PERSONALITIES HELP FIND MORE WOUNDED PERSONALITIES

Let's say that at this point, a group of thirteen personalities had been found and saved through their caretaker reporting them. At such a time, share with the saved and healed group of personalities that based on the Word of God, we can do all things through strength in Christ Jesus. Therefore, He can use them to accomplish His will. Explain to them that since they are now new creations in Christ Jesus, they can work in God's power, see with the eyes of Christ, hear with His ears, and comprehend with the mind of Christ.

Then, show the healed personalities who are now new creations, the courtesy of asking if they are willing to work with you as a team to help any other wounded personalities, like they used to be, so that they can become new creations in Jesus Christ also. Ask, "Isn't it exciting to think of being used by the Lord Jesus to do this?" Upon their agreeing, pray this prayer:

"Lord Jesus, I want You to take the healed personalities that were formerly known as call out list names and ages of each wounded part who are now core personality's formal name, new creations in You, and place them on a riser, podium, or stage so they can stand up and see. I ask that You allow them to see with Your eyes, to hear with Your ears and have Your mind as they work with me to meet the wounded personalities remaining in this person's life.

"Now Lord Jesus, please bring all the wounded personalities in the system that we have not met and stand them before these healed personalities who are new creations in You. Lord, if a wounded personality doesn't want to come up, please make him come up. Lord Jesus, do not allow the enemy to render him mute or deaf and do not allow the enemy to intimidate him so that he is kept from coming up to meet me.

"Lord, if a wounded personality is afraid to come up, please take it by the hand and let it know that nobody is going to hurt, embarrass or be mean to him. Let him know that I just need to meet him so he can be healed and become a new creation in You Lord Jesus.

256

"Lord Jesus, if a wounded personality is in hiding and just does not want to come up for whatever reason, I ask that You please make it come up and stand before these healed personalities so that he may experience Your forgiveness, cleansing and healing, so this person may be truly complete for the first time in his life.

"Heavenly Father I thank You now that You will bring up all the wounded personalities that are remaining in the life of <u>core personality's formal name</u>, age of _____, saved at age _____ and stand them in front of the riser that all the healed personalities have been placed on."

TAKE TIME TO PRAY TO TEST FOR ANY DECEIVERS IN THE GROUP

At this point in the prayer, you need to ask the Lord to enable you to discover any **deceivers that have managed to mix in with the group of wounded personalities**—demons masquerading as wounded personalities, demon-clones, or demon-produced personalities. Continue praying as follows:

"Lord Jesus, because Satan can come as an angel of light and fool us all, I ask that You enable all the healed personalities, new creations in Christ, who are standing on a podium where they can see the wounded personalities who are not yet saved, that You allow them to see with Your eyes. **I ask that You put chains on all the beings standing before these healed personalities that are demons or are otherwise of Satan, whether they are demons masquerading as wounded personalities, demon-produced personalities or demon-clones customized, specialized for future development, even if they believe they are human.**"

Ask of the **saved caretaker/reporter personality** and the **once-wounded, now-saved personalities with new names** who are on the podium observing, **"Of the wounded personalities that we've not yet dealt with, do any have chains on them? Yes or no?"** If the reporter indicates that one—or more of them—have chains on them, then ask the Lord to deal with all that are chained as follows:

"Lord Jesus, I ask You to remove every demonic being that has chains on it. Take all the demon-clones, demon-produced personalities, and demons masquerading as wounded personalities, and bind them with blood-links of Jesus' blood, which cannot be broken to <u>Ancestral Demon core personality's formal name</u> so that they cannot interfere with us as we seek to meet genuine wounded personalities."

At this point, we will say that there was one deceiver in the group of thirteen in the caretaker/reporter's care, which the Lord has now bound with blood-links that cannot be broken to the ancestral demon carrying the formal name of the core personality.

Then, ask the caretaker/reporter and once-wounded, now-saved personalities: **"Are any left?"** You should **go through them again one or two more times to confirm that you only have genuine wounded personalities**. You want to make certain that neither you, the reporter, nor the now-saved personalities are not being conned, simply because the Lord warns us to test the Spirit to see if it is of Him. Don't ever forget that Satan and his demons are experts on deceiving and can sometimes even make you think you're hearing from God! It is your responsibility to be thorough in your "investigation" and "interrogation!" **In the midst of this, please understand that we are not questioning God! We are just obediently testing the spirits to make certain that they are of** <u>**God**</u>**! And God will most surely reveal truth to you if you will just take time to sit and listen to Him.**

Having tested the spirits and dealt with them, this leaves us with a total of twelve once-wounded but now-saved and healed personalities who are ready to be fused and integrated with the core personality. The coast is clear! We can now call upon the healed personalities to continue reporting what they see!

ASK ALL THE HEALED PERSONALITIES TO REPORT WHAT THEY SEE

Address all the wounded personalities who have been healed thus far:

> "All of you together, with a new mind in Christ, do you see anyone in there who is still wounded like all of you used to be?"

If any new wounded personalities are identified, then discover what brought them into being and what they do in the core's life, etc., and lead them to Christ. We will assume at this point that they were unable to tell us of any other wounded personalities. We will then move on to the next procedure, a final check inside the building!

I. FINAL SEARCH IN BUILDING FOR WOUNDED PERSONALITIES

Having identified and dealt with all the wounded personalities that the Lord Jesus has brought forth so far at this point, **it's time for the now-healed personalities and me to act just like firefighters who are moving upward from the bottom floor to the top floor, evacuating people from an office building that is on fire. Like firefighters, we will search floor by floor for anyone that may have been left behind.** I ask the healed personalities to help me by letting me know if they hear, feel, sense or see someone or something as we go through all the floors.

PRAYER FOR SEARCH, RESCUE, EVACUATION, FLOOR BY FLOOR

I do this by asking the Lord to take us **year-by-year** in our core personality to draw out anyone left behind, starting in the basement. For instance, **if the person is 53 years old**, his elevator goes from **"basement (conception to birth) plus 53 floors above ground."** I ask the Lord, **"Our Fire Chief,"** to use us like firefighters in search and rescue efforts, praying:

> "Father, we want to see this person completely healed and whole, therefore, we truly want to meet each and every wounded personality in his life so he can be saved and integrated with the core. Father, I ask You to intervene so that the powers of darkness will not be able to keep us away from any personalities we need to meet, including any who are mute or deaf. Do not allow the forces of the enemy to keep any down by intimidation and fear. If any genuine wounded personalities are there for any reason, I ask, Father, that You bring into the light any wounded personalities that are hiding in darkness so that I can meet them and see them brought to healing and salvation.

> "Father, I ask in the name of Jesus, that if there are demon-produced personalities, demons masquerading as wounded personalities or demon-clones customized or specialized for future development involved in the life of core personality's formal name, that feel human or think they are human, I ask that they not be allowed to answer or otherwise interfere.

> "Father, I ask You to bring up only any genuine wounded personalities in this person's life that we have not met yet that are between the ages of his conception through 5 years old. Father, although they may be fearful, reassure them that You will not allow them to be hurt, intimidated or harassed while they work with us. Let them know that I am not going to embarrass them or make fun of them—I just need to meet them and ask a few simple questions. I thank You, heavenly Father that You will rescue them and bring them forward. Heavenly Father, I thank You for shining Your light into each and every room on every floor of this precious person's life! I thank You for enabling us to accomplish this search, rescue, and evacuation mission—floor by floor!"

I then proceed to start in the basement, calling out and searching every floor, all the way to the top floor, and upon finding wounded personalities, I rescue each one by ministering to them as I go, bringing them to salvation, then continuing the search until I've searched the top floor in the building. My floor-by-floor process is as follows:

In the basement, between conception and the age of five I call out, "Is there anyone in there from between conception ("0"/basement) and age of five?" (On each floor, I announce that if anyone is there, we will not hurt or embarrass him, but we do need to meet him. I then ask, "Will you please come up and talk with us? Anybody between the ages of conception to five years old, come up and talk with us, because we need to completely evacuate the building because all the floors and elevators must be completely done away with. Anybody between the ages of conception to five years old, come up and talk with us, please!" While in actuality I call out to every floor, I call in "groups of floors" as follows, knowing they are all in hearing range!

1.   **Repeat the preceding process for basement/ages conception/0 through 5**

2.   **Repeat the preceding process for floors/ages 6 through 12**

3.   **Repeat the preceding process for floors/ages 13 through 19**

4.   **Repeat the preceding process for floors/ages 20 through 30**

5.   **Repeat the preceding process for floors/ages 31 through 40**

6.   **Repeat the preceding process for floors/ages 41 through 50**

7.   **Repeat the preceding process for floors/ages 51 through 53**

Upon finding any wounded personalities and leading them to the Lord, as I've explained the procedures earlier, **it is essential for all of the wounded personalities, from all the floors, to receive each other, recognize the core as the boss, and express their desire to be fused and integrated with the core if he will accept them. It is essential that they agree that they want to be in unity under the authority of the Lord and stand against Satan.**

At this point, twelve wounded personalities on the dark-side of the duplex who were saved and healed, plus the three that were found hiding during our search of the burning building—making a total of fifteen. Therefore, things are in order for fusing and integrating them all as one. Whether fusing and integrating **one healed personality at a time or an entire group** with the core, I begin by praying, asking the Lord to put the healed personality/personalities in a safe place with His blood hedging about him/them, as I've explained before.

J.   CORE'S CHOICE TO BECOME ONE, FUSED WITH HEALED PARTS

Knowing that the core has heard and been a part of the entire counseling procedure, it's time to ask the core if he is ready to have the fifteen healed personalities fused and integrated with him. So, I address him as follows:

> "Core personality, core personality's formal name, age ___, saved at age ___, please talk with me. Do I have core's formal name, age ___, saved at age ___?"

Upon his confirming that he is the core, I proceed to ask him:

"Core personality's formal name, now that all of the 15 personalities, call off the old negative names and ages of each of the wounded personalities on the dark-side of the duplex, have acknowledged and renounced all that their names meant, all that the names represented, and asked Jesus Christ to be their Lord and Savior, and are now core personality's formal name, new creations in Jesus Christ, fully submitted to the Lordship of Jesus Christ, filled with Jesus' abundant life, are you ready to have all the healed personalities fused and integrated with you?"

If the core agrees to be fused and integrated with them, I lead him to pray:

"Lord Jesus everything that list names and ages of the 15 healed wounded parts were, all that their names meant, and all that their personalities represented, I take full responsibility for them. I call all of it my sin and ask You to forgive me and dump it on Your Cross, with all its emotional fall out. I ask You to forgive me and cleanse me, and I gratefully receive Your forgiveness and cleansing.

"Lord Jesus, I command that the ancestral demon carrying my formal name, core personality's formal name and his demon network and blood-linked demons, give me back the ground that was surrendered to them. By Your precious blood, saturate all that ground, heal, cleanse and totally restore it. Heal my mind, body, soul, and spirit. Heal my emotions, all the negative effects, past, present and future. I ask You Lord Jesus to seal off all the doors to those memories and their negative effects. Any demons that stood on that ground to manipulate or motivate me no longer have rights, ground or authority to torment me! Heal all my damaged emotions and restore all the wounded parts of my soul by fusing and integrating the wounded parts of my soul who have been saved and healed. I thank You, Lord Jesus, for doing this!"

I then lead the core to invite the wounded personalities to be made whole, fused and integrated, with him by the power of our Lord Jesus.

"Wounded personalities who were on the dark-side of the duplex, call off old negative names and ages of each of the "fifteen" wounded personalities, now that you have received the Lord Jesus into your lives and you are core personality's formal name, new creations in Jesus Christ, fully submitted to His Lordship, and filled with His abundant life, I invite you to come and be a part of my life."

261

Then, I lead the core personality to pray:

> "Lord Jesus, by Your precious blood, I ask You to fuse and integrate <u>core personality's formal name</u>, new creations in Jesus Christ, fully submitted to His Lordship, filled with His abundant life, who used to be <u>call off old negative namesand ages of each of the "fifteen" wounded personalities on the dark-side of the duplex</u>. Now that they are new creations, please make them one with me, <u>core personality's formal name</u>, age ___, saved at age ___.

> "I confess the demons no longer have rights, authority, or ground to stand on. Lord, when You are ready, I want them all in the abyss, the lake of fire or for You to annihilate them with the breath of Your Holy mouth—depending on how they have cooperated or interfered with us. I break all ties and claim back all ground given to the ancestral demon that carries my formal name.

> "Lord Jesus, I thank You that all the negatives that were connected to <u>list names and ages of healed wounded parts</u> no longer belong to me, for they were placed on Your Cross. With a childlike faith, I thank You for doing this."

I then ask the core personality this:

> "When we asked the Lord Jesus to fuse and integrate the fifteen healed parts, what did you **sense** if anything?"

If the core says that he didn't sense anything happening at all, or if he senses something negative—anything bothering him, then something is hindering the fusing and integrating. Therefore, I ask the Lord to allow me to speak to one of the fifteen personalities. Upon one acknowledging that he is there, ready to talk with me, I will ask him if all or only some of them are there, and why. **Then I will go through the process of dealing with them until the work is complete.**

If the core's answer is something like, "yes, I feel a peace, it's quiet, I feel together, whole" then we know the work has been done. And the time has come for us to confront the ancestral demon carrying the core personality's formal name and make him tell us whether or not he still has any right, ground, or authority in the core's life. The procedures for doing this are found in the next chapter, eleven.

BEFORE YOU MOVE ON DOWN THE ROAD
PLEASE REMEMBER THREE VERY IMPORTANT THINGS!

1. **If the person has children under 20 years of age, word of caution: before making the ancestral demon and his network and all other blood-linked demons depart from this dear person, it is necessary and very beneficial to deal with his children in order to pull all of the ancestral demon's ground from their lives!** You recall that I discussed **the age of accountability** in chapter two, **"Four Pillars Supporting the Biblical Counseling Platform" in "A. The Ancestral Demon Pillar."** When work is complete except for dealing with the ancestral demon, as you study chapter eleven, **"Tools for Dealing with the Ancestral Demon and his Network,"** you will find procedures in **"J. Time to Liberate Parents' Children Under Age Twenty."** From there, you will find instructions on how to complete the work—the liberation of precious souls including the precious children under 20 years of age!

2. **If the core personality, his flip-side and wounded personalities have been thoroughly dealt with:** you are ready to complete the work by dealing with the ancestral demon, so **continue to study the entire eleventh chapter where you will find more information about the ancestral demon** and the **procedures for your counselee**—through which he can attain victory over him. **You will find some very unique bargaining tools to use with the ancestral demon!**

3. **If your counselee has chosen to start with the ancestral demon, then START WITH CHAPTER ELEVEN. However: a) at "C. CHOICE OF ALTERNATE ROUTES:" you will be instructed to work through "D. And E.".** Then, b) you will be instructed to go **BACK to chapter nine** which helps you deal with a broken part of a core—if there is one—and the flip-side. **Then, c) work through the procedures in chapter ten,** for the the core and wounded personalities. **Then, d)** you will need to **RETURN to chapter eleven, at letter "F."** to continue following the procedures to bring the counselee to victory.

How grateful and excited we are at this point because the core (in chapter nine) has had the broken part of his core and the flip-side saved, healed and integrated with him, which **reclaimed 90 percent of the core's ground from the enemy!** And, now, in this tenth chapter, the core has also been fused and integrated with all of the once-wounded, now-saved personalities, which **reclaimed the remaining 10 percent of the ground held by the enemy!** So we know that **we can march forward boldly with our King, as Christian soldiers dressed in the whole armor of God, and defeat the enemy–and make him to vacate the premises!**

Chapter Eleven
TOOLS FOR DEALING WITH THE ANCESTRAL DEMON AND HIS NETWORK

"For whatever is born of God overcomes the world. And this is the victory that has overcome the world–our faith." (I John 5:4)

As you know by now, I always give my counselee three choices of starting points as he begins his journey toward victory: **(1)** the flip-side, **(2)** a wounded personality, or **(3)** the ancestral demon carrying the core's formal name. As you begin your journey from any of the three starting points, you will eventually intersect the other routes, travel each of them, deal with all the issues found along the routes and with the Lord leading you all the way, you will end up defeating the enemy and claiming victory!

EXCEPTION TO THE TYPICAL
A LIFESTYLE POWER DEMON—NOT AN ANCESTRAL DEMON

When starting one's search, it is far more common to find an ancestral demon. But take care to remember what I shared in chapter four, "Understanding the Core, Flip-side, Wounded Personalities and Categories of Demons," about there being two different types of power demons, **"ancestral demons"** and **"lifestyle power demons."** **In my experience of over 30 years of counseling, there has been either one or the other—not both!** With my knowing that the core personality has demonic activity going on in his life, yet after asking the Lord to bring up an ancestral demon carrying the formal name of the core personality to no avail, I then move on, asking that **"a lifestyle power demon"** be brought up for me to interview. This kind will be found to have come into the person's life due to his yielding consistently to a particular sin which became a lifestyle—thus **iniquity**—leaving the door wide open for Satan to claim ground! On this ground, Satan placed his **"lifestyle power demon."** The power demon then began luring the core into further sin—thus building his own network of demons! Like the ancestral demon, a power demon will be found to be boss over the system. We should make the counselee fully aware of the fact that while he did not have "iniquities of the fathers" passed down to him, he is now a vessel through which **that power demon becomes an ancestral demon if he is passed down to the next generation**! This should cause any parent who loves his children extremely eager to be set free of his demons!

Please note in the following counseling procedures where I illustrate addressing "the ancestral demon carrying the core's formal name," if I find a lifestyle power demon instead, then I would use "the power demon name reflecting ground claimed." If the Lord has brought forth a **"power demon who is boss over the system that came about through a sinful lifestyle,"** I gather information from him just as I would from the ancestral demon pertaining to the wounded personalities.

A.   UPON MEETING AN ANCESTRAL DEMON

Upon moving forward now, I will illustrate how to go about meeting and dealing with an ancestral demon carrying the formal name of a core personality who is the **power demon in charge**. He will be the only demon that I deal with unless the Lord tells me otherwise, because he is the boss over all the ground that he holds in the person's life. He is the one who has the authority to give out information, as well as making the other demons in the system obey what they are ordered to do.

When you meet an ancestral demon (or the lifestyle power demon) you can be assured that the Lord will let you know when the "power demon" is up and available to give you information. It is typical to see evidence of an ancestral demon/lifestyle power demon's response to you simply by a very stern expression on the core personality's face and his giving answers in a matter-of-fact way. There are times when the face of the counselee will reflect anger or meanness and his body becomes stiff or he takes on a pose of haughtiness. There have also been times when a counselee's facial expression reflects nervousness and others yet, mischievousness! There have been a few times that the ancestral demon actually twisted the person's body about like a writhing snake, stretching his neck and turning his face back and forth as he looked around, but such times are rare! Always remember that through Jesus Christ, you and your counselee have full authority and power over the ancestral demon and his network to make them stay in the chair and behave themselves and provide the necessary information! Do not be intimidated by them!

COUNSELOR PRAYS FOR THE CORE
BEFORE MEETING THE ANCESTRAL DEMON

Before asking the Lord to let us meet and deal with the ancestral demon, I pray for the core personality in this way:

> "Father, I want core personality, <u>core personality's formal name</u>, age ____, saved at age ____, not to be allowed to interfere, yet to be permitted to hear all that goes on. **Place him in a safe place with the Lord Jesus with a shield of the blood of the Lord Jesus** separating everything else from him so that we meet and deal with the ancestral demon and his network."

COUNSELOR PRAYS TO CONTACT THE ANCESTRAL DEMON

Through the authority I have in Christ, I pray, asking the Lord Jesus to bring the ancestral demon up to meet me so that I can interview—or more accurately, interrogate him!

"Lord Jesus, I ask through Your authority and power, that You make <u>Ancestral Demon core personality's formal name</u>, come up and do business with me immediately. Do not let him waste and burn our time by hesitating to come up. Do not let him slip another demon in front of himself to hide behind, such as a demon-produced personality, demon-clone or demon masquerading as a personality, unless You wish to teach us something."

Remember that sometimes ancestral demons, in attempts to delay the inevitable, refuse to respond immediately. You may see by the core's expression that the ancestral demon is up but he's just not talking. With his arrogant silence, he is challenging your authority! And, when one does this, I command him as follows:

"<u>Ancestral Demon core personality's formal name</u>, my authority is not of my own, it is through the Lord Jesus Christ. With your trying to test me, you will soon see if you and Satan really have more authority that I do in Jesus Christ! Now, in the name of the Lord Jesus Christ, get up here and talk to me! <u>Ancestral Demon core personality's formal name</u>, by the blood of the Lord Jesus, the King of kings and Lord of lords, and by the finger of Almighty God, I command you to come up and talk to me. I call you to attention now by the name of the Lord Jesus Christ!"

[**Extra note if you are working with an SRA victim:** while I typically use the above prayer, if I am working with an SRA victim and find the ancestral demon to be stubborn about communicating with me, rather than using the name "Lord Jesus Christ" in the prayer, I use **Jesus' Hebrew name, "Yeshua"** and often include "**ha Mashiach**," denoting, **"Jesus the Messiah"**. I do this because I have found that some of the cunningly deceptive demons in mockery to our Lord Jesus, have taken on names for their Satanic worship rituals such as: **Jesus, Lord, heavenly Father, Savior, and Holy Spirit**, but I have never found one named **"Yeshua"** or **"Yeshua ha Mashiach"**! During a counseling session this year, it was confirmed to me by an ancestral demon that **no demons are permitted to use that name**.]

After commanding the ancestral demon to come up and speak to me, if he doesn't answer right away, I may have to command him two or three times before he begins communicating with me. They sometimes just stall to try to waste time and avoid being dealt with! When he acknowledges that he is there, then I command through my authority in Jesus Christ that the ancestral demon answer my **first question**:

"Is your name <u>Ancestral Demon the core's formal name</u>? Yes or no?"

No matter what he answers, then command him to tell you whether or not his answer stands as **truth before the eternal throne of the Lord Jesus Christ [or Yeshua or Yeshua ha Mashiach if dealing with an SRA victim] where only truth can stand.**

WHEN YOU GET A "NO!" ANSWER

If the demon's answer was "No"—that his name is not the same as the core's formal name, and you learn that he is telling you the truth, then he is not the ancestral demon. Take advantage of the situation and ask him, **"Why did you come up?** I just want to speak to the boss of the system of demons—the ancestral demon carrying the formal name of the core!" Most of the time, such a demon will answer, **"I was told to come up!"** When I ask who told him to come up, the typical answer is, **"The ancestral demon did!"**

BLOOD-LINK THE "BLOCKER" DEMON

By his answer, I know that the ancestral demon tried to use him as a blocker to hinder me from meeting him. Therefore, I pray, asking the Lord to blood-link this blocker-demon with blood-links made of Jesus' blood, which cannot be broken, to his boss, the ancestral demon carrying the core personality's formal name. I always stay on the alert for an ancestral demon to pull some antics like this to try to hinder the work being done. When this happens while you are working, do not be discouraged! Remember that you and the core personality have authority through the Lord Jesus Christ to force him to talk to you—no ifs, ands, or buts—you are in charge because the Lord has placed you in authority over all the demons! You can be assured that soon—if there is an ancestral demon—he will have to admit who he is and that he carries the core personality's formal name.

B.   BARGAINING TOOLS FOR USE ON ANCESTRAL DEMON

Take care to remember that God is a God of justice. He laid down the protective love-rules for Adam and Eve, and the rules came coupled with a warning of serious consequences if they disobeyed the rules. Likewise, there were rules in heaven, which a third of the angels in heaven chose to disobey—thus they suffered the consequences and were cast out of heaven. While these fallen angels, demonic beings, are for a time tempting and tormenting humans, there are some rules with which we can confront them. As we explain these rules to the ancestral demon (or power demon) and his network, we can warn them of consequences if they don't obey our rules—**our bargaining tools rules!**

Upon meeting the ancestral demon carrying the core's formal name, I firmly warn him not to attempt to mess with the core, nor with me while we work! I am aware that all the demons already know they are guilty as charged and that God has sentenced them "in the end," to spend eternity in the lake of fire. With them so full of vengeance—hating God and His children—they are actually more vulnerable for us to use bargaining tools—our weapons of war—on them to prod them to cooperate! So, I proceed to tell the ancestral demon about **our tools rules—our weapons of war!** I will explain to him that there are three different conditions of sentencing—all are based on how cooperative he is in answering my questions. **The measure of the severity of his sentencing will be equal to the choice he makes among the three conditions of judgment.**

I explain my first bargaining tool to him, which will appear more merciful to him in comparison to the others: "Ancestral Demon, you have three choices. **Choice number one contains the lighter sentence:** If you choose to cooperate with me and answer me truthfully, and not waste my time nor mess around, the sentencing will be passed upon you **that you will be shown some mercy by allowing you to go to the bottomless pit, the abyss.** There, Abandon is going to come one day with the key to the abyss, and will let you and the other demons out and you will all be allowed five months to torment people on the earth."

I explain my second bargaining tool to him: "Ancestral Demon, **choice number two contains a heavier sentencing**: If you choose not to cooperate with me by failing to tell the truth, wasting time and causing problems for the core and me, the sentencing will be passed upon you **that you will be shown less mercy. Because, this person will be the last person you will ever get to torment, for you cannot go to the abyss and torture all those other people—you will go straight to the lake of fire where you will stay forever!**"

I explain the third bargaining tool: "Ancestral Demon, **choice number three contains a far greater sentencing**. If you choose not to cooperate with me, waste time, misbehave and mess with the core and me, the sentencing will be **that you be given no mercy, by my asking the Lord to completely blow away and annihilate you and all the other demons involved in the core personality's life. This way, none of you would ever be able to even imagine tormenting people again!** Personally, I hope you chose number three, for just the thought of your complete destruction thrills my soul and spirit, so you better understand that I will be looking for any opportunity and justification to ask my Father in heaven for your complete annihilation!"

The third bargaining tool is based on God's judgment passed on His people who were adamantly rebellious against Him which we read about in both Old and New Testaments:

> "...*I will gather you and blow on you with the fire of My wrath, and you shall be melted in its midst. As silver is melted in the midst of a furnace, so shall you be melted in its midst; then you shall know that I, the LORD, have poured out My fury on you.*" (Ezekiel 22:21-22)

> "*And then the lawless one will be revealed **whom the LORD will consume with the breath of His mouth** and destroy with the brightness of His coming.*" (II Thessalonians 2:8)

If God would deem it necessary to do this to His precious people—why would He not all the more deem it right to the evil, rebellious demons? Of course, in any three of these judgments, they can no longer tempt and torment others!

Having forewarned the ancestral demon, I question the ancestral demon carrying the core's formal name in this way:

"Ancestral Demon core personality's formal name, do you understand that if you mess with me or waste any of my time spent with core's formal name, age _____, saved at age ____, you will not be allowed the "privilege" of going to the abyss? Do you understand that a privilege comes by your going to the Abyss, but you can have that privilege only if you behave yourself and answer my questions with truth! Do you agree to cooperate?"

"Ancestral Demon core personality's formal name, do you understand that when I am ready to send you and your blood-linked demon network to the Abyss because you will have said that you have no more rights, no authority or ground to remain in the core personality's life, you must go? I want you to understand that after the core personality and I have prayed, asking the Lord Jesus to do that, we will come back and test the spirit to see if it be of God (I John 4:1-3). We are coming back to see if you are still there—not because we doubt God but to obey His scripture! You need to know that nothing can mute you, render you deaf, hide you or block you from answering me! When I call your name, if you have tried to cunningly appoint a little peon, "a nothing," no-god of a gatekeeper to stand in your place so that you don't have to answer me, I will find out the truth and catch you! Then I will ask my Lord Jesus Christ to give me the right to make you and your blood-linked demon network subservient to the little peon, "a nothing," no-god of a gate keeper by blood-linking you and your blood-linked network to him. Then I'll let you see that it is done before the Lord Jesus Christ—who will then annihilate you and the network demons with the breath of His Holy mouth!

"Ancestral Demon core personality's formal name, I am putting your boss, Satan himself, on notice that if he tries to leave anything behind, there will be a high price for the demonic realm to pay. For I will be given the authority to reek even more damage on his forces besides annihilating you and your network! Do you understand what you have been told?"

Having laid down the bargaining tools rules and the ancestral demon has answered that he understands the choices and says that he will cooperate, we move to the next step.

C.   CHOICE OF ALTERNATE ROUTES: EITHER "D. AND E." OR "F."

ONE: **If you BEGAN counseling with the flip-side first and have finished dealing with him and the wounded parts (chapters nine and ten), then SKIP these two sections: "D.   CONTACTING THE ANCESTRAL DEMON" and   "E.**

COMMANDING ANSWERS FROM THE ANCESTRAL DEMON" which are below, and travel on down the road, passed them to the section: **"F. CROSSROAD THAT MEETS WITH THE ALTERNATE ROUTE"** where you will then find instructions on how to interrogate the ancestral demon to gather some valuable information before bringing the counselee to total freedom.

TWO: IF YOUR STARTING POINT IN COUNSELING WAS WITH THE ANCESTRAL DEMON, CONTINUE ON THIS ROUTE.

D.   CONTACTING THE ANCESTRAL DEMON

If for some reason your counselee felt strongly about starting with the ancestral demon carrying his formal name and you have already begun this procedure and you and your counselee are still comfortable heading in this direction, then continue on your way. However, it is good for you and the counselee to keep in mind, that **"if the road gets bumpy" and things are not moving along smoothly enough, then, ask the Lord to bind up the ancestral demon and his network, and drive right on over to one of the other two routes and relax and start with the flip-side or wounded personalities (in previous chapters nine or ten).** Remind your counselee that he will eventually arrive at his destination—freedom, where peace and joy reside! **For now, before traveling back to deal with the flip-side and wounded parts, we will proceed down the ancestral demon route.**

Having already established that there is an ancestral demon carrying the core's formal name, it's time to call him up and begin gathering information from him. Begin with this prayer:

"Lord Jesus, as we work today, I ask You not to allow any demonic attacks or schemes to get loose that might hurt core personality's formal name, age ___, saved at age _____. I ask You, Jesus, that you prevent Satan and his demons from magnifying or amplifying the wounds that are already in core personality's formal name, and that You direct our minds and hearts as we work together with You. Lord Jesus, don't allow me to say a thing to core personality's formal name that would not bring praise, honor, and glory to You.

"And, Lord Jesus, I ask that You do not allow the ancestral demon, carrying the full formal name of core personality's formal name, to be mute or deaf and make him come up and do business with me."

"Lord Jesus, I praise and thank You for having shed Your precious blood on behalf of core personality's formal name and me. And, I thank You for graciously anointing us and giving us the right to operate in Your name. Lord Jesus, I need to speak and

271

do business with the ancestral demon that carries the formal name of the core. Lord Jesus, I ask that You prohibit the ancestral demon from hiding behind any demons by shoving them up to masquerade as the ancestral demon. I ask that You keep him from sending forward a demon-produced personality, a demon masquerading as a personality or a demon-clone, including a demon-clone of himself, to serve as an imposter of the ancestral demon. And, this includes all other categories of demons, demon-produced personalities, lifestyle demons, gatekeeper demons, demons shared from within and any demons shared from without, and of whatever nature or of whatever hierarchy. Lord Jesus, this includes any demon-clones that are specialized or customized for future development. This also includes any demons that may be muted or hiding.

"Lord Jesus, the core and I again thank You that You have given us permission to deal with all the ancestral demons and their networks, whether they carry the formal name of this person or whether they carry this person's family names or names of works. Lord Jesus, You know who all of the demons are and what they do in the life of <u>core personality's formal name</u>. And, I thank You that You will keep all of the demons from blocking me from talking with the ancestral demon, unless You want to use the demons in some way to help us learn some important information. Otherwise, I ask that You dull the hearing of all the other demons and keep their mouths shut until I ask to speak with them! And, Lord Jesus, I ask You, with Your blood, to blood-link the demons and the ancestral demon carrying the formal name of the core, together with chains that cannot be broken. And, I ask You to please shut them all down and render them all bound, gagged, and inoperative so that I can speak only with the ancestral demon carrying the core's formal name.

"And now, Lord Jesus, bring <u>Ancestral Demon core personality's formal name</u> to attention and "keep his feet to the fire" as we work today. Manifest Your presence even now in such a way that he knows we are here to do Your business in the life of the core and that I am here strictly as Your authorized representative."

E. COMMANDING ANSWERS FROM THE ANCESTRAL DEMON

Command that the ancestral demon answer the following questions:

1. **"What do you do—your work—in the core personality's life?"**
2. **"What else do you do in the core's life?" (Repeat the question until he reports that there is nothing else.)**

After you are satisfied that those questions have been answered in truth before the eternal throne of the Lord Jesus Christ, then command the ancestral demon to give you the following information:

272

3. **"Give me the names of all the demons in your personal network."**
4. **"Tell me the work each one is responsible for carrying out in the counselee's life!"**

When the ancestral demon says he has given you all their names and has described what work they are responsible for in the core's life, once again, ask if it all stands as truth before the eternal throne of Jesus Christ. Warn him of the consequences of lying to you! Then question him further:

5. **"What are the gatekeepers' names?"**
6. **"Do any of the gatekeepers have networks?"**
7. **"Are there any additional demons that you have not yet told me about?"**

RETRIEVING INFORMATION
FROM THE ANCESTRAL DEMON ABOUT THE FLIP-SIDE

It is not essential for you to get this information from the ancestral demon, but it costs nothing to try. When you ask the ancestral demon for the flip-side personality's name, most of the time, it will not carry any part of the core's formal name. Flip-sides often use names like "I Don't Know," "Nobody," "Anger" and such.

When you are ready to gather information about the flip-side, inform the ancestral demon that carries the core's formal name, that all the other demons blood-linked to him by Jesus' blood, are not to interfere, and remind him of the serious consequences if he doesn't give you accurate, truthful answers! Then, pray, asking God to shut down all demonic activity except for the ancestral demon, and then begin interviewing him. Remember to have him acknowledge that he understands your requests before he answers your questions:

> "<u>Ancestral Demon core personality's formal name</u>, by the blood of the Lord Jesus and by the finger of Almighty God, I call you to attention for I'm going to give some very specific instructions that you will follow or suffer consequences. Do you hear the sound of my voice?"

8. **"What is the name of the flip-side?"** (Remember, he may or may not know this.)
9. **"How many wounded personalities are on the dark-side of the duplex?"**
10. **"What are the names and ages of the wounded personalities?"** (NOTE: Sometimes he knows the names and ages of all the wounded parts—which often agrees with the information I gather from the flip-side and/or wounded personalities. Then there are times when he doesn't know. Thus, he cannot provide the information.)

WARN THE ANCESTRAL DEMON

Having finished gathering the information from the ancestral demon about the flip-side and the wounded parts, warn him by declaring, "Ancestral Demon, as I've warned you before, if you have been lying to me, you will reap consequences which you will not like! While I may not even know that you have lied to me, God Almighty will know and He is the One who will deal with you according to His will. Does your response to me stand as truth before the eternal throne of Jesus Christ where only truth can stand?"

NEXT: Upon being confident that some essential truths have been gathered from the ancestral demon—by testing the spirits again—it is time to travel on to gather information directly from the flip-side and wounded personalities. So, at this point: (1) Travel back to chapter nine that covers the counseling procedures for a broken-part of the core and the flip-side. (2) Continue on to chapter ten, for the core and wounded personalities. After you have completed followed the procedures in those two chapters: (3) Travel back here to "F. CROSSROAD THAT MEETS TOGETHER WITH THE ALTERNATE ROUTE" posted below, which will lead you to the finish line.

F. CROSSROAD THAT MEETS TOGETHER WITH ALTERNATE ROUTE

No matter if we started with the flip-side and wounded personalities first, or the ancestral demon, **we have now arrived at the location where we can meet with the ancestral demon to see if there are any other possible claims to ground in the core's life—and take care of any hidden, unfinished business.** Having dealt with the flip-side and all the wounded personalities, those battles have been won! How grateful and excited we are at this point! For, the core has not only been fused and integrated with the saved flip-side—which reclaimed 90 percent of the core's ground from the enemy—but the core has also been fused and integrated with all of the once-wounded, now-saved personalities—which reclaimed the remaining 10 percent of the ground held by the enemy!

At this point in our journey, we will interrogate the ancestral demon to find out if he and his network are holding onto any more ground in the core's life. In chapter four, under "G. Demon-Produced Personalities, Demon-Clones and Mind-Sets" where I shared five examples, I mentioned that mind-sets can sometimes be detected through reviewing the counseling form, during the first counseling session, or while interrogating the ancestral demon before sending him out. Concerning the demon-clones, while you may find them while working, it's more typical to find them upon the ancestral demon's refusing to leave, which exposes that he has ground in a clone. Therefore, I thought this would be the most appropriate time to explain how to deal with them—while approaching the time to make the demons leave!

Remember that if the counselee has children, it's important that these issues are dealt with before dealing with matters pertaining to iniquity and curses passed down to his children. Then, after searching out and dealing with any hidden issues or unfinished business, then the journey will at last lead us to our destination—sending the ancestral demon and his network to the abyss, the lake of fire or annihilating them all if He chooses to do so! Then, the core and I will thank the Lord for blessing the core with victory—peace and joy!

G. INTERROGATING THE ANCESTRAL DEMON CONCERNING UNFINISHED BUSINESS, INCLUDING DEMON-CLONES AND MIND-SETS

We will begin by asking the Lord to put the core in a safe place:

PRAYER FOR CORE BEFORE DEALING WITH THE ANCESTRAL DEMON

"Father, I want core personality, <u>core personality's formal name</u>, age ____, saved at age _____, not to be allowed to interfere, yet to be permitted to hear all that goes on. **Place him in a safe place with the Lord Jesus with a shield of the blood of the Lord Jesus separating everything else from him** so that we can meet and deal with the ancestral demon and his network."

COUNSELOR'S PRAYER BEFORE INTERROGATING ANCESTRAL DEMON

"Our heavenly Father, unless You wish to teach us something, I ask You to now bind, gag, and render inoperative Satan and all his demonic powers, including but not limited to <u>Ancestral Demon core personality's full name</u>, any other ancestral demons, lifestyle demons, power demons, territorial demons, and demons that desire to be shared in and those which desire to be shared out. I ask that You include all the demon-produced personalities, demon-clones, and demons that masquerade as wounded parts, including all their personal networks, plus demons of whatever nature or of whatever hierarchy. I ask that none of these be allowed to cause any confusion or misunderstanding, and that they cannot pretend to be the core, the flip-side or wounded personalities, nor can they misappropriate and block any truths being shared. I thank You for keeping them from interfering and messing with us as we work.

"Father until I need to talk with a particular demon, I ask that You dull all of the demons' hearing and keep them silent. Unless You wish to teach us something, keep them from speaking or otherwise interfering with us during this time."

H.   WARNING AND TESTING THE ANCESTRAL DEMON

After I've asked the ancestral demon if he still has any ground left in the person's life and he answers, "Yes!" then I have to find the reason why. For, he either **(1)** does have some legal ground that I don't know about—thus he has the right to stay, or **(2)** he's lying to waste my time—bluffing and testing me to see if I'm confident in the Lord Jesus, and can figure out that he really doesn't have any legal ground left to claim. Therefore, I warn him again about the bargaining tools-rules.

> "Ancestral Demon, you had better not be lying to me or you will reap consequences that you will not like. You remember my bargaining tools-rules, the abyss, the lake of fire and the annihilation by the breath of God's Holy mouth! I may not even know that you have lied to me, but God Almighty will know and He is the One who will deal with you according to His will. Will your response, stating that you have (or don't have) ground, legal right in the life of <u>core personality's formal name</u> stand as truth before the eternal throne of Jesus Christ where only truth can stand?"

Because demons do lie frequently, I cannot stress enough how critical it is that every time he answers a question that you always ask him: "By the blood of the Lord Jesus, does that answer stand as truth before the eternal throne of Jesus Christ where only truth can stand?"

When I am certain that the ancestral demon has no more ground and admits it by declaring, "No!" then I move on down the road!

But we will say at this point that an ancestral demon said he has ground and told the truth, that there are apparently one or more hidden issues—unfinished business—that he's still legally claiming. Therefore, I will pose some questions to him in order to discover what they are and deal with him accordingly!

I.   QUESTIONS TO ASK THE ANCESTRAL DEMON

I begin interrogating him by stating: "<u>Ancestral Demon core personality's formal name</u>, age _____, saved at age _____, I've already warned you what will happen to you if you lie to me or otherwise mess with me or the core. I am going to ask you some questions and your answers had better stand as truth before the eternal throne of Jesus Christ or there will be consequences that you will pay."

1.   **"Do you have any ground or legal right to remain in his life pertaining to <u>clones</u>?"**
2.   **"Do you have any ground or any legal right left in the life of <u>core personality's formal name</u> in any way, shape or form pertaining to or concerning his <u>health</u>?"**
3.   **"Do you have any ground or any legal right to remain in the life <u>core personality's formal name</u> in any way, shape or form pertaining to or concerning <u>curses</u>?"**
4.   **"Do you have any ground or legal right to remain in his life pertaining to <u>mind-sets</u>?"**

276

5. **"Do you have <u>any ground or legal right left</u> in the life of <u>core personality's formal name</u>, age ____, saved at age ___? If so, state your ground!"**

Upon the ancestral demon's carrying the core's formal name, stating that he doesn't have to go because he still has some legal ground and I learn that his claims match up with issues that have already been dealt with through the flip-side or wounded parts, I have a clue that there may, indeed, be a hidden issue. If I learn that there are no hidden wounded personalities, then I ask the Lord Jesus to bring up the one that represents the ground that the ancestral demon still claims. Most of the time, it will be the answer to one of the first four questions on the list—a connection to a clone, health issue, a curse or a mind-set.

A demon-clone: It may turn out to be a lifestyle, an ancestral demon-clone also carrying the core's formal name, a specialized/customized demon-clone for future development and assignments, or other ancestral demons connected to the core's family. I then ask the Lord to allow me to speak to that particular one claiming to hold ground. Upon learning what ground he holds—such as anger, hatred, or lust—I will ask the Lord to claim back the ground by pulling out every part of the demon-clone by the roots, from the age that it began to the core's current age. I would ask the Lord to blood-link it with His blood to the ancestral demon carrying the core's formal name, with blood-links that cannot be broken. With this being done, I then ask the Lord to saturate that ground with the blood of Jesus, and lead the core to thank Him for doing this for him.

Health issues: If the ancestral demon claims he has ground in the core's life connected to a particular health issue, I ask the Lord to pull it out by the roots, reclaim it from the ancestral demon carrying the formal name, and ask Him to blood-link it with His blood to the ancestral demon with blood-links that cannot be broken. I then ask the Lord to saturate that ground with His blood.

Curses: If any curses are found, find the ground, reclaim it from the ancestral demon, and ask the Lord, with His blood to blood-link the curses to the ancestral demon carrying the core's name, with blood-links that cannot be broken and saturate that ground with His precious blood.

A mind-set: Having dealt with any demon-clones, demon-caused health issues, and curses and blood-linked them to the ancestral demon, I will then question the ancestral demon again to see if he is standing on any other ground. As an example, we will say that I learned that he had done a wicked work in convincing the core personality that she was ignorant and a hopeless case—like "Jodie Irene (Ignoramus) Walker." (See Chapter Four, "Example #5 under Section G, Demon-Clone with Mind Set and Inherited Curse.) It is possible that the clone previously found held the same ground, but nevertheless, you find negative issues, the sins that are connected to the person's "mind-set" and lead them to confess that he has believed the Devil's lies rather than God Almighty's truth! Lead him to further confess that he has allowed those lies to become his mind-set, which is a sin against God. Lead him to take responsibility for the sin, confess and repent of it. Then, lead him to ask the Holy Spirit of God to pull that mind-set out by the roots from the age it began to his current age and place it on the Cross where the Lord Jesus paid that debt. Then lead him, through his authority in Jesus Christ to claim back the ground from Satan and the ancestral demon carrying his formal name. Instruct him to ask the Lord to saturate that ground with the blood of Jesus Christ, cleansing, healing and totally restoring that ground.

Ancestral demon has no more ground: Next, I would command the ancestral demon to tell me if he is holding any other ground in the core's life, and most of the time, he will answer "No!" Of course, I always ask if it stands as truth before the eternal throne of Jesus Christ—where only truth can stand! If he answers, "Yes!" I then threaten him that if he's lying to me, he could be annihilated. If he was telling the truth, I would deal with the issues until I was positive that the work was done. At this point, with all the core's ground having been reclaimed and cleansed, it's time to lead the core personality to pray a prayer of thanks to the Lord for what He has done for him thus far. However, **if he has any children, take care to lead him to include the part that mentions children in the following sample prayer**. For, it is essential to take time to deal with each of his children under the age of twenty and any curses upon those twenty and older. **(Note that it is wise to call in the ancestral demons from the children and attach them to the core's ancestral demon <u>before</u> sending him out.)**

CORE'S PRAYER THANKING GOD FOR WHAT HE HAS DONE THUS FAR

"Sweet Lord Jesus, I <u>core personality's formal name</u>, age ____, saved at age ____, thank You for allowing me to experience and endure all the things I've been through, and all the things I've caused others to endure, as I've had to go through all of this. I praise and thank You for it all and believe that You will work all of this together for my good and Your glory.

"Lord Jesus, I want to praise and thank You that You have given us authority in You to ask that all the demonic beings, demons masquerading as wounded personalities, demon-produced personalities, all the demon-clones that were specialized, customized for future development and placed in my life, and all demonic beings attached to, associated with or affiliated with my physical health **[and my children's physical health]**, and all other demonic beings, of whatever nature or hierarchy, and all their personal networks, and all curses that have been operating in my life, those known to me and those unknown to me, all the dregs, all the leftovers, illnesses, actions, attitudes, difficulties in communicating with others, anything and everything the ancestral demon tries to leave behind, and everything else that is not of You, to be blood-linked with Jesus' blood to the ancestral demon that carries my formal name. To the extent that we have not already asked, I ask now that You would blood-link it all, with blood-links that cannot be broken, to the ancestral demon that carries my formal name for it's all going where he is going.

"Lord Jesus, I ask that You take all the demon-clones that were specialized, customized for future development and placed in my life, and go back as far as You need to go, all the way back to my conception, and rip them out and attach them with blood-links that cannot be broken to the ancestral demon carrying my formal name.

"Lord Jesus, unless You wish to teach us something, I ask that You shut down the ancestral demon's plans and attempts to leave something behind. I thank You for doing it."

J.   TIME TO LIBERATE PARENTS' CHILDREN UNDER AGE TWENTY

If the counselee does have children under the age of twenty—the age of accountability—then he can claim back the ground that the flip-side and the ancestral demon and his network hold in the children's lives. He can also remove any curses that are upon any children he has who are twenty years old and older.

Having already explained to the counselee that this can be done through his authority in Jesus Christ, we begin the process of ministering to all of his children under the age of twenty. **We will begin with the oldest child and work our way down to the youngest one.**

COUNSELOR PRAYS
CONCERNING CORE'S CHILDREN UNDER AGE TWENTY

"Heavenly Father, in the name of Your Beloved Son, our Lord and Savior, Jesus Christ I ask that You keep the children of <u>parent/core personality's formal name</u> safe as we work. Do not allow Satan or any of his demonic powers to mess with them in any way during this time. I ask You to bind, gag and render inoperative any and all demonic powers that would seek to intimidate, harass, manipulate, deceive or otherwise mess with the children of <u>parent/core personality's formal name</u> while we work. Father we want all the demonic powers that are active in the lives of the children of <u>parent/core personality's formal name</u> shut down as we work.

"Heavenly Father, in the name of Your Beloved Son, our Lord and Savior, Jesus Christ, I ask that You take the flip-side of <u>full name of oldest child belonging to parent/core</u> and present his/her flip-side to the Lord Jesus and give him a new name of "healed by the mercy and grace of the Lord Jesus".

"Heavenly Father, having given the flip-side of <u>full name of oldest child</u> a new name of "healed by the mercy and grace of the Lord Jesus," I ask You to fuse and integrate the flip-side with the core of <u>full name of oldest child belonging to parent/core</u> so he/she will no longer be a double soul, but one soul as You created him.

279

"Heavenly Father, in the name of Your Beloved Son, our Lord and Savior, Jesus Christ, I ask that You take all the wounded personalities of <u>full name of oldest child belonging to parent/core</u> that have been created since his/her conception, all the way to the present and present them to Jesus. I ask You Heavenly Father to heal them and give them all new names of "healed by the mercy and grace of the Lord Jesus".

"Heavenly Father, having healed and given all the wounded personalities of <u>full name of oldest child belonging to parent/core</u> new names of "healed by the mercy and grace of the Lord Jesus," I ask You to fuse and integrate all of them with the core of <u>full name of oldest child belonging to parent/core</u> so he/she will be complete for the first time in his/her life just as You created and intended him to be.

"Lord Jesus, I want the <u>Ancestral Demon parent/core personlity's formal name</u> called to attention right now."

K.   COMMAND THE ANCESTRAL DEMON TO ANSWER MORE QUESTIONS

"<u>Ancestral Demon parent/core personality's formal name</u>, through my authority in Jesus Christ, I command that you come up and talk to me. I've already warned you what will happen to you and all those attached to you if you lie to me or otherwise mess with me. I want to know all that is going on in the life of <u>full name of oldest child</u>. I want to know the names of all the demons involved in the life of this child and I want to know what they do. I want to know about each and every curse that has flowed down into the life of <u>full name of oldest child</u>. I want to know what iniquity has passed down from this child's parents and other ancestors into the life of this child.

"Ancestral Demon, I will test everything you tell me so you had better be telling me truth and nothing but truth! If you lie to me or otherwise mess with me, the core or this child, you will be burned—you will surely reap serious consequences. Do you understand me?"

After he answers me, then I ask him the following questions:

1.   **"What illnesses flowed down into <u>full name of the oldest child</u>?"**
2.   **"What curses flowed down into <u>full name of oldest child</u>?"**
3.   **"What iniquity flowed down into <u>full name of oldest child</u>?"**

COUNSELOR PRAYS

"Lord Jesus, I want the ancestral demon that goes by the formal name of full <u>name of oldest child</u> called to attention right now.

"Lord Jesus, You know who all of these demons are and what they do in the life of <u>full name of oldest child</u>. Lord Jesus, I thank You for giving me the right to issue commands to all ancestral demons, whether they carry the formal name of the child's family or names of works, illnesses, or curses. Lifestyle demons, gatekeeper demons that are ancestral or lifestyle with their networks are also included. Any demons that have shared out to other people are included. Lord Jesus, I want them called in and blood-linked with blood-links of Your blood that cannot be broken, to the ancestral demon carrying the name of <u>full name of oldest child</u>. I want any demons that have been shared in from other networks. I want them entrapped so that they cannot go back "home," and I want them to be blood-linked with blood-links that cannot be broken to the ancestral demon carrying the name of <u>full name of oldest child</u>. I want any demons that may be muted and/or in hiding, or any demons that are masquerading as personalities, demon-produced personalities, demon-clones that are specialized/customized for future development, any dregs and everything that is attached, affiliated or associated with <u>call off known curses and works such as OCD, bipolar, ADD, ADHD, etc</u> as well as unknown curses flowing down into the life of this child, and everything that is attached, affiliated or associated with <u>call off iniquities that were identified</u> and any unknown iniquities to be blood-linked with blood-links that cannot be broken, to the ancestral demon carrying the name of <u>full name of oldest child</u>.

"Lord Jesus, in the life of <u>full name of oldest child</u>, I ask You to gather up each and every wound and hurt in his/her life, anything and everything that has caused him hurts, wounds and anxieties, anything and everything that has kept this child from being all that You have created and called this child to be, anything and everything this child's father and mother have done that has hurt or wounded this child, anything and everything done to this child by anyone else that has wounded, hurt or caused anxiety in this child's life, including but not limited to <u>known abuse</u> done by <u>name/s of abuser/s</u>, gather it all up and attach it with blood-links that cannot be broken to the ancestral demon who caries the formal name of <u>full name of oldest child</u>.

"Lord Jesus, I ask You to pull the ancestral demon that carries the formal name of <u>full name of oldest child</u> and everything that is attached to this child's ancestral demon and attach everything to the <u>Ancestral Demon parent/core personality's formal name</u>, for they are all going where that ancestral demon is going!"

CONFRONT THE ANCESTRAL DEMON WITH MORE QUESTIONS

I continue by warning and questioning the ancestral demon by saying: "<u>Ancestral Demon parent/core personality's formal name</u>, I've already warned you what will happen to you if you lie or otherwise mess with me. Now I command that you answer these questions with truth!"

1. **"Do you have any ground to hold the father/mother of <u>full name of oldest child</u> pertaining to any curses?"**

2. **"Are there any legitimate rights or any manner of legal ground for Satan and his demons remaining in this child?"**

3. **"Are there any gatekeepers remaining in the life of this child?"**

4. **"Are there any demons masquerading as wounded personalities remaining in the life of this child?"**

5. **"Are there any demon-produced personalities remaining in the life of this child?"**

6. **"Are there any clones customized/specialized for future development remaining in the life of this child?"**

7. **"Are there any demonic dregs of any kind remaining in this child?"**

8. **"Will all of your answers stand as truth before the eternal throne of the Lord Jesus Christ where only truth can stand?"**

WARN ANCESTRAL DEMON AGAIN

I give the ancestral demon this further warning: "Now, Ancestral Demon, if you are lying to me, when we are done with you, I am going to ask the Heavenly Father, who knows whether you are telling me the truth or not, to annihilate you with the breath of His Holy mouth if you are lying to me. Do you understand me?"

1. **"Ancestral Demon, I'll ask once again, did everything come over from <u>full name of oldest child</u>?**

2. **"Ancestral Demon, will your answer stand as truth before the eternal throne of the Lord Jesus Christ where only truth can stand?"**

COUNSELOR PRAYS
FOR INDIVIDUAL CHILDREN UNDER AGE OF TWENTY

Having peace that the ancestral demon, indeed, has no more ground in the precious child's life, then I pray the following prayer, thanking the Lord!

"Dear Lord Jesus, I praise You and thank You that with Your blood, You have blood-linked with chains which cannot be broken, all the demons of whatever type or hierarchy operating in the life of <u>full name of oldest child</u>, and all of the curses, those known to us and those unknown to us, in the life of <u>full name of oldest child</u>, and all of the iniquities, those known to us and those not known to us, with the <u>Ancestral Demon parent/core personality's formal name</u> and they're going where he is going."

Reminder: Repeat the above instructions for every child under the age of twenty belonging to the parents. Once you have dealt with each one, and then check with the ancestral demon that carries the formal name of each parent to make certain that everything came over for each of the children.

UNBORN AND NEWBORN CHILDREN

If there is a child in the mother's womb, pray the previous prayer for <u>the child God knows</u>, asking the Lord to heal any hurts, wounds and anything else, and the same applies for a newborn baby, using his/her formal name.

PARENTS PRAY, REMOVING DEMONIC
FROM CHILDREN UNDER AGE TWENTY

When counseling a father and mother of children under the age of twenty, I explain to them that it is very important for them to be in unity concerning dealing with their children in this matter. And with the father being the head of the home and the spiritual leader, each of them should pray the following:

"Lord Jesus, I want to praise and thank You that You have given me the authority to call out of my children all of the ancestral demons that were passed down to them that carry the name of <u>formal name of the father</u>. Lord Jesus I thank You for blood-linking with blood-links that cannot be broken, all the demon networks to the ancestral demons. Lord Jesus, I thank You for doing this!"

Note that the same applies to situations such as a mother who is a widow left to care for her children, a wife separated from her husband (who is in rebellion against God's will), or a divorcee who has custody of the children:

A WIFE PRAYING FOR CHILDREN WITH HUSBAND'S APPROVAL

When a mother with children under the age of twenty has come for counseling and has permission from her husband (whether present or not) to deal with these issues, then I lead her to pray this:

"Dear Lord Jesus, I know that I have the covering of my husband. Lord Jesus, I want to praise and thank You that because of my husband's willingness to be my headship, my covering today, I have the right to ask You that everything that is in our children—including anything ancestral connected to his side of the family—be called out and attached to <u>Ancestral Demon core personality's formal name</u>, with blood-links made of Your blood that cannot be broken.

"Lord Jesus, I want to praise and thank You that You have also given me power and authority in You to deal with the ancestral demon that carries my formal name and all the demonic beings and everything else blood-linked to him."

CURSES IN CHILDREN
TWENTY AND OLDER AND OTHER FAMILY MEMBERS

Please remember that **unlike his children under the age of twenty, a parent <u>cannot</u> attain freedom from Satan's captivity for his children who are of ages twenty and older. For these children are in the age bracket of "accountability!"** These children are responsible for their own choices of behavior. They will answer to the Lord for their own sins and sinful lifestyles they have chosen! **However, through his authority in Jesus Christ, the parent can remove curses from his children under the age of twenty and ages twenty and older! On rare occasions with very unusual circumstances, God has given the counselee and me authority to remove generational curses from other family members.** I pray like this pertaining to the curses:

"Heavenly Father, I ask for wisdom and discernment in regards to reaching out to the family members of <u>core personality's formal name</u> and the curse/s of <u>call out list of curses</u>.

"Heavenly Father, <u>Ancestral Demon core personality's formal name</u> said these curses flowed into the lives of the family members of <u>names ancestral demon provided</u>, and I asked this demon whether his claims would stand as truth before Your throne where only truth can stand and he said it would.

"Dear Lord Jesus, we thank You in advance for whatever You choose to do in Your sovereignty. Believing that You have given me authority to call forth and ask, in Your name, that all the demons associated, affiliated or attached to these curses be pulled out and attached and blood-linked with Your blood, to the <u>Ancestral Demon core personality's formal name</u>, and pull out and attach those from the lives of <u>names of known family members</u> and from those family members of the core that I don't know, but You know that the curses flowed into. With child-like faith, I praise You and thank You for doing this.

"Heavenly Father, realizing that these family members may still have work to do of their own because of their own issues, I ask that You heal anything and everything associated, affiliated or attached to these curses in their flip-sides, wounded parts and core. I ask that their healing and freedom be noticeable in each of these family members that have suffered from these curses. I acknowledge Your sovereignty, but ask for Your grace and healing on behalf of all these people in regards to these curses. I thank You for doing this, Lord Jesus."

RIGHT DECLARED TO REMOVE ANCESTRAL DEMON FROM CHILDREN

I lead the core personality in the following **responsive declaration to the ancestral demon** that no longer has any ground to stand on in the counselee's life. The core has the authority to ask the Lord Jesus to remove him from his life and the lives of his children under twenty, along with the curses in his age twenty and older children and any specific family members—then send him and his network wherever He deems best!

"Ancestral Demon, based on my authority in the Lord Jesus Christ, I, <u>core personality's formal name</u>, age ___, saved at age ___, since you no longer have any legal-rights or ground in my life, nor in the lives of my children (and specific family members pertaining to curses), I command that you and your blood-linked demon networks, blood-linked with chains made of Jesus' blood, which cannot be broken, go to wherever God wants you to go, to the abyss, the lake of fire, or for Him to annihilate you with the breath of His Holy mouth!"

L.   COUNSELEE PRAYS, GOD'S WILL BE DONE IN OUSTING DEMONS

Now that the counselee has dealt with all his issues, I lead him to pray the following prayer, asking the Lord to remove all the demons and to send them out according to His will, whether that's to the abyss, the lake of fire, or to annihilate them and blow their vapor away with the breath of His holy mouth!

"Heavenly Father, because You are a just God, You do not allow us to ask that the demons be annihilated without first warning them and so in obedience we warned them repeatedly as to what would happen if they lied, interfered or otherwise messed with us. At times they did lie, while at other times, they cooperated with us. So I am asking that Your will be done in this matter. I ask in the name of the Lord Jesus that You take the ancestral demon that carries my formal name and every demonic being blood-linked with Your blood to him and everything else blood-linked to him, including his personal network; blood-link all the other ancestral demons that were operating in my life and their personal networks, whether they be ancestral demons of family names or works, all the power and lifestyle demons and their personal network. Blood-link to him all the demons masquerading like wounded parts, demon-produced personalities, demon-clones that were specialized/customized for future development, and all their personal networks.

"Also blood-link the gatekeepers and all their personal networks. Include all the demonic beings attached to, affiliated with or associated with attacks against my physical health. Include all the curses and all the demons attached to, affiliated with or associated with the curses, those known to me and those unknown. Blood-link to him all the demonic beings and curses pulled in and attached to the ancestral demon that carries my formal name from my children <u>call off names of all the children</u>, and all the demonic beings and curses pulled in and attached to the ancestral demon that carries my formal name from my wife/husband, and all the demonic beings and curses pulled in and attached to the ancestral demon that carries my formal name from <u>name each of his family members that apply</u>, and then in accordance with Your will, send them all to the abyss or to the lake of fire or annihilate them with the breath of Your Holy mouth. With a childlike faith, I thank You that it is done."

PRAYER IF GOD DEEMS IT RIGHT TO ANNIHILATE THE DEMONS

If the ancestral demon and his network were extremely uncooperative in spite of your warnings of using the tool of annihilation on them, then follow through with your threat and pray as follows:

"Heavenly Father, because You are a just God, You do not allow us to ask that the demons be annihilated without first warning them and so in obedience we warned them repeatedly as to what would happen if they lied, interfered or otherwise messed with us and they kept lying, interfering and messing with us. So in keeping with the declaration made to them that we would ask You to annihilate them, I ask in name of the Lord Jesus that You take the ancestral demon that carries my formal name and every demonic being blood-linked with Your blood to him and everything else blood-linked to him, including his personal network, all the other ancestral demons that were operating in my life and their personal networks, whether they be ancestral-demons of family names or works, all the power and lifestyle demons and their personal network; all the demons masquerading like personalities, demon-produced personalities, demon-clones that were specialized or customized for future development, and all their personal networks, gatekeepers and all their personal networks, caretakers, and their personal networks, all the demonic beings attached to, affiliated with or associated with attacks against my physical health, all the curses and all the demons attached to, affiliated with or associated with the curses, those known to me and those unknown, all the demonic beings and curses pulled in and attached to the ancestral demon that carries my formal name from my children, <u>name all of the children</u>, all the demonic beings and curses pulled in and attached to the ancestral demon carrying my formal name from my wife/husband, plus all of the demonic beings and curses pulled in and attached to the ancestral demon carrying my formal name from name each family member. We ask that You annihilate them with the breath of Your Holy mouth. With a childlike faith, I thank You that it is done."

Now, ask the core: "Without any editing, tell me what you hear, feel, sense or see. Tell me what's going on inside right now?"

1. The person may answer that they don't hear, feel, sense, or see anything negative, that they just sense quietness.
2. The person may answer that he has feelings of emptiness, heaviness, or an unsettling, disturbing feeling, but he "just can't put his finger on it".

No matter if the core reports that he senses a positive feeling or a negative one, it's definitely time to go checking to see if something demonic has been left behind. It's time to tests the spirits to see whether or not the ancestral demon and his network are gone!

M. COUNSELOR TESTS SPIRITS TO SEE IF ANCESTRAL DEMON IS GONE

We will test the spirits once again based on what I John 4: 1-3 says: *"Beloved, do not believe every spirit, but **test the spirits whether they are of God**; because many false prophets have gone out into the world. By this you know the Spirit of God: Every spirit that confesses that Jesus Christ has come in the flesh is of God, and every spirit that does not confess that Jesus Christ has come in the flesh is not of God; and this is the spirit of the Anti-Christ...."*

I remind the counselee: "I am not testing you nor am I doubting God, but **I'm going to obey the Lord as He instructs in I John 4:1-3**, and test the spirits to be on the safe side—double-checking to make sure all the demons are gone! As I've said before, Satan can come as an angel of light and can even make a person think that he is hearing from God. It is actually my responsibility to check it out. The Lord will reveal the truth to us if we just take time to sit and listen. I will pray, asking the Lord to test the spirits for us."

Prayer for the Lord Jesus to test the spirits:

"I ask You, Lord Jesus, to not allow the ancestral demon to be mute or deaf but make him come up and acknowledge his presence, if in fact he still remains in the life of core personality's formal name. He can fool us, but he can't fool You, so Lord Jesus, if Ancestral Demon core personality's formal name is still here, we ask You to drag him up so we can do business with him. Don't let him waste and burn our time or trick us by hesitating or refusing to come up."

287

Call the ancestral demon to attention:

"In the authority of the name and blood of the Lord Jesus Christ, King of kings, Lord of lords, Ancestral Demon core personality's formal name, come up and acknowledge your presence. By the finger of Almighty God, I command that you to come up and talk to me immediately. I call you to attention by the name of the Lord Jesus Christ. Acknowledge your presence by answering me with, 'yes, sir' and tell me why are you still here!"

Insist that ancestral demons answer you by saying "yes, sir" or "no, sir," or "yes, ma'am" or "no, ma'am". This "keeps them in their place", under "your authority in Christ" over them:

When commanding, through my power and authority in Jesus Christ, the ancestral demon to answer with a "yes" or "no"—especially when one is arrogant and stubborn—I often demand that he show me respect also, as God's servant! I order him to acknowledge whether or not something is true or not by answering either "yes, sir"—or "no, sir". Counselors who are women may insist he answer with "yes, ma'am" or "no, ma'am". If he answers with a "no" or is silent, you know he remains and perhaps he still holds some ground. I then confront him again, commanding him to tell me what his remaining legal ground is (as I've illustrated earlier). If I learn that he does still have some ground, then I lead the core to deal with the issue and reclaim his ground. Sometimes, he will simply be slow to admit that he has no ground before finally giving up his comfy housing!

I search further for any other demons left behind by commanding:

"In the authority of the name and blood of the Lord Jesus Christ, King of kings, Lord of lords, I call for demons remaining in core personality's formal name to come up and acknowledge your presence. If there is more than one demon remaining and there is one in charge, then I call for the one in charge to come up and talk to me.

If there is no demon in charge, then I pray:

"Lord Jesus, we ask You to bring up the demon You want us to deal with. Lord Jesus, do not allow any demons remaining in the life of core personality's formal name to be mute or deaf but make all that may still be there come up and talk to me. If in fact one or more demonic beings remain in core personality's formal name, they may be able to fool us, but they can't fool You, so Lord Jesus, if one or more demonic beings remain in the life of core personality's formal name, we ask You to drag them up so that we can do business with them. Don't let them hide, or waste and burn our time trying to trick us by hesitating or refusing from coming up.

"By the blood and name of the Lord Jesus, King of kings and Lord of lords, and by the finger of Almighty God, I command that any demons of any type remaining in the life of <u>core personality's formal name</u> come up and acknowledge your presence. I call you to attention by the name of the Lord Jesus. Acknowledge your presence by stating, 'yes, sir' and tell me why are you still here."

If any demons answer:

I demand to know why any demons are still there and what the legal rights are of each one. If I find that they do have any legal rights to stay, then I lead the core to deal with the issues and reclaim the ground.

After the core has dealt with any additional sin-issues:

With the core's dealing with any additional issues, I then lead him once again to pray, asking the Lord to blood-link with blood-links that cannot be broken, those demons connected to the issue, to the ancestral demon carrying the formal name.

If there is silence, no response from any demons, then I question the core:

With the core assuring me that there is silence—a feeling that nothing is left behind, then I ask the core once again, "What do you hear, feel, see or sense, if anything?" If the core says something like, "nothing, just quietness—just experiencing positives, nothing negative"—then, I make notations of what he reported. Then I lead him to pray the prayer in which he will ask the Lord to do as He pleases with all the demons—send them to the abyss, the lake of fire, or to annihilate them.

COUNSELOR ASKS THE CORE AGAIN

"<u>Core personality's formal name</u>, just let me know what you are hearing, feeling, sensing or seeing. If the Lord is bringing up anything demonic, that's ok, don't hesitate to tell me about it so that we can deal with it now. If the Lord is exposing anything demonic, it's for your good! So please don't hesitate letting me know for it is far more wise to deal with it now than for you to suffer later and have to come back to deal with it!"

N.   PRAYERS FOR PEACE AS EVIDENCE OF FREEDOM

If the counselee reports again that he is not sensing anything negative, and he reports sensing things such as a feeling of calmness, then I ask the Lord to let him have "peace" accompanying his freedom:

"Heavenly Father, I come, to You right now on behalf of <u>core personality's formal name</u>, age _____, saved at age ___.   John 14:27 tells us that Your Son, the Lord Jesus, does not give the kind of peace the world gives that is based on feelings. Rather, it is the manifested presence of the Your Person, which is Your peace. So I ask You Lord Jesus, if <u>core personality's formal name</u> is truly free that You overwhelm and fill him with the manifested presence of Your peace."

COUNSELEE IS LED BY COUNSELOR TO PRAY CONCERNING PEACE

With the counselee assuring me that he has peace in his heart, then I then lead him to pray:

"Lord Jesus, we read in John 14:27 that when You were on earth, You declared, *'let not your heart be troubled, and let it not be afraid.'* You declare in Your Holy Word that Satan, the world, flesh, or demons cannot counterfeit Your peace, because the peace that You give is a Person, not as the world gives, it is not a good feeling, it is the manifested presence of the Your Person, and that it is Your peace. Lord, if I am free, and all bondage has been broken, manifest Your peace in my life. But if I'm still in bondage and we've been fooled, make the demons manifest their confusion. I want to praise You and thank You, You are not going to give me a little peace plus a little confusion. You will either give me Your peace, or manifest the demons' confusion. I thank You, Lord Jesus for doing this."

COUNSELOR PRAYS FOR THE CORE CONCERNING PEACE

Upon the counselee saying that he believes there is peace and nothing negative going on, then I pray the following prayer on his behalf:

"Lord Jesus, fill and overflow him with a manifested presence of Your sweet peace. Nothing can counterfeit it or masquerade. So Lord Jesus with a child like faith I wait on You.

"Lord, if we are through, if all bondage is broken in the life of <u>core personality's formal name</u>, and this core personality is free [and his children are free], and all the curses and demons are gone, and all the demons that were involved with the attacks and harassments against his physical health are gone, [and all the demons that were involved with the attacks and harassments against his children's physical health are gone], and all the other demons are gone, then we know the core only has negative-learned behavior that he will have to deal with! So, if all the work is done, and he is free, I ask that You show us that it is truly done. If anything is remaining that You know we need to deal with, I ask that You bring into light what is in darkness. I ask that You speak to our spirits about anything that needs to be dealt with at this time. If we are done, then confirm it in the spirit of <u>core personality's formal name</u>, by giving him Your perfect peace."

"I ask You heavenly Father to put the core in Your intensive care unit [with his children and his wife]. Please hedge <u>core personality's formal name</u> about with the blood of Your precious Son. Set an encampment of Your angels about him. Allow nothing to get to him that doesn't first come through the blood of Christ, Father, for he needs some 'rehab' time. I ask You to just pull him up into Your lap, embrace and love him, and take care of him as he learns how to walk in Christ. It is in Jesus' sweet holy name, I thank You for doing this!"

TIME FOR THE CORE TO THANK THE LORD FOR HIS FREEDOM

With you, as the core's counselor also having a peace that the core truly has a peace and confidence that the Lord has given him victory over the enemy, then lead him to pray this:

"Lord Jesus, I ask You to take Your powerful blood and literally saturate my being from the top of my head to the soles of my feet, every crack and crevice of my life, body, soul, spirit, mind, and emotions. Lord Jesus, bring Your Shekinah glory and light up my entire life. My sweet heavenly Father, I want You to fill all the vacancies that have been left in my life with Your sweet Holy Spirit, starting with flip-side, all that his name meant and his personality represented, and continuing with the vacancies left by all the wounded personalities in my life, all that their names meant, and all that their personality represented, and then continuing with all the vacancies remaining that pertain to the ancestral demon that carried my formal name, and all the demons connected to him, no matter where they came from that were formally in my life, I want You to fill all those vacancies in my life with Your Holy Spirit. Fill me to overflowing. I praise You and thank You! I love You for it!

[**Add this for those who dealt with children under age 20:** "Heavenly Father, thank You for removing the ancestral demon and his network from each of our children. Thank You for healing them by the mercy and grace of Your precious son and my Lord, Jesus Christ. I thank You that You will seal off all the doors in their lives. Whatever is needed in the lives of my children, by Your sovereignty, fill all the vacancies in their lives with Your Holy Spirit."]

"With a childlike faith, I thank You for doing all of this. I ask these things in Jesus' sweet name."

THANK YOU, LORD JESUS, FOR BLESSING US
WITH VICTORY OVER THE ENEMY!

What joy the counselee and I experienced as the battle was won against the ancestral demon and his network! Our hearts were filled with gratitude and joy, indeed!

"Oh, sing to the Lord a new song! For He has done marvelous things: His right hand and His holy arm have gained Him the victory. The Lord hath made known His salvation...." (Psalm 98:1-2a)

With extremely thankful hearts, having reached our destination—freedom for the counselee—he is free to walk in God's will for his precious life. Will it be easy? Of course not, because the enemy is still in this present world, tempting God's precious Christians with hope of bringing them over to serve on his side of the war! While it may not be easy to remain stationed on this earthly combat zone, with the Lord all Christians can do all things—we can walk in victory over the opposing enemy! **Remember that God lovingly "convicts" us of our sins to bring us to repentance and restoration of fellowship with Him. Satan hatefully "condemns" us and puts us down—reminding us of our past sins which God has forgiven and has put them as far as the east is from the west!** (Psalm 103:12) So, when Satan casts words of condemnation remember, as it's been put so well, *"When Satan reminds you of your past, remind him of his future!"*

For the now-set-free Christian there are some spiritual training exercises provided by his King of kings that he can do to make him stronger so he can be a winner, not a loser in the midst of this spiritual war! However, it would do all Christians well to review these training exercises as well! With this in mind, as we move to the next chapter to share how to confront and defeat old negative-learned behavior patterns, we're going to liken it to enlisting in the military service and driving down the road a piece to "boot camp"—for Christian military service! We truly hope that all soldiers wearing the Christian uniform will be blessed with much hope, help, and encouragement as they study the next chapter!

Chapter Twelve
TOOLS FOR CONQUERING NEGATIVE BEHAVIOR, DISGUISED AS A DEMON

We hope that all Christians will commit to going through "God's boot camp," which offers tremendous blessings to new babes in Christ, to His Christian soldiers once held captive by the enemy and to all other Christian soldiers as well! For every Christian must choose—moment by moment—whether or not he will conquer negative-learned behavior and serve his King with honor. **Now over the years, many people have heard me say that while it is not a demon, "negative behavior" is like having one of the biggest demons possible! Why? It's because Christians are still housed in clay vessels—the flesh, the old man, human nature—that is so prone to do "what comes naturally"—or easiest to do!**

When a Christian chooses to act out negatively in the flesh, he can reflect behavior that is like the unkind, self-centered, evil behavior that is common amongst demons! When others observe his actions, **his negative-learned behavior may appear disguised as a demon!** We have come to believe that negative-learned behavior, on the person's part **takes far more effort to conquer than an ancestral demon and all his network**! Why? Because with the ancestral demon and his network, once the reasons are discovered that gave them legal ground in the person's life, and the person dealt with the sins, the ground was reclaimed and they lost their right to stay! Therefore, the demons were gone and no demonic activity remained within the person!

Until that set-free Christian moves into heaven, he is still housed in his clay vessel—the flesh, the old man that is still a part of his make-up. Therefore, this free Christian himself has the legal right to **choose how he is going to walk through life moment by moment, in the flesh or in the Spirit—in his new nature or his old nature—in the old man or the new man—through Jesus Christ!** Colossians 3:9b-10 says: *"...you have put off the old man with his deeds, and have put on the new man who is renewed in knowledge according to the image of Him who created him."* Each Christian is free to listen to and obey the Lord, or his flesh to whom Satan appeals! **He is still subject to temptation! He is not a Christian robot!** Whoever said **"Old habits die hard!"** most surely knew what he was talking about! Just as we think we have shot and killed an old negative habit, it suddenly rises from the dead to taunt us—or should we say "haunt" us? Can we not conquer it, kill it permanently?

To better understand this seemingly immortal flesh—old man—within us all, let's take a moment to examine **the make-up of lost people** who surely do not have the ability through Christ to walk victoriously over Satan, the enemy—nor to conquer their negative-learned behavior. All lost people are **prone to please their "flesh"—that old man**. Without a shadow of a doubt, that's exactly why God wisely and lovingly implanted in every human being's heart and mind **"a conscience"**—so that he would know right from wrong! Every person would be **convicted to pause before choosing to do right or wrong**.

> **The definition of "conscience" is:** "Knowledge or feeling of right and wrong; the faculty, power, or principle of a person which decides on the lawfulness or unlawfulness of his actions, with a compulsion to do right; moral judgment that prohibits or opposes the violation of a previously recognized ethical principle." (Webster's New Twentieth Century Dictionary, Second Edition, Copyright © 1975 by William Collins + World Publishing Co., Inc.; page 387)

> **The definition of "conscience" in the thesaurus in our WordPerfect 12 computer program is:** "motivation deriving logically from ethical or moral principles that govern a person's thoughts and actions; conformity to one's own sense of right conduct; a feeling of shame when you do something immoral."

Therefore, a lost person is without excuse—his conscience has brought matters to his attention, and he knows full well that he should do right rather than wrong, and he knows when he has sinned! He always has the freedom to choose between the two.

Now a grievous truth is that if a lost person chooses to repeatedly yield to temptation, and do wrong—do evil—rejecting his loving Creator, then more and more ground is given to Satan. As he continues to deliberately make such choices and continue to do evil, we read in I Timothy 4:1-3, that the Lord says the state of that person's conscience becomes like having it burned away: *"Now the Spirit expressly says that in the latter times some will depart from the faith, giving heed to deceiving spirits and doctrines of demons, speaking lies in hypocrisy, **having their own conscience seared with a hot iron**, forbidding to marry, and commanding to abstain from foods which God created to be received with thanksgiving by those who believe and know the truth."* God knows when a person has reached this point—has permanently chosen against God—"crossed over the unseen line of no return." Knowing this, the Holy Spirit ceases to woo him unto Himself.

When we were in the pastorate many years ago, we had a nursing home ministry. Rita and a dear sister-in-the-Lord had visited and witnessed to a particular elderly man who politely thanked them for their concern for him, but burst into tears, declaring, "I can never be saved!" Then with tears, pleading on their knees beside the man in the wheel chair, they explained that no sin was too great for God to forgive when a person sincerely repents, and that He loved him unconditionally! The man continued to weep bitterly, insisting that he could not be saved because he was one of those spoken of in the Bible who had **"rejected God and crossed over that unseen line!"** Future visits with the man remained grievous as he tearfully insisted, "It's too late! I cannot be saved! God no longer calls me!" Years later, upon looking back on that tragic scene, we knew that the man could have been right—that he did, indeed, step over that line. Because at that time, we had not yet learned how to deal with persons held captive by Satan, we were more prone to wonder if the dear old man was saved but was deceived and being held captive and tormented by Satan. We hope to meet him one day in heaven!

Now let us also **keep in mind that lost people can "do both good and bad things—yet both are done in the flesh."** For instance, a lost person is tempted, he ignores his warning conscience, and acts badly by saying hateful things to someone. Yet at another time, he makes a sizeable contribution to a charity. While he did a good thing—to whom was glory given? There are many morally good people in the world who do enormously good things, and please, understand that we are most surely not criticizing their good deeds! It has been grievous to know many lost people who have done many good works while delighting in the praises that it brought to themselves. It is of great concern that these "good acts done in the flesh will not earn for themselves rewards or a place in heaven!" We are told the truth of the matter in Ephesians 2:8-10: *"For **by grace you have been saved through faith**, and that **not of yourselves**; it is the gift of God, **not of works, lest anyone should boast**. For we are His workmanship, created in Christ Jesus for good works, which God prepared beforehand that we should walk in them."* We must add that **as Christians soldiers**, we are most surely **not without sin when we allow ourselves to be deceived into thinking that a person is saved based on the facts that he is morally good and he does good works**! We should be prayerfully alert for opportunities to witness to these precious souls!

It is through every person's conscience—this unique conduit—the Lord lovingly draws each person to desire to fill the void in his heart, to understand his need for the Savior. For every person who has chosen to receive the Lord, He moved into their hearts in the form of the Holy Spirit—who was joined with their God-installed conscience! The Holy Spirit lives in the hearts of every Christian to guide, teach, convict him of sin, warn of temptation, comfort, encourage, and give him strength to walk in the Spirit. All are capable of reflecting the fruit of the Spirit, found in Galatians 5:22-26: *"For the fruit of the Spirit is love, joy, peace, longsuffering, kindness, goodness, faithfulness, gentleness, self-control. Against such there is no law. And those who are Christ's have crucified the flesh with its passions and desires. If we live in the Spirit, let us also walk in the Spirit. Let us not become conceited, provoking one another, envying one another."*

It is also crucial for every believer to understand that he is as capable of yielding to temptation and walking in the flesh as a lost person if he does not choose to consistently submit himself to the Lord and resist the enemy. Prayerfully read this scripture found in Galatians 5:19-21b, and honestly answer whether or not you understand that a Christian can act out these fleshly acts: *"Now **the works of the flesh are evident**, which are adultery, fornication, uncleanness, lewdness, idolatry, sorcery, hatred, contentions, jealousies, outbursts of wrath, selfish ambitions, dissensions, heresies, envy, murders, drunkenness, revelries, and the like...."*

TRUTHFUL REMINDERS FOR SET-FREE COUNSELEES

Without a doubt, if a Christian consistently gives into temptation, he is perfectly capable of being taken hostage by the enemy! Because Satan cunningly tempts God's children, this is why some counselees who have been set free become discouraged when they find themselves being drawn back to some of their old ways—their "negative-learned behavior patterns"—those old bad habits that keep resurrecting themselves! The truth is that Satan knows "where they used to walk," so that's where he tempts them! So, it is essential that we encourage each one with God's truths! Remind him of how he experienced his wounded personalities getting new names—carrying their formal name and **"a new creation in Jesus Christ, fully submitted to His Lordship and filled with His abundant life."** Further explain that with his wounded parts being fused and integrated to him, **he is a whole person, nothing negative remains within him!** He should know that "his Christian uniform is clean" and that Jesus can train him up in the way he should go—and help him avoid stumbling through life! Remind him that Satan and the ancestral demons and his network and any blood-linked demons can no longer manipulate and control his life! They have no ground in his core personality that God created! Remind him that **his ancestral demon and all his demon network lost all the ground they once held legally! All ground has been legally reclaimed— and those demons cannot re-enter him!** Remind him that Jesus did the same for him that He did for the little boy when He cast the ancestral demon out of him and declared, *"...enter him no more!"*

It is important that every now-free person understands that if he consistently begins to yield to temptation—listens to and obeys Satan's suggestions, thus venturing into a sinful lifestyle—then he is swinging the door wide open for Satan to set up housekeeping again—just using new, different demons! **He needs to know that he may find himself confronted with certain "negatives" which are like his "old negative-learned behavior patterns" that were very much a part of him when he was in bondage.** He needs to know that some of his negative behavior is more prone to be "automatically acted out without thought—like approaching a door and turning the doorknob." We declare again, **"Old habits die hard!"** However, **each counselee needs to be assured that with the Lord nothing is impossible—he can overcome—he can keep shooting those old habits down the instant they try to rise from the dead!** What joy to know as Christians that—if we choose to act on it and walk in the Spirit rather than the flesh—*"...we are more than conquerors through Him that loved us. For I am persuaded that neither death, nor life, nor angels, nor principalities, nor powers, nor things present, nor things to come, nor height, nor depth, nor any other creation, shall be able to separate us from the love of God, which is in Christ Jesus, our Lord."* (Romans 8:37-39)

It is essential that we Christians never forget that until the day we die, we are still housed in our "old man," our "flesh." For now-free Christians—and Christians who have never been in bondage—who struggle from time to time with negative behavior, it is not impossible at all to be trained in how to defeat negative-learned behavior—patterns that appear as demons in disguise. It is like going to God's boot camp of which we spoke earlier—and with determination and training, it is possible! It will be worth all the effort! If one is faithful to apply all that our King, our Lord Jesus Christ instructs, strength will abound even when the attacks come from the enemy in the combat zone, on the front lines!

Spiritual boot camp is very much like physical military boot camp! For, when a person has enlisted to serve in the military, before he is put on the front line he must go to "boot camp" where he will put aside his civilian clothes, and be given military clothes—and combat boots—and he will go

296

through many rigorous training exercises so that he will be physically fit. He will be fed balanced meals that will give his body nourishment. Upon willingly submitting to serve in the military, he will fully understand the importance of obeying the commanding officer's orders, even when it's hard and his flesh longs to be doing something less strenuous! Nevertheless, he will choose to obey, for he fully understands that the rules are not only for his own safety, but for the safety of those fellow soldiers who are also heading toward the front lines! He will also be taught how to use a variety of weapons. He will also be equipped with some special tools—such as a shovel to dig a "fox hole" to drop into so that he's less vulnerable to the enemy's weapons! Out of his love for his country and the freedoms it offers, he is wholeheartedly committed to serve on home base or on the battlefield until his enlistment is complete.

Likewise, as a person enlists in the Lord's military and finds himself in the midst of the Holy War, if he is not already physically fit, he soon finds, upon engaging in the strenuous military, spiritual exercises, that they are extremely difficult to do! His flesh will sometimes beg him to give up—go AWOL! **The exercise regiment is grueling.** It will do us very well to always remember what Paul said in Acts 24:16: *"...I myself always strive to have a conscience without offense toward God and men."* In some other translations, the word in place of "strive" is **"exercise!"** Indeed, if we are going to fight this earthly battle with the strength of Christ, then we Christian soldiers must purpose to exercise our minds to become like the mind of Christ! Why are we to exercise, and for what purposes? It is quite interesting that also in the book of Acts, we find Jesus' last recorded words that came to be known as **the Great Commission:** *"You shall be witnesses to Me in Jerusalem, and in all Judea and Samaria, and to the end of the earth."* (Acts 1:8) Indeed, **all Christian soldiers have been commissioned by Jesus upon His issuing the order for us to *"Go into all the world and preach the gospel to every creature."* (Mark 16:15)

If a Christian soldier loves his King—and appreciates the fact he will one day dwell in His Kingdom—and sticks to the program and follows His orders—he will never regret it. During boot camp, he will find that those exercises will become much easier to do, too! His reflexes will become far quicker! He will have strength to march through trials in the combat zone without fear, and he will effectively use the weapons the King has provided for him.

As you have observed through the years, there have been some Christian soldiers who have chosen to give up while others have chosen to fight the good fight to the finish! Sadly, there have also been Christian soldiers who have been hit by the enemy's fiery darts and left wounded by the wayside. Some fellow Christians have responded like the Good Samaritan, taking time to stop and minister to their fallen, wounded brethren. On the other hand, as you've probably heard it said, "Some Christians are known for shooting their wounded"—rather than seeking to minister to God's fallen soldiers! Oh that we stronger Christians will be more sensitive to tend to our brothers and sisters who have engaged in battle with the enemy and lost—and lay wounded by the wayside.

Some of the fallen soldiers on the wayside are those who are so wounded that they have come to believe that they cannot overcome, they cannot be victorious! We must tell them that if they deny that it's possible for them to conquer their learned behavior and temptation that comes from the enemy, then they are not believing their "Commander in Chief" and are actually calling God a liar! We read in I Corinthians 10:13, *"No temptation has overtaken you except such as is common to man; but God is faithful, who will not allow you to be tempted beyond what you are able, but with the temptation will also make the way of escape, that you may be able to bear it"!*

THE APOSTLE PAUL BATTLING OLD HABITS

Let's take a moment to look at our brother, the Apostle Paul's testimony on the subject of bad habits and the need to exercise to become stronger. He expressed a struggle he was having within himself. Clearly he was describing a battle he was engaged in on a daily basis—to do good—or to act contrary to God's will! He was battling that demon-like negative-learned behavior just as precious Christians battle it today! For read what he says:

> *"For what I am doing, I do not understand. For what I will to do, that I do not practice; but what I hate, that I do."* (Romans 7:15)

Now remember, this is the man who held the coats of men as he watched them persecuting and murdering Christians—before God got his attention and he chose to repent and accept the Lord Jesus as his Messiah, Savior and Lord! This is the man God called to be His missionary, whom He also used as His instrument to write fourteen books of the New Testament—if we include Hebrews, since the writings are so similar to Paul's style. After his salvation, in spite of the battle within himself, why does Paul's testimony throughout his life reflect that he more consistently obeyed the Lord rather than his flesh? What spiritual tools—weapons—did Paul possess to enable him to overcome the flesh? For one thing, Paul was humble. Apart from acknowledging his inner struggle with sin, Paul never forgot from whence he came—a sinner, saved by grace—for he declared: *"...Christ Jesus came into the world to save sinners, of whom I am chief."* (I Timothy 1:15) All Christians should carefully do likewise—never forget from whence they came—for none are found to be less guilty than another, which is clearly stated in James 2:10: *"For whoever shall keep the whole law, and yet stumble in one point, he is guilty of all."* Indeed, all of God's people are equal with one another—from Adam and Eve to the last person to be born on this earth before the Lord puts an end to it!

We Christian soldiers have the same spiritual weapons available to us that Paul had—thus, none of us has an excuse not to win the battles within us far more often than we lose them! As our example Paul did, we should be humble and accept the truth that the battle between the spirit and the flesh and external temptation will continue until we are housed in our new bodies in heaven! Just as our dear brother Paul's testimony reflects, through Christ he was able to conquer more of his inward battles than he lost—and we can also!

These truths are reflected in the book of James—which by the way, was written to Christians! Amidst the amazing, living testimony of our brother Paul—who proved his love and dedication to our Lord Jesus repeatedly through his obedience to share the Gospel at all costs—we learned that he battled against his flesh—his old man, his old nature! What a responsibility he had to share truth—the whole truth and nothing but the truth. For all too many years, it has been grievous to see Christians blending unsound doctrine and traditions of men with the truth. Satan delights when he is able to convince God's precious soldiers to do this—for it leads the precious lambs into wrong and dangerous fields!   Therefore, it does not surprise us **that our King instructed James, "the bondservant of God" to warn us all about the danger of yielding to temptation and mixing untruth with truth—thus losing the battle between the spirit and the flesh!**

Let us take care to heed our brother James' warning here: *"**My brethren, let not many of you become teachers, knowing that we shall receive a stricter judgment. For we all stumble in many things.** If anyone does not stumble in word, he is a perfect man, able also to bridle the whole body. Indeed, we put bits in horses' mouths that they may obey us, and we turn their whole body. Look also at ships: although they are so large and are driven by fierce winds, they are turned by a very small rudder wherever the pilot desires. Even so the tongue is a little member and boasts great things. See how great a forest a little fire kindles. And the tongue is a fire, a world of iniquity. **The tongue is so set among our members that it defiles the whole body, and sets on fire the course of nature; and it is set on fire by hell.** For every kind of beast and bird, of reptile and creature of the sea, is tamed and has been tamed by mankind. **But no man can tame the tongue. It is an unruly evil, full of deadly poison. With it we bless our God and Father, and with it we curse men, who have been made in the similitude of God. Out of the same mouth proceed blessings and cursing. My brethren, these things ought not to be so."** (James 3:1-10)*

Our Commander and Chief continues to give us instructions about our battle on this earthly mission field:

*"Who is wise and understanding among you? Let him show by good conduct that his works are done in the meekness of wisdom. But if you have bitter envy and self-seeking in your hearts, do not boast and lie against the truth. This wisdom does not descend from above, but is earthly, sensual, and demonic. For where envy and self-seeking exist, confusion and every evil thing are there. But the wisdom that is from above is first pure, then peaceable, gentle, willing to yield, full of mercy and good fruits, without partiality and without hypocrisy. Now the fruit of righteousness is sown in peace by those who make peace. **Where do wars and fights come from among you? Do they not come from your desires for pleasure that war in your members?** You lust and do not have. You murder and covet and cannot obtain. You fight and war. Yet you do not have because you do not ask. You ask and do not receive, because you ask amiss, that you may spend it on your pleasures. Adulterers*

299

*and adulteresses! Do you not know that friendship with the world is enmity with God? Whoever therefore wants to be a friend of the world makes himself an enemy of God. Or do you think that the Scripture says in vain, 'The Spirit who dwells in us yearns jealously'? But He gives more grace. Therefore, He says: **'Therefore submit to God. Resist the devil and he will flee from you. Draw near to God and He will draw near to you. Cleanse your hands, you sinners; and purify your hearts, you double-minded. Lament and mourn and weep! Let your laughter be turned to mourning and your joy to gloom. Humble yourselves in the sight of the Lord, and He will lift you up.'"** (James 3:13-18; 4:1-10)*

Clearly we Christians are encouraged to choose to submit to the Lord, be humble, resist temptation and defeat negative-learned behavior patterns! Just like people joining the military put off those civilian clothes and put on their military uniforms—we're to put off the old, put on the new! As we start off each day wearing our Christian uniform, it's left up to us to keep in step with the Lord, or carelessly stumble on the battle field and end up injured—bumps, bruises and a dirty uniform! A clean uniform represents a "right fellowship with God" and "a clean testimony" before others. Of course, we all have some choices to make. One choice is to go to bed in dirty uniforms and wake up in them, thus making ourselves more vulnerable to wearing them day after day, night after night. In doing so, our fellowship with the Lord is not as it should be and our testimony before others is dirty! The other choice is to sincerely repent before going to bed with the desire not to stumble again and awake wearing clean uniforms. We can start the day afresh in right fellowship with the Lord. Our testimony before others will be clean! The following scriptures found in Ephesians teach how to practice changing from our uniform and putting on a clean one—how to replace negative behavior with Christ-like behavior!

The new man, a renewed mind, true righteousness in Christ: *"This I say, therefore, and testify in the Lord, that you should no longer walk as the rest of the Gentiles walk, in the futility of their mind, having their understanding darkened, being alienated from the life of God, because of the ignorance that is in them, because of the blindness of their heart; who, being past feeling, have given themselves over to lewdness, to work all uncleanness with greediness. But you have not so learned Christ, if indeed you have heard Him and have been taught by Him, as the truth is in Jesus: that you **put off, concerning your former conduct, the old man which grows corrupt according to the deceitful lusts, and be renewed in the spirit of your mind, and that you put on the new man which was created according to God, in true righteousness and holiness."*** (Ephesians 4:17-24)

HOW TO PUT OFF BAD BEHAVIOR AND PUT ON GOOD BEHAVIOR

All of the negative behaviors mentioned in that scripture reflect the opposite of Christ-like behavior. God gives us a wonderful illustration that teaches us the true meaning of how we are to "put off bad behavior and put on good behavior". It is found in Ephesians 4:28: **"let him who stole steal no longer, but rather let him labor, working with his hands what is good, that he may have something to give**

300

him who has need." This lesson takes us far beyond a sinful thief repenting and no longer stealing. It takes us to the opposite extreme, for the repentant thief is to find a job and do it with a tremendous goal in mind—to not only provide for the needs of his own household, but for others along his pathway of life who are in need! This is what putting off something bad and putting on something good is all about! It is a powerful lesson that illustrates the duty of every good Christian soldier. When he fights the good fight—wearing Christ-like behavior—it is not only for his own personal, spiritual welfare, but for others as well! For our orders from our Commanding Officer are: ***"Therefore let us pursue** the things which make for peace and the things by which one may **edify** another."* (Romans 14:19)

HOW TO PUT OFF LYING AND PUT ON TRUTH
HOW TO BE ANGRY YET NOT SIN

We find the Lord making it very clear that we are to put off lying and put on truth and that it is okay to be angry yet we're not to sin as we read Ephesians 25-27; 29-32: *"Therefore, **put away lying,** 'Let each one of you **speak truth** with his neighbor, 'for we are members of one another. '**Be angry and do not sin'**: do not let the sun go down on your wrath, nor give place to the devil...let **no corrupt word proceed out of your mouth, but <u>what is good for necessary edification,</u> that it may impart grace to the hearers.** And **do not grieve the Holy Spirit of God,** by whom you were sealed for the day of redemption. Let all bitterness, wrath, anger* [unrighteous anger], *and clamor, and evil speaking be put away from you, with all malice. And be kind to one another, tenderhearted, forgiving one another even as God in Christ forgave you.*

Now the choice for a Christian to determine in his heart to **put on truth and put off all lying** is very easy to understand. The bottom line is, if a Christian loves the Lord with all his heart, mind and soul, he will slam on his spiritual brakes when tempted to lie, and obediently tell the truth—even if unpleasantries may come as a result!

But what does God mean when He says it's okay for us to "<u>be</u> angry" but for us not to let it result in sinful fallout? In **human reasoning,** this doesn't make sense, but with **the mind of Christ,** there is wisdom. For, the words **"be angry" carries a Godly, <u>justified type of anger</u> which is to only serve to motivate a Christian to respond in the Spirit, in love, with hopes of offering <u>help,</u> a <u>solution</u> to <u>what</u> birthed the anger in the first place, not <u>who.</u>** To do otherwise, as God says, if one has unrighteous anger—wrath—the Devil can gain a foothold, which can lead to his attaining a stronghold and gaining a captive! The Lord truly holds every Christian accountable to set Christ-like examples—to do the will of God from the heart. And if a Christian harbors anger within, while controlling their tongue and physical actions, often times, his facial expressions can expose the truth in his heart. For even though seated in silence, they can subtly broadcast their inner thoughts. God truly holds us accountable to set Christ-like examples before others. That's why the Lord also warns His children to deal with their unrighteous anger immediately and not take it to bed with them!

A good example of righteous anger is that of parents who lovingly warned their **little boy** not to venture into a yard where a septic tank was leaking harmful sewage that had formed a large, slimy puddle. Much to their discouragement, the little boy sneaked off and stomped around, slipping and sliding in the sewage. **Justified anger** stirred within the parents' hearts when they saw their son's **actions—his negative behavior—his sin** that put **him** in danger. They **lovingly** confronted **him,** patiently explain the **serious dangers of disease,** with **hopes he would choose to believe them, take their warning seriously, repent and obey!** They both also **hoped that he would not choose to be an unwise repeat-offender, requiring a reinforcement of the lesson by way of a paddling!**

Likewise, God confronts His children, makes loving appeals, issues protective love-rules, and warns of Satan's deceptive lies and traps, with hopes they will choose to obey—for their own sakes! His patience is "long-suffering", as II Peter 3:9 says. **We need to understand that God's type of anger is capable of separating the sin from the sinner. His anger is holy. It is "righteous indignation"—"righteous anger"— well blended with His "righteous love", offering "righteous solutions".** As we Christians have seen in His Word, with Christ living in our hearts, He wants us to do likewise. With the mind of Christ, we are without excuse to have patience and compassion in our hearts for our Christian brothers and sisters as well as our enemies. If someone does anything to cause anger to rise in our hearts, may we all take seriously the need to slam on our spiritual brakes and **ask the Lord to transform the anger into righteous indignation and enable us to see, hear, understand and love the person as He does, apart from their sinful behavior!**

As Christian soldiers, we are to walk boldly and sacrificially in Christ's love with a sincere desire to please our Commanding Officer: *"Therefore be imitators of God as dear children. And walk in love, as Christ also has loved us and given Himself for us, an offering and a sacrifice to God for a sweet-smelling aroma. But fornication and all uncleanness or covetousness, let it not even be named among you, as is fitting for saints; neither filthiness, nor foolish talking, nor coarse jesting, which are not fitting, but rather giving of thanks. For this you know, that no fornicator, unclean person, nor covetous man, who is an idolater, has any inheritance in the kingdom of Christ and God. Let no one deceive you with empty words, for because of these things the wrath of God comes upon the sons of disobedience. Therefore do not be partakers with them. "* (Ephesians 5:1-7)

For a testimony to precious souls, we are to walk as children of light, for Jesus said: *"You are the light of the world; a city that is set on a hill cannot be hidden. Nor do they light a lamp and put it under a basket, but on a lamp-stand, and it gives light to all who are in the house. Let your light so shine before men, that they may see your good works and glorify your Father in heaven."* (Matthew 5:14-16) We are also told: *"For you were once darkness, but now you are light in the Lord. Walk as children of light (for the fruit of the Spirit is in all goodness, righteousness, and truth), finding out what is acceptable to the Lord, and have no fellowship with unfruitful works of darkness, but rather expose them. For it is shameful even to speak of those things which are done by them in secret. But all things that are exposed are made manifest by the light, for whatever makes manifest is light. Therefore He says: 'Awake, you who sleep, arise from the dead, and Christ will give you light.'"* (Ephesians 5:8-14)

Of course as Christian soldiers, we must march according to our Commanding Officer's orders—thus, with God's wisdom: *"See then that you walk circumspectly, not as fools but as wise, redeeming the time, because the days are evil. Therefore do not be unwise, but **understand what the will of the Lord is**."* (Ephesians 5:15-17)

How was Paul, who battled from time to time with the "old man" within him, able to refrain from "grieving the Spirit," refrain from "sinning," and instead, "walk in Christ's love" as a "child of light" and "understand what the will of the Lord was"? How was Paul, in spite of that battle within him, able to "keep his uniform clean" most of the time? We can, of course, find his God-given tools in the Word of Almighty God, the Living Word, and Jesus on whom the iniquity of us all was laid! As Romans 15:4 says: ***"For whatever things were written before were written for our learning, that we through the patience and comfort of the Scriptures might have hope."*** Let us go search out those tools that He has provided for us in His Word—in both the Old and New Testaments for us and generations to follow!

We must become well acquainted with our God-given tools—our weapons of war—written for our learning: *"Now this is the commandment, and these are the statutes and judgments which the LORD your God has commanded to teach you, that you may observe them in the land which you are crossing over to possess, that you may **fear the Lord your God** to **keep all His statues and His commandments which I commanded you, you and your son and your grandson, all the days of your life**, and that your days may be prolonged. Therefore hear, O Israel, and **be careful to observe it, that it may be well with you**, and that you may multiply greatly as the LORD God of your fathers promised you—a land flowing with milk and honey. Hear, O Israel: the LORD our God, the LORD is one! **You shall love the LORD your God with all your heart, with all your soul, and with all your strength. And these words which I command you today shall be in your heart. You shall teach them diligently to your children, and shall talk of them when you sit in your house, when you walk by the way, when you lie down, and when you rise up.** You shall bind them as a sign on your hand and they shall be as frontlets between your eyes. You shall write them on the doorposts and on your gates."* (Deuteronomy 6:1-9)

That scripture from the Old Testament is known as, **"The Greatest Commandment."** Surely we can see God's tools inside these passages in Deuteronomy! These tools are essential for all Christians in order to walk victoriously, conquering all negative-learned behavior patterns, having a Christ-like testimony on His pathways ahead! As we examine the teachings of our Lord, note that they are intended not only for the individual, but for the sake of that person's future generations as well! As we have clearly seen in the lives of counselees, we can understand God's wisdom in the matter, for they were sorely affected by the iniquities of their ancestors! Therefore, it is critical that after a once-bound counselee has reclaimed ground that Satan once held, he must go forth with a deep desire to gain understanding of God's instructions of truth and **possess the land on which God wants him to walk—rather than letting the enemy have it!** He should have a heart like David who said in Psalm 25:4-5: ***"Show me Your ways, O LORD; teach me Your paths. Lead me in Your truth and teach me, for You are the God of my salvation; on You I wait all the day."***

If he is not sincere in his respect for the Lord and his desire to be still and wait for the Lord to speak to his heart and obey Him, he leaves the door of invitation open for Satan to begin claiming <u>new</u> ground in his life! Like all other Christians, he should willingly choose to be properly equipped with several essential spiritual tools.

This heart-stirring old hymn so beautifully expresses the sincere prayer which should be that of every Christian soldier:

Open My Eyes, That I May See

Open my eyes that I may see, glimpses of truth Thou hast for me;
Place in my hands the wonderful key that shall unclasp, and set me free.
Silently now I wait for Thee, ready my God, Thy will to see;
Open my eyes illumine me, Spirit divine!

Open my ears, that I may hear voices of truth Thou sendest clear;
And while the wave-notes fall on my ear, everything false will disappear.
Silently now I wait for Thee, ready my God, Thy will to see;
Open my ears illumine me, Spirit divine!

Open my mouth, and let me bear gladly the warm truth everywhere;
Open my heart, and let me prepare love with Thy children thus to share.
Silently now I wait for Thee, ready my God, Thy will to see;
Open my heart, illumine me, Spirit divine!

(Page 251; The Broadman Hymnal; The Broadman Press, Nashville, Tennessee; Copyright–1940)

A.   TOOL #1: HUMILITY WITH REVERENTIAL FEAR OF THE LORD GOD

You recall reading in the first chapter of this book, "Legal Rights Tools of God, Satan, and Christians," that our most powerful tool is to know and reverentially fear our sovereign God, Jehovah, Jesus Christ—the Father, the Son, and Holy Spirit! **He is the only "power tool" who can mercifully give us total victory over the enemy, the enemy we are not to fear!** God's Word clearly urges every soul to **fear the Lord your God!**

> ***"The fear of the Lord is the beginning of wisdom**, and the knowledge of the Holy One is understanding."* (Proverbs 9:10)

304

You may have read in "Liberating the Bruised," chapter five, how I used God's wonderful lesson from His Word about His young King Josiah to teach us about the subject of "Restoring True Worship." His father, King Amon who reigned before him had done great evil in the sight of the Lord! He neither feared the Lord, nor was he humble before Him. In the high places, Satan reigned, and King Amon and a great many of his people made sacrifices to Satan and worshiped idols—and the Temple of the Lord was sorely in disrepair. King Amon was assassinated by his own people. Then his little eight-year-old son became king. During his reign, his behavior proved to be the opposite of his father. For during his reign, Hilkiah, the high priest, found the book of the law in the house of the Lord, and told Shaphan, the scribe, about it. Shaphan read it to King Josiah. Josiah came under conviction and repented. His fear of the Lord showed in his repentance and his humility. We know that Josiah tore down the things of Satan in the high places and he restored God's Temple. Indeed, what an inspiring story of a king who chose to love, honor, and obey the Lord! ***"And he did what was right in the sight of the Lord, and walked in the ways of his father David; he did not turn aside to the right hand or to the left."*** (II Chronicles 34:2) Because of his choosing to repent and willingly do what was right in the sight of the Lord, he heard his merciful, forgiving God speak these comforting words: ***"'Because your heart was tender, and you humbled yourself before God when you heard His words against this place and against its inhabitants, and you humbled yourself before Me and tore your clothes and wept before Me, I also have heard you,' says the Lord."*** (II Chronicles 34:27)

As Christian soldiers, we should take care not to treat our Commanding Officer, our reigning King irreverently—flippantly acting as if He is just a sidekick, down on our level! It has been heartbreaking to see some Christians treat Him this way! Instead, we should always keep in mind that we should humble ourselves before Him and remember that we are privileged to communicate with Him only because we have been made righteous through His Son Jesus! Perhaps we can see this in proper perspective as we think of how a little child who is curled up in his Godly father's lap perceives his father's love and tenderness while at the same time feels his awesome strength, his protection and complete control over him. This child is well aware of the fact that his father will never leave or forsake him. While this child feels very safe and secure, if he is wise he will understand with a deep, unwavering trust that he is not to be the one issuing orders to his Papa, but rather, the one following Papa's rules! This child fully understands he has no goodly reason not to love, trust, respect, honor, listen to and obey his loving father without question, at all times.

Such a wise child declares: *"...You have been a shelter for me, a strong tower from the enemy. I will abide in Your tabernacle forever; **I will trust** in the shelter of Your wings. Selah For You, O God have heard my vows; You have given me the heritage of those who **fear Your name**."* (Psalm 61:3-5)

Such a child yearns to learn and says: *"**Teach me Your way O LORD; I will walk in Your truth; unite my heart to fear Your name.** I will praise You, O Lord my God, with all my heart, and I will glorify Your name forevermore. For great is Your mercy toward me. And You have delivered my soul from the depth of Sheol."* (Psalm 86:11-13)

*"Let us hear the **conclusion** of the whole matter: **Fear God and keep His commandments for this is man's all. For God will bring every work into judgment, including every secret thing, whether good or evil."*** (Ecclesiastes 12:13-14)

Most surely, coupled with our fear of the Lord should always be humility, for the Lord says: ***"A man's pride will bring him low,** but **the humble in spirit will retain honor**."*** (Proverbs 29:23)

*"Therefore **humble yourselves under the mighty hand of God**, that He may exalt you in due time, casting all your care upon Him for He cares for you. **Be sober, be vigilant; because your adversary the devil walks about like a roaring lion, seeking whom he may devour.**"* (I Peter 5:6-8)

HUMBLY FEAR THE LORD—BUT NOT SATAN

Now we should all wisely view the meaning of "fear" in proper perspective. When one fears someone or something that means that he perceives that person or thing as something intimidating, more powerful than he. He perceives that this person or thing has a capability of bringing either good or bad—or both—upon him. Thus, it is good for every lost person to fear God and come to the understanding that God loves him and desires for him to trust Him and have a relationship with Him. But, coupled with that truth it is the need for the lost person to understand that if he chooses to rebel and reject God, that he is taking the responsibility upon his own self to sever the relationship himself, not God. For God's heart's desire is that all men be saved. The fact that God our Savior desires that all would choose to accept Him and be saved is reflected below in Timothy's words—to encourage lost souls to be saved and that saved souls would live Godly lives so that others can see Jesus in us!

> *"Therefore I exhort first of all that supplications, prayers, intercessions, and giving of thanks be made for all men, for kings and all who are in authority, **that we may lead a quiet and peaceable life in all godliness and reverence**. For this is good and acceptable in the sight of **God our Savior, who desires all men to be saved and to come to the knowledge of the truth, for there is one God and one Mediator between God and man, the Man Christ Jesus, who gave Himself a ransom for all, to be testified in due time.**"* (I Timothy 2:1-6)

The truth that God desires for all to be saved is also expressed when Peter states that there would be scoffers, people who would very unwisely choose neither to fear God, nor to accept Jesus as their Savior, which we read about in II Peter 3:9-18:

> *"The Lord is not slack concerning His promise, as some count slackness, but is **longsuffering toward us, not willing that any should perish but that all should come to repentance**. But the day of the Lord will come as a thief in the night, in which the heavens will pass away with a great noise, and the elements will melt with*

fervent heat; both the earth and the works that are in it will be burned up. Therefore, since all these things will be dissolved, what manner of persons ought you to be in holy conduct and godliness, looking for and hastening the coming of the day of God, because of which the heavens will be dissolved, being on fire, and the elements will melt with fervent heat? Nevertheless we, according to His promise, look for new heavens and a new earth in which righteousness dwells. Therefore, beloved, looking forward to these things, be diligent to be found by Him in peace, without spot and blameless; and consider that the longsuffering of our Lord is salvation—also our beloved brother Paul, according to the wisdom given to him, has written to you, as also in all his epistles, speaking in them of these things, in which are some things hard to understand, which untaught and unstable people twist to their own destruction, as they do also the rest of the Scriptures. You therefore, beloved, since you know this beforehand, beware lest you also fall from your own steadfastness, being led away with the error of the wicked; but grow in the grace and knowledge of our Lord and Savior Jesus Christ. To Him be the glory both now and forever. Amen."

B.   TOOL #2: TRUST THE LORD, FEAR NOT PEOPLE, THINGS, OR CIRCUMSTANCES

As Christians, while we are to fear God, we are not to retain fear when it strikes our hearts pertaining to Satan his demonic crew, or other people, things, and circumstances. When something "bad" suddenly happens, causing fearful thoughts and racing pulses, that is not a sin. It becomes sin if we "entertain" the negative, sinful thoughts connected to it! When fear strikes our hearts for whatever the reasons, the key to not giving way to considering Satan's suggestions that we worry, doubt and fear, is to immediately stop, be still and concentrate on listening to the Lord's voice in our hearts, and rebuke the enemy! *"Trust in the Lord with all your heart, and lean not on your own understanding; in all your ways acknowledge Him, and He shall direct your paths."* (Proverbs 3:5-6)

We should immediately trust that the Lord will give us wisdom, courage and strength to overcome and deal with whatever we're facing. When we have done this, and have resisted entertaining the Devil's suggestions, he will flee from us, as we're promised in God's Word: *"Therefore **submit to God. Resist the devil and he will flee from you.** Draw near to God and He will draw near to you...."* (James 4:7-8a) The Devil has to flee because God said so—unless we have begun walking in a sinful lifestyle! Upon resisting temptation to entertain Satan's suggestions for us to worry, doubt and fear, we should continue to stay engaged in conversation with the Lord, while thanking Him that He will give us wisdom, courage, and strength to get through whatever has happened! As Christians, we should establish a good, new habit of this in such a way that when worry, doubt, and fear strikes our hearts, it just becomes automatic to obey God's suggestion that we apply these truths:

"Behold, God is my salvation; **I will trust, and not be afraid**; *for the LORD, even the LORD, is my strength and my song; He also is become my salvation."* (Isaiah 12:2)

"In God have I put my trust; **I will not be afraid what man can do unto me**.*"* (Psalm 56:11)

"Do not be afraid of sudden terror, nor of trouble from the wicked when it comes; *for* **the LORD will be your confidence**, *and* **will keep your foot from being caught**.*"* (Proverbs 3:25-26)

This last verse means that when we choose to fear not and stand strong in Christ against temptation, the enemy cannot cause us to stumble and soil our clothes—literally, our testimony for Christ! Most surely each of us can declare: **"I can do all things through Christ, who strengthens me."** (Philippians 4:13)

Believing and acting on these truths enables us to overcome negative-learned behavior patterns and establish new, Christ-like behavior patterns! With humble Christians having been well equipped with a reverential fear of God, trust in the Lord Jesus as their Savior, and confidence that they can resist the enemy and walk in victory, we move forward to the next power tool that was included in "The Greatest Commandment"—"love" for the Lord—and all people!

C.   TOOL #3: LOVE THE LORD WITH ALL YOUR HEART, SOUL, MIND, AND STRENGTH

When trials and tribulations come, we discover how much we really love the Lord. Each of us is told: **"And you shall love the LORD your God with all your heart, with all your soul, with all your mind, and with all your strength. This is the first commandment."** (Mark 12:30) Let us read what our brother Peter did when he was facing a fearful situation, and try to imagine ourselves in his sandals! May each of us answer honestly—"to thine own self be true"—as we answer the question, "Would I have done the same or differently?"

After the Lord had risen from the dead, we find Him questioning Peter: *"...When they had eaten breakfast, Jesus said to Simon Peter, 'Simon, son of Jonah, **do you love Me more than these?**' He said to Him, 'Yes, Lord; You know that I love You.' He said to him. 'Feed My lambs.' He said to him again a second time, 'Simon, son of Jonah, **do you love Me?**' He said to Him, 'Yes, Lord; You know that I love You.' He said to him, 'Tend My sheep.' He said to him the third time, 'Simon, son of Jonah, **do you Love Me?**' Peter was grieved because He said to him the third time, 'Do you love Me?' And he said to Him, 'Lord, You know all things; You know that I love You." Jesus said to him, 'Feed My sheep. Most assuredly, I say to you, when you were younger, you girded yourself and walked where you wished; but when you are old, you will stretch out your hands, and another* *will gird you and carry you where you do not wish.' This He spoke, signifying by what death he [Peter] would glorify God. And when He had spoken this, He said to him, 'Follow Me.'"* (John 21:15-19)

When we read of Jesus' questioning Peter, was He not causing Peter to take time to examine his own heart to learn how much he really loved the Lord? For Jesus was causing Peter to take inventory of his own heart—look inward to determine the measure of his love for Jesus. He was also causing Peter to **"count the cost"** of surrendering totally to walk in God's will. Jesus not only asked Peter **(1)** if he was willing to resist temptation and give up some of the pleasures of life if called upon to do so, but He also asked **(2)** if his love was so great that he was willing to make sacrifices, endure difficult times. He questioned Peter further by asking **(3)** if he was even willing to suffer persecution and die in his service for Him if it came to that. Peter's life would reveal if he really loved Him enough to willingly walk on difficult, rocky and steep pathways—with much pain and suffering along the way. Peter's measure of love for Jesus would be recorded in God's Word as a testimony for future Christians.

We've read of Jesus' voicing to His disciples His impending crucifixion and that all of them would stumble—would scatter. Upon His sharing that, Peter adamantly declared that while the other disciples may stumble and scatter when the going got tough, he most surely would not! But Jesus shared more details with Peter, saying, *"Assuredly, I say to you that today, even this night, before the rooster crows twice, you will deny Me three times."* (Mark 14:30) We read that Peter was quite upset as he continued to insist that he would not stumble and deny being His disciple, *"But he spoke more vehemently, 'If I have to die with You, I will not deny You!'"* (Mark 14:31) As you know, when the going got tough, Peter would indeed hide and would deny Him—he even cursed as he angrily declared that he was not a part of Jesus' ministry, which is recorded in Mark 14:66-72. We read that Peter then heard the cock crow, remembered what the Lord had predicted, and wept bitterly. After Jesus' crucifixion and resurrection, out of Peter's deep love for the Lord, he persistently battled and defeated that old man within him and unashamedly and boldly proclaimed the Gospel of Jesus Christ until the very day that he, too, was crucified on a cross.

While we may not be crucified for willingly walking in obedience to Christ, it would be wise for all of us to pause and take inventory of our hearts by honestly answering these questions from Jesus: "Do you love Me? If so, how great is the measure of your love for Me? Is your testimony of Me to all others on your pathway important to you? Do you truly love Me with all your heart, soul, mind and strength?   Are you willing to listen to My instructions and make sacrifices if I ask you to do so? Are you willing to risk persecution, even to the laying down of your life for My cause—for the Gospel, so that others may come to know Me—even as Peter and Paul did?"

When a person has repented and accepted Jesus Christ as his personal Savior—and after a Christian has been rescued from Satan's captivity embraces the awesome mercy of God—out of enormous gratitude it would seem automatic to fall deeply in love with Jesus, would it not? Tears of eternal gratitude and joy should flood his soul! For, surely, when a Christian has an awesome, reverential fear of and respect for Almighty God, Jehovah and he comprehends the sacrifice Jesus Christ made for him on Calvary's hill—an enormous love for Him should permeate his heart!

D. TOOL #4: LOVE OTHERS LIKE JESUS LOVES THEM—AND US

The Lord gave us a new commandment to love one another like He loves us.

> *"A new commandment I give to you, that you **love one another; as I have loved you**, that you also love one another. **By this all will know that you are My disciples, if you have love for one another."*** (John 13:34-35)

How can Christians love others with the same compassion with which He loves all of us? What hinders Christians from loving others the way He loves? How can Christians refrain from being respecters of persons? Part of the problem with many Christians seems to be **that of failing to take this new commandment seriously enough**. As Ecclesiastes 3:4 says, there is, *"...a time to weep, and a time to laugh...!"* **Many neglect to take seriously the lost state of souls**—that they will go to hell without Christ. **Many neglect to take seriously enough the condition of some Christians who are held in Satan's stronghold. Many neglect to ask the Lord to enable to allow them to see people with His eyes! Many neglect to ask Him to enable them to hear people with His ears. Many neglect to ask Him to enable them to understand people and love them with His heart...use them to fulfill His will.** Why? I wonder how many Christians are guilty of looking the other way—in a direction where the subject matter is less serious, "easier on one's eyes" and "more pleasant to one's ears"?

I'm certain you agree that **the Devil himself is extremely serious about his mission of trying to get people to turn away from God and follow his leading, and he's serious about his endeavor to sidetrack Christians from God's will!** To the other extreme, without doubt our Lord Jesus is extremely serious about souls getting saved and souls being set free from Satan's captivity! **Questions come: "Are we as serious about our mission as Satan is about his? Are we really as serious about our mission as Jesus is?"** We're told that Jesus was not a handsome man as the world would deem handsome—so it was God's love radiating through Him coupled with His genuineness that people recognized as "sincere care, concern for them" which drew people to Him. Let us take a moment to look in God's Word describing our Messiah to come, our Lord Jesus and that serious part of Him:

> *"...He has no form or comeliness; and when we see Him, there is no beauty that we should desire Him. He is despised and rejected by men, a **Man of sorrows and acquainted with grief...surely He has borne our grief's and carried our sorrows...."*** (Isaiah 53:2b, 3a, 4a)

310

We find Jesus with a grieved heart over His people—precious souls—who have chosen to listen to and believe the Devil's lies instead of accepting Jesus as their Messiah, their Savior and Lord as we read: *"O Jerusalem, Jerusalem, the one who kills the prophets and stones those who are sent to her! How often I wanted to gather your children together, as a hen gathers her brood under her wings, but you were not willing."* (Luke 13:34) And again, we read of the depth of His sorrow—his seriousness: ***"Now as He drew near, He saw the city and wept over it."*** (Luke 19:41)

Oh that we, too, would take our mission on earth as compassionately and seriously as our Savior does. Oh that our sincere prayer would be: "Precious Lord, please show me if there is any sin in my life for which I need to repent so that Your will in my life is not hindered. Lord Jesus, I choose not to be afraid and instead, trust that You will enable me to share Your truths and love others with Your heart, for their sakes. And, moment by moment, I desire to submit to Your will and resist temptation from the enemy. And I thank You that through Your power and authority, he will flee. Please enable me to hear Your instructions clearly and take Your mission as compassionately and seriously as You do! Please enable me to see people with Your eyes, hear them with Your ears, and understand and love them with Your heart! I thank You, Lord, for doing this for the sake of souls! Amen."

> ***"There is no fear in love; but perfect love casts out fear, because fear involves torment. But he who fears has not been made perfect in love. We love Him because He first loved us."*** (I John 4:18-19)

What does **"he who fears has not been made perfect in love"** mean? It has a twofold meaning. If a person is not saved, he has not been made "complete" through the Lord Jesus, thus he cannot conquer his fears. Secondly, if a Christian finds that he cannot conquer his fears, he is either being held in Satan's stronghold and/or he has not "matured" in the Lord.

What does God say about our declaring that we love Him, while we have hatred in our heart for someone? ***"If someone says, 'I love God,' and hates his brother, he is a liar; for he who does not love his brother whom he has seen, how can he love God whom he has not seen? And this commandment we have from Him: that he who loves God must love his brother also."*** (I John 4:20-21) It is clear to see that this person either needs salvation or if he is a Christian, he needs to seek God's forgiveness and right his heart with the Lord.

When one hates another person—perhaps out of jealousy or due to the person causing emotional and/or physical pain to them, that hatred is connected to unforgiveness. And, the Lord says of those who hate and do not forgive others: ***"....whenever you stand praying, if you have anything against anyone, forgive him, that your Father in heaven may also forgive you your trespasses. But if you do not forgive, neither will your Father in heaven forgive your trespasses."*** (Mark 11:25-26) Until this person rights his heart with the Lord and forgives whomever he has ought against, by his sinful disobedience sweet communication with the Lord is broken. For God's Word says: ***"If I regard iniquity in my heart, the Lord will not hear me."*** (Psalm 66:18) You can be

311

sure the Lord can "hear" the person, but He will not carry on a conversation with him concerning other subject matters! For this soul's sake, the Lord withdraws sweet conversation from him. It is certain that the Lord will also continue to talk to this person, convicting his heart and sometimes, as a loving Father, even spanking him concerning his stubborn sins! Sweet communion will return only when the person seeks God's forgiveness and forgives the one who brought hurt to him.

Not only are we to love people unconditionally like Jesus loves them, we are to take care not to think them less important than ourselves! For we read that truth in God's Word:

> ***"Let nothing be done through selfish ambition or conceit, but in lowliness of mind let each esteems others better than himself. Let each of you look out not only for his own interest, but also for the interests of others. Let this mind be in you which was also in Christ Jesus."*** (Philippians 2:3-5)

Someone once expressed that we will experience the true JOY of Jesus in our hearts if we fulfill our Lord's instructions in this matter. We will have things in right order if we do not fail to put: **"Jesus first, yourselves last, and others in between!"**

Jesus Others Yourself = JOY!

Oh, that all Christians would live their lives unselfishly, as our Lord did and as so many of His servants have done. Over the years, we've observed many Christians who, while they are willing to make many sacrifices to walk in God's will for their precious lives, they put limitations on a few things that they count as personal pleasures.

> God says, *"This know also, that **in the last days** perilous times shall come. For **men [women] shall be lovers of their own selves**, covetous, boasters, proud, blasphemers, disobedient to parents, unthankful, unholy, without natural affection, truce breakers, false accusers, incontinent, fierce, despisers of those that are good, traitors, heady, high minded, **lovers of pleasures more than lovers of God**; having a form of godliness, but denying the power thereof: from such turn away."* (II Timothy 3:1-5)

One doesn't have to look far to see that we are surely in the midst of a world that displays people who are void of "natural affections"—lovers of themselves! This is a beautiful old hymn that expresses how Christians should pray concerning this and how we should love others with the nature of God:

OTHERS

1.   Lord, help me live from day to day, in such a self-forgetful way
         That even when I kneel to pray my prayer shall be for—Others.

2.   Help me in all the work I do to ever be sincere and true,
         And know that all I'd do for You, must needs be done for—Others.

3.   Let "Self" be crucified and slain and buried deep:
         And all in vain may efforts be to rise again, unless to live for—Others.

4.   And when my work on earth is done, and my new work in heaven's begun,
         May I forget the crown I've won, while thinking still of—Others.

Chorus: Others, Lord, yes, others, let this my motto be,
              Help me to live for others, that I may live like Thee.

(Page 77; The Broadman Hymnal; The Broadman Press, Nashville, Tennessee; Copyright–1940)

LOVE ONE ANOTHER AND FORGIVE ENEMIES

Oh, that Christians would not be selfish with the Gospel and share as enthusiastically as Stephen did as God directed his heart. Oh, that Christians would also readily forgive people like Stephen did! For as he shared the Gospel with people who were "stiff-necked and uncircumcised in heart and ears," we read their actions: ***"...they stoned Stephen as he was calling on God and saying, 'Lord Jesus, receive my spirit.' Then he knelt down and cried out with a loud voice, 'Lord, do not charge them with this sin.' And when he had said this, he fell asleep."*** At this time, Paul (then called Saul) was keeping the coats of those who were stoning him. What a testimony Stephen was in the eyes of Paul! What an instrument to help bring Paul under conviction of his lost state—his need for the Messiah, the Lord Jesus!

What a wonderful illustration Stephen was of what Jesus meant when He said: *"You have heard that it was said, 'You shall love your neighbor and hate your enemy.' But **I say to you, love your enemies, bless those who curse you, do good to those who hate you, and pray for those who spitefully use you and persecute you,** that you may be sons of your Father in heaven; for He makes His sun rise on the evil and on the good, and sends rain on the just and on the unjust. **For if you love those who love you, what reward have you?** Do not even the tax collectors do the same? **And if you greet your brethren only, what do you do more than others? Therefore you shall be perfect [mature in the Lord], just as your Father in heaven is perfect."* (Matthew 5:43-48)

313

E. TOOL #5: HAVE AN ATTITUDE OF GRATITUDE AT ALL TIMES

Prayerfully read I Thessalonians 5:17-19: *"Pray without ceasing, **in** everything give **thanks;** for this is the will of God in Christ Jesus for you. Do not quench the Spirit."* Three points here are: **(1)** we are to stay tuned in constantly with our Lord, listening to His voice in our hearts. And, **(2)** if we truly love and trust the Lord with all our hearts, then we will have a large measure of thankfulness at all times! With hearts of gratitude, we will trust Him to give us strength and wisdom to get us through any trials and tribulations that may come our way. He is, indeed, trustworthy, therefore, we can trust Him emphatically. Even though we are experiencing a very unpleasant time, if we are in tune with Him "The Comforter" will comfort us, thus we will have a goodly measure of thankfulness. However, **(3)** if we yield to worry, doubt and fear, we "quench the Spirit!" Colossians 3:15 says: *"And let the **peace** of God **rule** in your hearts, to which also you were called in one body; and **be** **thankful**."*

Surely, we should take care not to allow the enemy to influence us in such a way that we fail to be grateful! We should faithfully *"...give thanks to the LORD! Call upon His name; make known His deeds among the peoples!"* (Psalm 105:1) Oh, *"Thanks be to God for His indescribable gift!"*— Jesus! (II Corinthians 9:15) Indeed, *"...thanks be to God, who gives us the victory through our Lord Jesus Christ!"* (I Corinthians 15:57)

F. TOOL #6: WILLINGLY SUBMIT TO GOD AND RESIST THE ENEMY

Persons who lack proper measures in their hearts of humility, reverential fear, gratitude, trust and love toward the Lord make themselves vulnerable to the deceitful lies and snares of the enemy! But for those who trust like a little child in his father's lap, they can walk in victory! When Christians submit to God, draw near to Him in a listening spirit, then they can hear the voice of God speaking truth to their hearts, then it is left up to them to choose to obey Him—partly or completely. Every Christian should pose these questions to himself: **"Do I put limits on my willingness to listen to and obey the Lord in all things? When the road ahead appears rough with unpleasantries on either side, do I come to a screeching halt, hold my willingness in reserve, and take a detour?"**

It's crucial for all Christians to keep in mind that if they repeatedly choose to walk in the flesh in disobedience—while they will still go to heaven when they die—during their stay on earth, they will rob themselves of the peace and joy that they would have if they choose to walk in God's plan instead of their own. By choosing not to be still and listen to God's instructions in their hearts before acting on things, they will rob themselves of sweet fellowship with the Lord until they repent.

We should not ignore the fact that Christians can regularly attend church and be involved in many "good" activities in the name of Christ, but it doesn't necessarily mean that they are in God's will! Christians can do many "good" things but if they are neglecting to do the "good" things that God has told them to do, they are being disobedient—rebellious! **Doing good things out of the will of**

God is sin! Example: the Lord has asked you to take a moment from your busy schedule to call and check on someone who is quite unpleasant to converse with. Instead you sidestep and call a dear friend who has had surgery to check on him. Even though calling your friend was not a "bad" deed, it was a sin because it was not **what** God asked you to do, nor **when** He asked you to do it! God knew it was the **best time** for you make that unpleasant phone call, to bless that other person! It wasn't about "self".

Likewise, and grievously so, there have been many "good things done out of the will of God" amongst congregations in churches. You may have heard, as we have over many years, very active churchgoing Christians—both in leadership and non-leadership roles—all adamantly declaring— from the two sides—that they've heard from God as to things that should or should not be done in the church. When the matters are put to the vote, disunity bursts forth—sadly enough even to verbal wars! Oh what grievous examples the children—the next generation—observe! Our hearts have broken upon hearing Christians on one side of the divided house adamantly declare about an issue that they know they've received "a word from God," while those on the other side declare hearing "a quite different word from God." In this divided house, no unity will be found—no peace. How grievous it must be to God's heart that His people have not all, in unity, humbled themselves with clean hearts, and sought His wisdom. All too many times, such has ended in the divided house by putting the issue to a vote—human reasoning kicks in, majority rules. It would have been wise not to do anything until all were in unity. Does this not remind you of today's political arena?

Chapter Thirteen
TRAVELING LIFE'S HIGHWAYS AND BYWAYS

Upon viewing the divisions amongst Christianity and the wavering willingness of some Christians to obey and walk in God's will with gladness in their hearts, these questions come: Are some Christians like spoiled children who take their blessings for granted and grumble when they believe they're short on blessings? Do they not love the Lord enough to be willing to walk with Him when the road gets rough? Do they not have an attitude of gratitude?

A. GRUMBLING OR GRATEFUL WHILE TRAVELING LIFE'S HIGHWAYS?

Our dear example, **Brother Paul** comes to mind, who out of his gratitude to the Lord, willingly served Him faithfully, in good and bad times—throughout the ups and downs of his travels—to his death. For he said: *"...I have learned in whatever state I am, to be content: I know how to be abased, and I know how to abound. Everywhere and in all things I have learned both to be full and to be hungry, both to abound and to suffer need. I can do all things through Christ who strengthens me."* (Philippians 4:11-13) Likewise, as new creations in Jesus Christ, we should take care to resist temptation to grumble and be grateful for all blessings as we travel life's highways. Paul tells us about the **"Character of the New Man"** in Colossians 3:12-17, which as you will see, includes, along with **the love of Christ living in us—a thankful heart**: *"...as the elect of God, holy and beloved, put on tender mercies, kindness, humility, meekness, longsuffering; bearing with one another, and forgiving one another, if anyone has a complaint against another, even as Christ forgave you, so you also must do, but above all these things **put on love** which is the bond of perfection. And **let the peace of God rule in your hearts**, to which also you were called into one body; and **be thankful**. Let the word of Christ dwell in you richly in all wisdom, teaching and admonishing one another in psalms and hymns and spiritual songs, singing with grace in your hearts to the Lord. And whatever you do in word or deed, do all in the name of the Lord Jesus, giving thanks to God the Father through Him."* When one finds himself thinking "ungrateful thoughts," he should "slam on his spiritual brakes" and start counting his blessings instead of his troubles!

LUXURY CARS AND FREEWAYS

Often as I have preached, I've explained that after people get saved, it certainly does not mean that life will be like God putting them in luxury cars on freeways with no bumps! Life is not bump-free for anyone—lost or saved! Because our heavenly Father says that *"...He makes His sun rise on the evil and on the good, and sends rain on the just and on the unjust,"* it is very critical that we remember and teach precious counselees who have been set free that **while we**

317

Christians are not of the world we are still in the world, and we are traveling steep roads and winding highways with bumps until we move into heaven! We should encourage them to know that through Christ they can do all things, and that they need to continue trusting even if they can't see over the next very steep hill!

We should teach them that not only are Christians blessed to have the Word of God in writing, but we have the Holy Spirit—Jesus, the Living Word living in our hearts—our personal built-in GPS! We can all clearly hear the voice of the Lord within us, directing our lives! Therefore, it's crucial for us to stay tuned in 24/7 to our GPS! Of course, one thing that's wonderfully different from a GPS is the fact that we can all be assured that God will not tell us to turn the wrong way as He faithfully navigates our way upon His paths of righteousness! If we aren't paying attention and get off on the wrong road, He will mercifully direct us back onto His highway! It is also important for us to recognize that if the pathway leads to a detour which we have no control over, we should not panic but rather trust that He's still with us! Perhaps He will teach us some necessary things while we're on the back roads—or even long after our journey is done! We may never know the purpose for which the Lord allowed us to travel different roads—perhaps using us without our knowledge for a testimony to the other travelers on that road. When He doesn't reveal His purposes—we should just leave it with Him, stay tuned in and travel on.

We find Jesus praying for his disciples—His "followers" through whom He trusts to spread the Gospel—and expressing His desire for them to have His joy fulfilled in them and states that He has given them God's Word! This prayer applies to us, His followers today! His prayer also clearly reflects that He has not placed any of us in luxury cars on freeways with no bumps—and no detours. We find Jesus expressing His desire that we all be kept from the evil one—have wisdom to recognize when he is tempting us! While our salvation is permanently in tact, safe from the enemy, our Lord knows that we are all vulnerable to temptation. He knows that Satan makes a practice of observing everyone's track record to learn their strengths and weaknesses with hope of gaining and claiming ground in our lives. Satan, indeed, knows "where everyone runs—where everyone travels!" Therefore, he knows quite well when, where, and how to more effectively use his temptation tactics! We see evidence of all these truths in Jesus' prayer to the heavenly Father when He prayed for His disciples and future Christians as read John 17:13-19; 20-21:

> *"...Now I come to You, and these things I speak in the world, that they may have My joy fulfilled in themselves. I have given them Your word; and **the world has hated them because they are not of the world**, just as I am not of the world. **I do not pray that You should take them out of the world, but that You should keep them from the evil one.** They are not of the world, just as I am not of the world. **Sanctify them by Your truth. Your word is truth.** As You sent Me into the world, **I also have sent them into the world**. And for their sakes I sanctify Myself, that they also may be **sanctified by the truth**...I do not pray for these alone, but also for those who will believe in Me through their word; that they all may be one, as You, Father, are in Me, and I in You; that they also may be one in Us, **that the world may believe that You sent Me." We are sent to save those who are lost!***

318

It truly grieves our hearts that every single Christian does not realize how very important he is in his daily walk, and that he is an instrument of the Lord, useful or not, until he steps into heaven! How sad that many do not fully comprehend that as every Christian shares their testimonies as the Lord places people on their pathways, they are God's valuable tools! Therefore, we should teach them that they will surely make the enemy unhappy, but to stand strong against him and not let him rob them of the joy of sharing the good news about Jesus with others! Every new Christian and every counselee who has been blessed with freedom from the enemy should be encouraged in this truth! The choice is left to them whether or not to submit to the Lord, resist the evil one, cause him to flee, then walk in God's will!

Satan is well aware of the fact that all Christians are missionaries on a wide range of mission fields—duty bound to share the Gospel. That's why he is so intense about trying to accomplish his own mission! That's exactly why Jesus warns us to put on—and keep on—the whole armor of Christ. It should motivate every Christian to be even more serious about desiring to please the Lord, knowing that Satan surely isn't shy—while he yet has time—about pridefully going back and forth to the throne of God, tattling on us all about his accomplishments! Our heavenly Father already knows of our wrongdoings, but Satan delights in dashing back and forth, boasting of how God's children listened to and obeyed his leading instead of God's. Oh how patient God is with us! This should drive us all the more to not give Satan reason to tattle!

How awesome to know that we can one day find release in knowing that Satan and his prideful arrogance will be no more. Even though Satan was a creation of God in heaven, he was most surely not a creation of higher value than humans. How tragic that he became so prideful about how beautiful and talented the Lord had made him, that he edified himself as a "god," desiring to reign over God. How tragic that God had to use His authority over him and cast him out of heaven. What a relief it is to know that in the not-too-distant future, he will be cast into the lake of fire, never to tempt God's people again. His pride brought him down, as we read: ***"...Now salvation and strength, and the kingdom of our God, and the power of His Christ have come, for the accuser of our brethren, who accused them before our God day and night, has been cast down."*** (Revelation 12:10) Not only will he and his defeated army be cast down, but as we read in the book of Isaiah, he will be exposed as one who is unworthy for anyone to even spend time remembering that he was once a wise, beautiful, and talented creature! **He will be out of sight, out of mind**, for we read this in Isaiah 14:12-19: *"How you are fallen from heaven, O Lucifer, son of the morning! How you are cut down to the ground, you who weakened the nations! For you said in your heart: 'I will ascend into heaven, I will exalt my throne above the stars of God; I will also sit on the mount of the congregation, on the farthest sides of the north; I will ascend above the heights of the clouds, I will be like the Most High,' yet you shall be brought down to Sheol, to the lowest depths of the pit. Those who see you will gaze at you, and consider you, saying: '**Is this the man** who made the earth tremble, who shook kingdoms, who made the world as a wilderness and destroyed its cities, who did not open the house of his prisoners? All the kings of the nations, all of them, sleep in glory, everyone in his own house; but you are cast out of your grave like an abominable branch, like the garment of those who are slain, thrust through with a sword, who go down to the stones of the pit, like a corpse trodden underfoot."*

Ours is the victory over this wicked enemy! These truths should inspire every Christian all the more to desire to please the Lord in every way! What joy to know that while traveling life's steep roads and winding highways, our Lord can "keep us from that evil one" if we call upon Him! As we obey Him, we can be "kept" from giving the enemy ground in our lives when we obey the Lord's instruction in James 4:7 to: *"Submit yourselves unto the Lord, resist the devil and he will flee!"* It can't be stressed enough that we are responsible for our own actions, moment by moment as we travel life's road all the way to our heavenly home! Until we get there, we should stay on the alert and determine in our hearts not to give Satan any cause to tattle on us! It is critical that we teach newly-freed Christians to watch out for the "tattletale's" traps—pot holes in the road ahead!

HOW TO AVOID POT HOLES OF NEGATIVE-LEARNED BEHAVIOR

After a precious lady we know received freedom through our precious Lord Jesus, she compared her battles with her old negative-learned behavior patterns as hitting deep pot holes in the road. She further shared that as she prayed about it, she was inspired by the Lord to make a list of the types of deep pot holes that could possibly keep appearing in the road ahead. This allowed her to study the list more intently—like memorizing a game plan—to help her more readily recognize the opponent's trap so she could be prepared to slam on her brakes! She enthusiastically listed the pot holes of negative behavior to which she was so prone to hit and go out of control! She listed pot holes such as fear, insecurity, hopelessness, and helplessness. Having received her freedom and purposing in her heart to obey the Lord out of her deeper love, trust and gratitude to Him, she began to recognize a pot hole more quickly and swerve around it in plenty of time. She joyfully came to the realization that as she submitted herself unto the Lord and resisted—or rather swerved to miss the opponent's pot hole—she did, indeed, have full authority over the enemy. How grateful she was to have this privilege of authority in Christ! She more and more consistently obeyed His instruction to act on His truth to *"...submit to God. Resist the devil and he will flee."* Therefore, Satan had no victory and his pot holes disappeared! Much to her delight, she did not lose control of her clay vessel when she trusted in and obeyed her Potter! She grew stronger and began growing to maturity in her trust and faith in the Lord.

This should be a priority lesson in the lives of now-set-free counselees (as well as ministers and counselors personally)! Therefore, it's critical that each of our counselees is made aware that "potholes of negative-learned behavior patterns" will appear from time to time in the road ahead! Like this precious lady, he too can swerve around the pot holes that the opponent digs on his roads! He doesn't have to hit those pot holes fast and hard, thus lose control! We believe strongly that this is one of the most vital things you can teach the counselee they step out in freedom, and will most surely find themselves confronted not only with pot holes of old negative-learned behavior, but also with external temptation that every Christian is faced with until moving to heaven! They need to be made aware that while **the enemy surely cannot read their minds, Satan just knows their track record**, so he is most sure to tempt the person in the areas where the counselee is most vulnerable. He needs to be encouraged to do what all Christians should do—stay tuned into the Lord's voice in his heart 24/7—and do more listening than talking—and be prepared to swerve and miss pot holes or slam on his brakes! Having Jesus in the form of the Holy Spirit living in his heart—His built-in GPS—if he leaves it on, he can miss every pot hole, and resist all temptation! He can be assured that in doing this, the Lord will lead him on roads of righteousness! As a set-free Christian, he can be assured that Jesus will *"...not lead us into temptation but deliver us from the evil one!"* The more consistently he obeys God's instructions, the stronger he will become and the enemy will eventually give up on digging the same kind of pot holes! Of course until his doom's day, the cunning enemy will seek to come up with other ideas with which to lure souls from God's pathway onto his!

WHEN DETERRENT BOXES APPEAR IN THE ROAD

I am reminded of a time, years ago, while I was attending seminary and pastoring First Baptist Church of Chita, Texas, on the weekends, almost five hours away. Rita and our three precious children were traveling to that church, and there was a box on the highway ahead. Seeing that I was headed straight for it, Rita said: "Hon, watch out for that box!" I estimated that I could just drive right over it without a problem. I was wrong! The box hit the oil line and the oil began to rapidly drain out. The engine started sputtering and running rough, and the red light came on, indicating the engine was hot! How grateful we were that just in the nick of time, before the engine could burn up, I was able to pull into a service station where a new oil line was eventually installed, oil was replenished, and we resumed our journey. However, my choice not to avoid the seemingly harmless box was a little costly and time consuming as well! Rita never said, "I told you to watch out for that box!" but you can be assured when we see a box in the road today, we both chuckle while remembering a lesson well learned! By the way, I've not run over another box since then—no matter its size!

Like that seemingly harmless box on that highway, whether persons are strong Christians who were never held in Satan's stronghold or if they are now-set-free Christians who were tightly bound by Satan, all should be aware of Satan's subtle way of throwing deterrent boxes in the highway! With the word "deterrent" meaning something seemingly immaterial that interferes with or delays action or progress, you can imagine how Satan, the cunning one, delights in using such! Most surely, no Christian is exempt from being deceived if he doesn't stay keenly alert as he travels life's highways! We Christians should acknowledge that sometimes, when we least expect it, small deterrent boxes can lie just around the corner, right in the middle of our lane! The Lord is available 24/7 to warn us to slam on our brakes, hear His words of wisdom, and swerve around deterrent boxes—sparing us from troublesome times! It is also good to remember that while traveling life's roads that we may be tempted in areas in which we've never been tempted before. When such temptation comes there are times when we need to simply pull around it—while at other times, we need to take time to pull over to the side of the road, be still and seek the Lord's wisdom and He will direct our pathways from that point!

While I was attending seminary, working, and pastoring the little church every weekend, my body grew very tired at times. Upon remembering His love and mercy upon me, it gave me determination to fulfill His calling upon my life. I kept remembering His mercy in saving my soul when I was age ten. I also kept remembering that He never gave up on me while I was running from His will, His calling on my life to preach the Gospel and share His Word with others. In spite of my bringing shame to His name through my materialism, alcoholism, and rebellious lifestyle, He did not leave or forsake me! When I cried out, repenting, He was right there to forgive and to restore. Though I would surely make mistakes along life's road, I was so secure in His love that I truly desired to please Him. I kept on keeping on, determined to complete my studies and serve Him in His will.

During those nearly five hours every Friday evening from our little duplex near the seminary to the little church—and back again on Sunday night, Rita, our three precious children and I passed the long hours listening to the radio and playing car-games. It was fun to see who could spot and "claim" the most white horses along the way. We sang a lot of songs, hymns, and *"Row, Row, Row Your Boat"*—and *"You Are My Sunshine,"* too! I lay no claim to composing music but during one of our trips, I began singing, making up a song from my heart. Once I completed my song and had sung it a few times, we were all singing it. How grateful I am that He continues to lead me all the way! Since our subject is about trusting the Lord to guide us on the highways and byways of life, I thought I would share the words to my song with you:

Oh, Lord, I Want to Know

Chorus:

Oh, Lord, I want to know,
Where Thou'd have me go,
What Thou'd have me do,
Lord, I'm trusting it all to You.

1. As I travel down this earthly road,
And meet my brother, carrying a heavy load.
Lord, teach me how to understand.
Lord, teach me how, to lend a helping hand!

Repeat Chorus

2. When this old world seems to let me down,
And not a true friend can be found,
Lord, lift me up and help me stand.
Lord, lift me up, in the hollow of Your hand.

Repeat Chorus

By Rev. Joe E. Allbright

How very grateful Rita and I are to have the privilege of knowing and serving our Savior, Jesus Christ! When we left that little country church every Sunday evening after church services, we would all load up the car and head back to our duplex near the seminary. A few miles down the road, I would switch the radio on to our favorite station. One of the programs quite appropriately started by playing the wonderful old Gospel song: *"Turn Your Radio On!"* to which we joined in singing. Some of the words were: *"Come and listen in to a radio station where the mighty hosts of heaven sing, turn your radio on, turn your radio on. If you want to hear the songs of Zion coming from the land of endless spring, get it touch with God, turn your radio on. Turn your radio on and listen to the music in the air. Turn your radio on, heaven's glory share. Turn the lights down low, and listen to the Master's radio. Get in touch with God, turn your radio on."* **This song causes us to remember that as we travel life's roads, we can find encouragement and guidance by constantly leaving our "Master's radio station" on, which is implanted in our hearts!**

That great Christian station always played another Gospel song that was quite fitting for all those miles we traveled! We would all join in, singing, ***"I Don't Regret a Mile I've Traveled For The Lord!"*** It's worth all the miles to see fruits of our labors—precious souls who accepted the Lord Jesus as their Savior—and tormented souls free and happy! Rita and I can say wholeheartedly, that we don't regret a mile we've traveled for our Lord on His highways—even when our clay vessels have grown weary! We thank Him for His faithfulness to give us many rest stops, too, where He refreshes us in His perfect timing!

Most surely we see that our example, Jesus, drew aside to rest and be alone to communicate with the Father. The crowds were "in the roads" pressing on Him, but when He knew the Father wanted Him to pull over to a secluded place; He did not let the pressing crowds intimidate Him into staying on the road! He never took detours from His Father's route or timetable! His departure and arrival time of each trip was in perfect timing! The Lord said that He came to do the Father's will—and He most certainly did not let "deterrent boxes" or "pot holes" in the road be costly to His purpose in life in any way! He consistently stayed in tune with the heavenly Father—drew **still** and **listened** for His Father's instructions! He promptly obeyed and traveled on down the road! We should take care to remember that Jesus was God in the flesh—housed in clay and **He got His orders from His heavenly Father!** Now if He did this—how dare we clay vessels neglect to take time to get our orders from our heavenly Potter—from our Holy GPS! As we mentioned earlier in this book, it's crucial that ministers and counselors stay tuned into God's voice, pertaining to time with family, church and ministry!

B. OUR HEAVENLY FATHER'S ROAD MAP

As we clay vessels travel life's highways and byways of life with our heavenly Potter, we should all take care to study His Word—His road map—so we can stay on the right roads! We should declare, ***"Your word I have hidden in my heart, that I might not sin against You!"*** (Psalm 119:11) We should take seriously the fact that we must keep scriptures in proper balance with one another—in context—so that we don't wander off God's road and get stuck in a swampland. Our hearts have been grieved as we learned of some Christians—including ones in leadership—taking scripture out of context and becoming prideful and arrogant with the Lord. We're sad to say that we've observed some precious, well-meaning Christians getting "cocky" with the Lord—about who they are in Christ. There was a time when the disciples were so excited over casting out demons that even though they were casting them out in Jesus' name, they were revealing that had been tempted and were entertaining prideful thoughts. Let us take a moment to review the lesson that holds two purposes: **(1)** Truth was confirmed that **Jesus was God Almighty in the flesh, holding power and authority over everything**. **(2)** Jesus warned them against **getting so caught up in the ministry of leading people to freedom from the enemy that they were getting cocky, feeling prideful, and beginning to take some of the credit**. Therefore, Jesus had to warn them of this danger, which we read about in Luke 10:17-20:

> *"Then the seventy returned with joy, saying, 'Lord, even the demons are subject to us in Your name.' And He said to them, 'I saw Satan fall like lightening from heaven. Behold, I give you the authority to trample on serpents and scorpions, and over all the power of the enemy, and nothing shall by any means hurt you.* ***Nevertheless do not rejoice in this, that the spirits are subject to you, but rather rejoice that your names are written in heaven.'"***

It is critical that we, too, remember that it is He who does the work through us and for us to humbly remember that it is by His grace that our names are even recorded in heaven! Pride is a dangerous road to travel, for the Lord says: ***"The highway of the upright is to depart from evil; he who keeps his way preserves his soul. Pride goes before destruction and a haughty spirit before a fall.*** *Better to* ***be of an humble spirit*** *with the lowly, than to divide the spoil with the proud.* ***He who heeds the word wisely will find good, and whoever trusts in the LORD, happy is he.''*** (Proverbs 16:17-20)

It's sad to say, when some Christians read God's travel guide—His Word—they are very selective about where they want to go, what they want to do. They choose to travel on the smoothest of roads, avoiding as many bumps as possible! They want the scenic route—no dry and barren lands! They steer away from remembering that our beloved, dedicated missionary Paul suffered horrific pain and rejection until the day he died! How dare any of us think ourselves qualified to be spoiled children, while others endure hardships? Too many are pleased to quote only John 14:14, for it says: ***"If you ask anything in My name I will do it."*** It's needful for them to back up and read God's travel guide more carefully which includes the preceding verse 13, which says: "And whatever you ask in My name, that I will do, **that the Father may be glorified in the Son."** This means that our all-wise Potter will answer "yes" only if He knows that in doing so, it will bring glory to the Lord! We also read in I John 5:14-15: *"Now this is the confidence that we have in Him, that if we ask anything* ***according to His will, He hears us.*** *And if we know that He hears us, whatever we ask, we know that we have the* ***petitions*** *that we have asked of Him."* In other words, if we are offering up petitions to Him that are in His will, we can be assured that He listens to them, and He will answer us with His all-wise, "Yes," "No," or a "Wait a while"!

As His clay vessels, a couple of serious questions come, **"Do we trust our Potter to be the wiser of the two of us and answer according to what's best 'according to His will'? Is He not trustworthy?"** As we've discussed before, every Christian should be willing to humble himself before the Lord and take time to be still and listen to Him. We should keep our spiritual ears open 24/7, eager for our Potter (who so conveniently lives in our hearts in the form of the Holy Spirit) to minister to and teach us. He truly is our Wonderful Counselor, Master Teacher—if we let Him do what He longs to do in our lives. We should frequently draw aside to take time to read and study His travel guide of encouraging words—relax with Him, listen to Him, and enjoy sweet fellowship with Him. He's the best friend we could ever have!

C. UNAVOIDABLE HIGHWAYS OF TRIALS AND TRIBULATIONS

We know that all of the examples written in God's Word are to teach us things that we should and should not do. Most Christians acknowledge that as they live their lives, they should also be setting examples before others—Christ-like examples! While they know they should set Christ-like examples before others, how many stop short of setting Christ-like examples in the midst of trials and tribulations?

We read in I Timothy 4:12b: *"...be an example to the believers in word, in conduct, in love, in spirit, in faith, in purity."* When we Christians feel that our bed of roses has suddenly been transformed into a bed of thorns and we're tempted to get under our pity-me-trees, it's time to review I Peter 2:18-25: *"Servants, be submissive to your masters with all fear, not only to the good and gentle, but also to the harsh. For this is commendable, if because of conscience toward God one endures grief, suffering wrongfully. For what credit is it if, when you are beaten for your faults, you take it patiently? But when you do good and suffer, if you take it patiently, this is commendable before God. For to this you were called, because Christ also suffered for us, leaving us an example, that you should follow His steps: who committed no sin, nor was deceit found in his mouth; who, when He was reviled, did not revile in return; when He suffered, He did not threaten, but committed Himself to Him who judges righteously; who Himself bore our sins in His own body on the tree, that we, having died to sins, might live for righteousness—by whose stripes you were healed. For you were like sheep going astray, but have now returned to the Shepherd and Overseer of your souls."*

We are certainly without excuse as we face the truth that we are to set Christ-like examples to others—and to teach them to do the same. For again, we see "The Golden Rule" in God's Word: *"...whatever you want men to do to you, do also to them, for this is the Law and the Prophets."* (Matthew 7:12) And we should all ask ourselves: **"Am I willing to make great sacrifices that are not at all easy to make if the Lord calls upon me to do so?"** As each of us prayerfully study the following example of Job, our brother of long ago, and imagine our feet in his shoes, may each one of us honestly answer whether or not we would have reacted as Job did to all the sufferings that he endured.

OUR EXAMPLE, BROTHER JOB

As you read in chapter one of this book, our dear brother Job had great understanding of the difference between himself and sovereign God Almighty. He saw himself in lowly esteem, reflecting his humility. We read of his voicing his sorrowful thoughts—how he felt when he was in such physical torment and anguish—in Job 3:3: *"May the day perish on which I was born, and the night in which it was said, a male child is conceived."* Later, in Job 9:2b, he says: *"...how can a man be righteous before the Lord?"* In Job 9:14-15: *"How then can I answer Him, and choose my words to reason with Him? For though I were righteous, I could not answer Him; I would beg mercy of my Judge."* He continues in Job 9:32-33: *"For He is not a man, as I am, that I may answer Him, and that we should go to court together. Nor is there any mediator between us, who may lay his hand on us both."* He declares in Job 28:28: ***"Behold, the fear of the Lord, that is wisdom, and to depart from evil is understanding."*** We then find him remembering how good life was before all his trials and tribulations came. He is reminiscing about how happy he was when he felt the nearness of God in the "good old days." In the midst of the tremendous physical suffering and emotional cruelties from all the words of condemnation blasted at him by his self-righteous wife and friends we read some of his sorrowful words in Job 29:2, 5: *"Oh, that I were as in months past, as in the days when God watched over me...when the Almighty was yet with me."* Do you see with the weight of the hurts, the afflictions, and sins of his wife and friends cast upon him, that he yielded to entertaining negative thoughts—as if God was afar off, as if He had forsaken him. After God preached a good long sermon to him (Job 38 and 39), Job replied:

> *"I know that You can do everything, and that no purpose of Yours can be withheld from You. You asked, 'Who is this who hides counsel without knowledge?' Therefore I have uttered what I did not understand, things too wonderful for me, which I did not know. Listen, please, and let me speak; You said, 'I will question you, and you will answer Me.' I have heard of You by the hearing of the ear, but now my eye sees You, therefore I abhor myself, and repent in dust and ashes."* (Job 42:2-6)

As much as Job loved God and desired with all his heart to please Him rather than being a man-pleaser, he wisely recognized that even if he kept the whole law and was guilty of only a tiny sin—he was guilty of all. (James 2:10) Job rightly perceived the difference between the holiness of God and his unrighteousness—as should we all. Job displays what it is to be "broken" before the Lord! We find David's prayer of repentance, that expresses what condition our heart is to be in before the Lord as we read Psalm 51:16-17: *"...You do not desire sacrifice, or else I would give it; You do not delight in burnt offering. The sacrifices of God are **a broken spirit, a broken and contrite heart—these, O God, You will not despise**."*

This reminds us once again of when Christ hung on Calvary's tree in our place, when He paid a debt He did not owe because we owed a debt we could not pay! In our place Jesus cried: *"...My God, My God, why have You forsaken Me?"* (Mark 15:34) It is important that we understand why Jesus expressed that He felt the absence of God as He hung on the Cross—all of mankind's horrible sins and accompanying fall out from them, such as afflictions, filthy sins and horrific cruelties He had taken upon Himself. He was being persecuted in our place, bearing the weight of our sins upon Himself. Our sins, our iniquities were covering Him, thus all the sins of the world since Adam and Eve were upon Him, therefore, He was experiencing for us the horrible void of being separated from sovereign God, Jehovah! What amazing grace, God has offered to us through His Son! Indeed, He declares: *"For God so loved the world that He gave His only begotten Son that whoever believes in Him should not perish but have everlasting life."* (John 3:16)

Jesus was our propitiation and atonement for our sins! He satisfied the debt of our sins before His Father! There is a beautiful old hymn that invites us to focus on what He did for us on Calvary. It brings Christians under conviction to be willing to obey Him, to desire to satisfy Him with our living testimonies!

Satisfied With Jesus

1. I am satisfied with Jesus, He has done so much for me,
   He has suffered to redeem me, He has died to set me free.
2. He is with me in my trials, best of friends of all is He;
   I can always count on Jesus, can He always count on me?
3. I can hear the voice of Jesus, calling out so pleadingly,
   "Go and win the lost and straying;" is He satisfied with me?
4. When my work on earth is ended, and I cross the mystic sea
   Oh, that I could hear Him saying, "I am satisfied with thee".

CHORUS: I am satisfied, I am satisfied, I am satisfied with Jesus, but the question comes to me, as I think of Calvary, is my Master satisfied with me?

(Page 375; The Broadman Hymnal; The Broadman Press, Nashville, Tennessee; Copyright–1940)

Among large numbers of Christians, a wide variety of behaviors can be observed. Some Christians are still babes in Christ even though they've been saved for many years. Others have matured to what we might call "a teenager level." Some have grown to adulthood Christianity, while others are wiser and more diligent yet in their dedication and obedience to Christ. Upon prayerfully pondering, "Why, Lord, are there such high numbers of immature Christians when so many have had the same opportunity to know You well? For years, they have had Your Bible close at hand, have attended Bible institutions, Bible study classes, and have heard the preaching of the Word for years—and have even had some Christ-like examples on their pathway, too. Why do some grow to maturity while others never grow up—even though their hair is gray?" Then the Lord spoke much truth: **"It depends on the measures of Christians' love for, trust in, and gratitude to Me, their Lord and Savior! You will see when the three measures are added together, the sum will be equal to the measure of Christians' willing obedience to Me."**

Therefore, it seems important for every Christian to seriously ask of himself, **"How much do I really love the Lord who paid in full my debt of sin?"** Does my daily life reflect that I am obedient to the first commandment *"...love the Lord, thy God with all thy heart, and with all thy soul, and with all thy mind...."*? (Mark 12:30) What would my answer be in truth to Jesus' question, *"Lovest thou Me?"* (John 21:17) Oh that it would be, **"Yes, Lord, I love Thee with all my heart, soul, and mind!"** Then I should willingly obey His instructions that followed that question: **"Feed My sheep"—and share my testimony of what Jesus has done for me and what He has taught me.** Should that not also include a willingness to share that Jesus can set souls free from Satan's strongholds? Am I truly willing to take time to make any form of sacrifices the Lord asks of me? Am I willing to even endure physical or verbal suffering in any form for Jesus? Do I display in my lifestyle both privately and publicly that my beloved Jesus is worthy of my service to Him in spite of sufferings that may come on this battlefield?

Am I like Paul, **"...content in the state I find myself"** in spite of not living life like unto being in a luxury car on a freeway with no bumps? No doubt about it, our dear brother Paul encountered quite a few "bumps" on his mission fields. Along with enduring a great deal of mockery and imprisonment, "some" of his trials and tribulations included these sufferings: five times, he received "40 stripes, save one" (39) which adds up to 195 stripes. Three times, he was beaten with rods, one time, stoned and left for dead. He was ship wrecked three times, and he spent one and a half days in the deep. He suffered many more troubles besides these, all of which confirmed his enormous love for and dedication to our Lord Jesus and his compassion for lost souls and his brothers and sisters! He willingly gave up all worldly pleasures to walk in God's plan for his precious life.

This brings us to consider how <u>our</u> hearts measure up to the second portion of that scripture: *"...love the Lord, your God with all your heart, with all your soul, and with all your mind. This is the first and great commandment. And the **second** is like it: 'You shall **love your neighbor as yourself.**' On these **two commandments** hang all the Law and the Prophets."* (Matthew 22:37-40; Mark 12:30)

Let us back up even further, before Paul's time and focus on some points within the lesson of the story about Adam and Eve: (1) They lacked nothing in that perfectly beautiful garden setting and were only told to leave that **ONE** thing alone—the Tree of Knowledge of Good and Evil. **(2)** In spite of God's warning that something bad would happen, they chose out of their fleshly desires to listen to and obey the serpent and partake of the ONE thing that their loving God warned them about. **(3)** Not only did they suffer the consequences of their wrong, sinful choice, their children and all generations to follow suffered the consequences.

Let us apply those points in the Adam and Eve lesson to us as Christians: (1) We truly lack nothing that we cannot live without on our God-appointed earthly mission fields, while walking on His straight and narrow pathway. **(2)** Is our gratitude to, trust in, and love for Him so great that we are willing to consistently choose to obey His loving warning and resist the Devil's suggestion for us to take the exit onto a broad pathway that leads to a field of pleasure for our flesh? A field that offers to satisfy **ONE** specific lust of the flesh. **(3)** Is that one fleshly pleasure so important to us that we are not only willing to run the risk of suffering unpleasant fall out from it, but also willing to run the risk of one day weeping upon learning that we have caused our weaker brothers and sisters to stumble and suffer? Our Lord's question comes to each of us again: **"Lovest thou Me? Lovest thou Me more than these, my child, what will your answer be?"**

We read in I John 5:1-4, that if we truly love the Lord, then we will obey Him, for the two go hand-in-hand! We read: *"whoever believes that Jesus is the Christ is born of God, and everyone who loves Him who begot also loves him who is begotten of Him.* ***By this we know that we love the children of God, when we love God and keep His commandments. For this is the love of God, that we keep His commandments. And His commandments are not burdensome.*** *For whatever is born of God overcomes the world. And this is the victory that has overcome the world–our faith."*

Jesus said: *"...**If anyone loves Me, he will keep My word**; and My Father will love him, and We will come to him and make Our home with him.* ***He who does not love Me does not keep My words****; and the word which you hear is not Mine but the Father's who sent Me. These things I have spoken to you while being present with you.* ***But the Helper, the Holy Spirit, whom the Father will send in My name, He will teach you all things, and bring to your remembrance all things that I said to you.***" (John 14:23-26)

Christians who love the Lord deeply, their **LOVE for the Lord will be joined to the equal measure of their GRATITUDE to the Lord.** With great measures of love and trust, they can remain in an attitude of gratitude even through storms, trials and tribulations of life, just as our brother Job did! *"Make a joyful noise unto the Lord, all ye lands.* ***Serve the Lord with gladness****; come before His presence with singing. Know ye that the LORD, He is God; it is He who hath made us, and not we ourselves; for we are his people, and the sheep of His pasture.* ***Enter into His gates with thanksgiving, and into His courts with praise; be thankful to Him, and bless His name. For the LORD is good; His mercy is everlasting, and His truth endureth to all generations.***" (Psalm 100)

A powerful statement is made concerning gratitude in Ephesians 5:20 that says that Christians should be *"**Giving thanks always for all things** unto God and the Father in the name of our Lord Jesus Christ."* Now Christians with smaller measures of love for and gratitude to the Lord would balk at that passage because instructions for Christians to be "thankful" for "all" things doesn't leave anything out—including "unwanted" things! Having small measures of love for and gratitude to the Lord when they read further instructions such as *"...we know that all things work together for good* [in the long run] *to them who are the called according to His purpose."* (Romans 8:28)

Christians having smaller measures of love and gratitude reflect that they have an equally small measure of **TRUST**. The measure of their **TRUST** in the Lord should be so great even when "bad" things happen on their pathway; they immediately pause and listen for God's instructions in their heart! The measure of their TRUST in the Lord should be like unto this scripture: ***"Trust in the LORD with all thine heart, and lean not to thine own understanding. In all thy ways acknowledge* [submit to, trust] *Him, and He shall direct thy paths. Be not wise in thine own eyes; fear the LORD, and depart from evil."*** (Proverbs 3:5-7) When going through "bad" times, the enemy will most certainly bombard Christians with temptations of worry, doubt, and fear!

It is very tragic that all too many Christians so readily entertain Satan's suggestions that they **doubt** what God has said. They do not understand that when He said to **"be thankful in all things"** and when one of the "all things" was something unpleasant or even "bad," He does not mean for them to excitedly jump up and down laughing hysterically with joy. What He does mean is that we Christians should have such great measures of love for, gratitude to, and trust in Him, that when unpleasant, bad things come along, that **upon submitting to Him, we trust Him so completely that we experience His joy, for that is part of Him!** We can then rebuke the enemy when he bombards us with evil suggestions—worry, doubt, fear—and we can hear the Lord directing our hearts, giving us peace concerning the matter. "Bad times" can be converted into unique tools that cause us to snuggle up to Him closer for His help. If we listen to and obey Him, we will grow stronger and more mature as a Christian! He will also use the bad times to get our attention—to draw us to repentance if we have sinned. He will tell us if He allowed the enemy to attack us, just as He did with our dear old brother Job—for a time of testing—proving the measure of Job's faith before others. Out of Job's love for, gratitude to, and trust in the Lord, God Almighty displayed through his testimony in such enormous measure, his friends and so many other souls were blessed—and the Lord rewarded him greatly! What a reputation! What a testimony! From long ago times up to this age, when persons describe an extremely patient person, they declare, "They have the patience of Job!"

I believe a **good measuring tool for all Christian soldiers** is found in James 1:2-3: *"My brethren, **count it all joy** when you fall into various trials, knowing that the **testing of your faith produces patience**. But **let patience have its perfect work, that you may be perfect** [mature] **and complete, lacking nothing**."*

As we said earlier, it is not that we are to excitedly and happily jump up and down over bad things that come our way, but rather we should understand what "joy" means! It means that we should not only have large measures of trust and gratitude, but also have a large measure of **willing obedience and count it a great privilege and pleasure to go through anything for our Lord and Savior, Jesus Christ**! As His Christian soldiers, our measures of love for, gratitude to, and trust in our King will be reflected on this earthly battlefield through the measure of our willing obedience.

Considering the critical spiritual condition that this world is in today, it surely appears that Jesus will soon give the order for Satan to be bound for a thousand years! After that, he will be loosed for a short time to once again have opportunity to deceive the world and then, the final judgment of Christ will place him in the lake of fire where they will be tormented day and night. (Rev. 20:10) Then after our Lord Jesus' thousand-year reign, we will all go to live with him forever in our New Jerusalem! Until that glorious day, He tells us to be busy tending to His business!

Here in America, Christians still have the freedom to meet together in churches, and can share the Gospel. However, threats and limitations on our legal rights are on the increase! The thought of the true Church's—God's entire family of believers—being persecuted more severely for their faith, like the church spoken of in Revelation 2:10, is becoming less and less hard to imagine! To that persecuted church, God said: ***"Do not fear any of those things which you are about to suffer. Indeed, the devil is about to throw some of you into prison, that you may be tested, and you will have tribulation ten days. Be faithful until death, and I will give you the crown of life."***

Christians look forward to the day when this earth is no more and we're living in heaven with no more battles with the enemy—no more sorrow, pain, death or wars. We're to "occupy" until the Lord comes for us, individually or cooperatively! Meanwhile, questions come for each of us as we ask of ourselves: **"Will I be found walking in His will—reflecting my love for, trust in, and gratitude to Him through my willing obedience? If I see hard times come, will I be found faithful to Him? What are the measures of my love for, trust in, and gratitude to the Lord? What is the measure of my willing obedience to Him? What will my honest answer be when He asks: 'Lovest thou Me?'"**

D. AM I MY BROTHER'S KEEPER OR A STUMBLING BLOCK ON HIS HIGHWAY?

Since Jesus would surely pose the same questions to us as He did Peter, let each of us pause to ask of ourselves some serious questions. How much do I really love the Lord? Do I put restrictions on Him, obeying some of His orders—disobeying others out of my self-centeredness in spite of knowing I may very well be a stumbling block to others? Am I willing to make any sacrifice that the Lord calls upon me to do in order to "be my brother's keeper"? Am I willing to resist what my flesh—the old man, the old nature—in me is luring me to do that is contrary to what my new nature—Christ in me—is pleading for me to do? Let's take time to look at God's lesson taught through two brothers: **(1)** Cain (a tiller of the soil) who chose to disobey the Lord and give an unacceptable offering. And **(2)** Cain's younger brother, Abel (who tended sheep) who obeyed the Lord's will and gave an acceptable offering. When the Lord confronted Cain about his disobedience, out of jealousy, he struck and killed his brother Abel. Of course, God was well aware of his wicked deed. Let us read His questions posed to Cain, and how He responded to Cain's answers. **Through this conversation, in Genesis 4:9-15, we will see how important and critical it is to God for us to be obedient to Him and to be "our brother's keeper":**

*"Then the LORD said to Cain, **'Where is Abel your brother?'** He said, **'I do not know. Am I my brother's keeper?'** And He said, 'What have you done? The voice of your brother's blood cries out to Me from the ground. So now **you are cursed from the earth**, which has opened its mouth to receive your brother's blood from your hand. When you till the ground, it shall no longer yield its strength to you. A fugitive and a vagabond you shall be on the earth.' And Cain said to the LORD, 'My punishment is greater than I can bear! Surely You have driven me out this day from the face of the ground; I shall be hidden from Your face; I shall be a fugitive and a vagabond on the earth, and it will happen that anyone who finds me will kill me. And the LORD said to him, 'Therefore, whoever kills Cain, vengeance shall be taken on him seven-fold.' And the LORD set a mark on Cain, lest anyone finding him should kill him."*

While we see the judgment of Holy God, we also see the mercy of Holy God. However, **through this powerful lesson, we clearly see that we are to be "our brother's keeper"—that we are to willingly sacrifice as God directs to encourage and minister to others**. We read further of this truth in the New Testament, in I Corinthians 8:9-13:

*"...**beware lest somehow this liberty of yours become a stumbling block to those who are weak**. For if anyone sees you who have knowledge eating in an idol's temple, will not the conscience of him who is weak be emboldened to eat those things offered to idols? And because of your knowledge shall the weak brother perish, for whom Christ died? But when you thus sin against the brethren, and wound their weak conscience, you sin against Christ. Therefore, if food makes my brother stumble, I will never again eat meat, **lest I make my brother stumble**."*

Oh that all of us as Christians, would love the Lord so much that we desire with all our hearts to be obedient to Him—determine in our hearts to be well pleasing in His sight. Oh that we would want to have Christ-like testimonies at all times—for which we shall be given or lose rewards according to the measure of our obedience to Him. We read in II Corinthians 5:10: *"**For we must all appear before the judgment seat of Christ, that each one may receive the things done in the body, according to what he has done, whether good or bad.**"*

God tells us to love and pray for lost souls—to even love and pray for our enemies—witness to them when opportunity comes. We are our brothers and sisters' keepers, and the Lord also holds us accountable for how we treat them! He also holds us accountable for how we treat lost people! That's why He tells us to love and pray for our enemies. How serious He is about how we treat others—how careful we should be not to do or say anything that would be a stumbling block to others! God puts His perspective of the negative behavior of people quite strongly in this passage of scripture:

"...the disciples came to Jesus, saying, 'Who then is the greatest in the kingdom of heaven?' Then Jesus called a little child to Him, set him in the midst of them, and said, 'Assuredly, I say to you, unless you are converted and become as little children, you will by no means enter the kingdom of heaven. Therefore whoever humbles himself as this little child is the greatest in the kingdom of heaven. Whoever received one little child like this in My name receives Me. But **whoever causes one of these little ones who believe in Me to sin, it would be easier for him if a millstone were hung around his neck, and he were drowned in the depth of the sea.** *Woe to the world because of offenses! For offenses must come, but woe to that man by whom the offense comes!"* (Matthew 18:1-7)

Hopefully, all Christians would do such things as "bite their tongues" when someone says something rude and unkind to them. Perhaps all would even agree that we should not engage in arguing with persons who may very well be wrong but insist that they are right! Hopefully, all would respect others' right to be wrong! How many Christians are willing to "turn the other cheek" if someone strikes them? They may even be forgiving if someone cheats them out of something. Perhaps most would forgive a person who still owes them sizeable amounts of money he borrowed years ago—whether he did not even intend to pay him back, or he fell on hard times. **To let the person know their debt is forgiven is a testimony of the new-nature of Christ within Christians.** The list of "what-if offenses" could go on and on, to which each of us would have to choose to walk, moment by moment, in our old man—or in our newness in Christ Jesus.

In the primary department of many Sunday schools, the little children were taught a little song to encourage them to behave like Jesus wanted them to behave. Perhaps "O Be Careful, Little Eyes" should be sung in "big-people church" often, as a reminder to us all! Here are the words:

O Be Careful, Little Eyes

(1)   O be careful little eyes what you see.
O be careful little eyes what you see.
There's a Father up above
And He's looking down in love.
So, be careful little eyes what you see.

Four verses followed the first by replacing "**eyes** what you see" with **(2) ears** what you hear, **(3) hands** what you do, **(4) feet** where you go, and **(5) mouth** what you say.

It is critical that a Christian remembers as he lives his life that his example will truly appear before others in one or more of these three categories: **(1)** as a brother and sister's keeper, **(2)** an aloof, self-centered, uncaring Christian, or **(3)** a stumbling block, inviting souls to take a fall into the clutches of the enemy!

333

In many years gone by, in the movies smoking cigarettes was made to look "cool" or make a man look macho—like a "tough guy." Of course some of the younger generation wanted to look cool or tough, so they started smoking. Few escaped becoming addicted to the nicotine, which the medical field and death itself have proven causes cancer. The addiction is so strong that we have witnessed some who lay dying with lung cancer just kept on smoking until their date with death. How many dads have offered "a smoke" to their sons, or an older brother to his younger brother when they reached their teens? **As I'm sure most people reading this would agree that the person setting the poor example was not deliberately trying to do harm to the victim of their example. The enemy just portrayed it as a fun, harmless thing to do. Nevertheless, harm was done, the victim stumbled and the addiction came with a threat to his health—as well as to many innocent people in homes and public places forced to breathe the second-hand smoke.** It's truly sad to say, that there have been many Christians—including those in leadership—who display their addiction between Bible study and church services as they smoke their cigarettes between the buildings. They were not hidden from the eyes of the teenagers and children passing by. When one fails to resist temptation and chooses to be a stumbling block, he is much like a domino stood on its end at the end of a long winding row of other dominoes. As that domino at the front of the line tilts over onto the next domino, it tilts over onto the next and so on—until they all fall.

It is with much gratitude that I am able to inject this testimony: You recall my telling you that I was an alcoholic, but I also smoked from the time I awoke in the morning until I put that last cigarette down before bedtime—coughing in between. When I repented of my disobedience to Him in the midst of running from His will all those years, He not only mercifully took away my desire for alcohol, he removed my desire to smoke—cigarettes, cigars, and pipes. However, consequences remained, leaving my lungs weaker. For His Godly reasons, He does not always choose to remove fall-out from sin! And to this day, when I pass someone smoking, it is extremely unpleasant—and I am also very concerned for the welfare of the smoker! How grateful I am for His mercy upon my soul!

Along that same "stumbling block" line, perhaps it is because we have seen "close up and personal" as well as "close up through ministry" the devastation, the fallout alcoholism brings to a person, we take the subject very seriously! We have seen so many souls who have repeatedly kept trying to "drown their sorrows in a bottle"—while loved ones stood by with broken hearts. How many people have lost loved ones killed by a drunk driver? Most of those drunk drivers would not even consider killing someone if they were in a sober state, yet they have to live with that guilt the rest of their lives! How many families have been torn asunder due to an alcoholic family member? How many marriages have "gone down the tube" because of alcoholism? As we covered in chapter three, "Victory Over Addictions and Negative-Learned Behavior," concerning alcoholism—it's like cigarettes, cigars and pipes—alcohol can most surely become an addiction. We strongly believe this is a subject that should be taught as an act of kindness, "a loving warning to our brethren in hopes of 'keeping them' from falling!" We firmly believe that Jesus served non-fermented wine at the marriage supper; otherwise, it would contradict God's many words warning against the alcohol trap in both the Old and New Testament! Like so many other Christians who hold tight to these beliefs, we have been mockingly called "Hard-shell Baptists." We do not take it as an insult. Instead, we translate "hard-shell" to mean that we know we should try to obey the Lord and "keep the whole armor of God on so that we can better stand against the enemy!" We believe we would be selfish if we did not take time to share our Creator's warnings on this subject in this book. As we begin sharing them, we hope that you will see these scriptures as powerful tools to help you as you continue to be your brothers and sisters' keeper—removing stumbling blocks from their pathways!

Bottom line—we are to live Christ-like testimonies out of our love and gratitude for the Lord and for the sake of others! We benefit ourselves when we walk in God's will—we have peace and joy as we willingly answer this call: *"I beseech you therefore, brethren, by the mercies of God, that you* <u>*present your bodies a living sacrifice, holy, acceptable to God, which is your*</u> <u>*reasonable service.*</u> *And do not be conformed to this world, but be transformed by the renewing of your mind, that you may prove what is that good and acceptable and perfect will of God."* (Romans 12:1-2)

Let us remember: **Christians are "The King's kids"—our King's princes and princesses!** And, **The King says:** *"...it is not for kings to drink wine, nor for princes intoxicating drink; lest they drink, and forget the law, and pervert the justice of all the afflicted."*—perverting their testimony before their weaker brethren and those without Christ! (Proverbs 31:4-5) As we shared in chapter three, we should remember that we are of a royal priesthood!

> [7941] **sekar:** A masculine noun referring to strong drink; beer. It refers to an intoxicating drink and is usually understood as some kind of beer. Priests were not to drink it when serving at the Tabernacle or Temple (Lev. 10:9). The Nazarite was not to touch it (Num. 6:3; Judg. 13:4, 7, 14). The drinkers of strong drink (sote sekar) were none other than drunkards (Ps. 69:12 [13]; Isa. 5:11, 22; 28:7; 29:9; 56; 122). Such drinking causes violent behavior (Prov. 20:1); kings should stay away from it (Prov. 31:4); though it may be a sedative for the dying and bitter (Prov. 31:6: Isa. 24:9). It is used in a context of mockery by Micah (2:11). (The Complete Word Study Dictionary Old Testament Baker; Carpenter. Page 1142, A.M.G. Publishers, Chattanooga, TN 37422, U.S.A.)

Our old brother **Noah is listed in the "Hall of Faith"** in the New Testament, and we will surely meet him in heaven one day. (Hebrews 11:7) **Sadly though, in Noah's latter years, he let his guard down and allowed his testimony to become tainted, and his downfall came through drunkenness.** (Genesis 9:20-25)

In Numbers 6:3-4, we read that **a person who separates himself, like a Nazarite, to be used of the Lord is given instructions not to drink any alcoholic beverages.** As Christians, are we not to be separate from the ways of the world? We read truth in II Corinthians 6:16-18; 7:1: *"...you are the temple of the living God. As God has said: 'I will dwell in them and walk among them. I will be their God, and they shall be My people. Come out from among them and be separate,' says the Lord. 'Do not touch what is unclean, and I will receive you. I will be a Father to you,* *and you shall be My sons and daughters,' says the Lord Almighty."* **He is talking about every Christian, not just ones in ministry!**

We're told that **our dear brother Timothy** had a stomach ailment—perhaps an ulcer. He was told: *"Drink no longer water, but use a little wine for thy stomach's sake and thine often infirmities."* (I Timothy 5:23) It implies that the fresh fruit of the vine—grape juice—helps to bring healing to persons experiencing stomach problems. Another point is that if water in a person's area was deemed unsanitary, fresh grape juice was a good solution to prevent dehydration—healthy for them to drink.

What did the Lord tell Zechariahs when he and his wife were to have a son, **John the Baptist**? He said: **"For he shall be great in the sight of the Lord, and shall drink neither wine nor strong drink; and he shall be filled with the Holy Spirit...."** (Luke 1:15)

Now we will see what the Lord has to say in these verses: *"Therefore **let us pursue the things which make for peace and the things by which one may edify another.** Do not destroy the work of God for the sake of food. All things indeed are pure, but it is evil for man who eats with offense. **It is good neither to eat meat nor drink wine nor do anything by which your brother stumbles or is offended or is made weak.** (Romans 14:19-21)

In God's Word we also read: *"See, then, that ye walk circumspectly, not as fools but as wise, redeeming the time, because the days are evil. Wherefore, **be ye not unwise but understanding what the will of the Lord is.** And **be not drunk with wine, in which is excess, but be filled with the Spirit.**" (Ephesians 5:15-18)

God lovingly warns us not to "hang around in places where our reputations as Christians, our testimonies are at risk. I Thessalonians 5:22 says: **"Abstain from every form of evil."** **Some translations say to abstain from the "appearance" of evil.** We are told in I Corinthians 5:11: **"...I have written to you not to keep company with anyone named a brother, who is sexually immoral, or covetous, or an idolater, or a reviler, or a drunkard, or an extortioner—not even to eat with such a person."** We must prayerfully guard our testimony, for Satan would delight in destroying it with his rumors, his lies! **This verse clearly warns us not to be a stumbling block— that we are our brother and sister's keeper:** *"Woe to him who gives drink to his neighbor, pressing him to your bottle, even to make him drunk, that you may look on his nakedness! You are filled with shame instead of glory. You also—drink! And be exposed as uncircumcised! The cup of the LORD'S right hand will be turned against you, and **utter shame will be upon your glory.**"* (Habakkuk 2:15-16)

Upon examining God's Word, there is no room left for argument, for He clearly does not want Christians to partake of alcoholic, fermented beverages. He surely expresses how critical it is for Christians' testimonies to reflect their convictions unashamedly about the matter—for the sake of others. As we've said before, "Give Satan an inch and he will take a mile," so you would probably agree that if he can tempt a soul to "take a sip, he may very well end up drinking the whole bottle!" While Satan has been delighted that many Christians drink alcohol, he has also been greatly disappointed that such a high number of Christians abstain totally from drinking fermented wine, liquor, and beer. While we're on the subject, there is one particular use of alcohol that Satan would rather we not mention at all. We are very keenly aware of Satan's sly strategies to destroy his victims, and have felt great sorrow in observing some first hand—personally as well as in our ministry. Therefore, I believe it absolutely necessary for us to draw attention to and expose this coveted area that Satan holds. It is one that he delights in scribbling his stamp of approval "Enjoy! No Harm Done!" You recall that the Lord tells us to abstain from the "appearance" of evil. Therefore, for Christians to have bottles of wine in their houses to cook with—or beer to make "beer batter"—if only one "little brother" or "little sister" sees this, it will surely appear to be the cook's stamp of approval on alcohol. Little eyes are watching! Lost people are watching! Babes in Christ are watching—as are the rest of the Christian family.

One step further, just suppose they never see that bottle in your kitchen, but you find yourself in situations where you are asked what you believe about the subject—will you tell the truth, or lie about your stash in the kitchen? Were you to make comparison lists between "the good that alcohol does" and "the bad that it does," which list do you think would be the longest? The results of the comparison would reveal that the list of "the bad that it does" is the longest. **Without a doubt, the conclusion of the biblical study is that not one drop of wine, liquor, or beer on one's tongue is worth risking one single, solitary life being led to drown in "the bottle." The choice remains ours, to be a stumbling block or keeper of our brothers and sisters!**

Now this is a very grievous, true story: There was a young Christian man who to this day sorely regrets that he offered his older brother his first beer. When they were very young, they suffered a great deal of heartbreak and abuse. Each one reached a point in time during which they became alcoholics. However, later in life, the youngest brother who had influenced his older brother to start drinking, chose to repent of his lifestyle that was so contrary to God's will. He fell in love with the Lord and began walking more closely with the Lord, and later he even surrendered to God's call on his life to preach the Gospel. What joy it was when he eventually led his dear elder brother to the Lord!

However, with great sorrow, in talking with his elder brother, it became clear that he was tormented by painful memories of the past, and he was full of anger, bitterness, hatred and unforgiveness. Beer remained a daily refuge from life's unpleasant realities, and it was clear that Satan had a stronghold on his life. He was fired from numerous jobs due to his short temper. In drunken states, he got into serious brawls in beer joints. He repeatedly got into trouble with the law and was jailed on various occasions. He, his wife, and two sons were educated, intelligent and talented people, and really had wonderful God-given personalities. However—tempers flew—feuding, fighting, and fussing were the main, daily activities in the house. Both of their teenage sons chose lifestyles of alcohol, drugs and theft—both went to prison for very lengthy times. One remains there today for accidentally killing a man while robbing him at gunpoint—while the other son's health has been destroyed from the use of illegal drugs. About two weeks before that dear elder brother died of sclerosis of the liver and lung cancer from his chain-smoking, he sat with his younger brother and wept bitterly in repentance to the Lord. He took responsibility for destroying his life, his marriage and his sons by his sinful choice to follow Satan's plan rather than God's. He declared so mournfully that he did not deserve for God to forgive him, though he knew that merciful, blessed assurance was his—that he would even go to heaven when he died. He also wept in gratitude. **Dear folks, it is I, Rev. Joe E. Allbright, the younger Christian brother, who bought his precious elder brother his first beer.** I am extremely glad and grateful to know that upon my sincere, sorrowful repentance, my dear Lord forgave my sinful deed—for causing my elder brother to stumble! Oh that I could walk back in time and do what God wanted me to do way back then—truly be "my brother's keeper" and set a Christ-like example before him. What sweet consolation is mine though, in knowing I will be with my now-healed, now-free brother in heaven for eternity—with only happy times ahead for us!

Having shared God's truths with you concerning fermented beverages, if you are a Christian who finds personal pleasure in fermented beverages, please ask this question of yourself and answer honestly before the Lord: "Am I willing to give up this pleasure for the sake of others? Do I care so much about other souls that I will willingly sacrifice this pleasure so that I am not a stumbling block to both lost and saved souls? Am I willing for the sake of others to even "abstain from the appearance of evil"—not have a bottle on the premises? Am I willing to stand strong and unselfishly share God's truths on this subject for the sake of others as God directs my heart?"

We have heard testimonies of numerous Christians—including counselors—saying that the Lord had brought them under conviction that fermented beverages were not to be a part of their lives in any way, and until they chose to sacrifice that pleasure, they would be hindered from being used effectively in their walk with Him. They shared that they knew if they disobeyed, they would be robbed of the peace and joy that accompanies obedience.

As each of us meditates on the importance of being our brothers and sisters' keeper and teaching others to do the same, upon nearing the end of this book let us seriously examine three key things that will assure us that we can walk strong in Christ and victoriously over the enemy. You recall that Jesus kept asking Peter how much He really loved Him. **No doubt, like us, you have more than likely observed that (1) some Christians seem to have <u>a greater love for the Lord</u> than other Christians do. (2) Some Christians seem to have <u>a greater trust in the Lord</u>, as well as (3) <u>a greater gratitude to the Lord</u> than other Christians. Ones with greater measures of love for, trust in, and gratitude to the Lord have <u>a greater willingness to obey the Lord</u>. Indeed, combined measures of a Christian's love for, trust in, and gratitude to the Lord will be equal to the measure of the person's willing obedience to the Lord.**

We then determined the reasons, for it has to do with Christians' **choices to grow up or not.** Christians have the freedom to remain babes in Christ all the days of their lives if they so choose, and sadly, we've observed too many of them. We've observed some who have grown—but only like unto teenagers. We have also happily observed those who have chosen to grow-up to adulthood—and be examples to the younger Christians and lost souls. It's sad when Christians choose to remain babes or teenagers, for they are more vulnerable to Satan's deceptive traps. It's critical that we recognize they are vulnerable to the "ways of the world," but they are also left vulnerable to "religious traps." Look what God has to say to the "Christian babes and teenagers in Christ"—who truly love the Lord, trust Him, and are grateful to Him **for their salvation**: *"...we should no longer be children, tossed to and fro and carried about with every wind of doctrine, by the trickery of men, in cunning craftiness of deceitful plotting, but speaking the truth in love, may grow up in all things into Him who is the head—Christ—from whom the whole body joined and knit together by what every joint supplies, according to the effective working by which every part does its share, causes growth of the body for the edifying of itself in love."* (Ephesians 4:14-16)

How dangerous it is for these precious Christians who remain spiritual babes and teenagers. What a large responsibility it is for mature Christians to take every opportunity to "train them up in the way they should go"—edify the body in love. Oh that all Christians would desire to mature—grow up—in the Lord so that the Church **body is healthier and together show the world that we are not of the world—that we are different, that we love God, that we trust God, and that we are grateful to God!** Sadly so, there are so many churches with sinfully poor testimonies before the world, not only containing babes who have chosen not to grow up—but divisions instigated by the enemy. How tragic—how grievous to behold. Therefore, it is our hope that more Christians in these latter times will turn their eyes upon Jesus, fall more in love with Him, trust Him more, and be grateful to Him for His mercy and grace upon them!

Our hope is that the measures of Christian brothers and sisters' love for, trust in, and gratitude to our Lord will increase beyond the fact that "God has given them 'fire insurance'—assuring them that they'll live in heaven when they die." Oh that they would joyfully share their testimony of what Jesus did for them on Calvary. Oh that they would not be ashamed of the Gospel of Jesus Christ! What a testimony they would be if they truly love the Lord their God with all their heart, not just a small measure of it. Oh that they would truly get to know Jesus better—so that greater measures of love, trust and gratitude would be in their hearts. How wonderful it would be for these precious babes and teenagers to lean not to their own human reasoning and to cease appearing as if they think life's all about them—and begin edifying others better than themselves. How marvelous it would be for all the spiritual babes and teenage Christians to grow up and help the mature Christians on this critical mission field where the laborers are still all too few. What a unique, beautiful testimony each one has to share in this needy world. Oh that all would be willing to be "living sacrifices"—willing to make any sacrifices the Lord asks us to make so that others may see Jesus in them and have opportunity to know The Way, The Truth, and The Life and go to heaven when they die. Oh that many souls may know God's truths that can set them free from Satan's captivity. How powerful the living-messages are of grown-up Christians when they go through trials and tribulations—turbulent times pertaining to people, things, and circumstances—as they display the measures of their love, trust, and gratitude to their Savior, Jesus Christ. Through loss of health, loved ones, employment, properties, etc., plus verbal persecutions, how powerful their testimony can be when they point to

Jesus in whom they trust to give them wisdom and strength to get through it. The choice remains for each member of the body of Christ to choose to put on the Christ-like behavior set forth in these passages of scripture in Colossians 3:12-17:

Precious brothers and sisters: *"...as the elect of God, holy and beloved,* **put on** *tender mercies, kindness, humility, meekness, longsuffering; bearing with one another, and forgiving one another, if anyone has a complaint against another, even as Christ forgave you, so you also must do, but above all these things* **put on love** *which is the bond of perfection [maturity]. And let the peace of God rule in your hearts, to which also you were called into one body; and* **be thankful**. *Let the word of Christ dwell in you richly in all wisdom, teaching and admonishing one another in psalms and hymns and spiritual songs, singing with grace in your hearts to the Lord.* **And whatever you do in word or deed, do all in the name of the Lord Jesus, giving thanks to God the Father through Him.***"*

Dear fellow servant, as you stay snuggled up to the Lord, listening to and obeying Him, may your life reflect in word and deed the words to this wonderful old hymn:

LIVING FOR JESUS

1.   Living for Jesus a life that is true, striving to please Him in all that I do,
      Yielding allegiance, glad hearted and free, this is the pathway of blessing for me.
2.   Living for Jesus who died in my place, bearing on Calvary my sin and disgrace,
      Such love constrains me to answer His call, follow His leading and give Him my all.
3.   Living for Jesus wherever I am, doing each duty in His holy name,
      Willing to suffer affliction or loss, deeming each trial a part of my cross.
4.   Living for Jesus thro' earth's little while, my dearest treasure, the light of His smile.
      Seeking the lost ones, He died to redeem, bringing the weary to find rest in Him.

CHORUS

      O Jesus, Lord and Savior, I give myself to Thee; For Thou, in Thy atonement, Didst
      give Thyself for me; I own no other Master, My heart shall be Thy throne, My life I
      give, henceforth to live, O Christ, for Thee alone.

      (Page 373; The Broadman Hymnal; The Broadman Press, Nashville, Tennessee;
      Copyright–1940)

As we determine in our hearts to live for Jesus, may each of us yield completely to our beloved Potter and sincerely desire for Him to have His way with us—His little chunks of clay, as we read the words to this beautiful old hymn:

HAVE THINE OWN WAY, LORD!

1. Have Thine own way, Lord! Have Thine own way! Thou art the Potter, I am the clay. Mold me and make me, after Thy will, while I am waiting, yielded and still.

2. Have Thine own way, Lord! Have Thine own way! Search me and try me, Master today! Whiter than snow, Lord, wash me just now, as in Thy presence humbly I bow.

3. Have Thine own way, Lord! Have Thine own way! Wounded and weary, help me, I pray! Power—all power—surely is Thine! Touch me and heal me, Savior divine!

4. Have Thine own way, Lord! Have Thine own way! Hold o'er my being absolute sway! Fill with Thy Spirit till all shall see, Christ only, always, living in me!

(Page 254; The Broadman Hymnal; The Broadman Press, Nashville, Tennessee; Copyright–1940)

As we now approach the last chapter of this book, **we find our hearts longing for all our brothers and sisters to stand strong in unity before the eyes of the lost world, so that they may be more strongly drawn to seek and find Jesus in these latter days**. We long to see greater numbers of Christians more boldly fulfilling **"the Great Commission"**: *"Go into all the world and preach the gospel to every creature."* (Mark 16:15) **Our hearts are greatly burdened that until "the world" sees greater evidence of unity—of our love for one another—and a sincere longing for the Lord to have His own way with us as a family, stumbling blocks remain in their roads. "United we stand! Divided we fall!"**

As you know, we're to all have the mind of Christ. He knows what we're thinking all the time, should we not be still and know His mind and will? The question comes—are each of us in unity with Him? Only if we seek to do this can unity come among brothers and sisters—as each allows Christ's mind in them to be in control! Oh, that all would sing out: *"Have Thine own way, Lord! Have Thine own way! Hold o'er my being absolute sway! Fill with Thy Spirit till all shall see, Christ only, always, living in me!"*

We hope that you perceive that the previous chapters and now, our last chapter has been our love-letter, not only to Christian individuals, and families, but to our entire, beloved "Church family." We desire that our love letter serves to encourage all our brothers and sisters to stay snuggled up so tightly to the Lord as they walk with Him moment by moment, that Satan's weapons are continually rendered inoperative! What joy it will be to someday have the awesome privilege of hearing our Father say to all of them as they arrive at their appointed times in heaven, *"Well done, thou good and faithful servant!"*

Chapter Fourteen
THE CHURCH–THE BRIDE OF CHRIST
SPIRIT VS. FLESH

"Let us be glad and rejoice and give Him glory, for the marriage of the Lamb has come, and His wife has made herself ready. And to her it was granted to be arrayed in fine linen, clean and bright, for the fine linen is the righteous acts of the saints." (Revelation 19:7-8)

The book of Genesis is the book of beginnings while the book of Revelation is the book of consummation. From Genesis through Revelation we are taught through the examples of people. God prompts our hearts to learn from both the good and bad examples, then choose to walk out good examples. James 4:14 says: *"...what is your life? It is even a vapor that appears for a little time and then vanishes away."* How often it's been said: **"Time flies!"** And God says in Ephesians 5:16: *"See then that you walk circumspectly, not as fools but as wise, redeeming the time, because the days are evil."* We heard someone make a very accurate statement: **"Time is a daily treasure which attracts many robbers!"** How true! Looking back over a great many years from the first church to our present time, we are brought to **wonder if the Bride of Christ—the Church—has wisely and obediently spent her time doing righteous acts**? The second chapter of Revelation gives us a tool, a ruler to use in determining how the acts of past to present generations of the Bridegroom's Bride measure up to His protective love-laws. As the Bride walks about in this present day and age, "signs of the times" are 'round about. The coming of the Lord is drawing nigh!

A wise man once looked back in time, moving forward, decade by decade to the present time. After comparing them, he declared how tragic it was to see that with each new decade, some good things had been lost and left behind, with morals continually declining. We believe as you prayerfully look back in history, you will agree that this is grievously true. Oh how drastically far America's moral condition has declined. 'Round about us we see signs of the times and the end of the age. There are vast numbers of people without natural affections. Reports come in daily about moral decay in families—even parents killing their children, children killing their parents as foretold in Mark 13:3-13 as the time of tribulation approaches. In the midst of it all, we clearly see **evidence of the war between good and evil—disunity—spirit vs. flesh**. It is heartbreaking to see such **great division in our beloved America**, for the Lord says in Matthew 12:25: *"...Every kingdom divided against itself is brought to desolation, and every city or house divided against itself will not stand."* America is not exempt from this possibility. She's in danger of falling!

A.   IDENTITY THEFT

Nikita Khrushchev once said that America will not be destroyed by physical weapons of war, but rather, it will very subtly self-destruct from within—forfeiting her identity as a Christian nation. For one not to see this as a truth in action, he would have to be in a state of denial. **Of course, we know that our enemy Satan is the subtle instigator of this battle. America was founded on the principle of "...one nation under God, indivisible, with liberty and justice for all." The divisions arose when one group of people chose to <u>remain</u> under God and His protective love-laws while the other group chose to <u>combine</u> what they liked about those laws with their own new rules that suited their flesh. Is that not what we see in America's political arena today? Do we not see ourselves in the midst of a holy war? Is America in need of being liberated from Satan's strongholds? There is no doubt about it that people who are following his orders are literally destroying themselves and one another. Jesus said that He must come one day for His people before mankind destroys himself. Let us take great care to remember that our Lord also said that there would come a day when souls fall away from the faith. Until each of us departs for heaven, Christians should not roll over and play dead—or stick their heads in the sand! Each of us is called according to God's purpose—we have a job to do, a race to run until our Lord says, "It is finished!"**

Let's back up a few decades ago and moving forward, study the spiritual conditions on our mission field. Peering through the "window to the world"—television—there was a time when all that was heard and seen through that window was carefully guarded by strict, morally clean rules. All the programs promoted good morals—some with biblical teachings. At the slip of a tongue, an employee of that window could be fired at will! The managers took great care and pride to provide programs that were wholesomely safe for children to watch. But as time passed, slowly but surely, bad morals subtly and successfully worked their way into television and movies. Times changed—evil increased, good decreased. Little time is spent while flipping television channels in search of a wholesome program or just watching a commercial, before one sees signs of widespread immorality, decades in moral decay. While watching national and world news, it's clear that Satan has had his way with many souls. Filthy language, violence, and sexual perversion are common. Programs and movies created for children warn parents to screen them for "inappropriate" content!

Sadly, both Christians and non-Christians being viewed by the eyes of the world frequently use bad language in spite of knowing they will probably be "bleeped"—which does not cover their sin. It only serves to point out that they said an inappropriate word. In spite of the "bleep," their reputation is tainted. Upon confronting such Christians about their misbehavior, some chuckle, shrug their shoulders and voice an insincere, "Sorry!" Too many Christians being seen through that window speak with double tongues, alternating between spirit and flesh, one minute praising God for doing something wonderful, and the next minute, spewing inappropriate words to express their frustration and anger about a matter. In daily conversations, some Christians habitually use words that in generations past were considered "gutter" or "sewer" language coming from "dirty mouths." New nicknames have been given to some of the filthiest words, as if by using them, they've cleaned up the word—making it appropriate. The old deceiver is so pleased when he dupes people into attempting to disguise dirty as clean. Upon frequently hearing "bad" words, some people yield to temptation, becoming desensitized, eventually even verbalizing the words. Tragically, many children use "bad" words without knowledge of their meanings. This is the way the enemy works, using desensitizing tactics to gain ground subtly, little by little. Many Christians bear guilt of having become desensitized to Satan's subtly evil war tactics, resulting in arrows penetrating their armor and tainting their testimonies. Throughout generations, America's residents have forfeited a huge number of good morals, and this crucial question comes to us as Christians—the Bride of Christ: Does the scripture declaring "a divided house will fall" apply to "God's house"—that morals have declined in some of His family members who meet together in church buildings? Has God's family lost "good—Godly" things while allowing "bad" things to take their place? Timothy warns us:

> *"I write so that you may know how you ought to conduct yourself in the house of God, which is the church of the living God, the pillar and ground of truth. And without controversy, great is the mystery of godliness: God was manifested in the flesh, justified in the Spirit, seen by angels, preached among the Gentiles, believed on in the world, received up in glory. <u>Now the Spirit expressly says that in latter times some will depart from the faith, giving heed to deceiving spirits and doctrines of demons, speaking lies in hypocrisy, having their own conscience seared with a hot iron.</u>"* (I Timothy 3:15-16; 4:1-2)

In the "old days" there were very high percentages of **non-Christians with "good morals"—were good-mannered, respectful and courteous—doing kind deeds for others**. There was a sense of respect for one another between Christians and non-Christians. Back then it was sometimes hard to tell a morally good person from a good Christian. Is this the case today? Being well up in years, through many decades we have grievously observed the decline in morals of both non-Christians and Christians—so much so that sometimes you still can't tell the two apart. What does the Lord ask us to do about this concerning our weaker brethren? **If we do nothing, by our silence we are guilty as charged for refusing to confront souls in love.** We believe this scripture points to the heart of the problem:

> *"A good man out of the good treasure of his heart brings forth good; and an evil man out of the evil treasure of his heart brings forth evil. For <u>out of the abundance of the heart his mouth speaks.</u>"* (Luke 6:45)

The serious matter at hand is "heart trouble connected to a tongue in one's mouth." So, we can well understand why the Lord appointed our dear old brother James to deliver a crucial lesson, warning us all to take care how we use our tongues. As you recall, the book of James was written to Christians. **In the third chapter, all Christians are taught and warned about their "untamable tongues"—which can only be bridled as one willingly allows the Lord to hold the reins at all times. To leaders, those who teach God's Word, there is an additional warning of consequences, "a stricter judgment," if they teach error to others. So it is crucial for one to teach truth—and their talk should match their walk!** Some Christians have "titles" attached to their particular calling that indicates they are ministers, missionaries, teachers, counselors, and such. **However, the heart-tongue issue applies to all Christians.** We are all to guard against carelessly neglecting our call to go into all the world sharing our personal testimony of salvation through Jesus Christ. There is no excuse for us not to treat others the way we would like to be treated. Jesus did that!

To be effective, all of us must have daily checkups with our Great Physician—our Cardiologist—and let Him voice to us the true condition of our hearts. His prescription reads: *"Beloved, if God so loved us, we also ought to love one another."* (I John 4:11) As you read the following statement, do you deem it **true or false**? **"Considering the number of churches from coast to coast in America, a large number of them fall short on unity and Christ-like love for one another."** Grievously, the answer is, "true." Oh that all would willingly submit to our Great Physician for the surgical removal of all stumbling blocks that are imbedded in hearts so we can peacefully and joyfully enter His sanctuary together in loving unity. Oh that we would all strive to remember and obey our Bridegroom's desire:

> *"...Assuredly, I say to you, inasmuch as you did it to one of the least of these My brethren, **you did it to Me**...assuredly, I say to you, inasmuch as you did not do it to one of the least of these, **you did not do it to Me**."* (Matthew 25:40, 45)

We should all ask our Great Physician—our Cardiologist—to permanently install this scripture into us like a heart's "pacemaker": *"Create in me a clean heart, O God, and renew <u>a steadfast spirit</u> within me."* (Psalm 51:10) Without short-circuiting, we can be shining examples to our immediate family and souls beyond on our pathways. Not only do we see divisions and parting of ways in churches, but in individual homes. None can deny the enormously high—and growing—numbers of divorces, including many in Christian couples. It has been said: **"As the family goes, so goes the Church!" How tragic to view the truth, that decade by decade in each generation many of God's people have been deceived and robbed of some invaluable tools. How heartbreaking it has been to see the divisions, the void of true, Christ-like love, the wars between spirit vs. flesh within the Bride of Christ.**

Sadly, it has been truthfully said that some behavior and activities in the church have become so much like the world, one can't tell the difference. **A story is told of a self-centered, greedy man who owned a small piece of property. He then purchased more land on each side of the property. After claiming more and more land this way, someone asked him if he was trying to buy up all the property in that territory. He replied, "No, I just want what's adjacent to mine!" Thus is Satan's subtle plan as he gains as much "ground" as he can "seize" from the lives of souls, including Christians—especially those teaching and preaching the Gospel! So many Christians have fallen for Satan's deceitful plans to lay claim to ground that's "adjacent to his." His compromising suggestions have come: "if churches would just start offering a more loose setting in their sanctuaries, with only soothing messages and perhaps some entertainment, too, perhaps that would draw some lost and unchurched people to God's** house." This **appears like a small and innocent idea** but it's Satan's clever line to begin claiming ground, just what's adjacent to his. Coast to coast, in a vast number of churches, such plans have taken flight by majority rules—not unanimous votes. For a long time, such ideas have been made to remain on the flight plan in spite of repeated warnings of turbulent headwinds. Spirit vs. flesh, and disunity grows.

These days, we often hear of **"identity thefts"** of persons having personal information stolen from them that literally robs them of their own personal identity. It often causes them to lose complete control of their holdings and transforms their lives into a very critical legal battle. **The victim exists within his own "positive" perception of himself but has lost his legal rights to his personal identity, along with his financial status. The sinful imposter also exists and lives out "negative" behavior as he bears the name of the victim. The situation is much like the "core personality" and the "flip-side."** Tragically, the "flip-side" has taken possession of the controls and is "running the show," bringing much shame to the core personality's identity. The core has two choices: **(1)** Passively surrender to the sinful imposter. Say nothing. Let the flip-side keep the legal rights and bring increasing shame to his assumed identity that once bore a good name. **(2)** Aggressively take a stand in his legal rights to restore his good identity by turning to someone in high authority for legal help to deal with the identity thief—thus restoring his good name. Tragically, if the "core personality" does not choose to speak up, confront and legally deal with the flip-side, he will never regain control of his invaluable personal identity—his good name. Proverbs 22:1a declares: *"A good name is to be chosen rather than great riches...."*

Not unlike this, amidst God's Church, within church walls of a wide number of denominations, many precious souls have become **victims of the identity thief**. Sadly true, individuals and those in leadership have been deceived by the enemy who has manipulated his way into their lives and tainted their reputations—the good names that are supposed to shine forth from those walls. **With each passing decade in God's family, the true identity of the Church has been stolen right out of their hands before the eyes of the world!** If "the world" would make comparisons between the original first Churches, to spiritual conditions inside Christ-based churches down through the decades, what would their conclusion be? Would you not agree that in simply comparing **all the names and the various doctrinal statements they project**, they would see disunity amongst God's people beneath their steepled roof tops alone? **Satan still relentlessly attacks individuals and families—the Church because God's people hold the truth about salvation through Jesus Christ. Some also share truths about how souls can be set free from Satan's strongholds. Down through the ages, Satan has been an identity thief, bringing sorrow and shame to Christians. Like a core personality with a flip-side, iniquity has been found in the Bride of Christ, allowing shame to come upon her face! An example of this very thing is found in what Daniel was praying about many long years ago:**

> *"...I set my face toward the Lord God to make request by prayer and supplications, with fasting, sackcloth, and ashes. And I prayed to the Lord my God, and made confession, and said,* **'O Lord, great and awesome God, who keeps His covenant**

*and mercy with <u>those who love Him</u>, and <u>with those who keep His commandments</u>, <u>we have sinned and committed iniquity</u>, we have done <u>wickedly and rebelled</u>, <u>even by departing from Your precepts and Your judgments</u>. Neither have we heeded Your servants and prophets, who spoke in Your name to our kings and our princes, to our fathers and all the people of the land.   **O Lord, righteousness belongs to You, but <u>to us shame of face</u>**, as it is this day...**O Lord, <u>to us belongs shame of face</u>**, to our kings, our princes, and our fathers, because we have sinned against You.   To the Lord our God belong mercy and forgiveness, though we have rebelled against Him. We have not obeyed the voice of the Lord our God, to walk in His laws, which He set before us by His servants the prophets...now therefore, **our God, hear the prayer of Your servant, and his supplications, and <u>for the Lord's sake cause Your face to shine on Your sanctuary, which is desolate</u>.** O my God, incline Your ear and hear; open Your eyes and see our desolations, and the city <u>**which is called by Your name**</u>; for we do not present our supplications before You because of our righteous deeds, but because of Your great mercies. O Lord, hear! O Lord, forgive! O Lord, listen and act! Do not delay for Your own sake, my God, for Your city and **<u>Your people are called by Your name</u>.**'" (Daniel 9:3-7a; 8-10; 17-19)*

As our Lord declared: *"**Unless the LORD builds the house, they labor in vain who build it; unless the LORD guards the city, the watchman stays awake in vain.**"* (Psalm 127:1)

With such increased crime these days, a high number of home owners and churches have taken extreme measures and spent much money to assure that their **homes and church buildings are well armed with burglar alarms to protect material possessions. However, many of them have left the "spiritual doors" wide open for the enemy to attack precious members of our Good Shepherd's flock.** (See John 10:7-18) **We find Jesus saying, "...*I am the door of the sheep.*" But many have neglected to learn, apply, and teach that Jesus has laid down His life for His sheep. He says that He hears the voice of His sheep and they can hear His, therefore, by His authority, they can stand strong against the enemy who comes to steal, kill and destroy. Sadly, with the enemy gaining entry, taking up residence and bringing in so much disunity, the world receives extremely confusing messages—that both true and false identities exist as one—core vs. flip-side—no unity, no peace, no joy.**

How grievous it is that too many Christians have let their guard down and lost sight of who they really are in Christ—representatives of Jesus Christ. The term "Christian" means "little Christ." But many have dropped their shields and **the enemy has attacked stolen, divided and conquered reputations!** Every single Christian makes up "God's entire family"—"the Church body"—the Bride of Christ. **All Christians are an intricate and vital part of "the Bride of Christ," and out of our love for our beloved "Bridegroom" we are to display what His loving, trusting, grateful and willingly obedient Bride is to look like.**

B.   CALL FOR UNITY—PUT OFF FLESH, PUT ON SPIRIT

As we said earlier, with each decade, something is lost—something good is left behind while something bad takes its place. Sadly enough, this **does apply to the Lord's family congregating in church buildings. It's been truthfully stated: "the Devil goes to church!" He is not a shy visitor. He contributes far more than his "two cents worth" of ideas, then the world learns of our disputes, declaring that people gathering within church walls are no different than those in secular gatherings. They surmise that it's okay not to be "on the same page"—just "agree to disagree!"** With thousands of denominations containing God's truths mixed with man's human reasoning born of the flesh, the world continues to see negative-learned behavior patterns mixed in with Christ-like ones! With such a vast conglomeration of "negative-learned behaviors and men's traditions" coupled with Christ-like behavior, no wonder the lost world isn't clambering to go to church in search of the Lord we are supposed to love so dearly. Grievously, there are high numbers of "church families" splitting up—with some declaring that they will never enter a church building again. Some wrongfully become angry and bitter, while others are simply so deeply grieved over the disunity and hypocrisies, they worship the Lord in private to avoid risking more painful experiences with their brethren. The two extremes please the enemy—along with the abundance of disunity within the church walls.

Truth is that God wants His entire Church family to come before Him as Daniel did with his people. With humility, he came with repentance of sin and negative-learned behavior issues. He asked God to forgive them, to wash the shame from their faces—their reputations—and restore their Godly identity. In so many church walls, the Lord is calling for His Church to **put off the flesh, the old man, and put on the new man, Christ-like behavior patterns.** Just as it seems in our divided America inch by inch, the Devil keeps claiming ground, taking away good morals and freedoms, sorrowfully, we have observed all too many times that leaders of God's people are yielding to the negatives and forfeiting the positives. **God wants to be head of the Church and govern His people who will agree to agree with Him, thus be able to vote in unity—unanimous votes! God does not want to govern the majority of a church body while the minorities sit silently out of the way in a corner! God's call for repentance and unity is a serious matter. He holds His ministers—under-shepherds of the flock—accountable for preaching and teaching the whole truth. He also holds Christian men, heads of their households, accountable, for they are to love their wives like Christ loves the church, enough to sacrifice, give his life for her.** (Ephesians 5:22-33) **If Satan continues to be given the rights to claim more and more ground on the home fields and in the fields where all the sheep graze together, we shudder to think of what the future holds!**

Eli the priest is a good example of the consequences of weak, sinful leadership: In the third and fourth chapter of I Samuel, we find God's message to Eli the priest: ***"...I have told him that I will judge his house forever for the <u>iniquity</u> which he knows, because his sons made themselves vile, and he did not restrain them."*** Eli's sons were amongst the Israelites to whom the Ark of the Covenant belonged. But they were disobedient to God, in disunity with Him and unrepentant. The

349

Philistines came, battled and defeated the Israelites and took possession of the Ark. A man of Benjamin had escaped the battle and brought word to ninety-eight year old Eli that his two sons, Hophni and Phinehas had been killed and the Ark of the Covenant had been captured. Eli's heart trembled upon hearing of the capture of the Ark, and he fell back, broke his neck and died. Upon hearing all the terrible news, Phinehas' wife went into labor and gave birth to a son. Her grief was three-fold, for we read: *"...she named the child **Ichabod**, saying, '**The glory has departed from Israel!**' because the ark of God had been captured and because of her father-in-law and her husband."* And she died.

This story of old holds an important message for us today. Because, in places designated for meeting with God, it still remains a serious matter for all of God's people to confess all sins, be in unity with God and each other, and love one another. For if this is neglected, the enemy finds open doors of opportunity to gain ground and take possession. God did not tolerate the rebellious band of Israelites, and while we are living in the period of grace, He will not tolerate for long our lack of repentance for sins—for iniquities. We have sadly observed such iniquities and divisions in some churches that it became evident that the Holy Spirit was no longer meeting in those places. It was evident that God had written Ichabod on each one: "My glory is departed from this place." With grief, members of some churches, that for a great many years had carried the name of Christ in such a way that large numbers of souls were drawn to Christ, failed to seek God's will concerning new pastors. They ended up with hirelings who eventually took down their churches. We felt much grief as the Spirit of the Lord in our hearts sensed the Holy Spirit's absence in those places—where we knew the Lord had stirred so many hearts. (A hireling is one in ministry only for financial gain and self-edification, not for the sake of the "flock"; see John 10:7-18)

Oh that all Christians would take care to obey God's message that we find Paul preaching to Christians who were divided on various issues: *"Now I plead with you, brethren, by the name of our Lord Jesus Christ, that **you all speak the same thing**, and that there **be no divisions among you**, but that you **be perfectly joined together in the same mind and in the same judgment.**"* (I Corinthians 1:10) Oh that all would remember: *"**If I regard iniquity in my heart, the Lord will not hear.**"* (Psalm 66:18) As long as a person allows iniquity to remain, he can hear only God's voice convicting him. Only when humility and repentance comes will sweet fellowship with the Lord return. Only when each individual rights his heart with God, and obeys His instructions can unity come in God's house, for the Lord says:

> *"**If My people who are called by My name will humble themselves, and pray and seek My face, and turn from their wicked ways, then I will hear from heaven, and will forgive their sin and heal their land.**"* (II Chronicles 7:14)

Sadly, in this day and time, it is no wonder that so many lost people view the church buildings no differently than secular country clubs. Why? As Christians, we are not to forsake the assembling of ourselves not only for the purpose of worshiping the Lord, but to love and encourage one another, to study God's Word together, and give forth a mature-in-Christ testimony as the Church body—showing lost souls, the babes in Christ and the world that we are different. We are in the world but not of it. **We are to demonstrate to the world our true love for God and one another, and that we are in unity with God, thus in unity with one another!**

> *"Behold, how good and how pleasant it is for brethren to dwell together in unity! It is like the precious oil upon the head, running down on the beard, the beard of Aaron, running down on the edge of his garments. It is like the dew of Hermon, descending upon the mountains of Zion;* **for there the Lord commanded the blessing**—*life forevermore."* (Psalm 133:1-3)

> As Paul wrote: *"I, therefore, the prisoner of the Lord, beseech you to walk worthy of the calling with which you were called, with all lowliness and gentleness, with longsuffering,* **bearing with one another in love, endeavoring to keep the unity of the Spirit in the bond of peace.***"* (Ephesians 4:1-3)

C. THE ENEMY'S CUNNINGLY DESTRUCTIVE TACTICS

Our evil enemy, the great deceiver, is quite clever at how he uses various things to draw Christians into his snares. We spoke earlier about the importance of knowing our enemy and his tactics and strategies so well, that we can wisely counter his attacks and defeat him. Deeply in our hearts, we know that the Lord has called upon us to expose—for the sake of all our brothers and sisters—what we firmly believe to be some of his subtle tactics. It is our earnest prayer that you will understand the true intents of our hearts—that we long to edify God's people, build them up, not tear them down! We want the enemy's "tactic of disunity" to be torn down in God's "temple." The only way to contribute toward the building up of the body of Christ is to tell them the whole truth in love—in God's love, which is declared in I John 3:18-19: *"My little children let us not love in word or in tongue, but in deed and in truth. And by this we know that we are of the truth, and shall assure our hearts before Him."* God is love. If He is love, we are to be a reflection of His love, therefore, CHRIST'S LOVE IS OUR TRUE IDENTITY.

With peace in our hearts, we now address some issues that we see as **cunningly destructive forces against God's people and their appointed mission on this earth**! Our desire is to present our Bridegroom's teachings with hope that His Bride will readily embrace these truths and walk in her true identity with peace and joy! **Oh that God's people will turn the Church's buildings back over to the Lord and allow Him to be the Watchman and fill His houses with His glory! There is hope for the Church's identity to be reclaimed—then unity amongst brothers and sisters would increase and lead to revivals within God's family.** In our old age, what a joyful blessing it would be to see spiritually healthy congregations spring up across this land, with many souls being led to Christ, and souls set free from Satan's captivity! A wonderful old song comes to mind, expressing how revival begins with each person humbling himself before the Lord, praying: *"Lord, send a revival, and let it begin in me!"*

A FAMINE OF THE WORD

Within the body of Christ is a sorrowful truth: Our Lord warned us in the eighth chapter of Amos that a day will come when there will be a famine—but He is not speaking of a famine of food. Instead, He is speaking of a far worse matter—a famine of His Word! Like the shadow of a gradual approaching storm cloud, this famine of God's Word now looms darkly overhead, growing more and more threatening with each passing moment. Evidence is seen that the enemy has been allowed—little by little—to convince many Christians to water down God's Word—pick and choose the "easier to obey" instructions. It's a surety that the enemy is quite prideful about his accomplishments in congregations around the world. **Some Christians say they don't like the "hell fire and brimstone" preaching. Yet, the loving warnings from God about the reality of hell through His bold, truth-telling preachers are the very messages that drew many lost souls to come under conviction and take seriously the Word of God and seek and find the Savior! How tragic that some preachers soft-pedal with God's words of warning, thus making it much easier for the subtly whispering agent of war to inject his lies.**

There are many church members and leaders who love the Lord with all their hearts, minds and souls and are striving to please Him in all that they do. God's light still shines brightly from such church houses while His light is made to flicker and grow dim in others as the spiritual conditions inside deteriorate. With God's light being dimmed in those, our sorrow has swelled to deep grief. Large crowds gather in some of the churches where the "basics" of the Gospel are preached and taught, yet the light of truth flickers because some truths are missing—**"they have left their first love."** (Revelation 2:4)   God's loving rules on how His Church family and individual families are supposed to function have been permeated with fleshly reasoning and men's "religious traditions" rather than "righteous traditions of God!" While some ministers know full well that God wants them to preach those "missing truths," they have steered away from the controversial subjects because they know that "some" people in the congregation don't want to hear them.

Some preachers, including those viewed through the media, have chosen to "compromise" rather than to be "controversial"—like our Lord Jesus and many of His followers were!   They have chosen "popularity" over "preaching the whole truth" because it comes with risks of suffering rejection and criticism by souls who "don't like" some of God's truths, including those who have sinfully destructive lifestyles. Some preachers have even voiced praises, words of approval, for particular persons in the political arena in spite of their living a self-destructive lifestyle. They slink past their responsibility to share God's truths—telling the world that they really don't care about those persons—their iniquity is acceptable. If they truly loved them with God's heart, they would share God's truths for their sakes—so that they have opportunity to be saved, to be set free from Satan's stronghold. How tragic that they've ignored the love-laws of God, to whom they must give an account, and deprived themselves of the joy of fulfilling His will. With an urgency, our imprisoned brother Paul writes to Timothy, about the seriousness of such situations:

> *"I charge you therefore before God and the Lord Jesus Christ, who will judge the living and the dead at His appearing and His kingdom:* **Preach the Word!** *Be ready in season and out of season.* **Convince, rebuke, exhort, with all longsuffering and teaching.** **For the time will come when they will not endure sound doctrine, but according to their own desires***, because they have itching ears, they will heap up for themselves teachers; and **they will turn their ears away from truth**, and be turned aside to fables. But you **be watchful in all things, endure afflictions, do the work of an evangelist, fulfill your ministry.*** (II Timothy 4:1-5)

God said that His House should be a "house of prayer"—His people **communicating** with Him, **listening and learning from Him**. In His House, His Word is to be preached **in its entirety** along with abundance of Bible studies, discipleship, and ministries to those with spiritual needs, as well as physical needs. Family members with bruised souls should feel welcome and safe to come to their church family. **For the sake of God's precious flock, church discipline should be exercised for rebellious ones when necessary. We should not "wink" at their sin and neglect to minister to them in love! Nonetheless counseling is a necessity—confronting with scripture out of love to bring about a needed change to precious souls.**

How can Christians reclaim their identity—put off the bad and put back on the good identity? Too often the very things the Lord asks His people to do for one another are ignored—disobeyed. It's clear **all too much of the *"lowliness, gentleness, longsuffering, bearing with one another in love—in the bond of peace"* has been forsaken and left behind in years gone by**. While we hasten to say that many in God's family shine forth such Christ-like testimonies, all too many do not. **Grievously one of the reasons for disunity is that many in God's family are immature and self-centered—not excluding many who are in places of leadership.** When those in leadership refuse to mature in the Lord, then they hinder their flock from growing up—for which God will hold them accountable. It has truly been grievous to learn that many in leadership are giving wrong, unwise counsel to their church members. We are to be a family with spiritually healthy leadership, sound in doctrine and working in unity together—each blessing one another by obeying the Lord's will. Oh that all would take care to be: *"...speaking truth in love... **grow up in all things into Him who is the head—Christ**—from whom the whole body, joined and **knit together** by what every joint supplies, according to the effective working by which **every part does its share, causes growth of the body for the edifying of itself in love.***" A choice to repent and "grow up" should come. **Then immaturity would be put off and maturity put on, which will lead to being capable of putting off disunity and putting on unity.**

Many Christians voice that they love one another, yet their actions are a contradiction. As **"the love chapter"** says in God's Word: *"Though I speak with the tongues of men and of angels, but have not love, I have become sounding brass or a clanging cymbal. And though I have the gift of prophecy, and understand all mysteries and all knowledge, and though I have all faith, so that I could remove mountains, but have not love, I am nothing. And though I bestow all my goods to feed the poor, and though I give my body to be burned, but have not love, it profits me nothing. Love suffers long and is kind; love does not envy; love does not parade itself, is not puffed up; does not behave rudely, does not seek its own, is not provoked, thinks no evil; does not rejoice in iniquity, but rejoices in truth; bears all things, believes all things, endures all things. Love never fails. But whether there are prophesies, they will fail, whether there are tongues, they will cease; whether there is knowledge, it will vanish away. For we know in part and we prophesy in part. But when that which is perfect has come, then that which is in part will be done away. When I was a child, I spoke as a child, I understood as a child, I thought as a child; but when I became a man, I put away childish things. For now we see in a mirror, dimly, but then face to face. Now I know in part, but then I shall know just as I also am known. And now abide faith, hope, love, and these three: but the greatest of these is love."* (I Corinthians 13)

NEGLECTING GOD'S PURPOSE

In studying God's Word, it is clear that He is the head of us all—for which we shall be eternally grateful! We are all called according to His purpose for our lives. As our Potter's clay vessels, we are to listen to and obey His will in our individual lives. Like a business has an owner, a boss with a secretary, a supervisor, and many others laboring to make the company run smoothly in order to be a success, so is God's purpose pertaining to His people on this mission field. It's about promoting proper balance. If each of God's children labor in their God-given abilities and talents in the section of the fields to which He has appointed them, He will be pleased and they will be blessed to feel the joy of fulfilling their purpose in life. The issue is so crucial that the Lord warns all women, whether single or married, not to stray from their vital purposes on this mission field, in I Timothy 2:11-12: **"Let a woman learn in silence with all submission. And I do not permit a woman to teach or to have authority over a man, but to be in silence."** How very tragic that Satan has duped so many women into misreading, misinterpreting that scripture as an insult, a "negative" rather than the "positive." Too many have only focused on the words "be in silence" instead of the positive, complimentary word, "learn!" God counts women extremely valuable! In addition to that, while some women are "serving the Lord," doing "good things," if these things are out of God's will and His order of operations, they've robbed themselves of the joy of being as fruitful as God intended. It is truly heartbreaking today to see some women taking on the roles that men should hold and neglecting to fulfill the roles for which God made them.

Oh that women would seek and find God's wisdom inside those two little sentences in I Timothy 2:11-12. **For God is calling His precious women on this mission field to <u>be still, listen and learn truth</u> from God and from His Godly men so they can apply the lessons to their own lives and pass the lessons on! With their having learned truth and matured in the Lord, we learn** of their purposes on this mission field in Titus 2:1-5: *"...Speak the things which are proper for sound doctrine: that the older [mature] men be sober, reverent, temperate, sound in faith, in love, in patience; <u>the older [mature] women likewise</u>, that they be reverent in behavior, not slanders, not given to much wine, teachers of good things- that they <u>admonish</u> the young women to love their husbands, to love their children, to be discreet, chaste, homemakers, good, obedient to their own husbands, that the word of God may not be blasphemed."* **Behold! The truth of this scripture is that <u>God has called women to be nouthetic counselors to women and children</u>, confronting with scripture out of love to bring about a needed change to precious souls. What a privilege to be called to such a mission field!**

In Ephesians 5 and 6, men and women are told to walk in love, be the light of the world, walk in wisdom, and we are also given God's love-laws about how a Christian family is to operate. **With God as the head of the household, the husband is overseer—protector—of his helpmeet, the husband and wife are to function as one, with their roles being equally vital to the spiritual health of the marriage. Together, they should be a beautiful reflection of Christ, our Bridegroom and us, His Bride!** Tragically, the Devil has lied and convinced some that the role of the "bride" is not the privilege that it truly is! **Look how powerful our Bridegroom counts the Christ-like walk of a wife before a lost or back-slidden husband** in I Peter 3:1-4:

"Wives, likewise, be submissive to your own husbands, that even if some do not obey the word, they, without a word, may be won by the conduct of their wives, when they observe your chaste conduct accompanied by fear [of the Lord]. Do not let your adornment be merely outward—arranging the hair, wearing gold, or putting on fine apparel—rather let it be the hidden person of the heart, with the incorruptible beauty of a gentle and quiet spirit, <u>which is very precious in the sight of God.</u>"

Her testimony can be powerful on her home mission field! What a privilege she has to teach her children—boys and girls—other children and other women. **How awesome to think that those precious little boys can grow up to be men who serve our Lord Jesus!** What an awesome responsibility to train boys and girls up in the way that they should go, knowing when they choose to grow-up in the Lord, they will not depart from His will! **Oh that all women would readily accept their awesome callings and out of their love for the Lord obey and fulfill them.**

FILTHY RAGS VS. BEAUTY OF HOLINESS

God's Word in Isaiah 64:6 states that we are all as filthy rags. Indeed, there is none righteous, no not one, but through salvation in Jesus Christ, we are made righteous. Covered by His blood we are accepted as "holy." But, as the Bride of Christ, does our behavior display honor and obedience concerning this scripture? *"Give to the Lord the glory due His name; bring an offering, and come before Him, Oh, worship the Lord in the beauty of holiness! Tremble before Him, all the earth...."* (I Chronicles 16:29-30a) You recall when **Moses** was told to **take off** his sandals (which represented **fleshly attitude**) because **he was on Holy ground as he appeared before the Lord** concerning the people for whom he would be responsible to lead out of captivity. In Exodus 35, we read of God's very precise regulations concerning the Sabbath, the building of the Tabernacle, and the beautiful priestly garments. We find in Leviticus 6:10-11; 16:23 where many of His Laws are found, He was telling **His priest Aaron** to **put off and put on garments** pertaining to various duties. Remember that "Christians" are "little priests"—servants of Christ. Concerning a day to be set aside to worship Him and rest, He strongly laid down the Law when He said: ***"Work shall be done for six days, but the seventh day shall be a holy day for you, a Sabbath of rest to the LORD. Whoever does any work on it shall be put to death."*** (Exodus 35:2) Did He also mean for us to worship Him today "in the beauty of holiness...trembling before Him"—reverentially coming before Him? **How serious is this matter of reverence with clean hearts?** When a priest went into the Tabernacle to offer various offerings to the Lord in the Holy of Holies, he was dressed in his priestly garments and **a rope was tied around one ankle with the tail of it extending out of the Holy of Holies area of the Tabernacle**. Why? If the priest was not **spiritually clean** before the Lord, he was struck dead. By grasping the tail of the rope, a **spiritually unclean** person could drag his body out from the Tabernacle without entering the Holy of Holies—where he would be struck dead as well! **We are in the period of grace today, nevertheless, should we not have that same attitude of reverence when we come together as God's family before Him? Oh that we would take seriously the truth that we as a corporate body are entering to worship the Lord together—like the priest entering the Holy of Holies!**

Let us take a moment to look at one of the garments our Lord Jesus wore, which held the symbolic significance that He was the Alpha and Omega—eternal, without beginning or end:

> *"Then the soldiers , when they had crucified Jesus, took His garments and made four parts, to each soldier a part, and also the tunic. Now **the tunic was without seam, woven from the top in one piece**. They said therefore among themselves, 'Let us not tear it, but cast lots for it, whose it shall be,' that the Scripture might be fulfilled which says: 'They divided My garments among them. And for My clothing they cast lots.' Therefore the soldiers did these things."* (John 19:23-24)

We read of how we are to come before the Lord in Hebrews 12:28-29: *"...since we are receiving a kingdom which cannot be shaken, let us have grace, by which we may serve God acceptably with reverence and godly fear. For our God is a consuming fire."*

Tragically, we have observed that the "atmosphere" in God's house has changed drastically over the years—and not for the best. **We have observed a continual decline in the measure of reverence for our Lord, God, the Alpha and Omega, in many, many church settings.** Over and over again, we have heard many other Christians express their deep concern about the irreverence in many churches. Over many years, we fondly remember that the atmosphere in a great number of churches gave forth testimonies to the world of the members' awesome, reverential fear of and love for God. Let us be quick to say that apart from those positive testimonies, the atmospheres of some other churches were generated by congregations who appeared as cold as ice—many just stiffly going through the motions. We have observed others who have been so hyper that they could not hear the voice of the Lord seeking to communicate with them. God doesn't want us to be either of those extremes. We are definitely not speaking of the need for people to sit perfectly still with their emotions locked away, forbidden to feel and express great joy and comfort at home in God's house. We **are** saying that it is needful for God's family to have a Godly balance, take time to **"be still and know God"**—to reverence Him—amidst the teaching and preaching of God's Word and by singing psalms, hymns and spiritual songs. It is also needful to sing praises to Him for the mercy and grace He has given to us—worship Him in truth with gratitude and joy.

Does God still yearn for His people to put off irreverence and put on reverence? Let us look at God's viewpoint, God's truths concerning this matter in order to edify our brothers and sisters—for their sake as well as for the sake of lost souls and baby Christians watching us. In recent years, have you noticed a decline of reverence for the Lord in His meeting places? Have you noticed with the attitudes of irreverence that they are often mirrored in the garments worn? Sadly, attire for church seems to be a touchy subject for some of our Christian brothers and sisters, for upon the subject coming up, they have attempted to make the term "legalism" apply. Someone once stated that **"legalism is strict conformity to the letter of the law <u>rather</u> than its spirit." This implies that while the law may be kept "in the flesh" if it is not walked out according to the leading of the Holy Spirit, it will fail to reflect the fruit of His Spirit. Godly talk should match our walk:** *"...love, joy, peace, longsuffering, kindness, goodness, faithfulness, gentleness, self-control. Against such there is no law. And those who are Christ's have crucified the flesh with its passions and desires. If we live in the Spirit, let us also walk in the Spirit. Let us not become conceited, provoking one another, envying one another."* (Galatians 5:22-26)

The point is that out of our love for the Lord, **we should all desire to obey Him** in the matter **rather than follow human opinion.** Therefore, we encourage all Christians to take time to evaluate the subject of our "attire" thoroughly. For starters, what would be among some of the first things that would pop into your mind if someone were to call and invite you to a very special occasion, perhaps a wedding. Besides wondering what gift you should give the couple, would you wonder, **"What should I wear?"** Let's answer a few other questions. Do clothes often "tell you" what activity a person is about to participate in, whether it's a casual occasion such as a ball game, a picnic, or trip to the zoo? Do some clothes "tell us" that they have ceased to be in good enough condition for "going out in public" but they're still good for doing yard work or painting the house? Are there other clothes that aren't made for public display, such as pajamas—perfect for sleeping comfortably? Are there other clothes that "tell us" that they're being worn for a very special occasion that's something worth "dressing up for!" **Would you consider it to be an extremely wonderful occasion—something worth taking time to put on your "Sunday best"—if you're going to step into the Holy of Holies to meet with the Lord?**

As we prayerfully ask the Lord to open our eyes to the truth of the matter, we see that, as usual, Satan is behind the scenes, offering his suggestions on every subject, including our "attire." Our eyes are open to the truth that Satan delights in luring Christians to either of two extremes—if he fails to succeed luring a person one way, he tries the other. He is a pro! He doesn't want Christians walking as Christ-like examples united in love—on God's "straight and narrow" pathway—between Satan's two extremes. Please take time to prayerfully consider these truths: in present times, when people go to weddings, funerals, and many other special occasions, **both Christians and non-Christians still "dress up."**

Even in the midst of this nation's state of moral decay—while it doesn't apply to all—we still see many news reporters, sports officials and people gathered for special events—men in suits and ties and women dressed in modest, feminine attire. We even see large crowds of men dressed in nice suits and women dressed up, wearing fancy hats for horse racing occasions. **Their clothes "tell us" that it is an exciting occasion for them.** When attending loved ones' graduations from school, "dressing up" for the occasions shows the graduates that people believe there is something very special to celebrate. It "goes without saying"—without questioning—that people invited to a wedding know it's disrespectful to sashay in nonchalantly wearing blue-jeans and T-shirts, carrying their cappuccino treat. Instead, they will wear their "Sunday best"—their clean, nicest "dress-up" clothes in celebration and respect of the couple getting married and their family.

The question comes: While God's people gather to meet with Him corporately, should their attitude fit the occasion whole heartedly with clothes to match? The garments of a gathering crowd carries a message to onlookers—telling the purpose for which they have taken time to get together. It may be declared that there is a funeral, a wedding, or a baseball game to attend—all are dressed to fit the occasion. As we look at the overall view of Christians gathering at a church today cooperatively, are they sending mixed messages? Do they voice that they are gathering in "unity" to meet with the Lord in the beauty of holiness? Or, as the onlookers gaze upon the group gathering at the church, are they puzzled when they see some in their "Sunday best" and others dressed as if many of the groups are headed outside for dinner on the grounds? Does the visual message say, "Come join us to meet with God"?

Please do not hear what we are not saying! We agree with the Lord who warns us against being respecters of persons in chapter two of James. So we are not saying that the most filthy, shabbily dressed person—lost or saved—should not be welcomed to the front pew in God's house by God's people with open arms, loving hearts and a joyful willingness to help him—and to buy him new clothes and fill his other needs. A Christian has no right to "look down" on a person who wears "poor" garments, nor to look upon those who are wearing their "Sunday best" with critical judgment. Hearts set with Godly intentions do not dress "in Sunday best" to show off garments but rather to come dressed in garments that demonstrate the reverence they have in their hearts for Holy God. As they gather with other Christians, their attitudes, their countenances "match" their "respectful" garments. God warned us all about the opposite behavior of pridefully strutting about, displaying "holier than thou" attitudes in Luke 20:46-47: *"Beware of the scribe, who desire to go around in long robes, love*

358

greetings in the marketplaces, the best seats at feasts, who devour widows' houses, and for a pretense make long prayers. These will receive greater condemnation."

Therefore, the information that we are sharing does not come from our personal opinions or human reasoning. Instead, it is found in the Bible, along with God's love-laws for His people. He included very detailed, specific instructions on how His people were to dress. **If you want to see how important the Lord considered what one wears when they come before Him turn to Exodus 39 and read the entire 43 verses describing the very detailed instructions He gave for Aaron's extravagantly expensive and awesomely beautiful priestly garments. Each intricate part held special meaning. We should take care to remember once again that Christians are "little priests!"** God's awesome dress codes for His people went far beyond the patterns for men and women's clothing and their wide range of beautiful colors and various fabrics from which they were made. One point is that Aaron was "obedient." He was told to do it. He did it. The Zondervan Pictorial Bible Dictionary, Zondervan Publishing House, Grand Rapids, Michigan, page 225 reads:

> *The clothing worn by the Hebrew people of Biblical times was graceful, modest, and exceedingly significant. They were considered so much a part of those who wore them that they not only told who and what they were, but were intended as external symbols of the individual's innermost feelings and deepest desires, and his moral urge to represent God aright. With certain kinds of cloth and with astonishingly vivid colors of white, purple, scarlet, blue, yellow, and black, they represented the state of their minds and emotions. When joyful and ready to enter into festive occasions, they donned their clothing of brightest array, and when they mourned or humbled themselves, they put on sackcloth—literally cloth from which sacks were made—which was considered the poorest kind of dress, and quite indicative of their lowly feelings.*

Sadly, in many churches today, it is a rarity to see an entire congregation in God's sanctuary dressed "respectfully" in their "Sunday best," displaying their **"innermost feelings and deepest desires, and their moral urge to represent God aright."** Has leadership yielded to the whispers of the enemy to an extreme? Have they announced: relax, come as comfortable as you like—that's the point—"don't worry, be happy"—just so YOU are comfortable, that's what matters most? While advertising in this way, a false impression has been given to the lost, the babes in Christ, the weaker vessels, that a "casual attitude" also means a "casual meeting with God and His people." Just as God says there is a time to work and a time to play—there is a time to worship in the true sense of the word and there is a time for God's people to fellowship—have picnics, dinner on the ground, ice cream socials! Instead of a spiritually healthy balance—the two have been merged. In doing so, the true sense and quality of worshiping the Lord has been diluted. **The casualness has brought about a false impression that God's nature is down on our human level.** Gradually, along the way **disrespect began to replace respect—irreverence replaced reverence.** Sadly, some of the words in the wonderful old hymn "Just As I Am" have been tweaked to apply to a person's outward appearance, his clothing—"come as you are"—rather than applying it to the "lost condition of a person's soul." It's an invitation to come before the Lord in your filthy spiritual condition and allow Him to cleanse you! Truly the words to that old hymn lovingly convicts a soul and draws him to plead for Jesus to "rid his soul of one dark blot by the blood He shed for them." Oh how awesome it has been to see, as those words were being sung by God's people, many souls walking the aisle, broken, weeping, repenting and trusting in Jesus—and Christians rededicating their lives to Him.

Clothes do carry a message of Christians' attitudes toward the God they have come to worship. Consider this, when some people enter the sanctuary, do their countenances and garments reflect that they are aware they are entering the Holy of Holies? Grievously, it appears that a great number of Christians have become desensitized concerning this matter, for some stroll in dressed very sloppily—even with some of the women who profess to be Christians wearing shorts, skin-tight clothes and showing more "skin" and "shape" than God wants them to show. Some women seem unaware that dressing in such a way is not only a bad testimony to others, but they can serve as a means of temptation to any persons with lustful eyes. This has proved to be the case all too many times in too many churches. When people look at a woman, should they not first be prompted to look at her face that reflects her countenance, her heart? So whether she wears a dress or slacks with a proper length blouse or jacket, bottom line, all women should snuggle up to the Lord and ask Him what He wants them to wear! Upon neglecting to ask the Lord for His opinion, poor examples are set for others. It is also possible that even though some scantily dressed women profess to be Christians, out of love and concern, we need to be prayerfully alert for opportunity to minister to them pertaining to their salvation and/or the possibility that they are in bondage.

GOOD AND BAD FIRST IMPRESSIONS

You have probably heard the expression that **"first impressions count."** When you meet someone or enter a place, a first impression is established in your mind whether good or bad. In the old days, as you saw a steeple atop a building, pointing to the heavens, you knew it was a church. When stepping into a foyer leading to a church's sanctuary, we fondly recall that the foyers gave us a sense of calling us to be still in our hearts, inviting our hearts to worship and listen to and heed the preaching of the Word. It was typical for foyers to hold things that "said something important to everyone," such as open Bibles displayed on tables with vases of lovely fresh-cut flowers beside them, and crosses. It was not uncommon for the lovely painting that represented Jesus praying for us in the "Garden of Gethsemane" to be hanging on a foyer wall. Another typical picture was one representing Jesus with children joyfully gathered around Him. And three others portrayed Jesus knocking at the door (of one's heart), Jesus crucified on Calvary's tree, and Jesus' return, coming through the clouds for His people. These items in foyers and other hallways and rooms in the church building were so different from worldly things, for they drew attention and verbalized what the meeting place was all about. Even lost people knew that in that place, God was the center of attention. There, He was inviting souls to meet with Him—to draw aside from the busyness and troubles of the outside world and learn from Him and worship Him.

Some foyers still contain such meaningful items that welcome God's people and invite them into the sanctuary. However, from coast to coast, many of today's churches typically give a first impression that is like "Starbucks"—a coffee and sweet rolls house where folks are invited to be casual, to just sit back, relax and please their taste buds as they gather with God's family. It appears that God is no longer the center of attention. In days of old, the sanctuary served the purpose of feeding on God's Holy Word and worshiping the Lord in songs of praise and music that ministered to souls. It was typical for a beautiful painting of Jesus to be over the baptistry, encouraging souls to focus on Him. "Fellowship Hall" served the purpose of God's family gathering to enjoy fellowship together over ice tea, lemonade and tasty homemade "pot luck" main dishes and desserts. There were games to be played, fun skits to be acted out, and songs to be sung.

Today, when God's people meet in the sanctuary together before our awesome Heavenly Father, is it not **an extremely small sacrifice** for God's family to set things of the world aside and sit together in respect for the Lord—in the beauty of holiness—without people having cups of coffee and beverages and distracting other people by getting up and down for refills? Such behavior of the "example-setters" seems to make the scene appear like any other casual gathering. Such a very small measure of time is allotted for worshiping the Lord and focusing on very serious matters concerning the spiritual conditions of God's family. In comparison, far more time is spent in fellowship and other activities than with God in the sanctuary. Therefore, it seems for the sake of family members and spiritually needy souls, it would be wise to avoid any unnecessary distractions. While some Christians may be spiritual healthy and content in the state they find themselves, many others may be sitting in the congregation, silently hiding turmoil inside. During the services, members and visitors should most surely be invited to times of fellowship—playtime in fellowship hall. **There is a time to worship, a time to play—to have dinner on the grounds and a good old fashion ice cream social!**

Just as God urges us to put off negative behavior and put on good behavior, He longs for the Church family to choose to **put off irreverence and put on reverence** and lovingly worship Him in the beauty of holiness—trembling—with great respect before Him. **God would not have told His "priests"—His people—to put off and put on certain garments, plus have clean hearts if it wasn't critical!** While God has a heart-code for us all, He also has a dress-code, which is a partner with our mouth that speaks of how much we adore and respect our Holy God. We are to set examples of our awesome identity—the Bride of Christ—before the eyes of lost people, babes in Christ and our other brothers and sisters. Oh that God's people would have the same sacrificial compassion reflected in the behavior of the "Good Samaritan" rather than like the priest and Levite who had no compassion on the man who was robbed, stripped of his clothes, wounded and left on the road, half dead. Oh that Christians would choose to **put off flippant attitudes and put on "the beatitudes!"** Hebrews 12:28b-29 says: ***"...let us have grace, by which we may serve God acceptably with reverence and godly fear. For our God is a consuming fire."***

ADMONISHING HAS BEEN STOLEN

There is point of great concern within God's family that should be connected with all the other issues we've mentioned. Along with the need for more reverence for the Lord, and love and unity in the family, plus the whole truth of God being preached and taught, including spiritual warfare, sadly, there is a lack of respect for the whole body of Christ. All His people should be found obeying His instructions to be *"admonishing one another in psalms and hymns and spiritual songs, singing with grace in their hearts to the Lord."* (Colossians 3:16) While "admonishing others"—Christians will be drawn to grow up in the Lord, wanderers will feel welcome to return home, and by their examples, lost sheep will find salvation therein. Isn't this the true picture of what Christian meeting places should be today? When this happens, the testimonies—and reputations— of God's family shining forth as the body of Christ will, indeed, draw others to want to come and find such a pleasant, ministering and uplifting dwelling place. **This is the behavior that God wants His people to put on—after putting off the old negative-learned behavior patterns:** *"Do unto others as you would hope they would do unto you"—"the Golden Rule"!*

On the subject of "psalms, hymns, and spiritual songs," let us first state that we know that THE LORD CONTINUES TO INSPIRE SONGS TODAY to be written from the hearts of His people. Clearly that verse declares that there are a variety of categories of Christian songs. Music is such a marvelous instrument in itself—a gift from the Lord to us! We humans even have music built into us—we can sing, hum, whistle and even make other unique sounds. As we listen to music blended with God's messages, it soothes our souls—like melting butter—so that our hearts are more receptive to God's wondrous messages of truths being sung and preached. Music was created by God and He has inspired His people since biblical times to create melodies and lyrics. We even read in I Samuel 16:23, that when God's man David played the harp for King Saul who was a demonically tormented soul, it soothed him: *"And so it was, whenever the spirit from God was upon Saul, that David would take a harp and play it with his hand. Then Saul would become refreshed and well, and the distressing spirit would depart from him."*

This reveals evidence that Godly music is an amazing gift from God through which souls can be ministered. In years gone by there was an awesome balance as we gathered to "be still and know God" better. There was the preaching of the Word and songs sung in praise and worship to our Lord, and how marvelous for one's soul to actually experience how God-inspired music transports His messages so uniquely softening one's heart, making it more porous to receive His truths. We cannot count high enough to number the souls that have been drawn to repentance through songs transporting an invitation to God's plan of redemption through Jesus' shed blood. Calls to specific ministries have been delivered to hearts through heart-softening messages in song, with evidence revealed as surrendered souls walked the aisles.

Through a variety of music we can witness, share biblical truths that draw souls to repentance and praise to our Lord for His merciful goodness. We can even see that Satan and his demons do not find pleasure in sticking around when Godly music resounds amongst God's people. What a wonderful way to let them know that they are not welcome in God's house! **Because music is such a precious gift from God, we never would have imagined that music would be an instrument used to bring division between Christians—even to the splitting of churches. Nevertheless, this very creation of God, "music," is actually being used like a sharp sword, dividing asunder God's people in many, many churches!**

As we share, please take care to understand that we truly love all Christian music leaders despite all the dividing musical issues in these present days. **Please know that we are making an appeal to all Christians to prayerfully join us in seeking God's perspective on the matter of music—plus His solutions to the sorrowful disunity that it has brought. Oh that God's people would join forces to defeat the enemy in this critical matter!**

Recalling what the man said about losing something good with each decade, we are reminded of the sorrow that filled our hearts many years ago when a couple of students of music ministry announced about ceasing to use certain hymns. **They declared, "Who would want to put their hand in a nail-scarred hand or sing about blood?" Hundreds of persons had been drawn to accept Christ as they heard the heart-stirring words,** *"Put your hand In the nail-scarred hand"* **and** *"What can wash away my sins? Nothing but the blood of Jesus. What can make me whole again? Nothing but the blood of Jesus! Oh precious is the flow, that makes me white as snow! No other fount I know nothing but the blood of Jesus!"* **Were it not for Jesus' shed blood and His willingness to be nailed to Calvary's tree those students could not enter into the kingdom of heaven. They were deceived into listening to Satan's suggestion and obeying---watered down God's truths. Satan continued pushing his wares through future decades—down through generations.**

Little did we know that this was only a glimpse of what was to come in a larger portion! Like so many other brothers and sisters, we were deeply troubled as hymns were sung less and less. Hymnals disappeared from so many church buildings all over America—and were replaced by large screens. **Without a doubt, we know that the disappearance of the hymnals grieves the heart of God for He is the One who inspired the thousands of hymns—just as He inspired the Bible.** It's as if these treasures have been stolen and buried, now hindered from fulfilling the purposes for which they were created. Those amazing hymns are partners with the Bible, transporting biblical truths through music. One can learn so much about God by only <u>reading</u> the words in hymns—such priceless tools, indeed! A great number of them were inspired of God in the hearts of Christians who were going through horrible storms in their life. In 1873, one dear Christian man, his wife and four daughters had suffered great financial loss, and in an effort to give his family a pleasant reprieve, he planned a trip to Europe for them—where he would also assist in a revival meeting being held there by Moody-Sanky. However, he had to let his wife and daughters sail on ahead when an urgent business matter arose. Half way across the Atlantic, an English vessel struck their ship, which sunk in twelve minutes. Sadly, 226 people drown, including all four daughters, but the wife and a few others were rescued. As this dear man stood on the deck of a ship carrying him to his sorrowing wife, as he neared the place where his precious daughters drowned, he wept to the Lord and found comfort only God could give and he was inspired to write this well-known, beloved hymn:

It Is Well With My Soul - by Horatio G. Spafford

"When peace, like a river, attendeth my way, when sorrows, like sea billows roll—
Whatever my lot, Thou hast taught me to say, It is well, it is well with my soul.

"Though Satan should buffet, though trials should come, let this blest assurance control,
That Christ hath regarded my helpless estate, and hath shed His own blood for my soul.

"And, Lord, haste the day when my faith shall be sight, the clouds be rolled back as a scroll;
The trump shall resound and the Lord shall descend, 'Even so'—it is well with my soul.

> ***Chorus:*** *"It is well with my soul; it is well, it is well with my soul."*

Our refuge, hope and peace are truly found in our Lord Jesus! So many others were most surely inspired of the Lord to minister to future generations. Why have the approximately 8,000 hymns—so packed with biblical truths for "everyone" —that were written in the 1800s by our beloved, blind sister, Fanny Crosby, suddenly been counted as no longer useful in ministering to younger generations living today? How can this be? People whose hearts have been blessed and ministered to through the vast number of inspirational hymns would surely deem them as priceless treasures from God that should not be discarded and hidden in basements. Perhaps many have never had the privilege of having those melodious messages convict and minister to their souls. **Those old hymns long faithfully bore God's "fruit of the spirit" to souls in various spiritual conditions—lost lambs, Christians who've strayed from God's will, souls going through trials and tribulations, and Christians just lifting up their hearts to the throne of God while making melodies of gratitude for the promises of heaven.** Those invaluable hymns have brought so many souls under conviction, welcoming them into God's family. Oh how heart-stirring—heart-moving those services were. **God's presence was felt as hearts were being still before God as He was moving, speaking to souls—young people and adults.** How awesome it was to see so many souls walking the aisle for various reasons. The question comes to our hearts, why can't God's family continue to be blessed by those God-inspired, truth-packed hymns, along with the great Gospel songs and other newer Christian songs that have followed? **Can't we all share and share alike—take turns with one another?**

Being deeply troubled about the disunity concerning music disunity, we sought God's wisdom—to see it from His perspective. He then reminded us that our enemy, the Devil himself, is the instigator of this matter! You know how clever he is about making suggestions and coating them with enough truth that God's people readily embrace them. God reminded us of what he was like before he chose to rebel against God and was cast out of heaven. He was not only awesomely beautiful, God told him, ***"the workmanship of your timbrels and pipes was prepared for you on the day you were created."*** (Ezekiel 28:13b) God created musical instruments inside him—timbrels (small drums) and wind instruments. Does it not seem logically true that this musically talented leader of a band of rebellious angels who continually seeks to get back at God by misleading His children, also tempts God's people to be in disunity in the area of music? **Without a doubt, Satan delights in distorting truth, as well as music that transports it. Why would Satan not purpose to and delight in distorting God's amazingly beautiful creation, "music"?**

In the **"old days"** there were a large number of **secular songs that were wholesome**—for children and adults. Some even included God and Godly living in them. The enemy moved, influencing little by little, from subtle to blatant flesh-stirring music and lyrics. **Let's prayerfully look at some truthful things about the clever musical-instrument Satan, the leader of his once-heavenly orchestra: (1)** Satan knows that most people enjoy music and that it **can stir their emotions, their flesh**, so he cleverly composes music and lyrics to transport his messages—none of which would woo a person to the Lord. **(2)** Satan knows that **Godly music can stir and soften persons' spirit, their hearts**, wooing them unto the Lord. He also knows that Godly music can minister to Christians' spirits powerfully whether they're walking in a valley or on a mountain top. He has not been shy about entering homes with his concerts, so why would he not desire to also stage them in meeting places of God's family? Has he succeeded in doing this, little by little, from subtle to blatant—"pulling the wool over the eyes" of some of God's people? Sadly, the answer to that question is, "Yes".

Oh that God's people would join together in unity to seriously face this reality while seeking the mind of God in the matter. Oh that all spiritual eyes would be open to see that Satan has cunningly succeeded in convincing some of God's people that a method of drawing more people to the church house "to find Jesus" is through more up-beat, entertaining music—like the secular world offers. While their intentions appeared to want to "help people find the Lord" and "make worship more fun for Christians"—"give them what they want"—why then has this caused such an enormous amount of dissension and division amongst God's people? Over and over we have heard souls voicing that in the midst of this world of turmoil they've gone from church building to church building, searching in vain to find a place of refuge offering hope of peace and joy and sweet fellowship with other Christians. **We wonder how many persons in leadership have become insensitive to the needs of people beyond the church walls. We wonder how many have allowed human reasoning to govern their hearts rather than the Holy Spirit who lives in their hearts.**

One visitor told a pastor and music director that he wouldn't be interested in attending church there because he liked more upbeat music, the band playing, more entertaining contemporary music. The leadership listened and heeded—thus, one of the reasons why some churches have gotten rid of the hymns, the hymnals, the organs and pianos, and replace them with keyboard, drums and amplified, electric guitars and such. **Is God's way that of giving "some" people what they want or what they need?** Wise parents do not always give their children candy just because they want it. **Therefore, we must take care to seek God's wisdom as to what souls need!**

To our sorrow, we once heard an evangelist tell the music leader, **"Let's get this show on the road! Go pump them up!"** Is that what meeting with God in His house is all about, stirring up their emotions—ministering to their flesh? Sadly, while we do not deny at all that some Christians in the congregation are most surely worshiping the Lord in their hearts—in their spirit—often, it appears that "worship" has been transformed to be like the world of entertainment—stirring emotions rather than spirits. The pace seldom slows to give souls time to seriously mediate and let God minister to hearts. When choirs once stood in some churches, dressed alike in their robes as they sang, they blended into the reverent atmosphere, encouraging God's family to just focus on the words delivered by the soothing, uplifting melody. God's awesome gift of voice ranges both in the choir and congregation enhanced the family's worshipful setting—the men's bass, baritone, and tenor voices, the women's first and second soprano and alto in beautiful harmony. In settings more like entertainment—with drums and amplified guitars played loudly—such family harmony is smothered and reverence is often forfeited. Even some very inappropriate secular songs have been included in some "special occasion" services, as if God wanted them to "entertain" the guests.

How sad it has been when some persons' appeals were ignored after explaining that the drums and other instruments were so loud that they couldn't hear themselves singing. A number of people have stated that they've had to stick a finger in one ear in order to hear their own voice. Even more grievous it has been to learn of members wearing hearing aids appealing in vain for the volume of the instruments to be turned down a bit so their hearing aids don't ring in their ears. Some were flippantly told, "Just turn your hearing-aid off until the music is over." The rejected members left, seeking a new church family to worship with.

Now this brings us to the underlying serious concern about the matter, which is that of "negative behavior" contrary to Christ-like behavior on the part of some of God's family members—leadership—their unkind treatment toward some of their brothers and sisters. The respecter of persons comes into play. It is truly hard to understand how they can claim that God brought them to the conclusion and insistence that all the old music is no longer useful but theirs is. **One music director declared that the old hymns were "only meant for a particular span of time," in the past, but that is far from the truth because they are so full of biblical truths. The Bible never grows old, it applies to the present generation and the next and the next. Hymns never grow old! Since they were composed in the 1800s, they have held hands ever so tightly with the Bible! Even the secular world does not totally leave the old songs behind in the dust.** We are then left to question if some of today's music leaders been deceived by the enemy into adopting a new form of delivering them—a new style of "worship"? Is it a form "pumping up the emotions" of the people, like the evangelist said? **These days, the title of Music Minister has been traded for titles such as Worship and Arts Leaders. And have you noticed that the majority of the contemporary songs fall into the category of "worshiping the Lord"?**

Let's prayerfully seek how these matters measure up beside God's Word, in **Colossians 3:16**, that says we are to be letting *"the word of Christ dwell in you richly in all wisdom, teaching and <u>admonishing</u> one another in psalms and hymns and spiritual songs, singing with grace in their hearts to the Lord."* **We think it's extremely important to learn some hidden truths implanted in that verse. Connected with the instructions to operate with the riches of Christ's wisdom and <u>teaching</u> it to others, it instructs Christians to be "<u>admonishing</u> one another in psalms and hymns and spiritual songs." Do all Christians really understand the meaning of the word "admonishing"? In Ephesians 5:19, the word "speaking" is used rather than admonishing, which, if we are not careful, we will simply assume that God's people should be "lifting one another up, edifying, and encouraging"—taking our responsibility too lightly! Because the true meaning of "admonishing" goes much deeper and it's extremely important that we understand that this portion of the passage is directed at God's people. You recall earlier that we mentioned God calling mature Christian women to "admonish" the younger women. So this portion of the verse is not directed "at" God. You will see the reasons why as you take a moment to come and reason with the Lord about His word "admonishing" in this passage. Let's prayerfully examine His lesson to us:**

> <u>Admonish</u>, Gr., **nouthesia** (noo-thes-ee'-ah) [3559], meaning **calling to attention** , i.e. (by impl.) **mild rebuke or warning**:—admonition; **noutheteo** (noo-thet-eh'-o); from the same as [3559]; **to put in mind**, i.e. (by impl.) **to caution or reprove gently**:—admonish, **warn**. (The Complete Word Study New Testament Zodhiates with Greek Parallel, AMB Publishers, Chattanooga, TN 87422, U.S.A.)

How interesting that the words for **admonishing** in Greek, **nouthesia** and **noutheteo**, are related to the word **"nouthetic."** As you recall, **nouthetic counseling** is **"confrontation with scripture out of love to bring about a needed change"**.

Let us look now at the English translation of admonish, which agrees with the above:

> <u>Admonish</u>: **to warn, caution against specific faults; to reprove with mildness; to advise, to exhort; to inform or remind by the way of a warning. Syn.—caution, rebuke, counsel, censure, advise, reprove, forewarn, warn. Admonisher: one who reproves or counsels.** (Webster's New Twentieth Century Dictionary, Second Edition, Copyright © 1975 by William Collins World Publishing Co., Inc.; page 26)

Before moving further let us note two crucial lessons in Colossians 3:16:

The first portion of the passage **specifically pertains to us—God's people—instructing us to "admonish one another through music—psalms, hymns, and spiritual songs." With God's wisdom we are to TEACH AND GIVE FORTH COUNSEL BY WAY OF MUSIC. God-inspired music and lyrics are intended to convict the lost of their need for a Savior. Other purposes are to convict and encourage Christians to take care to walk the straight and**

narrow path and display the security, strength, peace and joy that they have in Jesus Christ—so that the world may have opportunity to know Him. We are instructed to share the Gospel of Jesus Christ. The inspirational old hymns and Gospel songs reflect obedience to this passage of scripture.

The second portion of that passage of scripture <u>specifically pertains to praise and "worship" of our Lord and Savior, Jesus Christ</u>. It instructs Christians to be "singing with grace in our hearts to the Lord"—with gratitude to Him for His mercy upon us. We are to be singing praises to Him. But even when our voices are still, we are to be making melody in our hearts toward Him, worshiping Him who paid that debt that He didn't owe because we owed that debt we could not pay!

With hymnals being so abundantly rich with God's truths, we remain grieved that they were put away by all too many churches, robbing huge numbers of souls of God's truths contained in the "psalms, hymns and spiritual songs" that minister to a wide variety souls—no matter what spiritual condition they are in. **Recalling that the beautiful old music in the hymnals minister to all of God's people, we turned to the back of the beloved old "Broadman Hymnal" (compiled in 1940) holding 500 pages of hymns and Gospel songs—some old and some new, all soul-stirring.** Behind the Responsive Readings section covering many scriptures pertaining to matters such as "Abstinence, Adoration, Benedictions, Childlikeness, Christ Accepted, Christ All and In All, plus many other important topics, we found its Topical Index. **There, we found 58 topics.** Along with many worship songs, a very large number of the hymns serve to minister to, teach and convict God's people. **Here are some of the topics listed above the names of hymns: Affliction; Aspiration; Assurance; Atonement; Baptism; Bible; Blood; Christ's Return; Christmas; Comfort; Confession; Conflict; Consecration; Cross; Devotional; Faith; Fellowship; Funeral Hymns; God; Grace; Guidance; Heaven; Holy Spirit; Invitation; Jesus; Joy; Lord's Day; Lord's Supper; Love; Missionary Hymns; Praise; Prayer; Repentance; Resurrection; Savior; Second Coming; Security; Social Service; Soul Winning; Stewardship; Temperance; Trust; Warning; Worship; and Youth Hymns (which actually apply to all Christians growing to maturity in the Lord).**

Along with our grief over the evidence of the robbery of these treasures, coast to coast in America, was the sorrow of <u>how</u> some of the pastors and music ministers went about eliminating them. Quite a number of "worship leaders" came to churches declaring that they believed in "balance"—the old mixed with the new songs. However, in time, their words were not kept, the hymns, the Gospel songs faded away and were replaced by some new songs. Some were truly inspired of God. Some came to be known as the "The Seven Eleven" songs though—only seven words sung eleven times. With a few of these being sung in a service, so much time was lost during which many admonishing lessons found in the hymns could have been delivered to the lost, the wanderers, the discouraged servant of God, and uplifting songs that took one's heart to the portals of heaven itself! Hymns packed with wisdom that ministered to all ages in God's family.

When some Christians appealed to one music director concerning the "Seven Eleven" holding less messages than many other songs richer in biblical truths, they were shocked and grieved when he responded very mockingly, saying "Well, the words, 'Oh, how I love Jesus, Oh, how I love Jesus' are repeated over and over in a hymn!" This was **not completely true** because those are only the words to the **chorus of "There is a Name I Love to Hear"** that has four verses of teachings along with expressions of Christians' love for Jesus. The man added that Christians who don't like the contemporary music can play tapes and CDs of the hymns they like while at home or riding in their cars. He further explained that those hymns were "not the ones mentioned in the Bible." Did he not reason that neither were the new songs the ones mentioned in the Bible? Repeatedly, in various ways by ones in leadership, the elder generations were told that they should "keep silent and tolerate what the rest of God's family—the younger generations—"want." Sadly, from time to time, comments were made that clearly served to remind them to be silent about the matter.

Rather than lovingly seeking God's wisdom to know how to bring about "unity," with human reasoning, some churches attempted to bring unity by dividing the Church family up, "traditional side" and "contemporary side." Rather than bringing about a solution, it has only served to build another barrier between God's people. Such negative behavior—unkind treatment of other brothers and sisters—causes us to be extremely troubled over the critical disunity in God's family! For we had long thought the Church was God's family—babies, children, teens, young adults, older adults, and grandparents—all offering valuable contributions to one another. We thought inside "God's family," there would be respect shown for one another—even one's elders. **God says in Philippians 2: 3-4:** *"Let nothing be done through selfish ambition or conceit, but in lowliness of mind let each esteem others better than himself. Let each of you look out not only for his own interests, but also for the interests of others."* With acts so contrary to this, the disunity in far too many churches remains very grievous to our hearts—and to many other brothers and sisters. Oh that God's people would put away childish things and humble themselves before Him, repent, turn from their negative behaviors and love one another as Christ loves us all—so that the world may know Jesus, our Lord and Savior—by our love for one another. Galatians 5:13-15 says: *"...you have been called to liberty; only do not use liberty as an opportunity for the flesh, but through love serve one another. For all the law is fulfilled in one word, even in this: 'You shall love your neighbor as yourself.' But if you bite and devour one another, beware lest you be consumed by one another."* Is this not the very thing the once-heavenly band leader, the Devil, delights in?

Have you ever observed children playing together when one of the children—who readily expresses his feelings—doesn't get his way and his "flesh" stirs within him and he aggressively takes action with intent to reverse the situation? Without reservation or apology, the little boy lashes out at one of the other little boys, snatching a toy, hitting, pulling hair, shoving, or even biting him. **How very humbling that our heavenly Father not only told us—His children—to put away childish things, He also deemed it necessary to warn us not to "bite and devour one another!"** Clearly, Christians have been told to put away childish things. Rather than being so aggressively competitive like the world of sports—**people vs. people**—oh that all Christians would truly **love one another and lovingly play, fellowship and worship peacefully and joyfully together—so that the world** can see glimpses of Jesus! Oh that all would "play fair"—love vs. love! In this "game of life," in offering God's love to the lost world, we may not "win" them all—but we should surely "die-to-self" trying!

The spiritual needs of people in this world have not changed—they still need our Lord's biblical truths. They still need Jesus and those same words, those same amazing hymns that minister to souls of all ages and spiritual conditions! While some of their words convict, some soothe, some lift one's heart to the heavens with rejoicing. **Those hymns have a God-inspired way of bringing souls "Face-to-face" with Jesus! Personally, we have witnessed persons who were <u>not</u> "brought up" hearing the hymns, upon their hearing some of them, they fell in love with them and longed to listen to more of them. Souls and their emotional and spiritual needs have surely not changed—only the condition of the world around them has changed!** We can't begin to adequately describe how awesomely the hymns and Gospel music minister to such a wide variety of needs in the lives of people. Those marvelous hymns and newer God-inspired songs that followed are lovely tools of the Lord as their melodies are played and lyrics are sung. They **(1)** woo lost souls to Jesus, **(2)** draw Christians who have strayed from God's pathway back home, like the Prodigal son, **(3)** comfort Christians who are going through trials and tribulations, **(4)** encourage Christian servants who have grown weary on life's mission fields, **(5)** stir Christians' hearts that are full of love, trust and gratitude to the Lord to just enjoy praising Him, and **(6)** cause God's family to rejoice and sing together about heaven—when we all live together in that "city foursquare." **(7)** And how uplifting it is to sing with our family—our brothers and sisters—in gratitude, praise and honor to our Savior, Lord, and King of kings. **Oh what joy it would be for us—our generation—to see revival come to God's family—so that the world can see the love of Jesus shining from God's house again—offering souls what they so desperately need. Oh that all God's people will say:** *"Lord, send a revival and let it begin in me."*

D. CALL FOR CHRIST'S BRIDE TO RECLAIM HER LEGAL RIGHTS FROM THE ENEMY AND THROUGH JESUS CHRIST HAVE REVIVAL!

What does the word "revival" mean? It carries a message of proclaiming:

> *"a bringing back into use, attention, or being, after a decline; a bringing back to life or consciousness; a stirring up of religious faith among those who have been indifferent, usually through meetings by fervid preaching, public confession of sins, professions of renewed faith; the coming again into activity and prominence; <u>the conversion of waste land into land suitable for use of habitation and cultivation</u>....*" (Webster's New Twentieth Century Dictionary, Second Edition, Copyright © 1975 by William Collins World Publishing Co., Inc.; page 1552)

Indeed, preaching and teaching God's Word brings revival when the listeners humble themselves and heed God's messages. Complete revival can come only to an individual church body if the members humble themselves and let God do a work in their individual lives. You

370

noticed in the definitions of "revival" that "land" was actually used as an example. **It is like Christians reclaiming ground to which the enemy laid legal claim!** As we read this passage of scripture again, we see how applicable this is to our sovereign God's statement:

> *"If My people who are called by My name will humble themselves, and pray and seek My face, and turn from their wicked ways, then I will hear from heaven, and will <u>forgive</u> <u>their</u> <u>sin</u> and <u>heal</u> <u>their</u> <u>land</u>."* (II Chronicles 7:14)

The Lord knows that revival is possible in individual churches that are crowded with divisions—but as His Word reveals, it's left up to the choices of His people to humble themselves and repent—or not. In order for the "whole body" to function as a spiritually healthy body, it is needful for it to be laid on our Great Physician's examining table and see if all the parts are "all there and in proper working order." Our Potter says in I Corinthians 12:12-21: *"...**the body is one and has many members**, but all the members of that one body, being many, are one body, so also is Christ. For **by one Spirit we were all baptized into one body**—whether Jews or Greeks, whether slaves or free—and have all been made to drink into one Spirit. For in fact the body is not one member but many. If the **foot** should say, 'Because I am not a **hand**, I am not of the body,' And if the **ear** should say, 'Because I am not an **eye**, I am not of the body,' is it therefore not of the body? If the whole body were an eye, where would be the hearing? If the whole were hearing, where would be the smelling? **But now God has set the members, each one of them, in the body just as He pleased.** And if they were all one member, where would the body be? But now indeed there are many members, yet one body. And **the eye cannot say to the hand, 'I have no need of you'; nor again the head to the feet, 'I have no need of you.'"** Yet, within those church walls are some missing parts of the body—parts as vital to the spiritual health of the Church body as any other part of the physical body.

As our Great Physician examines the conditions of these "bodies in Christ" serving in the midst of this Holy War down here, it's probably accurate to say that few would be issued a "clean bill of health." It is like an infection of stubbornness has spread in the body, like the Lord speaks of in Psalm 78: 8: *"A stubborn and rebellious generation, a generation that did not set its heart aright, and whose spirit was not faithful to God."* The true diagnosis is that the Church's immune system has been attacked and is in a declining state, thus susceptible to infection—and death. We read of the culprit—like cancer—in **the spiritual health report posted for Christians** in James 4:1: ***"Where do wars and fights come from among you? Do they not come from your desires for pleasure that war in your members?"*** Just as an individual has a battle between "spirit vs. flesh," so the church—the Bride of Christ—is engaged in battle! It breaks our hearts that there are spiritual wars going on inside church walls—amongst God's soldiers! When Christian soldiers fail to keep their armor on—resisting the attacks of Satan—their unit will fall into disunity, leaving "the entire fort" vulnerable to the enemy. If some of the soldiers are missing from the unit, they fall short-handed in the battle, leaving spaces in the fort, weakening the defense further. Sadly, this has happened far too many times in far too many churches over the years!

We're told in Hebrews 10:24-25: *"...**let us consider one another in order to stir up love and good works**, not forsaking the assembling of ourselves together, as is the manner of some, but **exhorting one another and so much the more as you see the Day approaching**."* We are living in such critical times—signs of the times round about us—the fields are white unto harvest, so much work needs to be done in God's fields. Upon our appealing to our beloved, fellow Christian brothers and sisters, **our hope is that we will truly see revival come and the enemy defeated amongst God's people**! Oh, that all Christian soldiers who are "out of step" with God, will for their own sakes as well as for others, obey the Lord's appeals for them to: *"...**submit to God. Resist the devil and he will flee from you. Draw near to God and He will draw near to you. Cleanse your hands, you sinners; and purify your hearts, you doubled-minded. Lament and mourn and weep! Let your laughter be turned to mourning and your joy to gloom. Humble yourselves in the sight of the Lord, and He will lift you up.**"* (James 4:7-10)

Oh that God's people will all love the Lord their God with all their heart, mind, soul and strength, and their neighbor—brothers and sisters—as themselves. What joy it would be for all to see each other the way God does—with His eyes, hear each other with God's ears, and love and understand one another with God's heart. Revival will not come until each member accepts the truth that no member is more important than the other—for, no different from the human body—they are to function as one, bringing glory to their Potter. It's important that the physical church building be kept clean as well as the hearts of the "Church body." Every member is a necessary part of the body of Christ, and each is to care for and love all the other members—understand and appreciate what their purpose is as part of the body.

The spiritual condition of the "church body" is truly a grievous sight before the Lord. There is hearing loss, vision impairment, crippled limbs, and missing limbs, all due to "sin" as a result of some of the members' succumbing to "propaganda of the enemy!" As we've said so many times, the "church building"—"our military base, our fortress"—is suppose to include a "hospital wing!" **It should be a place where members who have been attacked, ravaged and crippled by the enemy—or by "friendly fire"—can find healing for their souls!** It has long been common for church buildings to include church offices, break rooms, storage rooms, a foyer, a sanctuary—for preaching and admonishing one another in psalms and hymns and spiritual songs, singing with grace in our hearts to the Lord. There are rooms designated for Bible studies, and a kitchen connected to a big room for fellowship where we can break bread together. Some churches even have their own theaters, gymnasiums, bowling alleys, and restaurants. Many churches unselfishly give to many worthy missions far across the sea. Few have the sorely needed "hospital wing"—"rooms of refuge," "surgery rooms" and "intensive care units," where sound biblical doctrine is applied to bring healing to the wounded soldiers. All too few have allowed the "limbs, members of special forces" to be a part of the Church body.

Therefore, churches that are void of biblical and spiritual warfare counseling and teachings on how to rescue imprisoned soldiers are "missing these special-forces limbs." So many patients, burdened with hopelessness, have fallen by the wayside. Where are all the "medics" in God's house? As our

King has said: *"Where there is no counsel, the people fall; but in the multitude of counselors there is safety."* (Proverbs 11:14) **It is truly sorrowful that there aren't multitudes of counselors in God's houses, ready to lift the fallen and lead them out of captivity!**

Oh that we would all be so blessed to see revival come to the church house, that all the members would desire to be made whole so that together, the world would see a positive difference and want to have the same peace and joy of God's people. For those who frequent those church walls yet have strayed from God's commandments and statutes, for their sakes, our hearts long for our King's people to cry out: *"Have mercy upon me, O God, according to your loving kindness; according to the multitude of Your tender mercies, blot out my transgressions. Wash me thoroughly from my iniquity, and cleanse me from my sin...Purge me with hyssop, and I shall be clean; wash me, and I shall be whiter than snow."* (Psalm 51:1-2; 7) What peace comes when one is washed whiter than snow—legally claimed forever by our Savior and Lord, Jesus Christ! Legally rescued from Satan's captivity!

As we begin to close this "tool box," our hope is that God's people will truly allow revival to come. That we will all labor together to obey our loving Father's Word that says: *"Let this mind be in you which was also in Christ Jesus, who being in the form of God did not consider it robbery to be equal with God, but made Himself of no reputation, taking the form of a bond-servant, and coming in the likeness of men. And being found in appearance as a man, He humbled Himself and became obedient to the point of death, even the death of the cross."* (Philippians 2:5-8)

May we all strive to stand with clean hearts in our legal rights in Jesus Christ, our sovereign God, and refuse to let the enemy triumph over us! Out of love, adoration, trust and gratitude may we declare to our Savior: *"To You O LORD, I lift up my soul. O my God, I trust in You; let me not be ashamed; let not my enemies triumph over me."* (Psalm 25:1-2) *"Behold, God is my salvation; I will trust, and not be afraid; for the LORD, even the LORD, is my strength and my song; He also is become my salvation."* (Isaiah 12:2)

As you walk this earthly mission field in God's plan for your precious life, may we be in unity together, wholeheartedly, praying: *"Teach me, O LORD, the way of Your statutes, and I shall keep it to the end. Give me understanding, and I shall keep Your law; indeed, I shall observe it with my whole heart. Make me walk in the path of Your commandments, for I delight in it. Incline my heart to Your testimonies, and not to covetousness. Turn away my eyes from looking at worthless things, and revive me in Your way. Establish Your word to Your servant who is devoted to fearing You. Turn away my reproach which I dread, for Your judgments are good. Behold, I long for Your precepts; revive me in Your righteousness."* (Psalm 119:33-40)

Oh that all of us—the Bride of Christ—would run the race set before us like the Special Olympics group of down syndrome youth. As they were all running a race one of the youth fell down. Surprising the crowd of spectators, all the other youth stopped, turned and ran to the aid of their fallen friend. Then together, they resumed the race. As each of us run our

appointed race in life, may all of us have caring hearts like those youth, full of a willingness to take time to help our fallen brothers and sisters so they can stand again and continue running their race in life.

Our precious fellow servant, we earnestly hope this tools book has given you ample tools for your counseling tool box. We hope the tools supply you with much encouragement and enlightenment—whether you are a minister, missionary, counselor, or lay-counselor, desiring to learn how to lead souls in bondage to freedom, or if you are a person desiring to learn how to apply God's wondrous truths to your own life. God bless you as you walk with our Lord Jesus in His fields, filled with enormous measures of love for, trust in, and gratitude to Him!

As our dear brother Paul said—with great love for his brothers and sisters—after sharing words of instructions with the Philippians concerning Christian unity, we, too, say: *"Finally, brethren, whatever things are true, whatever things are noble, whatever things are just, whatever things are pure, whatever things are lovely, whatever things are of good report, if there is any virtue and if there is anything praiseworthy—meditate on these things. The things which you learned and received and heard and saw in me, these do, and the God of peace will be with you."* (Philippians 4:8-9)

As servants of the Lord, out of our love and gratitude to Him, may we all fulfill His charge found in II Timothy 2:15: *"Be diligent to present yourself approved to God, a worker who does not need to be ashamed, rightly dividing the word of truth."* What joy it would be for each of us to one day hear Him say as we step into heaven:

"Well done, thou good and faithful servant!"